Mill Power

Mill Power

The Origin and Impact of Lowell National Historical Park

Paul Marion

ROWMAN & LITTLEFIELD
Lanham • Boulder • New York • London

Published by Rowman & Littlefield
A wholly owned subsidary of The Rowman & Littlefield Publishing Group, Inc.
4501 Forbes Boulevard, Suite 200, Lanham, Maryland 20706
www.rowman.com

16 Carlisle Street, London W1D 3BT, United Kingdom

British Library Cataloguing in Publication Information Available

Library of Congress Cataloging-in-Publication Data

Marion, Paul, 1954–
    Mill power : the origin and impact of Lowell National Historical Park / Paul Marion.
        pages cm.
    Includes bibliographical references and index.
    ISBN 978-1-4422-3628-8 (cloth) — ISBN 978-1-4422-3629-5 (pbk.) —
    ISBN 978-1-4422-3630-1 (electronic)
    1. Lowell (Mass.)—History. 2. Lowell National Historical Park (Lowell, Mass.)
3. Urban renewal—Massachusetts—Lowell—History. 4. Deindustrialization—
Massachusetts—Lowell—History. 5. Community development—Massachusetts—
Lowell—History. I. Title.
    F74.L9M27 2014
    974.4'4—dc23   2014016218

∞™ The paper used in this publication meets the minimum requirements of American National Standard for Information Sciences—Permanence of Paper for Printed Library Materials, ANSI/NISO Z39.48-1992.

Printed in the United States of America

To Everyone Who Helped (1966–2012)

There is a clear arc to the Lowell story. In many ways the lower Merrimack Valley is a microcosm of the whole American story.

—**Jane Brox**, author of *Here and Nowhere Else*
and *Brilliant: The Evolution of Artificial Light*

Under the free enterprise system, useless items are discarded in favor of more productive ones. How do you discard a city?

—**Paul Tsongas**, Lowell native, U.S. senator, and presidential candidate,
from *The Road from Here: Liberalism and Realities in the 1980s*

If there is a lesson other aging industrial cities can learn from Lowell, it is that revitalization begins with the kinds of changes in a community's self-image that project a palpable sense of confidence and direction. The catalyst for such changes is what preservationists have called a sense of place.

—**Lawrence D. Gall**, former assistant superintendent,
Lowell National Historical Park, from "The Heritage Factor in Lowell's
Revitalization," in *The Continuing Revolution: A History of Lowell, Massachusetts*

Contents

FOREWORD   xi

ACKNOWLEDGMENTS   xv

INTRODUCTION: LIGHTNING STRIKES TWICE   xix

CHAPTER ONE: THE INTENTIONAL CITY   1

    Pawtucket and Wamesit   1
    "Wonderful Machine"   2
    Waterpower   5
    Mile of Mills   6
    First Blood of the North   10
    Battered Hive   12
    Neighborhood Nations   13
    Running on Empty   16

CHAPTER TWO: URBAN LABORATORY   19

    Model City   19
    Revitalization   22
    Mogan Speaks: Collected Wisdom   23
    Living History: David McKean   29
    College Town   33

CHAPTER THREE: MAKING THE PARK   39

    "Lowell Has Done It"   39
    A National Park Stands Apart   39
    Stairway to Park-dom   41
    From Alternative School to Urban Cultural Park   42
    Building the Park: First Moves   51
    The Park Bill Becomes Law: A Staff Diary   52
    An Act Establishing a Park   54
    Taking Shape   58
    Realizing the Idea   60
    The Canalway and Beyond   66
    Into the Twenty-First Century   69
    Yellowstone and Lowell   76

CHAPTER FOUR: BRICKS AND MORTAR, THEN AND NOW   81

    Lowell Manufacturing Company   82
    Moody-Whistler-Francis House   85
    Fiske Building   86
    Darius Young House   89

Boston and Maine Railroad Depot   91
Appleton Block   92
Bon Marché Building   96
Wetherbee, Kelley, Rose, Maynard, and Day Houses   100
Boott Cotton Mills   100
Boott Cotton Mills Boarding House   105
Suffolk Manufacturing Company   108

CHAPTER FIVE: THE ECONOMICS OF HERITAGE   111

Urban Destruction   111
Fear Not Preservation   114
Adaptive-Reuse Economics   117
"The Long View"   120
Lowell: By the Numbers   121
Heritage Reclamation: Public-Private Sectors, Investment/Development 121
Preservation Tax Credit Tool   124
Two Cases: Market Mills and Hamilton Canal District   126
Standoff at the Dam   135
Public-Private Partnership   138
High-Tech Hive   139
Creative Place-Making   146
Gathering the Lowell Honey   151

CHAPTER SIX: TELLING THE STORY   155

If the Falls Could Speak   155
A Counter-Narrative   160
"The Danger of a Single Story"   163
The Power of Water   165
Riding the *Paul Moody*   167
Mill Work   174
Walk This Way: A Canal Hike, 2010   176
The City as a Classroom   180
Moulin Rouge   181
"The Everywhere School"   184
Tsongas Industrial History (and Science) Center   185
Lowell Folk Festival   196
Traditions Connect Us   206
Cultural Affairs   208
Lowell Summer Music Series   210
Sculpture Trail   212
Kerouac Comes Home   221

CHAPTER SEVEN: STEWARDSHIP AND LEADERSHIP   231

Youth Stewardship   231
Public Matters   233

BIBLIOGRAPHY   241
INDEX   255
ABOUT THE AUTHOR   267

Foreword

Celeste Bernardo, Superintendent, Lowell National Historical Park
Kevin Harkins

The National Park Service will be 100 years old in 2016. To help the agency's leadership refresh the system, the National Parks Second Century Commission in 2008 visited six of the 391 parks to see what shape they were in. Lowell National Historical Park was on the short list. Former U.S. Senators Howard H. Baker Jr. of Tennessee and J. Bennett Johnston of Louisiana cochaired the twenty-six-member Commission. Among the members were former justice of the Supreme Court Sandra Day O'Connor, Harvard University scientist E. O. Wilson, Milton Chen of the George Lucas Educational Foundation, and Maria Hinojosa of the Public Broadcasting System. The National Parks Conservation Association sponsored the project. After field visits, research, public hearings, and consultation with stakeholders, Baker and Johnston concluded:

> Our yearlong concentration on the national park idea convinces us that its evolution has been of exceptional value to the nation. Continued expansion of that idea should play a central role in solving some of our most daunting problems. Our recommendations capture strategies that will, if they are adopted now, strengthen education, reduce impacts of climate change, provide meaningful opportunities for young people, support a healthier and more interconnected citizenry, preserve extraordinary places that reflect our diverse national experience, and safeguard our life-sustaining natural heritage on land and sea. America stands at a crossroads. Down one road lie missed opportunities and irretrievable loss of our natural and cultural legacy. Down the other is a future in which national parks—protected forever and for all—help forge a better world.[1]

In addition to Lowell, the members toured Santa Monica Mountains National Recreation in California, Yellowstone National Park in Wyoming, Gettysburg National Military Park in Pennsylvania, Great Smoky Mountains National Park in Tennessee, and Essex National Heritage Area in Massachusetts. That Lowell has risen to this level of prominence attests to its compelling story and the successful way the park has taken shape in 35 years. About Lowell, the Commissioners wrote, "The park is woven into the rest of the community not just by its physical layout . . . but also by collaborations with local government agencies, private donors, colleges, and community service projects." Among National Park Service people around the country, Lowell is known as the "partnership park."[2]

The city of Lowell began as a grand industrial experiment in the 1820s and for a time captured the world's attention. America's Industrial Revolution grew to large scale here. What happened at the start, in between, and since Lowell was organized as a factory town continues to be important for our understanding of the American experience.

In 1975, the United States Congress created a federal commission to study Lowell's prospects for inclusion into the system of national parks. The commission's report is known as "the Brown Book" for the color of the cover, but often overlooked is the dominant cover image: a black-and-white photograph of the sturdy loom fixer Albert Biro standing among machines on a shop floor in one of the last textile mills. Superimposed on his grimy work shirt is a small circular badge imprinted with a diagram of the Lowell canal system. The message was clear from the start: the extraordinary account of canal-building and textile production in Lowell cannot be told without the central narrative about the people who built this city and gave it a soul.

What follows is an account of the origin and impact of Lowell National Historical Park, established in 1978; a look at the ways the park staff and community partners preserve, present, and add to the Lowell story; and an assessment of the impact of the park on the city's quality of life and economy since its establishment. The park has a thorough administrative history by George O'Har and Gray Fitzsimons that chronicles the park's development and operations in the first twenty-five years. This book frames the narrative for a broad readership and brings the story to the present

Albert Biro on the cover of "the Brown Book" from the Lowell Historic Canal District Commission
UMass Lowell Center for Lowell History

as Lowell continues to evolve and impress visitors and the people who know it best. In addition to its lively account of what has been achieved in Lowell, this book includes remarkable images that depict accomplishments in physical revitalization and cultural expression. The author, Paul Marion, is a former administrator with the U.S. Department of the Interior, when he was on the staff of the Lowell Historic Preservation Commission. He worked on this project with park personnel for a year through an interagency agreement with UMass–Lowell, where he is executive director of community relations. The story and analysis in *Mill Power* are his own. The then-and-now section on significant preserved buildings was written by Charles "Chuck" Parrott, longtime architect at the park and before that at the Preservation Commission. In undertaking this project, our objective was to create a document that will carry the story of the park and the city's revival to a new generation of readers. As Secretary of the Interior Ken Salazar said in 2012 after seeing the park for the first time, "Lowell has done it."

—Celeste Bernardo, Superintendent, Lowell National Historical Park, 2014

NOTES

1. Howard H. Baker Jr. and J. Bennett Johnston, *Advancing the National Park Idea* (Washington: National Parks Conservation Association, 2009), 2.
2. Baker and Johnston, 36.

Acknowledgments

I was honored when Superintendent Michael Creasey of Lowell National Historical Park (LNHP) asked me to write this book. Among ardent local supporters of the park and the veterans of the city's renaissance, there had been a refrain heard for years: Somebody has to write the real story. As the years went by, I thought more often the telling would be my assignment. One of the reasons I had been enthusiastic about the park is that the story is my family's story, ancestors on both sides having settled in Lowell around 1880, part of the vast migration of French Canadians to New England's redbrick cities, factory fortresses on rivers like the Merrimack. My mother's mother belonged to the International Ladies' Garment Workers' Union; my father worked in the wool industry for most of his life. The "Immigrants" museum exhibition in the Patrick J. Mogan Cultural Center includes a photograph of my grandfather's store in Little Canada in 1926: Marion's Meat Market.

The making of the park and revitalization of the city have been the subject of hundreds of newspaper and magazine articles, TV and radio reports, chapters in books, scholarly essays, and other accounts. We did not have one coherent narrative that traces the experience from the start to the present day—which of course is dated the day the manuscript is published. It was too rare an opportunity to decline. Michael Creasey asked UMass–Lowell Chancellor Marty Meehan if the park could add me to its staff on a half-time basis for twelve months. Thank you to Chancellor Meehan for supporting the plan and reinforcing the alliance of park and university. Thanks also to park Superintendent Celeste Bernardo, who embraced the book project when she took the helm in Lowell.

Vice Chancellor of University Relations Patti McCafferty endorsed the plan; Assistant Director of Community Relations Patty Coffey helped manage the office admirably in my absence. Other university colleagues contributed in various ways: Mary Lou Hubbell, Jack McDonough, Geoffrey Douglas, Tony Sampas, Dave Perry, Chris Wilkinson, Dimitrios Booras, and Brian Herrmann.

I had the best readers one could hope for when it was time to review the manuscript. The "expert readers" were author Jane Brox, a good friend who is an insightful storyteller and trusted book doctor; longtime National Park Service manager and former LNHP assistant superintendent Larry Gall; and Fred Faust, who helped write the legislation for the park and served as the first executive director of the Lowell Historic Preservation Commission (LHPC), where he hired me twice (for which I will be always grateful). In addition, the manuscript was reviewed by Mehmed Ali, LNHP's first director of the Mogan Cultural Center and former president of the national Oral History Association; Peter Aucella, assistant superintendent of LNHP and former executive director of the LHPC; Paul Brouillette, my oldest friend in the local history sphere; Jim Cook, executive director of the Lowell Development & Financial Corporation and Lowell Plan, Inc.; Gray Fitzsimons, former historian at LNHP and a coauthor of the park's administrative history; Richard Howe Jr., Register of Deeds of Northern Middlesex County and Lowell historian; former mayor and

Lowell city manager Brian Martin, now headmaster of Lowell High School; librarian Martha Mayo of the UMass–Lowell Center for Lowell History and veteran board member of the Lowell Historical Society; Sarah Peskin, a former planning director of the LHPC and National Park Service planner; Marie Sweeney, former president of the Lowell Museum Corporation and one of the "wise women" of Lowell; Robert Weible, state historian of New York and former historian at LNHP; Jim Wilde, executive director of the Merrimack Valley Housing Partnership and Lowell enthusiast; and John Wooding, professor of political science at UMass–Lowell and one of the founders of a master's program in which students and faculty explore the social and economic development of regions.

For economic research and analysis, I am grateful to economist John Edward of the economics faculty at Bentley University and UMass–Lowell; professor Bob Forrant of the UMass–Lowell history department and master's program in regional development; Chris Wilkinson of the political science faculty at UMass–Lowell; Lowell researcher James Ostis; and Lowell city planner Craig Thomas.

Senior administrators Sue Andrews and David Blackburn of LNHP not only read the manuscript, but also shepherded the project inside the park. Planner Chris Briggs of LNHP provided essential background on the Canalway, historic trolley system, and other construction projects; curator Jack Herlihy steered me through the park archives; and ranger Tess Shatzer shared her research on the park visitor experience. Former LHPC and NPS planner Nancy Woods shared her knowledge of the park trolley project. My former LHPC colleague Ray LaPorte generously allowed me to quote from his diary about passage of the park legislation. Ellen Anstey of the Tsongas Industrial History Center and Dan Brosnan of UMass–Lowell kept the business end of the project running smoothly.

I appreciated the openness of the people I interviewed or corresponded with, some of them from the park's founding generation and others who picked up the torch along the way: Adam Baacke, Steve Conant, Pat Cook, Doug DeNatale, Taya Dixon Mullane, Amy Glowacki, Pauline Golec, Anita Greenwood, Maggie Holtzberg, Lew Karabatsos, Sheila Kirschbaum, Duey Kol, Ray LaPorte, Michael Leary, Janet Leggat, John Leite, Bill Lipchitz, Rebecca Lofgren, Marty Meehan, Jim Milinazzo, Charles Nikitopoulos, Don Pierson, Theresa Park, Sovanna Devin Pouv, Bill Samaras, Corey Sciuto, Molly Sheehy, Linda Sopheap Sou, Michael Southworth, Steve Stowell, George Tsapatsaris, Bill Walsh, and Mike Wurm.

Thanks to museum educator Paul Levasseur of the Tsongas Industrial History Center and park ranger Krystal Vezina for allowing me to tag along with my reporter's notebook as they led groups through the park. I am indebted to George O'Har and Gray Fitzsimons, authors of LNHP's administrative history, which covers the period 1978 to 2003; their diligent effort added immensely to the section of this book titled "Making the Park." Charles "Chuck" Parrott is the enduring spirit of the park, having been on the ground before the beginning when the potential of Lowell was being studied, and then serving heroically on the staffs of the LHPC and LNHP as chief historic architect. His expert commentary in "Bricks and Mortar" was lifted whole cloth from *Lowell, Then and Now: Restoring the Legacy of a Mill City*, published by the LHPC in 1995.

On behalf of the park and myself, I offer thanks to Charles Harmon and his colleagues at Rowman & Littlefield for producing a fine book. We appreciate their confidence in this project from the start.

This is a work of words and pictures. There was a period in the middle of the twentieth century when Lowell history was not much noticed, but since the middle 1970s there has been an avalanche of publications—produced by scholars, students, community documentarians, creative writers, journalists, artists, and videographers and filmmakers. The books, articles, reports, pamphlets, and media were immensely useful; my extensive bibliography is a catalogue of the research. I am grateful to LNHP, UMass–Lowell's Center for Lowell History, Pollard Memorial Library, and the Lowell Historical Society for decades of stewardship of the Lowell story in the form of drawings, maps, photographs, newspapers, video and film, historical papers, and artifacts. The case for a national park in Lowell would have been much more difficult to make if thoughtful, imaginative, responsible people had not saved and protected the evidence of life in the city. Their efforts continue today, to the benefit of all. For his images of the Lowell revival, Jim Higgins deserves a lifetime achievement award. His photographs of the terrain, formidable structures, and vivid society in this national park convey its movingly humane, joyous, and profound qualities. Thanks also to Tim Carter, Tory Germann, Kevin Harkins, Ray Houde, Meghan Moore, Jennifer Myers, and Lou Neofotistos for permission to use their photographs. Lowell National Historical Park and the Lowell Historical Society generously provided images and documents.

This book is dedicated to "Everyone who helped," but Patrick J. Mogan and Paul E. Tsongas are at the top of the list. It is unlikely that I would be in Lowell today if they had not set out to save the city. I had the great good fortune to know both of them for many years and to work alongside them. They were inspirational mentors and friends of mine.

Last, I thank my family for their enthusiasm and patience as this book took form. My wife, Rosemary Noon, listened to a thousand reports of progress over three years and improved the manuscript with her questions and comments. One of the early park rangers, she dressed up like a mill girl on occasion to visit schools, walked people down the cobblestone streets, and brought her family's Irish-American heritage to her interpretation of Lowell. She went on to the LHPC cultural-affairs staff and later became the city's first cultural-affairs director. These days she is assistant director of the Lowell Plan, Inc., and coordinates the Public Matters leadership development program. Our son Joe has met a lot of the people who are in this book and has begun his own documentary and creative efforts in various media; he said he likes the "Stewardship and Leadership" section of the book for the passionate younger voices.

—Paul Marion, January 2014

Introduction

Lightning Strikes Twice

Park ranger Tess Shatzer tells tourists that Lowell has been a model city twice since its founding. In the first half of the nineteenth century, the city's redbrick mills pumped out massive quantities of woven cloth so efficiently that the factory production was considered revolutionary; and in the late twentieth century, the component parts of this distinctive industrial city were refurbished and reconnected to function as a new kind of national park encompassing an entire city, where Americans would experience their industrial past and pluralistic urban culture.

People tell Shatzer what Lowell means to them. Visitors respond to the physical evidence of early industry that they see on the street and touch as they climb stairs in a mill. One woman told Shatzer that her visit made her think "about our own families and how similar their stories might have been—and how work was for them." A man touring the Boott Cotton Mills Museum said, "You hear some of the same things today, like how we need to make more products in this country, but you see all the jobs going overseas." Another person said, "A lot of women came here to work, and you don't always learn about that in school."[1]

Between 1920 and 1976 there was no general history of Lowell published. During the same period, large sections of the city were dismantled, and much of the nineteenth-century architecture in the core of the city was obscured by modern makeovers or allowed to deteriorate in a method sometimes called "demolition by neglect." Starting in the 1960s, by ones and fives and tens, residents of the city began to realize they lived in an extraordinary place. Spanning six decades, their collective effort to preserve the historic structures and articulate their history set Lowell apart as a model of urban revival. Following is a condensed history of Lowell offered as background and context for the renaissance.

Mill Power documents the invention and growth of Lowell National Historical Park in the context of the city's revitalization in the period from the mid-1960s to the present. The starting point of the story is 1966, when the federal Model Cities Program for urban redevelopment was established. With the new aid, the community began to reclaim its place in physical form and its story as part of the American narrative. The book has seven chapters: The Intentional City; Urban Laboratory; Making the Park; Bricks and Mortar, Then and Now; the Economics of Heritage; Telling the Story; and Stewardship and Leadership. Photographs document the often astounding improvements in the historic environment. Images throughout the book capture the effervescent cultural atmosphere that has come to be a hallmark of Lowell life.

NOTE

1. Tess Shatzer, "The Boott Cotton Mills Museum: An Exploration of Meanings, Connections, and Sense of Place Outcomes" (master's thesis, Stephen F. Austin State University, May 2007), 55.

CHAPTER 1

The Intentional City

"Innovation never comes from the established institutions. It's always a graduate student or a crazy person or somebody with great vision."

—Eric Schmidt, Chairman, Google, on *60 Minutes* (2012)

"All was expectancy. Changes were coming. Things were going to happen, nobody could guess what."

—Lucy Larcom, *A New England Girlhood* (1889)

PAWTUCKET AND WAMESIT

Canadians call them the people of the "First Nations." They moved freely across northeastern North America. The Merrimack River Valley of central New England was home to Algonkian-speaking peoples from a variety of tribes. Native peoples lived in two settlements on the land that became Lowell: the villages of Pawtucket near Pawtucket Falls on the Merrimack and Wamesit at the confluence of the Concord and Merrimack rivers, roughly downtown Lowell today. They hunted, fished, and farmed, traveling in a region from what is now Concord, New Hampshire, to the lower Merrimack River area around Lowell. Historian Richard Howe Jr. fills in the picture: "Besides those who lived in what we now call Lowell year round, thousands of other Native Americans from across New England would travel each spring to the Pawtucket Falls where prodigious amounts of shad, alewife, and salmon could be collected for food and fertilizer."[1]

After 1620, European settlers spread from the coast of the Massachusetts Bay Colony to the interior. With these immigrants came strange germs that caused epidemics of smallpox and influenza, ravaging the local population until the natives numbered only in the hundreds. Local people traded with English colonists and sought a peaceful coexistence, recognizing the trend of expanded settlement. Late in the seventeenth century, leaders like Passaconaway and Wannalancit resorted "to land sales to maintain their consumption levels."[2] The Christian missionary John Eliot had begun visiting Pawtucket and Wamesit in 1647, and in 1653 he represented the interests of the indigenous tribes in requesting that the colonial legislature incorporate Wamesit as a town of their own. At the same time, several men from Concord and Woburn, Massachusetts, asked for a charter for a town called Chelmsford, just upriver from Wamesit. Some twenty years later, the side-by-side living of colonists and Native Americans came apart in a cataclysm called King Philip's War. Fighting tore through Massachusetts towns, including a few near Chelmsford and

1

From the air, the Merrimack River at Lowell
James Higgins

Wamesit. Howe notes that "in terms of the percentage of the population killed, this war was the deadliest conflict in American history."[3] The resulting hostility felt by settlers toward the diminished number of natives contributed to their decision to migrate to the New Hampshire frontier. The Indian town of Wamesit was signed over to a group of Chelmsford men, who folded the new property into their town in 1686. Worked mostly as farmland, this region drew the interest of Boston merchants about 130 years later.

"WONDERFUL MACHINE"

Bostonian Nathan Appleton was a successful importer of European products. In 1811, he met Francis Cabot Lowell (1775–1817), a distant relative and fellow Boston businessman, in Edinburgh, Scotland, where the two men were traveling. They discussed the prospects of cloth manufacturing in America. The newly independent nation was in a hurry-up mode, itching to compete with manufacturers in Britain. Alexander Hamilton had set the agenda in his "Report on Manufactures" of 1791: "To procure all such machines as are known in part of Europe can only require a proper provision and due pains. . . . The knowledge of several of the most important of them is already possessed. The preparation of them here is, in most cases, practicable on nearly equal terms."[4]

Near Edinburgh were the cotton mills in New Lanark, early adopters of the power loom, controversial because of its collateral impact on hand-weaving in the British countryside. At New Lanark, Robert Owen had not only refined the use of

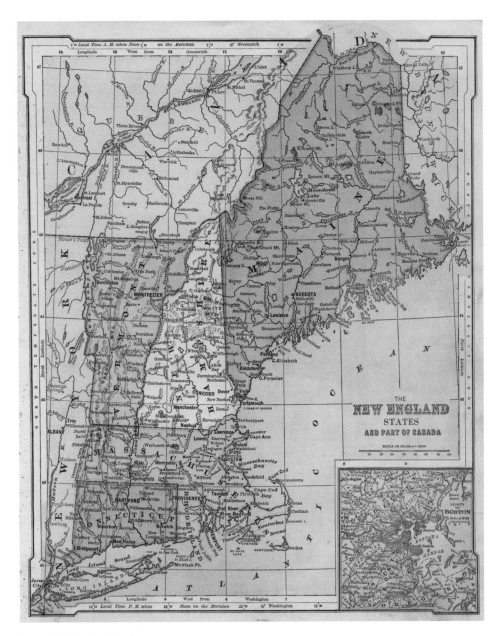

Lowell in New England
Lowell National Historical Park (LNHP)

The only known rendering of Francis Cabot
Lowell (1775–1817)
LNHP

the power-loom system, but also
introduced "a more humane industrial system"[5] with worker amenities
such as company housing, safe water, and schools. About the claim
that Lowell was influenced by Owen
in picturing more compassionate
management of his imagined mill
enterprise, one biographer writes,
"There exists no evidence that Francis Lowell actually met Robert Owen
or even visited New Lanark," and
asserts that Lowell's worldview dif-
fered from Owen's "utopian social-
ism"; he had been "raised to believe
that individuals had the capacity to
shape their own lives."[6]

On his tour of the United Kingdom, Lowell visited textile mills in
Manchester, England. British export
laws prohibited the sale of manufacturing equipment to American
buyers. Customs officials forbade
anyone from taking abroad representations of the high-tech Cartwright and Horrocks textile looms
made of iron. Lowell had seen the
power looms in action, and with
the machine in his mind's grip he
and his family sailed back to the
States. Lowell and the master mechanic Paul Moody then proceeded to build a
New England version of the English power loom in a Boston loft, a prerequisite to
launching Lowell's first factory venture. They patented the design in February 1815.

In its final form, Appleton saw his new business partner's American-made loom
as a kind of time machine that would transport them to a wealthy beyond: "I well
recollect the state of admiration and satisfaction with which we sat by the hour
watching the beautiful movement of this new and wonderful machine, destined, as
it evidently was, to change the nature of all textile industry."[7]

Journalist John Cassidy places Lowell in the first rank of American business
leaders:

> In 1814, Francis Cabot Lowell, a Boston merchant, founded the first public company,
> when he built a textile factory on the banks of the Charles River in Waltham, Massachu-
> setts, and called it the Boston Manufacturing Company. Lowell had smuggled a plan of a
> power loom out of England, and he intended to compete with the Lancashire mills. But
> he couldn't afford to pay for the construction and installation of expensive machinery
> by himself, so he sold stock in his company to ten associates. Within seven years, these
> stockholders had received a cumulative return of more than a hundred percent, and
> Lowell had established a new business model. Under its auspices, mankind has invented

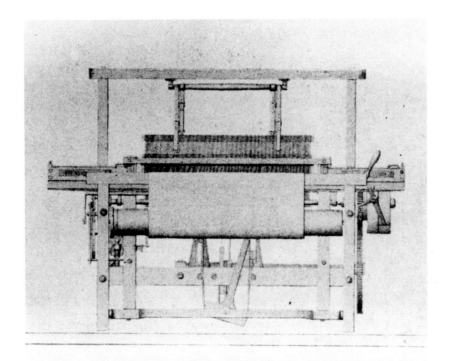

Lowell Loom with Wood Frame.

The "wonderful" power loom as illustrated in 1848, from a catalog of the Lowell Machine Shop

American Textile History Museum, Lowell, Massachusetts

cures for deadly diseases, extracted minerals from ocean floors, extended commerce to all corners of the earth, and generated unprecedented rates of economic expansion. . . . Unfortunately, there is no easy way to make sure that the managers [of a public company] don't slack off, or divert some of the stockholders' money into their own pockets.[8]

WATERPOWER

In November 1821, six men from Boston traveled by coach to the town of East Chelmsford, about twenty-eight miles northwest, to see for themselves the physicality of Pawtucket Falls on the Merrimack River. Here the river dropped more than thirty feet in less than a mile. The deep V of the river channel testified to the volume of liquid that had poured toward the sea for ages. Native people in these woodlands had named the river *Merroh Awke* or "strong place" for its natural force and constancy as a good fishing ground. On the overlook at the falls behind Captain John Ford's tavern, Appleton and Patrick Tracy Jackson imagined the power they could harness with a large stone dam at that very spot.

View of Lowell, Mass., taken from the House of Elisha Fuller, Esq. in Dracutt [sic], by E. A. Farrar, 1834
American Textile History Museum, Lowell, Massachusetts

Without the Wisconsin Glacier, there would be no falls at Lowell. Going back 70,000 years, ice a mile thick in some places sealed the American Northeast. When the glacier hiked its frozen hem about 10,000 years ago, the river emerged in its oddly bent and scraped-out form. The dip at Lowell rushes the current over rocky ribs toward a wide basin before the riverbed angles sharply toward the Atlantic, thirty miles east. Appleton, Jackson, and several others bought 400 acres at the junction of the Merrimack and Concord rivers, including rights to the Pawtucket transportation canal (1792), which they intended to convert into a power source to scale up the integrated cloth manufacturing operation (carding, spinning, weaving, dressing) they had piloted in 1813 on the Charles River in Waltham, Massachusetts. The new factory town was named for Francis Cabot Lowell, who had died in 1817, just forty-two years old. In October 1823, weaver Deborah Skinner turned out the first cotton cloth at her loom in the Merrimack Manufacturing Company. The Lowell Experiment was under way.

MILE OF MILLS

Early Lowell was praised by writer John Greenleaf Whittier as "A city springing up, like the enchanted palaces of Arabian tales."[9] Beyond its integrated textile production (figuratively, bales of cotton in one end of the mill, bolts of cloth out the other), Lowell gained prominence for its innovative approach to forming a labor force. The Lowell "mill girls" or factory operatives were a new phenomenon in the working world and in the social role of women. They left homes in rural middle New England and traveled to Lowell for money and a measure of self-determination.

The engineered power from the water drove a new phase of activity at the confluence of the Merrimack and Concord. Factory-based mass production of consumable textile products, city-building from scratch, cultural growth spurred by the pile-up of ethnically diverse peoples and rival economic classes—these marked the coming of an extensive urban laboratory, a venture between 1820 and 1850 on a scale that had not been seen before. An economy that had been dominated by agriculture took its great leap to one stoked by industry—factories, machines, and laborers. Great Britain was already there with the "satanic mills" abhorred by poet William Blake. But Lowell was meant to better the British model. It was pictured as factories on the frontier with content, healthy, right-living workers—Jefferson's yeoman-farmers' daughters reporting in for the first long shift at the mill. Lowell was the American imagination at work, Yankee ingenuity that would better the imperialists from whom "New" Englanders had separated. This was a declaration of industrial independence.

After the first corps of young women arrived in 1822, they added to their numbers by urging friends back home in nearby states to come to Lowell. An unsigned letter to Elizabeth A. Jackman in 1840 announces:

> i am a Factory girl and wish you Was one idont no But thar Will Be aplace For you in a fortnigh or three Weeks and as Soon as there is I Will let you no and as you Can board With me We Will have first rate fun getting up mornings in the Snow Storm . . . Elizabeth there is a lot of hansome fellows here my mother is going to Send me a Bundle this Week and you Besure to Write and put a letter in it.[10]

The women worked fourteen hours a day, six days a week, and fought to work only ten hours. Some of them organized one of the first unions in the country, the Lowell Female Labor Reform Association; some of them wrote for a literary journal, *The Lowell Offering*. Charles Dickens took 400 pages worth of *Offering* issues back to England with him after visiting Lowell on February 3, 1842, during an extended trip to the United States. He later said the Lowell day was his favorite on the trip—and praised the quality of the women's writing.

Here is Dickens after witnessing the Lowell scene, from his *American Notes for General Circulation*:

> Lowell is a large, populous, thriving place. Those indications of its youth which first attract the eye, give it a quaintness and oddity of character which, to a visitor from the old country, is amusing enough. It was a very dirty winter's day, and nothing in the whole town looked old to me, except the mud, which in some parts was almost knee-deep, and might have been deposited there, on the subsiding waters after the Deluge.[11]

The 1848 *Hand-Book for the Visitor to Lowell* is a slim volume with profiles of the eight major textile companies as well as the Lowell Machine Shop and Lowell Bleachery, to which visitors could gain admission if the proper "cards of introduction" were obtained from factory officials beforehand. In a 1982 reprint by the Lowell Publishing Company, the editors note that at its manufacturing peak, "A constant stream of visitors of all kinds came by the Boston & Lowell Railroad to see the new industrial paradise."[12]

The first phase of Lowell's industrial history, when for a time it was the second largest city in the state, retains an aura of ingenious success. These were the years

Lowell Offering, 1845
LNHP

when President Andrew Jackson, congressmen Davy Crockett and Abraham Lincoln, Emerson and Thoreau, and Edgar Allan Poe stopped in Lowell to see the model city and tap its cosmopolitan energy. Among the important city figures of the day were the transplanted Englishman Kirk Boott, a master builder and chief executive for the mill company owners; Reverend Theodore Edson, who championed public education; and, briefly, Major George Washington Whistler, father of the future famous painter and a sought-after engineer. When James McNeill Whistler was only three, his family left Lowell so that his father could take on projects such as building a railroad for the Czar of Russia. The artist's birthplace on Worthen Street is a museum where the staff has heard every wisecrack about "Whistler's mother," subject of one of the most familiar paintings in the world. At this address hangs a fair copy of Whistler's *Arrangement in Grey and Black* (the mother) made by a cousin of the artist from the original in the Musée d'Orsay in Paris.

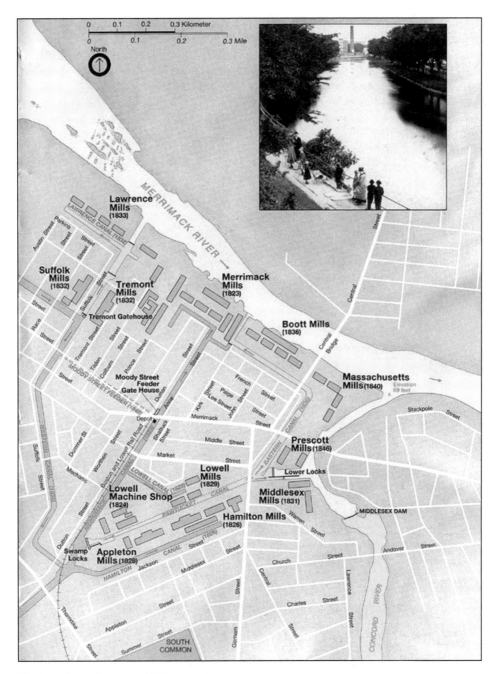

The Lowell canal system, 1850
LNHP

The Lowell founders' hope to avoid creating a "permanent underclass" as in England's factory cities was short lived. Competition quickly led to "speed-ups" (making machines run faster) and "stretch-outs" (forcing workers to tend more machines) on the shop floor. The women workers banded together and protested. Without success, in 1845 and 1846 they petitioned the state legislature for a shorter working day—ten hours instead of twelve. As the Lowell System was copied and improved upon elsewhere, the industrial experiment on the Merrimack lost its luster and hegemony. The initial corps of operatives began to diversify, with Irish immigrants filling more places in the mills.

FIRST BLOOD OF THE NORTH

In the years leading to the American Civil War, Lowell symbolized the cooperation between the "The Lords of the Lash and the Lords of the Loom," in the words of Senator Charles Sumner of Massachusetts. Writing about the Boston area's culture of that time in *The Metaphysical Club: A Story of Ideas in America* (2001), Louis Menand explains,

St. Patrick Church in the Acre neighborhood, 1854
LNHP

The mill towns that sprang up in the Merrimack Valley north of Boston around 1820 . . . were heavily dependent on Southern cotton, which they made into finished goods and then sold, along with footwear, machine parts, rubber goods, and other manufactured products, back to the South. The dependency ran in both directions, for the South had no real industrial base of its own: there were more cotton spindles in Lowell, Massachusetts, in 1860 than in all eleven of the states that eventually made up the confederacy combined.[13]

While the Lowell factories were noted for production of "Negro cloth," the coarse fabric used to make clothing for African slaves on Southern plantations, the city was also animated by abolition activities involving newspaper publisher and poet John Greenleaf Whittier, black antislavery activist Frederick Douglass, and reformer William Lloyd Garrison.

With the onset of war, Lowell found itself on the opening page of the drama; two Lowell men (Luther Ladd and Addison Whitney) were among the first few northerners to fall—during a riot in Baltimore as the troops made their way to protect the nation's capital. Soon after the cannons fired on Fort Sumter in South Carolina, the cotton mill companies halted production. Local historian Charles Cowley, a labor rights activist, painted April 27, 1861, as a black day: "[N]ine of the great corporations of Lowell, under a mistaken belief that they could not run their mills to a profit during the war, unanimously, in cold blood, dismissed ten thousand operatives, penniless into the streets!"[14] Conversely, the woolen mills picked up business as the demand for uniforms soared.

Joseph A. Nesmith's memoir offers a glimpse of Lowell's upper class during the war. The son of a wealthy businessman and land developer, Nesmith describes life at the family mansion on Belvidere Hill:

There was at the time of the Civil War, a group of young men and women hardly more than boys and girls who frequented our house, played croquet on the lawn and bowled in the long, low bowling alley, old when I remember it, and covered from chimney top to threshold with trumpet vines and rambler roses. . . . Henry Livermore Abbott was one of the boys who wrote his name in chalk on the walls of the bowling alley, and later wrote it large in the annals of the Civil War. Him alone among the young men I can remember. He was wounded early and sent home on a furlough; our garden was a pleasant place to convalesce in. He was a graduate of Harvard in the class of 1860. His brother Ned was killed in the battle of Cedar Mountain. Henry fought in the seven days fight before Richmond, Fredericksburg, and Gettysburg, in which his regiment won laurels, and fell in the Battle of the Wilderness: wounded three times, he did not leave the ranks. He was a lad of great promise.[15]

Lowell's best known Civil War figure is General Benjamin F. Butler, "The Beast of New Orleans." (Southerners so hated Butler that they manufactured chamber pots with his face on the inside bottom.) He was the brigade leader in Baltimore on April 19, 1861, and later administrator of captured New Orleans, where he issued the notorious General Order Number 28. Reacting to what he considered to be poor treatment of his troops, Butler directed that any woman who insulted a Union soldier be arrested for prostitution. In response, Jefferson Davis promised $10,000 to any man who would deliver Butler in chains. Butler is also reputed to have dismantled ornate cast iron fences around Southern mansions and packed them on northbound trains. The Confederates charged that he lifted silverware and other valuables from private homes as war booty, which earned him the nickname "Spoons."

The rebellious Virginians used slaves to construct battle fortifications. In 1861, at Fort Monroe in Virginia, Butler designated three young African American men who had escaped their slave masters and crossed into Union lines to be contraband of war. With this challenge to the Fugitive Slave Act, the Massachusetts lawyer set the United States on a path that would finally lead to the abolition of slavery.

In quick order, Butler had 500 black men, women, and children in his custody. His decision to keep them on the Union side of the line "proved a harbinger of things to come," according to historian Doris Kearns Goodwin. President Abraham Lincoln and the majority in Congress accepted Butler's interpretation of the escaped African Americans as contraband of war. Lincoln's position on emancipation was evolving toward a major new policy view. His Emancipation Proclamation would take effect on New Year's Day, 1863, certifying the freedom of more than three million slaves in the eleven Confederate States of America. Lincoln cabinet members John Hay and John Nicolay wrote about Butler's innovative response to the slaves showing up at his gate: "Out of this incident seems to have grown one of the most sudden and important revolutions in popular thought which took place during the whole war."[16]

By the end of the conflict, Lowell had sent 5,266 men to the battles, while many local women served in field hospitals.

BATTERED HIVE

Following the Civil War, Benjamin Butler represented Lowell in Congress and in 1882 was elected governor of Massachusetts. In the aftermath, Lowell was a changed city, economically and socially. The mill jobs were low-paying, but there was still work to be had. From the managers' viewpoint, the surplus of labor meant wages could be kept to a minimum. Semiskilled workers were as interchangeable as machine parts. There was tension among immigrant workers as competition for jobs heated up. A series of strikes added to the labor turmoil—skilled spinners went on strike in 1867 and 1875, with little accomplished. Corruption and corporate inbreeding undermined business in the city. A letter to the editor of one newspaper summed up the concerns: "Disband the oligarchy of office-holding which now rules supreme; which makes one man director of thirty companies and president of nineteen."[17]

Unlike the troubled textile industry, the patent medicine business was booming. What looked to some like snake-oil success, to others was patent medicine–mania. The Hood and Ayer companies of Lowell were giants in the field. The colorful J. C. Ayer became one of the city's prominent citizens, a salesman and tycoon known around the world. He even took on the corporate overlords of Lowell in his book *Usages and Abuses* and fought for legislation that would shine a light on secretive business practices that enriched the few at the expense of the many in the city.

Always provocative, it was Butler who said in 1876, "Our city has been a hive of industry, and, as a rule, the honey has been gathered by others."[18] Those without honey at the turn of the century might find themselves living at the City Poor Farm. Lowell suffered through the Depression of the 1890s, and found itself mentioned by Karl Marx in *Das Kapital*, where the grand theorist of communism rebutted Charles Dickens's earlier portrayal of Lowell as an example of capitalism benefiting

Bird's eye view of
the Spindle City
LNHP

the workers. In the second volume of his opus (published in 1885), Marx leaps on an economic report by the secretary of the British Legation in Washington, D.C., who describes the Lowell manufacturing and boarding house system with admiration. Marx's contrary analysis reads almost as if it were ripped from the headlines in 2013: "A reduction of wages and long hours of labor, that is the essence of the rational and healthy method which is to elevate the laborer to the dignity of a rational consumer, in order that he may create a market for the mass of objects which civilization and the progress of invention have made accessible to him."[19.]

NEIGHBORHOOD NATIONS

By 1910, 40.9 percent of Lowellians were foreign born. City neighborhoods had become ethnic enclaves, with the French speakers in Little Canada, the Irish Americans in the Acre alongside the Greeks, who dominated Market Street, and pockets of Polish, Swedish, Portuguese, and Jewish families elsewhere.

Yvonne Hoar remembered the tensions:

> The Irish were instigators. They were up across the common, the North Common. If you went up on the Common, they had swings and teeters and all that. There'd always be a fight between the French and the Irish. The Irish would come up, "Are you French?" They'd knock the stuffings out of ya. And the Greek kids would be recognized because they'd go to the Greek schools, and they'd wear sort of a blue pinafore uniform . . . so they got hell kicked out of them too by the Irish. But don't worry, the Irish got theirs too. On Saturdays when they'd come down to Hart's Bakery for their beans, many a bean pot was spilled and broken for the wallops we took during the week.[20]

"It is the boast of Lowell that it has no aristocracy,"[21] wrote Charles Cowley, but there was economic and social stratification. French Canadian Americans, for example, operated in a three-tiered class system. The low step on the ladder was cramped tenement life in Little Canada, the blocks jammed against each other on a wedge of land bounded by the Suffolk and Lawrence mill complexes and the muscular river. The middle step was across the river to the northeast, the area called Centralville, especially near St. Louis de France parish. A blue-collar family could rent a cottage or spacious flat. Topmost was the section to the west, Pawtucketville, which had been annexed from the town of Dracut years before. Here, the single-family homes or two-families boasted lawns and driveways.

The Bread and Roses Strike of 1912 put nearby Lawrence on the labor strife map; Big Bill Haywood and Elizabeth Gurley Flynn rallied workers in Lowell. Textile workers in the city won a 10 percent wage increase. Government spending during World War I boosted the local economy for a time, but the long decline resumed after the war. More factories closed. The over-reliance on one industry was a disaster. By the 1930s Lowell's economic woes were drawing attention nationally—*Harper's Magazine* published an article on "tragic" Lowell. Most of the mill corporations had ceased operations and some relocated in the South, where unions were fewer and the wage expectations lower. Instead of making improvements in the Lowell plants, companies were investing in modern equipment elsewhere. Nineteen thirty-six was a terrible time: a spring flood devastated low-lying sections of the city, and only two of the ten original mill companies were operating.

By increments through the twentieth century, Lowell had forfeited its place in the American chronicle. Historians still checked off Lowell in the "significant" category when writing new texts on U.S. history, but locally the epochal contributions of the early nineteenth century had become the province of flame-keepers, raconteurs, and the heritage clubbers. Still, even in the throes of decline, individuals with energy and imagination kept emerging.

Among the prominent Lowellians of the mid-twentieth century was Congresswoman Edith Nourse Rogers. Mrs. Rogers, as she was known, represented Lowell in Congress from 1925 to 1960. Her staunch support of President Roosevelt's New Deal programs and veterans' assistance that meant so much to her district was repaid at the ballot box. Born in Maine, Rogers had been a student at a private school for girls in Lowell and later married John Rogers, from one of the leading textile-industry families in the city. Her husband died while serving in Congress, and she ran successfully to fill his seat. Historian Mary Blewett writes:

Congresswoman Rogers was a liberal and an internationalist, typical of successful Republicans of the northeast. She voted for most of the key New Deal programs of the '30s—the Wagner Act, which protected union organization, the Social Security Act of 1935, and the minimum wage law of 1938—in line with the needs of her Lowell constituents, if not with the Republican leadership.[22]

From his office in the *Sun* newspaper building high over Kearney Square, Charles "Charlie" Sampas typed daily columns, "Sampascoopies," that mirrored Lowell life to his readers. His style was described as "Ideas cascading across the page like a wild river."[23] George Duncan grew up in Lowell reading Sampas; the future founder of Enterprise Bank and a leader of Lowell's revitalization credits Sampas with fueling his own enthusiasm for Lowell's unique character. For decades, Charles Sampas was the voice of the city, a proto-blogger, ever-optimistic that Lowell would regain its greatness. Always looking for the next star, he encouraged the literary prospects of the brain-trust at *Alentour* magazine (1935–1943) and took special note of a friend of his younger brother Sebastian's, an emerging talent, Jean-Louis Kerouac—known by his Americanized name: Jack.

The *Alentour* poets imagined that the same muses who had inspired Concord's Transcendentalist writers a hundred years before could rejuvenate Lowell. One essayist in 1940 pictured a twig dropped by Emerson into the Concord River floating all the way to the Merrimack:

> It would be good to think that as the twig finally reached the other river with the city of empty mills, the piles of dust, that perhaps a boy playing barefooted by the edge of the river picked up the twig, long from Emerson's hand, and planted it that later it would grow into a tree, bringing life to the ruins. And then because workers were idle and had time to listen, perhaps the birds would come to the tree to sing. Perhaps, again, the muse of poetry, weary from travel would rest a while beneath the tree.[24]

The dream of a cultural renaissance was not as far-fetched as it may have seemed then.

Lowell got an unexpected image boost from the Works Progress Administration, one of President Franklin D. Roosevelt's New Deal economic-stimulus programs that between 1935 and 1943 employed about eight million people on public works projects ranging from bridge-building to community theater. The Federal Writers' Project produced a series of state guidebooks. The 1937 *Guide to 1930s Massachusetts* included seven pages on Lowell. Here is the opening description:

> One hundred feet above sea level, on a plateau where the powerful Merrimack joins the sluggish Concord River, stands Lowell, one of the leading manufacturing cities of New England. Canals and grassy plots crisscross the crowded metropolitan business section. On the hill beyond are a city's homes from mansion to tenement. . . .
>
> After 1924, there was a general decrease [in prosperity], ending in the devastating debacle of 1929. . . . The whole textile industry of the city was reduced by 50 percent.[25]

The Lowell section has a street map and a tour route that starts on Appleton Street near the South Common ("22-acre recreational center") and then takes the visitor across town and over the Concord River to the "beautifully planted" Fort Hill Park on Rogers Street with its "birches, maples, beeches, poplars, oaks, pines, spruces, cedars, and tamaracks."[26] The next points of interest are the Gothic-style Immaculate

Conception Church on East Merrimack Street with "its great rosette window on the side reminiscent of the cathedrals of France"[27] and St. Anne's Church, "a plain Norman house of worship with a square tower, constructed almost entirely of small, irregular field-stone blocks." St. Anne's stands alongside Lucy Larcom Park, named for the nineteenth-century poet from Lowell; also in the park is a memorial section of track "laid in 1835 for the Boston and Lowell Railroad, the first steam railroad in New England."[28] Notable attractions include the first Byzantine-style Greek Orthodox Church built in the United States. The cluster of industrial architecture that is the city's reason for being does not warrant a mention; only "the Francis Floodgate" at the guard lock on the upper Pawtucket Canal is called out for the story about the huge gate from 1848 saving parts of the city during the flood of 1938.

Both Lowell State Teachers College (1894) and Lowell Textile Institute (1895) are on the list, with a highlight in the Textile Institute item describing a public "exhibit of the various processes undergone by cotton from the boll to the finished cloth. In connection with this exhibit are spindles and looms in full operation"[29]—this is decades before the community-driven Lowell Museum at the Wannalancit Mills and today's popular Weave Room in the Boott Cotton Mills Museum of the National Park Service.

One place of interest in the WPA guide is an area near the North Common in the Acre neighborhood, close to the yellow-brick Byzantine church, which the authors call "Little Greece, a center of humble nondescript frame dwellings and small variety shops bearing signs in modern Greek."[30] The 1930s closed out darkly for Lowell's Greek American community. With a federally funded housing complex destined for the Acre neighborhood, an area just west of City Hall, Greek Americans fought to protect their businesses and homes. With the assent of the City Council, more than 2,000 residents were evicted and 150 buildings demolished, destroying the traditional hub of the Greek community. While the new North Common Village provided badly needed public housing, the city's culture was permanently altered.

The razing of the Greek section of the Acre prefigured the federally funded Urban Renewal project in Little Canada, the densely populated French Canadian American area behind City Hall. In the early 1960s, the wrecking ball would smash dozens of blocks, scattering neighborhood residents, hundreds of whom regularly spent their week's pay in downtown stores, diners, and theaters.

RUNNING ON EMPTY

Lowell residents suffered through bleak years from the start of World War II to the mid-1960s, when the community saw the first stirrings of a movement to revitalize Lowell. The war economy in the mid-1940s boosted the local economy, but when hostilities ended in Europe and in the Pacific, the relentless slide continued.

After World War II, Lowell hemorrhaged human talent. Many veterans used their G.I. Bill benefits to borrow money to buy small ranch houses in the suburbs of Greater Lowell. Most Lowellians professed the Roman Catholic faith, and the Catholic Archdiocese of Boston continued its binge of parish-building in the boomtowns that ring the city: Billerica, Chelmsford, Dracut, Tewksbury, and Tyngsborough. Through the 1960s, the bishops followed suburban families instead of standing with the urban churches and their marvelous cathedral-like edifices. Conversely, the Greek Orthodox congregations remained largely faithful to the urban mother churches.

By 1963, Lowell's median family income of $5,679 was $3,000 lower than that in comparable cities around the state. Twenty-six percent of Lowell High School students went on to four-year colleges. Students interested in vocational and technical skills competed for only a few hundred slots at the high school level. On the horizon was a regional "voke-tech" high school. The schools were in the spotlight, as seen in a *Boston Globe* article by Ian Forman headlined "Lowell: Politics Before Education." Forman wrote, "Many members of recent School Committees haven't cared enough about education. They have been interested in the politics of administrative appointments, according to local observers."[31] There was hope for reform, which the reporter saw in two newly elected women on the Lowell School Committee, Helen Droney, a Radcliffe College graduate and math teacher with kids in the public schools, and Katherine Martin, who had taught in Newton, Massachusetts, and had four children in the Lowell schools. One of the women's first wins was to get professors from the Tufts University education program to lead workshops on teaching remedial reading.

The mill boarding house or "row house" controversy of 1965 triggered a community debate about the city's historic structures. The Merrimack Manufacturing Company's worker housing on Dutton Street fell to the urban-renewal wrecking crane, but not before a spirited back-and-forth played out in the daily newspaper. The row houses were slated to come down as the tail end of the demolition of the French Canadian American enclave called Little Canada. The bulk of the destruction took place in Little Canada, but it was the solid redbrick, dormitory-style buildings that caught the attention of nascent preservationists. Advocates for business expansion who favored a highway connection to a downtown industrial park pushed for demolition while a few voices were raised in support of rehabilitating the row houses for low-cost apartments. The loss of the row houses moved the preservation debate to

The core of Lowell's commercial district was crumbling in the decades after World War II.
Lowell Historical Society/Lowell Sun Collection

another level, setting the stage for imaginative proposals that called for transforming Lowell into a city-scale museum, an urban laboratory for lifelong, place-based, hands-on learning.

NOTES

1. Richard Howe Jr., "What Was Lowell Before It Was Lowell?" www.howlmag.com.
2. Robert Forrant and Christoph Strobel, *The Big Move: Immigrant Voices from a Mill City* (Lowell: Loom Press, 2011), 17.
3. Howe, "What Was Lowell?"
4. Peter Andreas, "Piracy and Fraud Propelled the U.S. Industrial Revolution," www.bloomberg.com/news/2013-02-01/piracy-and-fraud-propelled-the-u-s-industrial-revolution.html.
5. Chaim M. Rosenberg, *The Life and Times of Francis Cabot Lowell, 1775–1818* (Lanham, MD: Lexington/Rowman & Littlefield, 2011), 183.
6. Rosenberg, *Francis Cabot Lowell*, 183.
7. Arthur L. Eno Jr., *Cotton Was King: A History of Lowell, Massachusetts* (Lowell, MA: Lowell Historical Society and New Hampshire Publishing Company, 1976), 80.
8. John Cassidy, "The Greed Cycle: How the Financial System Encouraged Corporations to Go Crazy," *New Yorker*, September 23, 2002, 64.
9. John Greenleaf Whittier, *Prose Works*, vol. 2 (Boston: Ticknor and Fields, 1866), 288.
10. Lewis T. Karabatsos, ed., *I Am a Factory Girl: Documents of Lowell's 19th Century Working Women* (Lowell Museum Corporation, 1977).
11. Charles Dickens, *American Notes for General Circulation* (London: Penguin, 1985), 114.
12. Mary H. Blewett and Arthur L. Eno, *Hand-book for the Visitor to Lowell, 1848* (Lowell: D. Bixby and Company, 1848).
13. Louis Menand, *The Metaphysical Club: A Story of Ideas in America* (New York: Farrar, Straus and Giroux, 2001), 10.
14. Arthur L. Eno Jr., ed., *Cotton Was King: A History of Lowell, Massachusetts* (Lowell: Lowell Historical Society and New Hampshire Publishing Company, 1976), 141.
15. Joseph A. Nesmith, *The Old Nesmith House and Some of Its Guests* (Lowell: John Nesmith House Alumni Foundation, 1989), n.p.
16. Doris Kearns Goodwin, *Team of Rivals: The Political Genius of Abraham Lincoln* (New York: Simon and Schuster, 2005).
17. Eno, *Cotton Was King*, 143.
18. Eno, *Cotton Was King*, 145.
19. Karl Marx, *Capital*, vol. 2, part 3 (Chicago: Charles H. Kerr and Co., 1909), 21.94.
20. Mary Blewett, ed., *Surviving Hard Times: The Working People of Lowell* (Lowell: Lowell Museum, 1982), 134–35.
21. Eno, *Cotton Was King*, 218.
22. Eno, *Cotton Was King*, 187.
23. Paul Tsongas in Charles Sampas, *The Was the Way It Was*, ed. Marina Sampas Schell (Lowell: Marina Sampas Schell, 1986), n.p.
24. Paul Marion, "Alentour: One of the Lost 'Little Magazines' (1935–1943)," *Massachusetts Review* (Summer 2004).
25. Federal Writers Project, *The WPA Guide to Massachusetts*, 261, 263.
26. Federal Writers Project, 263.
27. Federal Writers Project, 264.
28. Federal Writers Project, 264.
29. Federal Writers Project, 265.
30. Federal Writers Project, 264.
31. Ian Forman, "Lowell: Politics before Education," *Boston Globe*, April 2, 1963, 16.

CHAPTER 2

Urban Laboratory

MODEL CITY

In the final quarter of the twentieth century, federal and state agencies, community development groups, and private investors spent more than $1 billion in Lowell to renovate old mills for businesses and apartments, fix streets and improve the water treatment plant, build a baseball stadium and civic arena for sports and entertainment, lay walkways along the river and canals, and construct houses, schools, and museums. More than 400 historic buildings were restored, creating a distinctive setting of vibrant rose-red structures, cobblestone streets, vintage lampposts, an esplanade and stage along the river, and contemporary sculpture on downtown greens.

One lead figure in the Lowell story emerged, a man who combined the seriousness of Yul Brynner's magnetic hired gunman in *The Magnificent Seven* with the quirky, metaphysical seer qualities of *Star Wars'* Yoda. Pat Mogan—Dr. Patrick J. Mogan—was not born in Lowell. There is extensive preamble to Mogan's passion for a restored Lowell. The subsequent successes link back to numerous fathers and mothers on various redevelopment boards and civic improvement committees. Still, more than forty years on, he remains the consensus choice for main actor, as in "taking action," at the start of Lowell's turnaround. Although he operated in concert with a variety of people—teachers, parish activists, planning consultants, city bureaucrats, politicians, neighborhood leaders, local historians—Mogan most clearly and most consistently described what the city could be and expressed a rationale for mobilization. Mogan and his robust band reconceived Lowell as a city-scale lifelong learning laboratory. The grassroots effort embodied the rock-ribbed American value of progress through education. The unlikely guru was an Irish-American reading teacher from Norwood, Massachusetts. With his marriage to Mary Pollard, he was embraced by a prominent Lowell family. Through a willful reshaping of community expectations, he made the place his own the way an author can take hold of a place with language and an artistic vision. *Boston Globe* reporter Forman had cited Mogan's success as a principal at the Reilly School in the Belvidere neighborhood, including constructive work with the Parent and Teachers Association. The Reilly School in 1963 was regarded as one of a few dams holding back a potential flood of families into the highly absorbent suburban towns.

Mogan composed the stump speech about Lowell's singular importance. He would recite the speech countless times between 1966 and 1978, and then some. The audience might be ten people in a church basement or a phalanx of congressmen at a Washington, D.C., hearing. He would tell them about merchants from

Boston who took a runaway river, a bankrupt canal, pilot technology, and an available labor pool of rural young women and created a template for industrial success. They connected parts picked up along the Merrimack River and fashioned a humming cloth production complex on a scale and of an efficiency never before seen in the United States. Plentiful falling water and a practical mill town combined to forge a hinge of history, the place where America could be seen transforming from a dominant agrarian culture to a society tilted toward factories, wage earners, and teeming cities.

To his parable about the past, Mogan added a balancing future side that suggested how Lowell could reclaim its special place in American history: the city would be reshaped into a museum without walls, a living exhibit of the process and consequences of the American Industrial Revolution—a place so compelling visually and expressively that visitors would fill city streets, scholars would come to write books, and chief executive officers would establish businesses in an inspiring, purposeful renaissance city. Mogan gave anyone who showed interest a homework assignment designed to push the project forward an inch.

Mogan was on the reclamation job by 1966. He had connected the prevailing negative community mindset in Lowell with lagging educational achievement and poor self-esteem among schoolchildren. "There appeared to be a complete disassociation between the present and the past," he said. "This was very serious, for scholars have been saying for a long time that people need 'roots' and a positive sense of being as prime ingredients for development."[1] Students in the inner-city neighborhood schools in Lowell were a year and a half behind the "educational norm"[2] when they reached the eighth grade. Lowell had hired fifty remedial reading teachers, but for many the improvement was stalled.

Young Martin T. Meehan, the future congressman, knew the educational opportunities in Lowell were unequal. He attended a school close to home in a working-class precinct in the southern end of the city. "When we got new books, we had to erase the names in the book—they came from other schools that got the new books. My father said it was wrong."[3] In the sixth grade he took a bus across the river to the Pawtucketville Memorial School, where he saw for himself what it was like in a neighborhood that got more attention. Former Lowell mayor Jim Milinazzo is about the same age as Meehan. As a boy he went to elementary school near home in Belvidere, an upper-tier section. Pat Mogan was his principal at the Reilly. "It was *the* school to go to," he said.[4]

In Mogan's analysis, "No single agency, including the schools, could meet people's needs."[5] They began talking about "a community-type school" that policy makers in the state education office dubbed "The Everywhere School." His answer for repairing the breach between "Who am I?" and "Where do I come from?" was to focus his thinking on the fact that Lowell was a place to be proud of because of the role it played in the formation of America. "Upon looking into Lowell's past and present, we found that Lowell had a very substantial and proud story to tell about mankind and his relationship to the environment," he said.[6]

Toward that end, Mogan and his allies pursued the goals of bringing a national historical park and heritage state park to the city. He always added that the parks themselves were a "means—not ends in themselves—for achieving the stated goals. These means were intended to utilize the physical environment and the cultural environment as two interrelated attributes worthy of being celebrated and shared with people around the United States and the world."[7] As a coda, he stressed this point: "We believed the cultural or 'people' element was our prime focus." Upon learning that the National Park Service and other decision makers in Washington, D.C., would be more at ease talking about the value of "the artifacts of the industrial city" as opposed to "the human story,"[8] Mogan and company, ever-pragmatic, stopped calling their project a "cultural park" and went with the more familiar historical park category used in the U.S. Department of the Interior. Mogan was the first to admit that the physical redevelopment was needed as "props" around which the people's story could be told. He knew the built environment was the strongest evidence of Lowell's unique character as much as he was convinced that the innovative new park's true value would be in enshrining the nation-building contributions made by generations of immigrant workers in Lowell.

Mogan urged Lowellians to flip their value assessment of the city's resources. The conventional wisdom inside and outside of the city limits held that outmoded mill buildings, a working-class labor heritage, and a mostly low-schooled multi-ethnic population were drags on the community efforts to climb the progress ladder. Mogan said, No, what you think is bad is really good—the perceived liabilities are actually assets, and the past is the gateway to a better future. People in Lowell did not shut down the city. They did not turn their backs on 92,000 people and the accumulated work of generations. They got started on the profound business of saving the place.

Pat Mogan wanted everyone to be an entrepreneur contributing to the renaissance. He would say, "Never underestimate the capacity that is in the average person to contribute to the common good." He liked to tell stories on himself, chuckling as he recalled this or that episode. One of his favorites went like this: "Years ago, a man standing near the Merrimack Canal said to me, 'Someone could make a good living by running a wire around the edges of the canal, attaching small boats like Boston's Swan Boats, and powering the whole system with a bicycle.' I said, 'You're crazy.' He laughed and said, 'Well, you're crazy, too!'"[9]

Much of the early funding for park planning came to Lowell through federal Great Society programs like the Model Cities Program and innovative state programs for urban revitalization, which Lowell qualified for because it ranked so high on the "misery index," explained Mogan's colleague at the time, Peter Stamas. A local Greek American and Harvard graduate, Stamas went on to teach mathematics and serve as headmaster of Lowell High School. All the while, he urged along the Lowell revival in various roles, from championing a vision of Lowell as "The Flowering City" while president of the Human Services Corporation to helping to create the Greater Lowell Community Foundation. Asked by the *Boston Globe* in 2002 about his community work that led to a national park, Stamas said he got involved in the beginning "to help the kids in the Acre neighborhood with education."[10]

Mogan was feted by the National Park Service on the thirtieth anniversary of the park. In one of the last formal photographs made of him, he is wearing a green NPS jacket in the front row among dozens of park staff members with the Patrick J. Mogan Cultural Center in the background. He died in December 2012.

Meeting at the Athenian Corner restaurant some months after Mogan's passing, two former school department leaders and colleagues of Mogan's reflected on their friend's legacy. Former Superintendent of Schools George Tsapatsaris and former Lowell High School Headmaster Bill Samaras, both of whom grew up in Lowell, noted that Mogan was extraordinary in the way he wanted to broaden people's thinking. Tsapatsaris's contact with Mogan linked back to the Model Cities Program days when he served on the crime task force. At the Model Cities Education

Component, "we started opening windows and doors," Tsapatsaris said. "We brought together teachers from the public schools with those from the Catholic and Hellenic American schools in the Acre neighborhood. People began to collaborate in new ways."[11] Later, as superintendent of schools (1977–1983), Mogan pushed for more collaboration among schools and teachers in the system and supported professional development opportunities for educators.

"Pat would say, 'Give me five disciples and I will change Lowell,'" Samaras said. "His legacy is in the people who took a piece of what he talked about and gave it structure, translating it into a concrete result."[12] Tsapatsaris added: "More than that, Pat was cognizant of what was fair and what was right, which had a lot to do with his personal history."[13]

REVITALIZATION

After President Jimmy Carter signed the Lowell National Historical Park legislation in June 1978, more than 5,000 people celebrated downtown. The park represented a $40 million initial commitment by the federal government. Fred Faust, a legislative aide on Congressman Paul Tsongas's staff, played a central role in crafting the

Dr. Patrick J. Mogan, right, with his wife, Mary Pollard Mogan, receiving a Lifetime Achievement Award from Secretary of State Michael Connolly, chairman of the Massachusetts Historical Commission, 1992
Lowell Historical Society/ Lowell Sun Collection

MOGAN SPEAKS: COLLECTED WISDOM

"The thinking prevalent in my youth was that to become something better you had to become something else. My section of the town of Norwood, Massachusetts, was called Dublin, and virtually everyone spoke Gaelic. We were referred to by the public schools as second-language problems. When you have an institution as powerful as the schools referring to your background as a problem, well, whether it was deliberate or a reaction to what the educational institution was saying, my people killed their culture so we could live better.

"You won't find much learning, you'll find instruction, in school. There's not a lot of learning in schools. Some people confuse knowing something with understanding something. You'll never understand anything unless you apply it in some circumstance and find out if it's working or not and whether you have to make a further accommodation. That's the only time learning occurs. Your learning is occurring with some kind of dialogue that is not happening in the schools but is happening outside the schools. The school is a small factor, maybe a twenty percent factor, in learning, and your home, neighbors, and peers combine for an eighty percent factor in learning. I had the concept for years of making that eighty percent factor a school, a school in a different sense, but a learning environment that was going to help people when they got into the twenty percent factor, the school. And I'm still consumed with that idea.

"Lowell was not considered a good address in the 1960s. Our industrial city aspect and our ethnic city aspect were looked upon as deficits. There was an alienation being built up between the people and their community.

"We created a process that enabled people of various disciplines to come to Lowell and work with the community to think, plan, and develop concepts, which allowed us to express a vision of the future. In our Model Cities program, we knew we were involved in a process that was going to take time to develop. We used the words of historian William Bundy, who said, 'Every great civilization (I say, every great city) has one thing in common—that's a positive sense of the future infusing the present with a sense of purpose, hope, and expectation.'"

—Patrick J. Mogan, 1995

legislation, and soon after its enactment became the first executive director of a new federal agency called the Lowell Historic Preservation Commission. He talked about the local response.

When the legislation passed there was a parade. It was not a contrived parade. It was a parade of people who were proud that their story had been recognized and that they had been part of that recognition. The idea of having a national park that really honored people for working and for carrying out the traditions of labor and for immigration met with resistance as we talked to the National Park Service and a lot of decision makers at the time. And probably for some good reasons, but I think there was some snobbishness and avoidance of change. This was a real victory for people in Lowell and for the cultures they represented.[14]

Faust said the Lowell advocates, particularly Mogan and his team at Human Services Corporation, were "relentless," and that "they grasped that people and their stories, their ethnic backgrounds, were important . . . and that the paradigm of a melting pot where everybody blended into one was not necessarily something that was good."[15]

Around the same time that the park was established, computer entrepreneur An Wang purchased land in Lowell to build an international headquarters for his growing firm. Born in China, Wang was the city's Francis Cabot Lowell of the twentieth century; both were pioneers of high technology. After earning a PhD in physics from Harvard, Wang invented a breakthrough memory device for computing that became the basis of his new computer company. Lowell would soon reap the benefits of Wang's rocketing success. In the early 1980s, Wang Laboratories hired thousands at its Lowell offices and manufacturing facilities. Wang's twelve-story, million-foot triplex off the Lowell Connector boasted 4,500 employees at its peak—and the firm supported legions of other workers in subsidiary and support companies that helped fuel the Wang engine. Annual revenue reached $3 billion in the late 1980s. By 1985, Lowell's three percent unemployment rate was among the nation's lowest. The majority of top U.S. corporations used Wang office systems. But an ominous echo soon sounded. The city was battered when Wang declared bankruptcy in 1992. The hard lesson that came from over-dependence on one industry wrote itself on Lowell streets one more time. At the ribbon cutting of the international headquarters in the new towers, An Wang had said, "We are not like the textile industry. We will be here for a long time."[16]

The company had misread the direction of the information sector. Wang executives favored proprietary software that isolated its word processing brand and, worse, they missed the customer base turning toward personal computers. Wang Labs had made its bones as an innovative maker of calculators and word-processing systems, aiming to surpass IBM. The company's insular bias proved to be a liability. One longtime Wang employee recalled an industry showcase in California when a young Bill Gates came calling with ideas of his own. What would have happened if the early word-processing heavyweight had gone a different route and the market-giant "Word" product had become known by a different "W"? Less well known in the Wang saga is that the company restructured in the 1990s with imaging software out front. Annual earnings climbed back into the billions before the business was bought by Getronics of the Netherlands and was then sold again to a U.S. corporation.

Lowell reinvented itself as a regional cultural hub, and, for a time in the 1980s, profited from the area's high-technology boom at the heart of what Governor Michael Dukakis called the Massachusetts Miracle. Dukakis, whose father was from Lowell, ran for president against George H. W. Bush in 1988, touting the state's economic "miracle" and pledging to replicate success stories like Lowell's across the country. Bush won the election, and Lowell took a second swing with the presidential bat three years later when native son Paul Efthemios Tsongas sought the Democratic nomination. On a rainy morning in April 1991, in front of a thousand people at Boarding House Park, Tsongas announced his run against President Bush. No fellow Democrat would challenge the president, who was soaring at a 90 percent approval rating in opinion polls following the Gulf War victory. Former U.S. Senator Tsongas took his David-like campaign on the road and shared stories about his comeback city with audiences in Iowa, Florida, and elsewhere. Having won

At Boarding House Park, Paul Tsongas announces he will seek the Democratic Party's nomination for President of the United States, April 1991
James Higgins

the New Hampshire primary and eight other state contests, Tsongas was the last Democrat standing in Arkansas Governor Bill Clinton's path; the pair was featured on the cover of *Time*, with a debate on economic policy inside. In the end, Tsongas folded his campaign tent, lacking money and the political surge that he would have needed to overtake Clinton. Lowell took a third cut with the White House bat in 2004, when Massachusetts Senator John F. Kerry, a former Lowell resident who had begun his political career in the city, carried the Democratic Party's banner against Texas governor George W. Bush. Despite winning more votes than any previous Democratic presidential candidate, Kerry lost to Bush, finding himself on the receiving end of vicious political attacks like those made on him by the conservative *Lowell Sun* newspaper in 1972, when he had run for Congress as an anti–Vietnam War candidate.

After graduating from college, Paul Tsongas spent two years in the Peace Corps in Ethiopia in the early 1960s. He remembered a *Sports Illustrated* article from that time. In a story about Adebe Bikila, the gold-medal marathon runner of the Olympics in Rome, the national hero of Ethiopia, the reporter compared the destitute hometown of the champion marathoner to down-and-out places in the United States. Paterson, New Jersey, and Lowell were offered as the abject examples. Tsongas never forgot how his hometown had been portrayed. "I remember vividly that the audience of *Sports Illustrated*, in reading that, would think that Addis Ababa was in terrible shape," Tsongas said.[17]

Tsongas had his own version of Lowell Economics 101. Arguing in favor of a pro-business platform for the Democratic Party in 1991–1992 when he was running for his party's presidential nomination against the likes of Governor Bill Clinton and Senator Bob Kerrey of Nebraska, Tsongas told his story in a plain gray pamphlet titled *A Call to Economic Arms*. The eighty-six-page publication was a campaign phenomenon for its tough-love talk about the American future. The candidate distributed hundreds of thousands to voters starved for substance. In it Tsongas wrote about growing up in Lowell:

> My childhood was spent experiencing the economic decline of my home city. . . . My father (a Republican) owned a dry cleaners and the entire family worked in the business. My father worked 6:30 a.m. to 6:30 p.m., six days a week, 51 weeks a year. Sundays were spent doing books and repairing the machinery. By any fair standard, this staggering workload should have resulted in just rewards for him. It didn't. No matter how hard he worked, no matter how conscientious he was, the forces of Lowell's economic decline were too much to overcome. The remembrance of those days has left me with an inability to view economic dislocation casually.[18]

A 1958 graduate of Lowell High School who went on to Dartmouth College and then Yale University Law School, Tsongas talked about a "psychological numbness," the feeling "that somehow there's not a lot going on and you are sinking into the mud. You don't want to be part of that, particularly if you are 18 years of age." The atmosphere suppressed the local ambition to do well in the city. Like many of his contemporaries, he decided that the way up was to "go on to the greater world and do what he could."[19] Ten years later, there was still a lot of that in the air. David Marion is a professor of political science at Hampden-Sydney College in Virginia. In the mid-1960s he attended St. Joseph's High School for Boys on upper Merrimack Street in Saint-Jean-Baptiste parish. He recalled the afternoon when one of the Marist Brothers who taught there walked in to his class and said, "Somebody should just drop a bomb on this place and start over." A couple of blocks away in what had been Little Canada, it looked like the bombs had already exploded.

Not everyone shared that view, not everyone sped out of town; even Paul Tsongas came back in the mid-1960s and was elected to the Lowell City

Paul Tsongas at Lowell High School, c. 1958
UMass–Lowell Center for Lowell History/
Tsongas Family Collection

Council. He would tell the story of riding in a car with a longtime councilor who thought he would take the rookie to school. The old "pol" said, "Remember, Lowell may be a dump, but it's our dump—and we control it."

Reflecting on what Lowell had been through, forty-year-old Senator Tsongas wrote:

> Under the free enterprise system, useless items are discarded in favor of more productive ones. How do you discard a city? Very simply—by allowing it to decay. Who makes the decision? Everyone. . . . Watching a city decline is like watching a fire dying out. The critical mass necessary for continued dynamism is no longer present: even while there is still both heat and light, the eventual outcome is obvious.[20]

Tsongas would jokingly refer to himself as a "pinko" when the talk came around to social issues, but he was as hard-headed as his Republican father the dry-cleaner when the topic was the importance of business and partnerships. He had seen his father struggle in economic quicksand. As proud as he was of the historical park bill, he was convinced that Lowell needed a vigorous business sector and a pro-business climate citywide to survive long-term. Tsongas is the one who said to his fellow Democrats, "You can't be pro-jobs and anti-business." He teamed up with then-City Manager B. Joseph Tully, a gruff but effective political boss-type who favored a cardigan sweater over a shirt and tie at the office—an unlikely dance partner for Tsongas. A former state senator, Tully was city manager from 1979 to 1986. They devised mechanisms to foster collaboration between government and business sector leaders. Veterans of the Lowell renaissance swap stories about Tsongas and Tully using their considerable powers of persuasion in two-on-one meetings with downtown landlords whose buildings were detracting from the city's overall progress, either in appearance or through down-market activity. Sometimes the agenda items were agreed to on the merits, but there are tales like the one involving a Public Works Department crew showing up unannounced on the street in front of a landlord's ranch-style home in an upscale neighborhood; the workers proceeded to excavate in search of a broken water pipe, shutting down service to the house. Message received. Tsongas liked that the manager could get results on the city side. Tully stepped down as manager in 1986, and he came to grief in court two years later as a result of malfeasance while in office.

Making notes one night on a napkin in a riverfront restaurant appointed like King Arthur's Court, Tsongas and Tully had outlined a strategy for cooperation among leaders in the public and private sectors. Out of this meeting in 1979 came the second of two related organizations: the Lowell Plan, Inc., a roundtable of business, government, and community leaders that Tsongas described as "a chamber of commerce that actually works." The first organization was a quasi-public banking entity called the Lowell Development & Financial Corporation (LDFC), founded in 1975, through which local banks pooled funds to make low-rate loans for local projects. With these innovative tools, leaders forged a collaborative approach to city development and aligned the private interests behind both business ventures and other initiatives that contributed to the public good, for example, a master plan for city development and an assessment of the public schools.

Complementing the efforts of the Lowell Plan and the LDFC were various community-action groups that tapped into the city's momentum and then fueled it with their own work. The Coalition for a Better Acre (CBA) was as sidewalk grassroots as

Journalist Charles Sampas of the *Lowell Sun* with the American Revolution Bicentennial Commission's Freedom Train in downtown Lowell in 1975. National enthusiasm about the Bicentennial reinforced local passion for rediscovering Lowell's history.
Lowell Historical Society/Lowell Sun Collection

the Lowell Plan was executive conference room. The CBA stretched its arms around the poorest, toughest neighborhood. The Acre began as property west of downtown set aside by the textile company management for rustic work camps for the Irish immigrants as early as 1822—and they stayed. The Acre became the place where newcomers got a foothold on Lowell turf and then jumped off to a better lot. Irish, Scots, French Canadians, Greeks, Syrians, and others were followed by Colombians, Lebanese, Puerto Ricans, Cubans, Laotians, Cambodians, Vietnamese, Cameroonians, Iraqis, and Burmese. Acre native, former park ranger, and now St. Patrick Church historian Dave McKean in 1993 told *Time* magazine that "At midnight Mass on Christmas Eve, 'Silent Night' is now sung in Vietnamese. For some it's a sign of unity. For others it hurts."[21]

McKean's involvement with neighborhood history took an interesting turn in 2011, when UMass–Lowell and Queen's University in Belfast, Ireland, teamed up for an archaeological dig on the green in front of St. Patrick Church. The largely undisturbed lawn promised to yield up pieces of the local-Irish past, dating from spring 1822 when a work gang of thirty immigrants led by Hugh Cummiskey walked to Lowell from Charlestown, Massachusetts, to dig canal trenches. The "Acre" was an actual acre of property given to the growing Irish contingent, land upon which a church (1831) and school were built. Passersby would shout to McKean, "Did you find any gold yet?" The modern-day diggers uncovered 1,352 artifacts, from a

LIVING HISTORY: DAVID MCKEAN

David McKean
Kevin Harkins

"The Acre was where my grandparents settled upon arriving in America. It was where I was raised and attended school. It is not where my children were born. At the time I grew up in Lowell, as today, each neighborhood had its own identity. The tenement in which I spent my early years on the corner of Broadway and Walker was similar to the places where my relatives and friends lived. We attended the same schools and church. Shopped at the same markets, belonged to the same clubs and teams, and everyone was related to everyone else. It was in the truest sense a community. What many of us didn't know was that we lived on the edge of poverty. That gives me a unique perspective on the park's early days.

"I'll be honest, mine was a political appointment. A fellow Acre resident with some influence approached me about joining the Park Service. Some Acreites thought the park was not utilizing the city's most precious resource—Lowell's residents, especially from some of the less affluent neighborhoods. Whether it was because of this or not, I was hired to be a part-time ranger.

"One part of our training was to tag along with veteran rangers and learn the variety of tours. One of the offerings was the Mill Girls & Immigrants tour. Rangers gave one or two variations of the tour. The first was a semi-mythical history of the first Irish with visions of 'No Irish Need Apply' nailed to every mill. That was a story, not the facts. Maybe a quick look at the Greek church, and then back to the Visitor Center. What about the rest of the story? What about the Acre of the day? I didn't hear much. The second version of the tour was often a quick walk-them-in and walk-them-out. I recall being at the information desk when a visitor said her family was from the Acre and she wanted to visit the old neighborhood. The ranger on duty told her that was not a good idea and suggested other tours, insinuating that it was not a safe place.

"The park superintendent at the time attended St. Patrick's Church in the Acre. Soon, festivals were taking place on Ecumenical Plaza, facing the church. Rangers had a key to bring visitors in to the church. I loved bringing people through the neighborhood. It represents Lowell's struggles and successes. Acre residents would stop to chat with visitors. Over time, better research and wider interest in diversity made rangers and guests more open to visiting a working neighborhood. The park and the Acre have grown up over time, learning from each other.

"Who defines what happens in the Acre today? How much influence should history have on what happens in the Acre today? The Acre of my father's time, the Acre of my youth, and the Acre of today are vastly different and yet continue through time."

—David McKean, 2013

clay-pipe bowl and buttons to oyster shells and rusty nails. UMass–Lowell student Dimitrios Booras, an immigrant himself, made a link to his past: "On the first day of the dig, we found clay marbles that would have been used by children in the 1800s, which reminded me of playing marbles as a little kid in Greece. The connection was instant, and I was hooked."[22] Students from Lowell and Belfast regrouped in Crossan, County Tyrone, in Northern Ireland to excavate at the site of Cummiskey's homestead. The rediscovery of Acre heritage is a long way from the desperate years when the neighborhood was a source of much distress.

Between 1975 and 1980, sixty-five buildings in one part of the Acre burned, many of the fires suspected to be the dastardly acts of arsonists. Community organizers rallied the mostly Hispanic families in the neighborhood. The CBA matured to become a major property holder, small business incubator, and the city's only true community development corporation—keeping community empowerment as its core objective. Along the way, the CBA became one of the stars in the local historic-preservation firmament, helping to keep intact the distinctive architecture and streetscape of the neighborhood. In their own words, the CBA leaders recalled their origins:

> CBA emerged from an urban renewal plan in 1982 that would have leveled much of the Acre and dispersed its residents. The community mobilized, beat the plan, then recognized that the opportunity for long-term improvement lay in coming up with their own plan for the neighborhood and doing whatever they could to make it happen. . . . Step 1 was to win site control of large tracts (vacant lots and dilapidated buildings) within the Acre neighborhood. Step 2 was to revitalize and redevelop them for residents of modest means, the Acre's residents from the neighborhood's inception. . . . CBA has facilitated more than 475 low- and medium-priced housing units, including the 270-unit North Canal Apartments complex, a low-income project built by the private sector and then left to decay.[23]

In addition to the rebuilding, the CBA started and spun off the Acre Family Day Care nonprofit organization, helped finance a manufacturing business that has meant 200 jobs in the Acre, and partnered with the Lowell Housing Authority on an after-school homework club for middle school students, and responded to the foreclosure crisis of the past several years by creating a counseling and assistance center that has helped hundreds of owners.

In the early 1980s, five years after the park opened and while visitors were being guided through the downtown and outlying historic areas, religious activists responded to deplorable conditions in many of the city's multifamily apartment houses and tenements by forming the Ethnic Covenant. Leaders released *Thirty Pieces of Silver*, a scathing report on housing conditions and abusive landlords, which was part of their "attempt to address a long-standing and shameful situation in our city, a situation that forces lower-income families to pay outrageously high rents for the privilege of staying in unsafe, unsanitary, slum shelter."[24] Charging that older neighborhoods were being ignored, they called for restoration of the city's rent review board, reorganization of the health and code departments, and increasing family housing, and then followed up by lobbying state legislators to create a housing court in the Merrimack Valley to expedite complaints and judicial action on behalf of tenants. The Northeast Housing Court in Lawrence, Massachusetts, still hears cases today.

Cambodian refugees at Boston's Logan Airport en route to Lowell, c. 1985
James Higgins

The Covenant also created the Merrimack Valley Housing Partnership (MVHP), which started out building affordable housing and has since pioneered new-home-buyer education. Offering programs in many languages, the MVHP has prepared thousands of people to buy their first homes. The staff works closely with the city planning department and LDFC to provide down-payment assistance to the new homebuyers.

Lowell's population changed dramatically from 1980 to 2000, a time during which some 17,000 refugees from Southeast Asia, most of them Cambodians, along with many Vietnamese and Laotians, resettled in the mill city. The predominantly working-class Catholic city almost overnight became, after Long Beach, California, the second largest Cambodian population center in America. Buddhist temples opened in Lowell and surrounds while the regional bishop demolished an empty Catholic church that had once brimmed like a cathedral on the outskirts of downtown: St. Peter Church. From wrenching relocation to assimilation and now the assumption of a place in the city's power structure, the Cambodian Americans repeated the experience of Irish, Greek, French Canadian, Portuguese, and other ethnic groups in Lowell. In November 1999, Lowellians elected the first Cambodian-born city councilor in America, Rithy Uong. Around the same time, headlines reported proceedings from Asian youth-gang murder trials. Efforts were made to quiet the streets where hard-core gangsters who had moved to Lowell from California were shooting each other. Councilor Uong worried about the spillover damage to the perception of the Asian community at large if Lowell was descended upon by immigration agency investigators and federal agents of the Drug Enforcement

Agency. With their children and grandchildren, the survivors of the Killing Fields of the Khmer Rouge genocide and the dangerous way stations in Thailand constitute one of the largest ethnic groups in Lowell. They have formed their own business-centric Cambodia Town, reminiscent of Little Canada or Greektown in the Acre, and are increasingly involved in civic affairs.

The city was changing in other ways. Local artists, writers, business chiefs, museum directors, patrons, and others joined forces in 1985 to write the state's first comprehensive plan for cultural development. In every corner of Lowell, people were organizing, planning, acting to shape the future. There was a palpable sense that people were reclaiming control over their lives and neighborhoods. People in the city believed that they could solve their own problems and create opportunities for themselves and their children—no small change. In his analysis of several northeast cities, *Renewing Cities*, urban affairs scholar Ross J. Gittell writes that Lowell's success is due in part to having the components needed to spark regeneration: motivating factors such as crisis conditions and a plan for change combined with the capacity to describe and diagnose the problem, effective leadership (individual and organizational), and the money needed to act.

Patrick Mogan often said that his goal was to make Lowell a "good address" again, and Tsongas claimed that Lowellians would know their city had attained the desired quality of life when young residents began choosing to stay and outsiders starting buying in. Real estate activity suggests that the change has come. The housing market leveled off but didn't completely collapse in the Great Recession, as it did in some other sections of the country. Low-cost rental units remain scarce. Artists are renting studios and buying lofts in the historic district. For a time, a banner topping a four-story building laced with scaffolding read: "Dutton Street Artists' Lofts—United Lowell Stands." Not far away, the five-acre campus of Western Avenue Studios, the largest complex of its type on the East Coast of the United States, exceeds 350 artists working in every type of media, plus a state-of-the-art recording studio determined to capture a "Lowell sound" to rival Liverpool's or Seattle's of the past. A $500-million redevelopment project, the Hamilton Canal District, wound its way through state-of-the-art community-planning and municipal-permitting phases during the economic slump and attempts to catch the economic cycle on the upturn. Massachusetts Governor Deval Patrick helped break ground for the district's first project, an artist live-work building that rose out of the historic remnants of the Appleton Mills.

A label stuck in the minds of many people who grew up in and around Lowell in the 1950s and 1960s—Depressed Area—an official public designation that clung like an old bumper sticker so sealed by the heat that you cannot scrape if off the back end. The city had recovered so well by the 1980s that visitors like Prince Charles of England and the mayor of Beijing traveled to the mill city much as Charles Dickens and Congressman Davy Crockett had once toured the Spindle City's pristine red-brick factories ranged along the Merrimack. In 1990, *Historic Preservation* magazine praised Lowell as "the premier rehabilitation model for gritty cities worldwide."[25] Urban experts consider the city a model of effective, innovative practices. Dignitaries and planners today come to hear about redevelopment strategies that can be custom-designed for their communities. In October 2002, Lowell received the highest honor awarded by the National Trust for Historic Preservation, recognizing twenty-five years of concerted work by partners in the public and private sectors. Speaking at the National Preservation Conference in Cleveland, Ohio, president of the trust Richard Moe said, "Lowell was always a working city, but preservation has given the phrase a whole new meaning: Lowell works."[26]

Lowell's open-ended reclamation project remained the city's key theme through the opening decades of the twenty-first century. Politics in the city is as hard-nosed but pragmatic as always. Paul Tsongas's widow, Nicola "Niki" Tsongas, left her administrative job at Middlesex Community College in Lowell to seek the Democratic nomination for Congress in 2007. Despite losing the Lowell vote in the primary election to the city's popular former mayor Eileen Donoghue, Niki Tsongas was elected district-wide in a special election to fill the same seat her late husband had held. She won the city overwhelmingly in the general election. She quickly identified urban issues as a policy focus and gained seats on committees on Armed Services and the National Parks, topics of essential interest in her district. She was reelected in 2008, 2010, and 2012. Niki had seized an opportunity created by the resignation of the seven-term, nationally known Martin T. "Marty" Meehan, who surprised many political experts by accepting an appointment as chancellor of UMass–Lowell, his alma mater, in the middle of his eighth term.

Lowell was not immune to the ravages of the Great Recession, which took 40 percent of the wealth from middle-income Americans between 2008 and 2012. Unemployment in Lowell reached the notorious 1975 high-water mark of 12 percent before receding. While the suffering was real in the mill city, the urban fabric did not look as damaged as it did in 1965 or 1975. Housing values fell, but the population remained steady. The most counterintuitive scenes were the construction cranes: projects valued in the hundreds of millions of dollars continued apace at Lowell General Hospital, UMass–Lowell, in the Hamilton Canal District, and at a state construction site for the new Richard P. Howe Bridge across the Merrimack. Hard hats, cranes, and dump trucks signaled that money was flowing again.

COLLEGE TOWN

The University of Massachusetts–Lowell's campus and programs have steadily spread from the riverfront to the heart of the city. Its faculty researchers work to solve the riddle of economic boom and bust that has plagued places like Lowell. In 1997, Chancellor William T. Hogan established a Department of Regional Economic and Social Development to promote the study of "best practices" in the field. Hogan grew up not far from the Tsongas homestead and attended St. Peter's Parish School on his way to earning a doctorate at MIT. He had seen lean years give way to better times, and knew it would take imagination and drive to break free of the ingrained economic cycle. Today, a commercial-ventures unit in the renovated Wannalancit Mill helps start-up companies to assemble capital and technical expertise to launch homegrown products.

Hogan worked closely with then-state Senator Steven C. Panagiotakos, who for a time chaired the influential Ways and Means Committee. Also a Lowellian, Panagiotakos is an attorney who attended Phillips Academy and Harvard University. His electoral road had run from the Lowell School Committee to the State House, where he helped move legislation important for Lowell's prospects, including the widening of Route 3, which linked Greater Lowell to the industrial belt outside Boston along Route 128. The route had been dubbed America's Technology Highway in the years before Silicon Valley burst into a supernova of innovation on the other coast. He also moved into position essential state economic development money, $35 million, that was the core funding for UMass–Lowell's $80 million Mark and Elisia Saab Emerging Technologies and Innovation Center, the largest university research facility north of Boston.

Panagiotakos has a deep affection for his hometown. On a cold night in February 2009, when the scale of the Great Recession was beginning to be understood in every city and town, Panagiotakos hosted a free breakfast at the Owl Diner for more than 100 community leaders. He expressed thanks for the contributions of nonprofit groups and neighborhood associations, which would be needed more than ever in the frightful economic times because state and federal governments were in such a deep fiscal ditch. The new congresswoman, Niki Tsongas, arrived from Washington, D.C., midway through the event with news of how Congress and the president were trying to help with a stimulus package. Everyone knew it was time to pull together. Panagiotakos added considerably to the city's social glue at a crucial moment, and people still talk about the scrambled eggs, French toast, and camaraderie. It felt as if all Lowell squeezed into the diner that night.

UMass–Lowell history professor Bob Forrant teaches the economic and labor history of Massachusetts, particularly postindustrial cities like Lowell. Among a dozen other responsibilities, he writes for the *MassBenchmarks* journal of the Donahue research institute of UMass and the Federal Reserve Bank of Boston. Citing Mario Polese's *The Wealth and Poverty of Regions: Why Cities Matter*, Forrant quoted Sir Peter Hall, "Places with a unique fizz, a special kind of energy will prove more magnetic than ever." He puts Lowell in that category—"It's a place with a walkable downtown, affordable housing, a growing entrepreneurial immigrant population, and vibrant cultural and community organizations, including churches, youth groups, and ethnic social clubs." Forrant added:

> In the mid-1990s, under then-Chancellor Hogan, UMass–Lowell focused on the development of a regional economy predicated on the notion that a sustainable economy required a skilled and ever-replenished workforce, innovative products, environmental protection, and strong public health and public education infrastructures. This work continues under Chancellor Marty Meehan. Faculty, staff, students, and the administration are more engaged than ever, with co-op learning, internships, and expanded study and service abroad. Engineering students all participate in service-learning, and the school is ranked with outstanding institutions on President Obama's Higher Education Community Service Honor Roll.[27]

In 2012, annual funded research at UMass–Lowell reached $60 million. Nanotechnology, laser optics, polymers—these are the fields where engineers and scientists are pushing the boundaries and creating new knowledge. The investigations are all geared to applying knowledge to solve problems or invent solutions, whether it is a new way to identify cancer cells or eliminate toxic materials from products. At the Massachusetts Medical Devices Development Center (M2D2) in Wannalancit Mills, a business incubator program occupies space once loaded with textile production machinery. The center opened in 2011 with several start-up companies whose products advance the care of wounds and the treatment of prostate cancer and other medical conditions. The center has helped more than twenty companies take new products from the laboratory through the patent process and to market.

UMass–Lowell now ranks among the top 100 public universities in America, according to *U.S. News & World Report*. In the first seven years of the Meehan administration, UMass–Lowell added nine new facilities, investing nearly $600 million: academic and research buildings, the downtown Inn & Conference Center (former hotel) and Tsongas Center (former arena), student and administrative center (former hospital), upscale residence halls, and parking garages on north and south campuses. The university is in the midst of an epochal revival. Enrollment exceeds 17,000; SAT scores for first-year students have risen 63 points; $85 million in financial gifts has been raised or pledged; research money has grown by nearly 70 percent; there are 100 new international partnership agreements; and all the athletic teams compete in NCAA Division 1.

UMass–Lowell Chancellor Marty Meehan
UMass–Lowell

UMass President Robert Caret said, "Lowell has been just about as aggressive, if not the most aggressive, of the five UMass campuses in getting private money."[28] About Chancellor Meehan, former UMass board of trustees chair Robert Karam said, "He's got the ability to galvanize people,"[29] and Jack Clancy, CEO of Enterprise Bank in Lowell, noted, "We're all standing a little taller."[30] Lowell has taken on a college town character in a way that is substantially different than at any time since two colleges were founded along the river in 1894–1895. Speaking at the Innovative Cities Conference in Lowell in June 2010, Meehan sketched a picture of Lowell as a place where the dominant motifs are learning, innovation, and inspiration:

> People should flow back and forth among educational, cultural, commercial, and recreational settings, from the Emerging Technologies and Innovation Center to the businesses at Wannalancit Mills, from the boathouse on the north bank of the Merrimack to Merrimack Repertory Theatre downtown, from the Tsongas Center's sports and entertainment events to the park Visitor Center's tours and exhibits. It's time to merge the heart of the city with its higher education institutions. The experience should be a seamless, campus-like feeling for students, residents, and visitors. The University is the knowledge hub of the region, with its programs at the apex of learning. Companies start up, grow, and often move. Higher education is the modern constant in cities.[31]

Middlesex Community College (MCC) was seventeen years old when its leadership opened a downtown Lowell campus in Wannalancit Mills, just north of downtown, where the Western and Northern canals come together. That was 1987. The school was young, the thirteenth community college in the state, and at the time had a main campus in Bedford, Massachusetts. Middlesex had been growing steadily since opening. With a push from Governor Michael Dukakis, who saw the advantage of an urban campus for the school, MCC made a leap northward. Dukakis was a cheerleader for the revitalization that he saw as a template for other small industrial cities in the Commonwealth. He made sure the state kept investing in the model.

Another key player was state Senator Paul Sheehy of Lowell, who as a state representative had been a strong advocate for the original legislation that created MCC. Sheehy, a former schoolteacher, saw an opportunity to fill a gap in educational offerings in the city. "We had a lot of people going into Boston to take certain courses," he said at the time.[32]

Starting with 392 students that first semester in Lowell, the urban campus enrollment of MCC now tops 5,000. MCC has earned a stellar reputation for its workforce development programs and international business education initiatives, the global reach exemplifying the vision of longtime President Carole Cowan. On the ground in Lowell, MCC quickly became an essential contributor to the city's revitalization, especially downtown. In 1990, trustees approved a move to a permanent home in Lowell in a contemporary hexagonal brick building that had been erected for Wang Laboratories' corporate education program. Wang had abandoned the building when its computer business collapsed a few years before. MCC rebooted the six-story building and then redeveloped other properties in the core of the downtown; President Cowan also acquired a surplus former U.S. post office across the street from its main campus and renamed it the F. Bradford Morse Federal Building in honor of the late Lowell congressman and high official of the United Nations. Each of these buildings had its rehabilitation challenges and requirements to meet explicit preservation standards, which MCC met effectively. A more ambitious preservation challenge faced MCC when Cowan seized the opportunity to acquire the nineteenth-century John Nesmith House, a mansion on Belvidere Hill that has become the college's showpiece venue for receptions and executive-level meetings. MCC continued to restore and renovate other historic properties downtown, such as the Pollard Building on Middle Street and the former Boston & Maine Railroad Depot (later the Rialto Theatre) on Central Street, which is slated to house the school's Fine Arts program. The B&M/Rialto represented a success for the National Park Service, which had fully rehabilitated the exterior, including replacing signature towers, before conveying it to MCC in a "Preservation to Education" ceremony.

Sheehy was also the architect of the legislation that called for the merger of Lowell Technological Institute and Lowell State College into the University of Lowell in 1975. His wife, Molly, a career educator, noted that her husband had taken to heart the big dreams that newspaperman Charles G. Sampas always had for the city, including the notion that bringing together the two colleges on either side of the river would lift Lowell to a higher orbit of cities and better serve people in the area. The contributions made by Sheehy toward the higher education sector in the city are enormous and in the long run could possibly exceed the impact of a national park. Combined, LNHP, MCC, and UMass–Lowell give Lowell an intellectual and cultural "gravitas" that is the envy of small, postindustrial cities near and far.

With its historic downtown beautifully restored, Lowell began to see a collateral benefit not anticipated by preservation advocates. The city is winning raves from Hollywood directors, among them Ricky Gervais, who filmed *The Invention of Lying*

(2009) at locations throughout the city. The movie bombed at the box office. In the summer of 2009, actors Mark Wahlberg and Christian Bale led a cast for the filming of *The Fighter*, a gritty biopic based on the story of Lowell boxer Micky Ward, whose epic bouts with Arturo Gatti gave HBO expanded audiences. When *The Fighter* was released in 2011, despite scenes of drug abuse and rough street life, it burnished Lowell's reputation as an exceptional American city. The film was nominated for seven Academy Awards, including Best Picture, and the cast won two: Best Actor in a Supporting Role for Bale and Best Actress in a Supporting Role for Melissa Leo. The city's boxing heritage maintains its allure, as evidenced in a 2012 "American Times" broadcast on the Travel Channel in the United Kingdom (seen in seventeen countries), which shone a spotlight on Lowell for its boxing, international cuisine, industrial history, and Jack Kerouac literary sites.

NOTES

1. Patrick J. Mogan, *Culture: A Celebration of Lowell, a Report on the Conference of November 22, 1986* (Human Services Corporation, 1986), 22.

2. Mogan, "Renewal Process in Lowell, Massachusetts: Toward an Ecologically Sensitive Educational Model," University of Massachusetts–Amherst, 1975, 2.

3. Marty Meehan, interview with the author.

4. James Milinazzo, interview with the author.

5. Mogan, "Renewal Process in Lowell," 4.

6. Mogan in *Culture: A Celebration of Lowell*, 22–23.

7. Mogan in *Culture: A Celebration of Lowell*, 23.

8. Mogan in *Culture: A Celebration of Lowell*, 23.

9. Page One Productions, *Patrick J. Mogan*.

10. James Ostis, "Peter S. Stamas: A Brief Biography for Consideration of the Lowell High School Distinguished Alumni Award," n.p.

11. George Tsapatsaris, interview with the author.

12. Bill Samaras, interview with the author.

13. Tsapatsaris, interview with the author.

14. Fred Faust, interview with Mehmed Ali.

15. Faust, interview with Mehmed Ali.

16. Martha Mayo, interview with the author.

17. Paul E. Tsongas in *Culture: A Celebration of Lowell*, 28.

18. Tsongas, *A Call to Economic Arms: Forging a New American Mandate* (Boston: The Tsongas Committee, 1991), 11.

19. Tsongas in *Culture: A Celebration of Lowell*, 28.

20. Tsongas, *The Road From Here: Liberalism and Realities in the 1980s* (New York: Knopf, 1981), 18–19.

21. Ann Blackman, "Lowell's Little Acre: For Centuries, One Neighborhood Has Served as a Gateway for Immigrants," *Time*, June 23, 1993, 34.

22. Dimitrios Booras, "Archaeology Reflections," 4.

23. Coalition for a Better Acre, http://www.coalitionforabetteracre.org/about-us/history.

24. *Thirty Pieces of Silver: A Report on Slum Housing in Lowell* (Lowell Ethnic Covenant, June 1983), 1.

25. Allen Freeman, "Lessons from Lowell," *Historic Preservation*, November–December 1990, 2.

26. *The Shuttle: A Publication of UMass Lowell*, "National Trust Honors City for Excellence in Preservation," 3.

27. Robert Forrant, e-mail to author, 2013.

28. Mary Moore, "Greetings from Martyville: UMass Lowell Chancellor Has Significantly Grown the School's Size." *Boston Business Journal* 33, no. 17 (May 17–23, 2013): 41.

29. Moore, "Greetings from Martyville," 41.

30. Jon Marcus, "Meehan's House," *Boston Globe Magazine*, August 19, 2012, 20.

31. Martin T. Meehan, "College Town Speech at the Innovative Cities Conference," UMass Lowell Inn and Conference Center, June 17, 2010.

32. Patrick Cook, *Middlesex Community College: Celebrating a Forty-Year Legacy of Learning* (Bedford and Lowell: Middlesex Community College, 2011), 35.

CHAPTER 3

Making the Park

"LOWELL HAS DONE IT"

For 9,000 jubilant people in the Paul Tsongas Center, U.S. Secretary of the Interior Ken Salazar sang a line in Spanish that his father had sung to him when he was a boy. The English words are, "I would love to leave to my children what I do not have." In May 2012, he was on the speakers' platform to receive an honorary doctorate of humane letters from UMass–Lowell. He praised the community for shaping a future out of its past. A former U.S. Senator and state Attorney General from Colorado, Salazar grew up in a large family on a farm where there was no electricity and for a long time no telephone service. Education was a path to success for him and his brothers and sisters, all of whom earned college degrees.

Secretary Salazar, whose department includes the National Park Service, had been invited to Lowell by Congresswoman Niki Tsongas. She had been at center ice on the opening night of this building in January 1998 when the captain of the UMass–Lowell hockey team presented her with a red-and-blue Tsongas jersey with the numeral 1 on the back. She acknowledged the crowd's warm feelings for her late husband as the ovation thundered. On this day, she introduced the secretary in the city's largest indoor gathering place. Presiding at the ceremony was Chancellor Martin T. Meehan, the former congressman who had championed the park during his fourteen years in Washington. Leadership history was looping in the building like the happy messages to the graduates on the electronic signboard that rings the seating bowl.

Salazar hailed what he had seen around the city: "Lowell has done it. You have shown what is possible in combining historic preservation and economic development. The success of Lowell demonstrates the power of an idea to transform a community, a state, and a nation. We can help all of America if we rediscover our past. Let's build on it! Create a renaissance in your own community!"[1]

A NATIONAL PARK STANDS APART

National Park Service Director Jon Jarvis asked "Where is the park?" on his first visit to Lowell in 2010, during an Innovative Cities Conference featuring speakers from Portland, Oregon; Asheville, North Carolina; and Belfast in the north of Ireland. Lowell is no conventional park unit. People looking for a craggy western vista or a battlefield guarded by Civil War ghosts will be disappointed. The best advice a ranger can offer someone who has stepped out of the Visitor Center on Market Street is "Stop looking for it. You're in it." Every square foot in the 142-acre park and overlapping 583-acre preservation district is its own kind of sacred ground, made so by the critical thinking and toil of everyone who helped transform a used factory-city into a new urban cultural park—all of them standing on the shoulders of generations of people who provided a collective pulse.

The park staff members in Lowell like to say it this way: "The park is the city, and the city is the park." The idea is that the park is about physical structures that are the manifestation of industrial development, as well as cultural traditions. The people involved are not presidents or generals, they are Americans, most of whom immigrated to this country and worked hard for a better life for themselves and their children. The park can be thought of as a receptacle of time and place defined geographically by the legal boundaries of the city at its edges and the stone crust of the earth—riven by water. Time is uncapped at each end. The park historian in the 1980s, Robert Weible, added another guiding concept when he insisted that the Lowell narrative transmitted by park staff should always reinforce the notion of "change over time."

There are pieces of the park creation myth that bear examination. Lowell is often referred to as the first urban national park, which is not accurate. The existence of Lowell as a national park tracks back to an announcement by Secretary of the Interior Walter J. Hickel in 1970. The plan was to create fourteen new parks in or close to large cities. Within the NPS, the first urban national parks are Gateway National Recreation Area in New York City and Golden Gate National Recreation Area in San Francisco.

Prior to the Gateway and Golden Gate parks, created in 1972, there were national park operations in cities, Ethan Carr writes:

> There were earlier urban national parks, including many of the public spaces of Washington, D.C., under the care of the National Park Service since Franklin Delano Roosevelt transferred their jurisdiction in 1933. Others included Independence National Historical Park in Philadelphia and the Jefferson National Expansion Memorial in St. Louis. . . . With the slogan "parks for the people, where the people are," the urban national parks of the 1970s originated in the idealism of the "New Conservation" of Steward Udall (Secretary of the Interior under presidents John F. Kennedy and Lyndon B. Johnson) and especially from the influential recommendations of the Outdoor Recreation Resources Review Committee published in 1962. . . . Like many of the environmental laws of the era, national urban park legislation was intended to increase federal responsibility in a critical area of environmental concern, in this case quality of life in the nation's cities.[2]

The director of the NPS in the early 1970s was George Hartzog. Eager to open up the culture at the NPS, he told an interviewer many years later, "We felt that the Park Service had to be relevant to an urban environment . . . if we were to survive as an institution and as a resource for America."[3] Hartzog, however, likely remained in the minority of the more traditional NPS employees.

Larry Gall is a former assistant superintendent at Lowell National Historical Park and was later Superintendent of Minute Man National Historical Park. He played a key role in building the foundation of the park in Lowell and was on the front line of early struggles to shape the park. He says, "The NPS leadership for the most part has been ambivalent on this issue: on one hand, they see the need to tap into an urban constituency for support; on the other hand, one gets the sense that they see urban parks as somehow diluting 'real' national park values and representing the threat of 'raids' on the NPS budget."[4]

When he read about Hickel's plan, Pat Mogan was not deterred either by the prospect that it was a big-city initiative or that cities like Lowell had received little or no national recognition. He immediately went to work on a local solution, urging Lowell Congressman F. Bradford Morse to act. In 1972, shortly before leaving Congress for a position at the United Nations, Morse filed legislation calling for Lowell to be designated a national park. At the U.N., Morse became Under Secretary-General for Political and General Assembly Affairs, where he served with distinction in that role and others.

Lawrence D. "Larry" Gall was assistant superintendent at LNHP and later superintendent of Minute Man National Historical Park in Concord-Lexington-Lincoln, Massachusetts, and associate regional director for stewardship and partnerships in the Northeast Region of the National Park Service. LNHP

STAIRWAY TO PARK-DOM

In 1966, President Lyndon B. Johnson's "Great Society" legislative broadside was well under way. The White House's urban agenda included a program called the Demonstration Cities and Metropolitan Development Act, intended to shore up the most troubled sections of older cities with multipronged support for infrastructure, social programs, employment, and schools. Lowell Mayor Edward J. Early Jr. moved to explore the new source of funding at the behest of Lowell City Councilor George F. O'Meara, a longtime supporter of the Kennedy political clan in Massachusetts who also had contacts in the Johnson administration. The mayor appointed a committee to follow up: city planner Jack Tavares, John Mahoney of Community Teamwork Inc., George Flanagan of the Lowell Housing Authority, William Kealy of the Lowell Redevelopment Authority, and Pat Mogan, then assistant superintendent of the Lowell School Department. Mogan was a rising star in the community, known particularly for his ability to obtain federal and state grants for education initiatives like his environmental education program in the Lowell-Dracut-Tyngsboro State Forest, in which sixth grade students applied what they learned in on-site encounters with nature and culture to their classroom experiences.

Lowell received funding via the Model Cities program of the national rehabilitation initiative for cities in 1967. Lowell and its region had "long been one of the eight major centers of the U.S. classified as one of chronic unemployment, and as late as 1965 the jobless rate was 50 percent higher than the national average."[5] From economic deprivation grew "deterioration, crime, neglect of the young and the elderly, poor physical and mental health, welfarism, and the steady withering of community involvement and spirit," as described in a Model Cities report.[6]

Tavares became the project manager and immediately assembled a neighborhood organization, as required in this new approach to urban renewal—a stark contrast to past top-down processes that Lowell and other cities had seen. The distressed Acre neighborhood was the prime focus of Lowell's Model Cities effort. The citizens' group was elected by residents and took the name Acre Model Neighborhood Organization (AMNO). More than fifty people, including representatives from businesses, labor groups, and social service organizations outside the Acre, were appointed to various issue-oriented task forces. The task forces handed recommendations up to AMNO for packaging as funded projects. State and local money was brought into the mix where possible. Mogan led the Educational Component of the Model Cities project. Two major strands emerged here: (1) the city as a classroom and (2) an experimental school with integrated services to provide holistically for student learning and well-being.

The 10,000-person Acre became a laboratory for community action in the areas of housing; public safety; elder and child care, including food security and health services; recreation and culture; information services; and education. For five generations the neighborhood had been the start-up zone for newcomers. People there could walk to the mills when there were jobs. Layers of ethnic occupation marked the area, from a few native Yankees and the original English to succeeding waves of people from Ireland, French Canada, Greece, and Latin America.

Model Cities had a five-year plan (1968–1972) to improve the quality of life and bring more jobs to Acre residents. The philosophy of Model Cities was a progressive theory of urban living:

> Through the centuries, man's basic needs have been intimately tied to the happiness and fulfillment he seeks from life. The complexities of present-day urban environments haven't changed this, for our aspirations are, in essence, as timeless as the natural cycle of birth and death. We seek adequate food and shelter. Outlets for our skills and our inborn creative talents. Health. Safety. Stimuli for learning and self-expression. The presence of open space—of sky above us, grass at our feet, and sunshine's warm embrace. Because we are interrelating creatures, we also seek the companionship, compassion, and understanding of our fellow human beings. The fundamental reason for a city's existence is to foster those human values.[7]

The hope of the task force overseeing the Model Cities activities was that they could demonstrate in the Acre some community redevelopment strategies that could be taken up citywide. That would be their greatest success.

FROM ALTERNATIVE SCHOOL TO URBAN CULTURAL PARK

In the same way that the Boston business entrepreneurs scaled up their prototype factory in Waltham to the massive industrial plant of Lowell, Mogan and company took the seed of an idea for an alternative school that stressed experiential learning in the local environment and hot-housed it into a standing hybrid tree whose young crown was a national park. In 1970, Mogan pictured a different kind of school, one that would be informed by every aspect of city life, this particular city's life because of Lowell's important heritage. The concept of the Center for Human Development and planning trail for an experimental school are described in detail ahead.

When Secretary of the Interior Hickel announced in September 1970 that the Park Service would look into creating fourteen new park units emphasizing recreation in the vicinity of large cities, the Model Cities education planners were surprised and excited. Their notion of environmental or place-based education seemed like a good fit for a federal agency that is the custodian of the country's most treasured heritage sites. The local people knew that Lowell was in every respected history textbook, no matter how brief the mention. The city was synonymous with the American Industrial Revolution. Nearby in Massachusetts, Salem Maritime National Historic Site (1938) and Minute Man National Historical Park (1959) in Concord and Lexington were on the list. To Mogan and his planners, Lowell did not seem out of their historical league.

To carry on the Model Cities Education Component when the federal funds stopped flowing, Mogan and his collaborators in 1971 formed the Human Services Corporation (HSC), a nonprofit corporation. HSC was organized "to ensure the continuation of programs and the preservation of a philosophy born of a faith in the citizens of Lowell, respect for those who made its history, and hope for a future which, phoenix-like, would arise from the ashes of the past to rekindle a once-great city and bring it to a new birth and prosperity built upon its most valuable resource, its people."[8] The mission was to "strive to build concrete economic and social programs that seem to offer a sense of hope and determination in all of the residents." They wanted the people of Lowell to benefit in their daily material condition as well as in their psyches. The original incorporators were Rev. Bernard A. Belley, Joseph T. Dillon, Angelike Georgalos, John F. Kirwin, Sister Lillian L. Lamoureux, Patrick J. Mogan, and Peter S. Stamas.

HSC became the primary vehicle for developing plans for what was being called an urban cultural park. From 1972 to 1974, with $100,000 from the New England Regional Commission, HSC advanced the park idea. The funds were filtered through the new Center City Committee, whose members included key downtown stakeholders. Urban planner Gordon Marker managed the park initiative. Working with consultant Robert Graulich of ACTION in Washington, D.C., Marker drafted the legislation calling for a park that was sent to Congressman Morse and filed as a bill in April 1972.

Park Service historian Barry Mackintosh made the original reconnaissance of Lowell in June, and was not won over by what he saw. He wrote to the director of the NPS Office of Archaeology and Historic Preservation to say that Lowell's early industrial activity was of national importance, but "the few remaining mill buildings and associated structures do not convey the impression of the industrial empire that was once here. With the company boardinghouses gone, nothing is left to interpret this distinctive aspect of the city's early social development." His recommendation? No national park for Lowell. He concluded that the city "most definitely" did not "meet the criterion of integrity required of a historical area" based on NPS standards.[9]

Larry Gall remembered that Mackintosh's analysis had staying power among NPS decision makers.

> Even after the park was authorized, the NPS historical "establishment" held to this view. I was on the master-planning team then, in mid-1979, and I recall arguing with the NPS'

From left, John Goodwin of the Lowell Historical Society, U.S. Representative F. Bradford Morse and Patrick J. Mogan, c. 1972
Lowell Historical Society/Lowell Sun Collection

Denver Service Center (DSC) historians and telling them that Lowell's significance was not confined to its early period, but also embraced its "representative" later history—which played out the consequences as well as the origins of the American Industrial Revolution. The DSC staff equated national significance with uniqueness. One planner said to me, "Well, by 1870, Lowell was just another mill town." Much of the language in the General Management Plan had to be carefully negotiated with the Denver planners, who mostly resisted those of us in Lowell who emphasized the decline and revitalization parts of the story. They saw Lowell's national significance confined to the mill girl era and believed the interpretation of immigrant workers, industrial decline, etc., should be handled by others who were concerned about local and state matters. I really pushed the idea of historical continuity and that Lowell should be interpreted as not simply "unique," meaning the pre–Civil War experience in the city, but rather as representative of industrialization.[10]

Unfazed, the Lowell organizers pressed the case. Mogan continued his weekly radio broadcasts about urban park planning on WCAP, one of two local AM stations with studios downtown. In October 1973, the Lowell City Council voted in favor of making the urban cultural park concept the central theme of the city's redevelopment efforts. The NPS sent more staff to Lowell to look again. They examined the topography from a helicopter. They toured the canal system in boats provided by the Proprietors of the Locks & Canals Company.

City Councilor Brendan Fleming, a mathematics professor at Lowell Technological Institute (one of the predecessor schools of UMass–Lowell), in 1973 led the council in voting to create the city's first historic district, authorized under state law, with oversight and controls over new construction, alterations, and demolition. Fleming had lived in Lowell all his life other than when he was in the military in World War II. When he was a Boston College student he enjoyed combing through the old bookshops in "The Hub" for volumes about his hometown, which he remembers in those days sold "for practically a pittance." Lowell titles are collectibles on eBay now.

Fleming was appointed to the Lowell Redevelopment Authority in 1963, when various urban renewal efforts began to gather steam. Fleming was distressed by the loss of the "beautiful" (in his words) Dutton Street row houses as part of the Northern Canal urban renewal project. He first proposed to the City Council that a historic district encompassing the canals be established in 1966.

> At that time, I was told that the history of Lowell best be forgotten. I'll never forget that statement being made. And I thought it was just so lacking in knowledge of the history of Lowell. I said at that point in time that I was going to try to do something about it. If I couldn't do it from outside the City Council, I'd try and see if I could do something within the City Council. So, in 1967, I ran for the City Council, and I came in tenth. But I ran again in 1969, and I got on the Council in 1970. One of the first things I did was to propose that we have a historic district.[11]

The new Locks & Canals Historic District was followed by a City Hall District soon after. Human Services Corporation (HSC), using New England Regional Commission funds, spent much of 1973 and 1974 preparing a fifty-page booklet, illustrated with photographs, maps, and charts, that detailed a plan for development of the "Lowell Urban Park."

They also made a slide-tape presentation to market the concept. About the twenty-five-minute slide-tape production, Mogan wrote: "Virtually every school child, church, service, and fraternal organization has seen and enjoyed the presentation which graphically portrays Lowell's past, present, and its great potential for the future. This and other programs gradually replaced the despair and apathy with a sense of hope and pride."[12]

Congressman Paul W. Cronin, who had succeeded F. Bradford Morse, knew how important the park project was to the largest city in his district. A Republican, like Morse, Cronin had defeated young Democrat John F. Kerry, who had survived a political street fight in the primary contest only to be savaged in *Lowell Sun* editorials for his anti–Vietnam War views during the fall campaign. As a freshman, Cronin had gained a coveted seat on the House Subcommittee on Parks and Recreation and reintroduced the park legislation as framed by Morse. Lowell made it over the first big hurdle when the Congress recommended Lowell as one of twelve places from among 115 proposals submitted for consideration as a new urban park. HSC acknowledged Cronin's leadership on page one of the booklet. The authors of the booklet concluded:

> America has not yet adequately come to terms with the Industrial Revolution as a process which we should identify with as much as with the American political revolution which began in Lexington and Concord. . . . Lowell more than meets the criteria of preserving a national cultural site and way of life. It more than meets criteria of significance in the heritage of the United States; especially in its potential to preserve and interpret a dynamic era of American history.[13]

Additional federal attention came in the form of a team from the NPS's Historic
Architectural Engineering Record Program and Library of Congress's Historic American Buildings Survey. The Locks & Canals Company donated work space for the
architects and historians. More interest groups in the city were getting on board.
Cronin was diligent in his efforts to move the project forward, but he was lashed
by strong political crosswinds in his second year in office as the Watergate political
corruption scandal turned the country against President Nixon and the Republican
Party. Nixon resigned in August of 1974, by which time former Lowell City Councilor and current Middlesex County Commissioner Paul Tsongas had announced he
would challenge Cronin for the Congressional seat.

Cronin's compromise bill calling for a federal commission to study Lowell's park
prospects rather than the establishment of a full national park was approved easily
in the U.S. House in October, but stalled in the upper chamber. The lack of action
in the Senate hurt Cronin's standing. Along with a wave of new members across
the country, Tsongas swept to victory with more than 60 percent of the votes. The
future of the park would be on his shoulders. As a city councilor he had not been
pro-preservation, having voted for the extension of a highway link into the city and
having suggested that the canals might be better covered over to make alternate bus
lanes around Lowell. In December, as Cronin was wrapping up his term, the Senate
finally passed the bill establishing the Lowell Historic Canal District Commission
with a budget of $150,000 to determine whether Lowell warranted being a park
and to recommend how that should happen if the answer was in the affirmative.
President Gerald R. Ford signed the legislation in January 1975. The lieutenant
governor of Massachusetts, Thomas P. O'Neill III, son of Speaker of the U.S. House
"Tip" O'Neill, was named to chair the Canal District Commission. During this same
period HSC worked with partners like the Lowell Historical Society on a proposal
to the National Endowment for the Humanities for a Lowell Museum and in 1976
helped prepare for a major dual celebration of the nation's Bicentennial and 150th
anniversary of Lowell's founding as a town.

On a parallel track, the local park activists were pursuing a state option in the form
of a heritage state park. In early 1974, Governor Francis Sargent had visited Lowell to
hear what the local constituents were proposing. He was pressed for a commitment
by the by-now highly skilled community organizers out of the Model Cities project
and AMNO, including Sister Lillian Lamoureux, a Lowell native and one of the HSC
founders. Sister Lillian at the time was with the Sisters of Charity of Montreal or "Grey
Nuns," a religious order whose members had been serving in Lowell since 1880,
when the sisters had come to teach and help the needy. In a public meeting she demanded of the governor "Something tangible and something financial!"[14]

In the fall, the state announced that Lowell would be the first in a series of her-
itage state parks in struggling small factory cities from Lynn to Holyoke. The state
Department of Natural Resources acknowledged Interior Secretary Hickel for pro-
moting the idea of urban parks nationwide. The budget was set at $9.4 million for
Lowell, and the focus would be the city's waterways. The state would be responsible
for creating parkland on the north bank of the Merrimack River above Pawtucket
Falls (Vandenberg Esplanade) as well as for managing certain canal-side properties.
This would prove to be a crucial step in making the federal case for a national park.
To see the state investing in this interlocking heritage site development plan allevi-
ated fears of some in Congress who were worried about its efficacy and burdens on
the federal government alone.

In Lowell, the leadership was immense. There were people like Franco-American community activist Armand W. LeMay, who used his construction company background to advocate for historic preservation of key buildings. He served as a city councilor and for one term as mayor. LeMay later joined the administration of Governor Michael Dukakis for a time, where he continued to advocate strongly for the city. They helped steer the state park idea in Lowell to reality. LeMay was an early appointee to the Lowell Historic Preservation Commission.

"Armand was literally out in the trenches all the time with the national and state parks, with Dukakis, with the Human Services Corporation folks, and with the City Council," Fred Faust said. The feeling in Tsongas's office was that if the federal decision makers saw Lowell and heard from the local people "who are really genuine, who understood the importance of history here, and had that passion for telling the story . . . once you got them together with the right people in the room, they bought into it."[15]

Faust started in the media world, and so he was always acutely aware of that aspect of the work. The support of a hometown newspaper is one of those intangible ingredients required for success that founding generation members of the Lowell park always stress when speaking to visiting officials trying to decipher the Lowell "mojo." The daily paper "really bought into the concept," Faust said.

> Brad Morse and Paul Cronin had a strong relationship with the *Sun*. Paul Tsongas had a mixed relationship with them because he got into some scuffles with publisher Clement Costello, as a lot of political people did. Costello was a character in his own right, but he wanted to build up Lowell. One day we would write an editorial about annexing Canada and Mexico to get their oil fields, but the next day he could talk about Lowell's marvelous idea for a national park or as the local people called it, an urban cultural park. Pat Mogan did a great job getting the *Sun* on board and making them understand the educational connections. The *Sun* was a key player in changing the environment and talking about the value of history. There were some good writers at that time, including Frank Phillips and Chris Black, a bunch of excellent reporters who went on to national careers—and Kendall Wallace was a strong supporter.[16]

Mary Ellen Pollard Fitzpatrick is another one of the Lowellians who has been involved with the park and revitalization for most of its long development arc. The daughter of prominent civic leader Samuel Pollard, she interned in Washington with both Senator Ted Kennedy and Congressman Philip Philbin of Massachusetts and earned a master's degree in political science from Boston College. The latter part of her career has been in the private sector as an executive with Enterprise Bank. She was an administrative assistant to Massachusetts Lieutenant Governor Thomas P. O'Neill III when the Historic Canal District Commission was formed. O'Neill had the federal-state relations portfolio in Governor Dukakis's administration, so he was a logical selection for chair of the Commission (and his father *was* "the Speaker"). Fitzpatrick had a front-row seat for this critical phase of work. Echoing Pat Mogan, who had married her aunt, Mary Pollard, Fitzpatrick said, "No one person really did it. It was a combination of a lot of factors that seemed to have come together at the right time. The story of Lowell on a lot of occasions is about . . . groups of people coming together at the same time with a common vision. That really was the success of the park."[17]

Political-science student Marty Meehan was an intern in the mayor's office in City Hall during the run-up to the vote in Congress. He recalled one veteran city councilor wondering, How are we going to have a park that glorifies horrible working conditions? Many old-line folks were skeptical, and not everyone "got" the vision at first glance. They thought Mogan was a dreamer. Meehan noticed something:

> The people who were smart were excited about the idea. Mogan was an intelligent man and connected to the community. He had credibility. The first published plan, "The Brown Book," changed the paradigm. Now people had a document, a study, which was an impressive piece of work. That made a difference, and got the community behind the park.[18]

While the Lowell park proponents were often condescended to by officials in Washington, D.C., whose reflex response was that the Lowell project was just another cut of pork for a clever congressman, Tsongas was adamant that the people whom he had to persuade see the larger concept. He also resisted attempts to minimize the scope of the project. Fred Faust recalled a discussion with NPS Director Bill Whalen, who pushed for an easy-to-manage operation with ten buildings owned by the federal government.

> Paul said, "No, you know, you're missing it. This is the living part. This is the story. There's a story that has to do with this. There are elements of the story that are all over the downtown. They're in the buildings, they're in the people." There were times when he could have got things through, but he was holding out for what was important.
> We had great people who were working on the ground. I mean we were talking to Pat Mogan every day, and he was lobbying people. I remember working with Bob Malavich in the city planning office. He was the technical point man. And it would be, Bob, you know, we need a better picture of this or a line drawing of that.
> We got the Congressional subcommittee to come to Lowell. We were pulling our hair out because that day it was forty degrees. Today, it's easy, you're on the canal. Well, I had to call Mel Lezberg [from the Locks & Canals Co.]. I said, "Mel, next Monday bring your boat up from Lexington [Massachusetts] because we're going on a canal ride." Mel said, "I have to cut the fence open," and I said, "Cut the fence open." And they were cooperative.[19]

Former park historian Gray Fitzsimons described the Historic Canal District Commission's work in an unpublished paper:

> [The Commission's work] was the result of combined efforts of a Boston-Cambridge group of consultants; the Lowell Team; and a subcommittee of Commission members representing the state, the U.S. Department of Transportation, and the National Park Service. Employing language and concepts used in earlier studies for a national park in Lowell, the report called for the creation of a "cultural park," though this was later changed to "historical park" at the behest of the NPS. [The Commission stated:] "The creation of a Lowell National Cultural Park by Congress . . . is the appropriate action for the federal government to take in order to preserve Lowell's historical and cultural resources and to interpret the city's special role in the American Industrial Revolution."[20]

Making the canal system the centerpiece of the plan, the Canal District Commission dodged the consistent skepticism within the NPS about the critical mass of historical structures in Lowell. The proposed park would have a "broad preservation zone and a smaller intensive use zone," which would be downtown-centric and the purview of the NPS. The preservation zone would be overseen by "a new management entity," which became the Lowell Historic Preservation Commission, charged with directing preservation and regeneration, both economically and culturally. The projected cost over the first ten years would be $40 million for development, not counting the annual operating budgets of the new park unit and allied LHPC.

> The Historic Canal District Commission recommended the most ambitious alternative of six sent to the Congress. The "Concentrated/Large" option would include several attractions that were expected to draw as many as 750,000 visitors annually, on a scale comparable to "major attractions in New England." The Summary Evaluation of this alternative indicated that "this scale of park should be sufficient to encourage substantial private investment such as that proposed for the Lowell [Market Mills] and Boott Mills centers. Park activities encircling downtown should improve the economic climate and provide a strong impetus for private restoration. Although this scheme would be among the more expensive to develop, its return to the city and to the federal government per dollar spent is likely to be the greatest."[21]

The march to a park took another large step forward in April 1977, when Congressman Tsongas put forward a bill to establish Lowell National Historical Park. Democrat Jimmy Carter was now president, having defeated Gerald R. Ford, who had ascended to the presidency upon Richard M. Nixon's resignation the previous summer—and then pardoned Nixon to "end the long national nightmare." At the same time that Tsongas had introduced legislation for the Lowell park, the Advisory Board on National Parks, Historic Sites, Buildings, and Monuments of the Interior Department rejected the advice of the Canal District Commission to make Lowell part of the national park system. The board members, appointive products of the two previous Republican administrations, preferred traditional parks and wild open spaces to the new urban ventures for which Secretary Hickel had argued. In the fall, the board met again, this time with a number of Carter appointees, and decided that the Lowell canal system was nationally significant.

Richard Arenberg was a premed student at Boston University in the late 1960s when he decided that politics was his true passion. After some grassroots work in Boston, he signed on with Tsongas's first campaign for Congress in 1974 and stayed with him through his Senate years. In 1975, Tsongas cast a crucial ballot in a contest for Democratic Majority Leader of the House of Representatives. In a five-way contest, Tsongas sided with California Representative Phil Burton, who eventually lost to Representative Jim Wright of Texas—and Tsongas had let Burton know how his "secret ballot" had been cast. Burton was a high-ranking member of the Interior Committee in the House, who became chair of the subcommittee on national parks. In Arenberg's telling:

> Burton held hearings on the park and moved it right through. The day that we were apprehensive about the mark-up, Burton came in and called the subcommittee to order, and said, "We're going to report the Lowell park bill today." Bang, bang, bang, hit the gavel, and out it went to the full committee.[22]

Arenberg stresses that it is important to understand what an achievement the Lowell park bill was for a second-term member of Congress. He said it was a tribute to his boss's "single-mindedness" about Lowell. That Massachusetts had a powerful congressional delegation in the 1970s was a huge plus, but the accomplishment was nonetheless extraordinary.

The House Interior Committee had a decidedly "western tilt" because of its oversight of vast tracts of public lands from the Mississippi River westward. Tsongas had proven himself to his colleagues from Wyoming, Alaska, Arizona, and elsewhere through diligent work on issues like hard rock mining. He had also gained respect for his leadership in preserving the environment in Alaska, legislation that he later steered through the U.S. Senate as the Alaska Lands Act of 1980 and which President Jimmy Carter described at the time as "the most important conservation legislation of the century."[23]

The National Parks Conservation Association goes further than Carter in describing the Alaska National Interest Lands Conservation Act (ANILCA):

> Often called the most significant land conservation measure in the history of our nation, the statute protected over 100 million acres of federal lands in Alaska, doubling the size of the country's national park and refuge system and tripling the amount of land designated as wilderness. ANILCA expanded the national park system in Alaska by over 43 million acres, creating 10 new national parks and increasing the acreage of three existing units.[24]

The day after his Valentine's Day birthday in 1978, Tsongas re-filed his bill with some changes, including a more robust role for what was now called the Lowell Historic Preservation Commission. The NPS staffers pushed back on the stronger LHPC, and Tsongas agreed to a ten-year limit for the innovative agency. There were a few more legislative hoops to get through. Tip O'Neill interceded before the final House vote. The first vote had failed to garner a three-quarters vote under suspension of the rules, a legislative means to fast-track passage. Now needing a simple majority to assure the bill's passage, O'Neill's staff volunteered to help—an insurance policy for a then-concerned Tsongas. They recommended that Tsongas prepare a letter restating the case for the members who had voted nay. Legislative aide Fred Faust worked the language for hours. What began as a carefully crafted, single-spaced one-page argument in favor of the bill was eventually revised by an O'Neill lieutenant to a one-sentence letter signed by the Speaker: "Paul Tsongas and I would appreciate it if you would vote for the Lowell National Historical Park legislation."[25] House passage came on April 11, 326 in favor and 76 opposed, and the Senate approved the bill on May 18. President Jimmy Carter signed Public Law 95-290 on June 5, 1978. It had been six years since Congressman Morse brought the matter to the floor of the House of Representatives; the community-bred idea dated from 1967.

Recalling her husband's efforts on the park bill, now-Congresswoman Niki Tsongas said:

> The work never stopped. He pursued anybody who could make a difference in getting the legislation through. It never stopped. . . .When the legislation passed he was just ecstatic, absolutely ecstatic. . . . And now, the park has done so much for old cities everywhere because people look at old buildings and instead of seeing things you want to tear down, they see things you want to save. You recognize their intrinsic beauty. And quite apart from the history of the Industrial Revolution, in terms of immigrant culture it has generated a lot more respect for what people contributed to the making of this country.[26]

Lillian Lamoureux of the Model Cities project and Human Services Corporation reflected on the process in 1991: "I am convinced that if we had not gone to all those meetings, if we had not written all those grants, then none of this would have

President Jimmy
Carter signs
the legislation
establishing Lowell
National Historical
Park, June 5, 1978,
with U.S. Senator
Edward M. Kennedy,
left, and U.S.
Representative
Paul E. Tsongas
LNHP

happened."[27] What began as a mission by teachers and local organizers to make life better for those in Lowell being left behind in the churn of callous economic and political markets had morphed into a citywide renewal strategy. A community had reconciled its past with its future. No longer did history, the long ago local story, emit a bad odor. What was heterogeneous now radiated positive value. Mogan always believed that the perceived liabilities could be turned into assets. Tsongas said it was immoral to kick the whole city into the ditch because it was broken. He did not use the term "generational responsibility" until he ran for president, but that is what he meant in the 1970s. Led by the Congress of the United States, the National Park Service took Lowell on board and now brags about it.

BUILDING THE PARK: FIRST MOVES

Five weeks after the June 1978 White House signing ceremony with Paul Tsongas and Senator Ted Kennedy flanking President Carter in the official photo, the Park Service had a man on the ground in Lowell: Marc Vagos. An experienced ranger from Boston National Historical Park, another urban park in the system, Vagos caused a stir on the main street with his iconic "flat hat"—the broad-brimmed, stiff straw Smokey-the-Bear lid. Living out of a veritable suitcase at the Human Services Corporation office downtown, he plunged into the heavy-duty partnership network in Lowell as the park's ambassador. In September, NPS Director William Whalen introduced Lewis Albert as the first superintendent. The NPS rented offices and a storefront at 169 Merrimack Street, which would be the first stop for visitors until a proper Visitor Center opened in the Market Mills complex in 1982.

The Lowell Historic Preservation Commission (LHPC) had its leadership in place by the fall also. Historian John B. Duff, president of the new University of Lowell,

THE PARK BILL BECOMES LAW: A STAFF DIARY

Ray LaPorte finished his master's degree requirements in political science at The New School in New York City in December 1977, and went home to Lowell for the holidays to figure out what to do next. At twenty-six years old, he needed a job and wanted to do something that counted. He had been away from Lowell at boarding school and college in Worcester, Massachusetts, and spent summers at his family's beach house in Seabrook, New Hampshire. Despite being a fourth generation Pawtucketville neighborhood native, and having played along the river as a kid, he did not feel rooted in the place. Bored at Christmastime, he became curious about the park chatter in the newspaper. His mother urged him to talk to Pat Mogan in City Hall. Without an appointment, he dropped in for a talk, but Mogan did all the talking: "I was spellbound by his enthusiasm, intrigued by the community planning efforts, and dumbfounded at how little I knew of Lowell's history. When he said that all further action about the Lowell park legislation was to be in Washington D.C., I knew where I was headed after New Year's Day."

LaPorte arrived in D.C. with no money, no place to stay, no job, and no plan other than to deal his "woeful deck of resume cards around Capitol Hill with enthusiasm and a smile." He roamed the halls of the Capitol until he found the office of his member of Congress, Paul Tsongas. The appointment secretary told him to come back the next day, which he did—waiting almost all day until Tsongas returned from committee meetings and floor votes. "In a flash, there I was sitting alone with Paul, who was fully engaged in my story and our shared Lowell childhoods and families." A week later he was an intern. Following are excerpts from a diary he kept during the run-up to the passage of the park legislation.

January 27, 1978: Lunch in the Members' restaurant with the Congressman. I was assigned to work with legislative aide Fred Faust on park legislation. We conferred with the House subcommittee staff about final draft language of the Lowell park bill.

February 16: Met Karen Carpenter of Human Services Corporation and Pat Mogan at the Health, Education, and Welfare Dept.'s Teacher Corps office; I ran back to office afterwards, so missed a surprise meeting they had with Interior Secretary Cecil Andrus! Got things ready for hearings. Met Lowell City Councilors Ed Kennedy and Ray Lord, City planner Bob Malavich, and Lew Karabatsos of the Lowell Museum.

February 17: Subcommittee hearings from 9 a.m. to 4 p.m. A love-in, favorable hearing. The NPS is supportive, but they want to do it their way, meaning scattered sites for park activities instead of an intensive-use zone covering the core of the city—and less money. Pat Mogan, Lowell City Councilor Sam Pollard, and mill operator Ted Larter were excellent.

February 23: With Fred, met with the Senate Interior Subcommittee. They were a bit stuffy, but seem to agree with us that the separate sites proposal by the NPS is inadequate, especially for the same amount of money, when we could have a more unified intensive-use zone. They suggested we start requesting money for FY '79.

March 7: Got proxy signatures for the Subcommittee hearing on Thursday.

March 8: NPS folks have accepted our positions in most cases and the $40 million!

March 9: National Parks Subcommittee unanimously reports the bill to the full committee!

March 21: The bill came up in full committee, but will be reported out tomorrow. I met with Paul, Fred, and senior Tsongas staffer Rich Arenberg on strategy, and met later with them, the NPS, minority and majority staff, and the Interior Department's Congressional Liaison. We worked on new amendments, and left at 7:30 p.m. Fred didn't finish until 5 a.m.

March 22: The bill came out of the committee this morning at 10 a.m., with amendments.

March 27: Worked on the legislative report; went to a Committee meeting with Fred. We set the scope of what should be the park. Rep. Clay won't give in, when clearly the Committee transcript and the agreed compromise included the intensive-use zone.

March 28: The committee compromise was settled. Rep. Keith Sebelius, a Republican from Kansas, agreed to the intensive-use zone for Lowell National Historical Park, including the canals. Now it's on to finish the report and to the House vote!

March 30: Worked on park matters, tying up loose ends, and preparing for the arrival of the Lowell officials. I must make sure that all goes smoothly.

March 31: The park plan ran into problems again with minority members. They want the Commission's name to be changed—a lot of b.s.—so now the amendment must be unanimously approved in a House vote on Monday.

April 3: Crap! The three-fourths suspension of the rules to ensure quick passage fell short by a few votes due to poor floor vote management. We took a political gamble and lost badly.

April 4: Licked wounds and started to assess strategy: letters, lobbying, etc. A floor vote is set for next week. We have a Rules hearing tomorrow.

April 5: Wrote letters and made calls. We got a letter signed by Massachusetts' Republicans, Sen. Ed Brooke and Reps. Margaret Heckler and Silvio Conti. I got their signatures to send around to the other Republicans. The Rules Committee motion passed. We talked off the floor, and Speaker of the House Tip O'Neill came by. Things look really good now. I picked up Lowell City Council members at the airport.

April 6: Got floor helpers set up, and started to collect support materials for next week. At the Senate Subcommittee hearing, Sen. Ted Kennedy, Sen. Brooke, O'Neill, and others spoke. Things look good.

April 10: *Washington Post* editorial today, favorable about the Lowell park bill.

April 11: House votes 326–76!! Enjoyed a celebratory dinner with Paul and others.

April 24: Senate committee hearings on Lowell postponed.

May 1: Lowell park bill vote postponed again. I am freaking out, to say the least.

May 4: The Lowell bill was up on the committee docket, and Sens. John Durkin (D-NH), Clifford Hansen (R-WY), and Dale Bumpers (D-AR) spoke to it; they have problems with the bill. There is a sense of trouble.

May 5: Tsongas office staff members from Massachusetts have come to Washington for the committee meeting.

May 8: Finally, the bill passes the Senate committee after more than two weeks delay. Forty-five minutes of debate and a final 15–2 vote!!

—Raymond LaPorte, "My Story: Lowell–D.C. and Back Again, a Journal"

AN ACT ESTABLISHING A PARK

Public Law 95-290
95th Congress
June 5, 1978 (H.R. 11662)
Lowell National Historical Park
16 U.S.C. 410cc.

An Act

To provide for the establishment of the Lowell National Historical Park in the Commonwealth of Massachusetts, and for other purposes.

Be it enacted by the Senate and House of Representatives of the United States of America in Congress assembled,

Findings and Purpose

Section 1. (a) The Congress finds that—

1. certain sites and structures in Lowell, Massachusetts, historically and culturally the most significant planned industrial city in the United States, symbolize in physical form the Industrial Revolution;
2. the cultural heritage of many of the ethnic groups that immigrated to the United States during the late nineteenth and early twentieth centuries is still preserved in Lowell's neighborhoods;
3. a very large proportion of the buildings, other structures, and districts in Lowell date to the period of the Industrial Revolution and are nationally significant historical resources, including the five-and-six-tenths-mile power canal system, seven original mill complexes, and significant examples of early housing, commercial structures, transportation facilities, and buildings associated with labor and social institutions; and
4. despite the expenditure of substantial amounts of money by the City of Lowell and the Commonwealth of Massachusetts for historical and cultural preservation and interpretation in Lowell, the early buildings and other structures in Lowell may be lost without the assistance of the Federal Government.

(b) It is the purpose of this Act to preserve and interpret the nationally significant historical and cultural sites, structures, and districts, in Lowell, Massachusetts, for the benefit and inspiration of present and future generations by implementing to the extent practicable the recommendations in the report of the Lowell Historic Canal District Commission.

The first superintendent of LNHP, Lewis Albert, seated, with assistant superintendent John Debo
LNHP

was the first chair, and one of Tsongas's top aides, Fred Faust, was hired as the executive director. Faust, twenty-nine years old, had extensive knowledge of the park through his legislative work and years as liaison to community leaders. The LHPC set up shop in the back room of the University's public relations office in Cumnock Hall across the river from downtown. It would not be long before the operation moved downtown to the old Lowell Gaslight Building on Shattuck Street.

Many years later, Faust recalled his first look at Lowell in 1968. He was in the Boston area, looking at colleges, and had driven to Lowell to see relatives.

> I must have been on the Lord Overpass above Thorndike Street when I saw the red mills along the Pawtucket Canal. I remember wondering what they were. I had never seen anything like those mills. Looking back to those first days at the Preservation Commission, I have to say we were incredibly bold about what we pledged to do—to imagine that five million square feet of underused mill space could be renovated and put to better uses in forty years. We were not fazed about the challenge.[28]

The "sister" federal agencies, as they came to be called in the city, each set to work on developing roadmaps for creating the park. Every NPS unit has a General

Fred Faust, center, first executive director of the LHPC, with then-University of Lowell President John B. Duff, chairman of the LHPC, and vice-chair Angelike "Kay" Georgalos, a Lowell educator who had worked alongside Pat Mogan on early park planning
Lowell Historical Society/Lowell Sun Collection

Management Plan that guides development and operations; the LHPC prepared its own plan. Both documents would require approval at the federal cabinet level. Another priority project was preparing an inventory of the structures in the Park and Preservation District, what was called the "cultural resources inventory." The park also needed a plan for presenting the Lowell story, an "interpretive prospectus." These founding documents would shape the growth and operation of the park through its first thirty years. Superintendent Albert was careful about managing community expectations, noting that a mature park operation could be about ten years away.

Lowell came into being as a very different kind of national park. The federal government had no intention of purchasing large sections of the city that would be classified as park territory for the enjoyment of day visitors and campers. The park was authorized to buy seven properties: The Linus Childs House at 67 Kirk Street (now the park headquarters); H & H Paper Company or the Boott Mills Boarding House at 42 French Street (now the Mogan Cultural Center); Old City Hall at 226 Merrimack Street (now leased to a leading local bank); the Merrimack Gatehouse at 269 Merrimack Street (now an interpretive site); Wannalancit Textile Company at 562 Suffolk Street (now home to the park exhibit "The River Transformed," including a working water turbine); and two nonhistorical buildings next to Old City Hall at 200 and 210 Merrimack, which were tagged for removal because they were inconsistent with the predominant architectural style on the street. The larger

Park rangers in a parade on Merrimack Street; second from right is Marc Vagos, the first ranger on the ground in Lowell in 1978.
LNHP

strategy, involving the Preservation Commission, was to encourage private property owners to renovate, reconstruct, or otherwise rehab their buildings in the historic district to knit together the area. If the Park Service was not going to own the mill and commercial district and portions of adjoining older neighborhoods, then the goal was to present a consistent, coherent look that says to those encountering the scene that this is a unified urban environment, a recognizable place.

Lowell had its challenges at the start, said Larry Gall, who was one of the first managers on the scene:

> I started working in Lowell in July 1979. In my first two weeks on the job, a crazed woman with a hammer smashed storefront windows up and down Merrimack Street and a drunk drove a car right into the front door of the NPS headquarters on the main street downtown. I thought, "What have I gotten myself into? Should I at least get combat pay?"[29]

The Preservation Commission was something new under the sun. The Park Service understood this going in because of the wording in the enabling legislation. "Had Congress intended that Lowell was to be managed in the way of the other units within the national park system, it could have conferred all management functions upon the National Park Service," wrote Roger Sumner Babb, an attorney for the Interior Department. Lowell, he asserted, represented "a departure from the usual paradigm in accordance with which most national parks have been established. . . . [I]t appears that Congress established the Commission with the intent that it have a measure of freedom and flexibility which the Park Service does not possess."[30] Those qualities would be invaluable over the seventeen years of the

Preservation Commission's life. Embedding a new national park into a functioning medium-sized city would prove to be complicated and sometimes maddening for the administrators and the public. One of the powerful tools on the agency's workbench was the authority to make grants and issue loans for both bricks-and-mortar projects and cultural and educational initiatives.

The Cultural Resources Inventory turned out to be a fourteen-volume opus containing history and condition descriptions for nearly 900 structures in the Park and Preservation District. The volumes were delivered in January 1980; later in the year the *Preservation Plan* was published with a memorable front-cover image in color: a reproduction of a watercolor painting of a Greek American neighborhood grocery store, Giavis Market. The artist was Vassilios "Bill" Giavis. Born in 1930, Giavis attended Lowell High School and later, like his older brother, graduated from Massachusetts College of Art. After college he went to work in the family store. He never stopped painting, however, and eventually opened a work space in the "Brush" studios at Market Mills. In 2012, Park Superintendent Michael Creasey named the eighty-two-year-old Giavis to be Lowell's first "Artist-in-the-Park."

Despite lengthy negotiations, the National Park Service was not able to acquire the Wannalancit Textile Company on the terms it deemed best for park operations and shifted its focus to the Lowell Manufacturing Company or Market Mills complex at the corner of Dutton and Market streets, closer to the center of downtown. The LHPC leadership supported this change, having been concerned about a visitor center at Wannalancit pulling visitors away from the downtown core. There were loud whispers about the Wannalancit becoming a Park Service fort on the perimeter of downtown with an isolated, self-contained operation. These comments came even though the locally managed Lowell Museum of the mid-1970s had occupied the same space. The push-pull between park staff and community park supporters was to be expected as both groups found ways to collaborate. In late 1979, the NPS and LHPC staff forged an agreement that they would develop a portion of the Boott Cotton Mills in the heart of the downtown for a high-profile use to be identified later. As it turned out, the NPS used a section of the Wannalancit for exhibits for school groups and visitors while the main industrial history museum, an extensive experiential education program, and related offices filled Boott Mill No. 6, in what many observers consider the iconic location of the park.

TAKING SHAPE

In early 1980, the NPS had Market Mills (Lowell Manufacturing Company) on Market Street in its sights for a Visitor Center that would introduce the public to the five topics around which the Lowell story would be told: The Industrial City, Labor, Capital, Waterpower, and Technology. Larry Gall, the park's lead planner, convened a group of people to discuss the "interpretive program." Participants came from the park; LHPC; University of Lowell, as it was known then; Merrimack Valley Textile Museum of Andover, Massachusetts (now the American Textile History Museum in Lowell); Lowell Museum; and elsewhere. He recalls a pivotal moment in the process: "We haggled for an entire day. Late in the afternoon, I looked around the room during a period of silence and saw nothing but glazed eyes. I took a chance and said, 'How about these five themes?' I wrote them on a flip-chart. Everybody agreed!"[31]

Simultaneously, the NPS had teamed up with the state's Department of Environmental Management (operators of the Heritage State Park in Lowell) to repair and restore elements of the Northern Canal, Francis Gate, and Guard Locks. This work was aimed at opening a portion of the canal system for boat tours. In the meantime, work progressed on improvements at the Linus Childs House, today's park headquarters. Superintendent Lew Albert assembled the primary park properties, including the Linus Childs House, Boott Mills boarding house, Old City Hall, Merrimack Gatehouse (Moody Street Feeder), and Wannalancit Mills.

Absent Wannalancit, these structures, plus Market Mills later and related intermediate properties, would add up to "a slice of nineteenth-century life." The buildings represented aspects of daily life in the city at the height of the mill era: mills, worker housing, management offices, canal features, government, religion (St. Anne's Church, 1824), commerce (Lowell Institution for Savings, 1829). A visitor would proceed from Market Street outside the Visitor Center, cross the street and walk up cobblestoned Shattuck, turn right on Merrimack and then take an immediate left on Kirk to the end, and then right on French, where the Boott Mills complex rose in front of the river. The concept of a massive mill complex as "the anchor" store of the historic district carried through the enabling legislation and subsequent plans.

John Burchill, a lawyer and former Boston schoolteacher who had worked for the U.S. Army Corps of Engineers and as a concessions manager at Yellowstone and Yosemite for the NPS, succeeded Albert as superintendent of the Lowell park in 1981. Burchill in three years moved park development forward another several big steps. With the General Management Plan (GMP) in hand as the official game plan, Burchill made final the decision to use the Boott Mills for the park's main exhibit area. This decision was consistent with a new downtown development plan spearheaded by the city administration and leadership of the Lowell Plan economic development group. Called the American Cities Plan because it was the product of American Cities Corporation, a national consulting firm, the new plan "saw the Boott rehabilitation as critical to the success of its downtown strategy, and NPS participation as vital."[32] The GMP called for park activity in three main areas of the historic district: Old City Hall, Boott Mills, and Wannalancit Mills. The NPS also decided to acquire property for a parking lot off Dutton Street behind Market Mills, a maintenance facility along the Northern Canal in the old Little Canada sector close to Wannalancit, and Tremont Yard, where the remains of a vast turbine operation stood (adjacent to Wannalancit and along the Western Canal). Another key property, the Boott Mills boarding house, was added to the NPS's ownership list in 1983. Ahead in chapter 5 of this book is a detailed look at the Market Mills development project, which opened in the summer of 1982 with a high-end Visitor Center for LNHP and the Heritage State Park, a food emporium called The Melting Pot with festival marketplace-type vendors, an artist studio co-op named A Brush With History, and a computer services company—all of this combined with apartments for families and senior citizens on the upper floors of the mill complex.

The public offerings of the park were growing incrementally in the early 1980s. Every fourth grade student in the Lowell public schools was being introduced to Lowell history through the Lowell Industrial Learning Experience, a school visit program with costumed education-rangers. Rosemary Noon, who later worked on cultural affairs at the LHPC, remembers students saying upon her arrival dressed as mill girl of the 1840s, "Here comes the pilgrim lady." The Suffolk Mill Turbine Room exhibit at Wannalancit opened in 1983. Traveling exhibits about "Negro

Historian Mary Blewett of then-University of Lowell, center, collecting stories from retirees on Mill Workers Day, 1985
James Higgins

Cloth" and the "Workers' World" were brought in. Rangers organized "Mondays at Market Mills" at the Visitor Center with talks, performances, and workshops.

In late 1984, Chrysandra "Sandy" Walter replaced Burchill as superintendent. She had started with the NPS at Pointe Reyes National Seashore, where she worked on a National Environmental Studies education project. After her time at Golden Gate National Recreation Area, she went to the LBJ Ranch at the Lyndon Baines Johnson National Historical Park in Texas.

When Walter was promoted to deputy director of the North Atlantic Region of the NPS in July 1992, the Lowell park was essentially complete in both bricks-and-mortar and core programs. During her tenure she led with imagination, ambition, and great vigor. When she arrived, the first big task was to get the arms of the park and LHPC around Boott Mill No. 6, the signature building of the park. Even today, the park's signature postcard shot is the yellow street trolley on the canal-side tracks in front of the great red wall of the textile factory, with the decorative clock-and-bell tower behind and smokestack rising higher.

REALIZING THE IDEA

Between 1987 and 1992, the park matured to its near current form. The annual Lowell Folk Festival (1987), Mogan Cultural Center (1989), Boarding House Park

(1990), historic trolley line expansion (1988), 3.5 miles of new canal walkways, and Boott Mills Museum (1992) filled out the conceptual outlines that had been drawn and redrawn since the late 1960s. Collectively, these sites connected by trolleys plus the expansive downtown festival answered the question, where is the park? The cultural center, performance park, and industrial history museum made a critical mass of "place" that anyone could point to as the symbolic hub of the unusual national park.

Federal funds flowed during these years as Senators Edward Kennedy and John Kerry, with Lowell's congressman Chester "Chet" Atkins, a member of the powerful House Interior Appropriations Subcommittee, made the case to Congress to the tune of nearly $37 million for the park over five years, an extraordinary pile of development money for a new park. (Atkins had succeeded Congressman James Shannon of Lawrence, Massachusetts, who served from 1979 to 1985; Shannon's position on the House Ways and Means Committee had been very helpful in his efforts to deliver funding for the park.) Transforming Mill No. 6 of the Boott complex into the Boott Cotton Mills Museum, the largest industrial history museum in the NPS system, cost $15 million. This all happened during a period when the National Park Service was defending against congressional budget cutters and the NPS funding was reduced. The larger Lowell revitalization effort had been fueled by $500 million in combined private and public dollars from 1978, the first year of park operations, to 1987, the start of the five-year growth spurt.

One of the essential steps forward in this period was the Heritage State Park's $1.5 million purchase of twenty-six acres of land, including canal gatehouses, conservation easements on the banks of the waterways, and air rights above the canals from the Proprietors of Locks & Canals. This acquisition ensured longtime use of the canals for tourism. Other pieces of the state park like the Vandenberg Esplanade and boathouse on the north bank of the Merrimack above the falls were already in place.

Steve Conant, principal planner for the Heritage State Park at the time, said, "This was huge—and it also illustrated how at the time the state park, national park, and Preservation Commission were joined at the hip. Everyone worked together to get the big things done. There was a strong sense of community and feeling of vibrancy in the city in that era."[33]

The Heritage State Park's main contributions to historic preservation involved gaining access to the canal system for tours and the development of the Mack Building and plaza on Shattuck Street for the state park headquarters. This prominent public space includes the unusual brick-covered barrel vault over the Merrimack Canal, a ghost arch tribute to the historic train station at the former location of Huntington Hall, and a pocket-park now named Mary Bacigalupo Victorian Park for a much-admired community activist. The plaza features the canal-worker stone fountain, based on the design of the original waterpower museum exhibit figures in the Mack Building. On the tracks running parallel to Dutton Street near the Mack Building, there is a vintage black locomotive on permanent display, maintained by the Boston & Maine Railroad Historical Society.

The state park's mission emphasized the water resources and hydropower history in Lowell. The headquarters in the Mack Building on Shattuck Street housed a museum exhibition about the power canals; along the Merrimack River, the staff maintained a popular esplanade with a performance pavilion, not far from the Lowell-Dracut-Tyngsborough State Forest, also managed by the same state agency.

This restored locomotive is a nod to the city's train history. The Boston and Lowell Railroad dates from 1835, one of the earliest lines in the United States.
Tory Germann

In the early years, national and state park staff worked in interpretive teams at sites like the Guard Locks on the Pawtucket Canal. In the early 1990s, a state budget crisis precipitated the de-funding of most of the Heritage Park system. The downtown waterpower exhibit closed, and the remaining staff concentrated its efforts above the Pawtucket Falls on the Vandenberg Esplanade, which had become the most popular public parkland in the city as health walkers, Rollerbladers, and families with strollers enjoyed the river vistas and sunset views. In 2009, the Bellegarde Boathouse was transferred from Heritage Park oversight to UMass–Lowell's Department of Athletics and renovated with $1 million in state funds.

From the state park, Steve Conant went on to work for Congressman Chester "Chet" Atkins, the City of Lowell planning office, and then to an environmental planning firm. (Of note during his state park days, Conant suggested to the Lowell Historic Preservation Commission that a planned sculptural tribute to Jack Kerouac be moved from a modest site along the Pawtucket Canal downtown to its present larger location off Bridge Street that was being redeveloped by the state and City of Lowell, as described ahead in chapter 6.) With Matt Donahue of Lowell, another former member of the local Conservation Commission, he cofounded the Lowell Parks & Conservation Trust in 1992. The city's only land trust is much more than that—with its urban forestry services, environmental education activities, white-water rafting program on the Concord River, and stewardship of the Spalding House, one of Lowell's last few eighteenth-century structures. The trust has more than 900 members.

On the tenth anniversary of the park, in June 1988, a stellar cast assembled to mark the occasion. U.S. Senators Kennedy and Kerry, former Senator Tsongas, U.S. Representative Atkins, NPS Regional Director Herbert Cables, former Lowell superintendents Albert and Burchill, and Superintendent Walter gathered at the new Lowell Hilton Hotel at Lower Locks. Topping the guest list was NPS Director William Penn Mott Jr. who knew success when he saw it:

The urban population will provide the public constituency and support which is essential to our parks in a democratic society. In our urban areas, the National Park Service can function as an agent of change, not only as a preservation agent, retrieving a sense of environmental harmony for lands entrusted to our care and providing opportunities for individual regeneration and recreation where none previously existed.[34]

Chief planner of the Preservation Commission Sarah Peskin said, "We've done all the major things we said we'd do, and each project has been better than the one before."[35] Superintendent Sandy Walter remarked that the National Park Service had helped lift the city's spirit and prospects, while former Preservation Commission boss Fred Faust added, "People are staying in Lowell because they see a future here for themselves and their families. But the revitalization won't be complete until it's a city where everybody can share equally." And it was only 1988.

A couple of weeks later, some 200 people cheered on the first trolley to leave the platform along Dutton Street near the Mack Building of Lowell Heritage State Park. Built by the Gomaco firm of Ida Grove, Iowa, streetcar No. 4131 was sent off in a shower of broken glass and champagne in tribute to Ted Santorelli de Brausch, the recently deceased founder of the Seashore Trolley Museum in Kennebunkport, Maine. De Brausch had supervised construction of the replica trolley, modeled on one made by the St. Louis Car Company for the Bay State Street Railway, circa 1913. The Bay State trolley empire at one time had cars running in cities from Nashua, New Hampshire, to Newport, Rhode Island.

It's not a stretch, in Sarah Peskin's view, to say that Lowell was a major impetus in the reappearance of trolleys around the country in the form of "old timey" but functional streetcars. When the Lowell Trolley project commenced, there were no known suppliers of equipment in the United States, which is why the LHPC called

Moving through the park by trolley
James Higgins

on its contractors for a custom design. After the system was proven to work and GOMACO got into the business of building the equipment, it was easier for other cities to copy Lowell.

June was a busy time that year. A week later, several hundred more people gathered in a new park along the Eastern Canal off Bridge Street for the dedication of the *Jack Kerouac Commemorative*, a sculptural tribute to the American author responsible for a counterculture groundswell with his 1957 novel of highway adventuring, *On the Road*. The evening before the dedication, a poetry reading drew 1,000 people to the Smith Baker Center, a former Congregational Church that functioned like a Lowell version of Sanders Theatre at Harvard University.

That same year, the LHPC completed construction of the Patrick J. Mogan Cultural Center or Boott Mills Boarding House on French Street. The boarding house was the last remaining of what had been eight matching structures set perpendicular to the Boott Mills just across the Eastern Canal. The Mogan Center represents one of the most dramatic transformations of historic buildings in Lowell. Park architect Chuck Parrott describes the process as a reconstruction. The effort began with the former H & H Paper Company building, whose top had been sawed off, leaving a structure that looked very little like the original boarding house with its distinctive "H" block end sections. Earlier, a study by the NPS had recommended against restoration, concerned that little of the original fabric remained to justify the work. It would open in early 1989, fully restored on the boarding house side and with a simple two-story "linking structure" filling the space between the boarding house and adjacent cotton storehouse. In fact, the careful restoration would anchor one of the most striking and active settings in the park.

"Reconstruction" is an important word to note, Larry Gall said:

> A reconstruction would never have been permitted by NPS standards because the building had lost its "integrity." This is a clear example of the wisdom of the enabling legislation that allowed so much latitude to the Preservation Commission. The NPS would have been stymied by federal standards of the day—yet restoring the boarding house was critical to telling the story of mill girls in relationship to the Boott Mills story of cotton manufacturing. Thus we overcame historian Mary Blewett's concern about "the tyranny of existing structures" in this important instance.[36]

The central element of the boarding house is an NPS museum exhibition about the lives of workers outside the mill. The two-part exhibit consists of a re-created 1840s-era living quarters for mill girls (dining room and kitchen downstairs and bedroom upstairs) with historical materials and commentary and an adjoining two-level display about the immigrant experience in the city. With timeline, artifacts, images, wall text, and short videos, the NPS presented the experience of immigrant peoples who had settled in Lowell. These paired exhibits focused on life outside the workplace, filling in the social history of the workers and families as a complement to the shop floor story conveyed in the Boott Mills Museum only steps away.

The Mogan Center also housed and continues to house the UMass–Lowell Center for Lowell History (CLH), a unit of the University Libraries that is the custodian of the treasured documents of Lowelliana. Here, the collections of the Lowell Historical Society, former Lowell Museum Corporation, and other allied entities are available for research and study. The NPS maintains its own research library in Lowell, but is one of the primary users of the CLH materials. The maps, papers, books, and photographs in the collections proved essential to planners, architects, historians, and others during the development phase of the park.

The building opened with the Preservation Commission and Park Service expecting that it would be a highly active community space. Through the years it has been the location for numerous events and activities ranging from temporary exhibits about aspects of Lowell history to lectures and performances. For many years it has been the home of Lowell's award-winning Angkor Dance Troupe, a youth arts program that was founded by master artist Tim Thou, a survivor of the Cambodian "killing fields" who brought his family to Lowell.

When the second phase of construction at Boott Mill No. 6 began in June 1989, Congressman Atkins said, "When this project is completed two years from now, we're going to have something that will ignite development in the city. Lowell used to be referred to as 'Oz.' Nobody in Washington but Paul Tsongas believed this day would ever happen. Now, Washington has a view of Lowell as a city on a hill."[37]

On that day, onlookers could only imagine the experience of entering the 7,000 square foot weave room filled with dozens of power looms and the enveloping cacophony of the machines banging out cloth. The Boott Mills Museum would open with the two-floor centerpiece exhibition on textile production, the Tsongas Industrial History Center for experiential education, the New England Folklife Center, curatorial space for the Lowell Historical Society, and offices for the Building Conservation Branch of the Northeast Cultural Resources Center of the NPS.

Former park employee and now freelance journalist Mike Wurm credits Superintendent Walter for pushing the Boott Museum project over the goal line.

Looms return to the Boott Mills, 1991
James Higgins

U.S. Representative Chet Atkins and LNHP Superintendent Chrysandra "Sandy" Walter at the opening of the Boott Cotton Mills Museum, 1992
James Higgins

> Sandy provided the fire along with decisive leadership for getting the Boott Cotton Mills Museum accomplished in the face of many bureaucratic and architectural challenges. I witnessed her ripping into architects, engineers, and consultants in order to get them "outside the box"—to embrace her vision for the old mill building coming to life with dynamic exhibits, cooperative partners, and what has become the state-of-the-art hands-on learning center.[38]

THE CANALWAY AND BEYOND

The run up to the Boott Cotton Mills Museum opening involved a number of complicated real-estate moves related to the development of the associated buildings in the complex—consistent with plans agreed to by the key public entities, the NPS, LHPC, and City of Lowell. In 1987, Congress Group Properties of Boston acquired the Boott with plans for offices, technology companies, and shops. Congress Group announced that it would spend $50 million to renovate the complex. Across Bridge Street from the Boott stands the Massachusetts Mills, itself deep into a planned $80 million conversion to apartments at the time. The LHPC helped the Boott project along in two ways: (1) by purchasing a surface parking lot in front of the Boott Mills from Congress Group, the proceeds of which were used to buy an adjacent lot from the city, providing the land for what would be a beautiful performance venue called Boarding House Park (the city then used the money to help fund the design of a new 1,000-car parking garage across the street to accommodate increased activity at

The Canalway at Lucy Larcom Park, which is named for the nineteenth-century poet, writer, and editor who had been a factory operative in Lowell
James Higgins

the Boott Mills complex); and (2) by providing $300,000 in grant funds for restoration of the four stair towers in the Boott Mills yard.

After signing up Alliance Technologies and EUA Cogenex Corporation, Congress Group's progress at the Boott stalled out in the recession of 1991. Not only had Wang Laboratories' large computer operation in Lowell collapsed a few years before, but the high-tech sector in eastern Massachusetts also contracted. Chase Manhattan Bank, the major lender to Congress Group, foreclosed on the mill complex in 1991. Bank executives promised to stick with the existing development plan, but the strategy did not yield results. Eventually, the majority of the space was redeveloped as residences, apartments, and condominiums. WinnDevelopment of Boston now oversees a complex with more than 292 residential units completed; they and Rees-Larkin Development have invested $37 million in the project. As of 2013, the total private investment at the Boott complex was $102 million. When matched against the $15 million in federal funding that brought the National Park Service to Boott Mill No. 6, the return-on-public-investment is astounding.

The LHPC was authorized with a ten-year lifespan in 1978, a compromise agreed to by Tsongas to disarm critics concerned about the proposed agency's unconventional powers to buy and lease property, award grants and loans, and operate broadly in the historic district. Visitors to the office of the first executive director, Faust, got a closeup view of a large, orange, stuffed-cloth carrot dangling from a long wooden stick. The message was not subtle, and the LHPC was known for its fidelity to the original intent of the park legislation. Not everyone in the city was a fan of the preservation ethic, but there was widespread respect for the agency's businesslike attitude about economics, architecture, and culture. It was clear, however, that the LHPC's work would not be done in Lowell by June 1988, which is why the commissioners had sought and gained reauthorization with a mandate to focus seven years of work on further development of Lowell's canal system.

Of note is that the LHPC's reauthorization was considered to be in line with President Ronald Reagan's "New Federalism" concept for public policy. While the proven Lowell park method of collaborating with state government and bringing on board private investment gained approval from the Reagan-era officials, the administration still did not recommend any federal funding for a reauthorized LHPC. Staff members in the Congress, however, were confident the reauthorization would pass. The Lowell bill had received the most favorable recommendation that they had seen from the White House on any previous National Park Service project. And, indeed, the LHPC was extended through 1995, with a budget.

The *Preservation Plan Amendment* of 1990 outlined the work to come in physical improvements and program initiatives aimed at drawing people to the canals themselves and contiguous city areas. The centerpiece of the plan was called the Canalway, a connected series of paths that would allow people to walk alongside long sections of the canal system. The system was divided into a downtown "Inner Loop" and an "Outer Loop" in the outlying areas. There was much to be done. A 1985 assessment of the canal system had determined that people viewed the canals as "dangerous, valueless, nameless back alley remains." For its part, the Preservation Commission held that the Canalway "should be promoted as a large, diverse system with many experiences, from compatible industrial to pastoral green areas that provide a respite from the pressures of life."[39] The Canalway blueprint called for bike and walking paths and places to fish, swim, skate, and even ride on a replica horse-drawn canal barge.

The LHPC concentrated its work on five areas, namely Swamp Locks at Thorndike and Dutton streets; the Upper Pawtucket Canal, which runs through a portion of the Acre and Lower Highlands neighborhoods; the Northern Canal Walkway below the Pawtucket Falls Dam; the Merrimack Canal in the heart of the downtown historic district; and Western Canal, which branches off the Pawtucket and cuts through sections of the Acre and downtown before emptying into the Merrimack at the foot of Suffolk Street near the Lawrence Manufacturing Company.

When the Preservation Commission came up against its second "sunset" date, another attempt was made to extend the agency. Since 1978, the LHPC had invested some $36 million in Lowell's reclamation. Then-Congressman Marty Meehan of Lowell succeeded in 1994 in getting the extension legislation through a Republican-controlled House of Representatives, but the effort was stymied in the U.S. Senate. Some observers felt that there was a sentiment among those in Congress who pay attention to national park activities that Lowell had been more than well treated since 1978. The timing was not right for a further extension of federal support. As a summation of preservation work during its seventeen years, the Preservation Commission in 1995 published an illustrated book, *Lowell: Then and Now*, which described the transformation of more than sixty structures in the historic district. The agency had awarded $5.4 million in grants and loans and generated $52 million in private funding, a $9.60 to $1 ratio. In twenty years, the vaunted public-private partnership strategy in Lowell had led to the rehabilitation of some

250 buildings. The last of the Preservation Commission's executive directors, Peter Aucella (1986–1995), wrote in the Introduction:

> When the proposal for federal participation in Lowell was before the U.S. Congress, its leading advocate, Paul Tsongas, promised his colleagues that, if approved, the development of Lowell National Historical Park would be done right. There was a commitment to quality in all undertakings that would make the nation proud. . . . This book chronicles some successes and some near successes.[40]

INTO THE TWENTY-FIRST CENTURY

The bricks-and-mortar component of the federal park was largely in place by the mid-1990s. Superintendent Rich Rambur succeeded Sandy Walter at the helm in Lowell. Faced with a lean budget, Rambur sought to consolidate gains and figure out how to function with fewer dollars. His 1995 goals were topped by an effort to expand visitation and followed by items like "seek and procure alternative sources of funding" and "achieve greater constituent involvement."[41] After years of expansion and flush budgets, the park was transitioning into an operations entity.

Rambur eliminated seventeen jobs from the payroll. Inside the park, "That got me off on the wrong foot," he said. "My first priority was to make sure we could maintain [the Boott Mills with its 500 windows], but we also had to find the funding level that would allow us to carry on good interpretive programs." He was blunt in his assessment of the visitor situation in 1994. "Lowell was one of those areas that was built under the idea that if you build it, they will come. Well, we built it, and they didn't come. We had high expectations. We're not even close to that yet." Planners in the 1970s had projected one million visitors a year. Despite his concerns, Rambur was sure about Lowell's value. "People really get the connection that exists between generations and see how this country developed."[42]

Former LNHP assistant superintendent Larry Gall has his own view of the visitation results:

> I always thought the projected visitation figures in early planning documents were wildly optimistic and setting us up for a perception of failure when we couldn't meet them. Supt. John Burchill was always pressing me for inflated figures when I was responsible for reporting them. When the media pressed me about visitors, I was at pains to say that the numbers were less important than the fact that the very existence of a national park in Lowell represented federal recognition of Lowell's national significance and encouraged both private- and public-sector investment, which was much more important than how many people spent a few dollars downtown. Sometimes the Chamber of Commerce had a hard time with that longer view.[43]

By the late 1990s, some 450,000 people were visiting the park in some form each year, counting big events like the Lowell Folk Festival, with numbers approaching 200,000, and Lowell Summer Music Series, topping 30,000, and school programs, which served 50,000 kids. As a combined attraction, by 2012 Lowell was exceeding one million visitors. Big draws that supplement specific visits to park facilities include the Southeast Asian Water Festival; minor-league Red Sox baseball at LeLacheur Park; UMass–Lowell's Hockey East games; major music stars at the Tsongas

Center at UMass–Lowell and Lowell Summer Music Series; Lowell Memorial Auditorium shows and Merrimack Repertory Theatre; and an array of street festivals,
regattas, parades, museums, and art studios. More and more, Lowell is seen as a
multiverse cultural hub. The systemic challenge of segmenting out the places where
people are stepping on park territory becomes unsolvable. In the end it is a benefit.
The park glow radiates above and around most anything Lowell. At the same time,
any trouble in the city rubs off a bit on the park, which adds to the anxiety of cultural tourism professionals in the city.

Finding ways to boost visitor numbers, offering new activities, and completing the
Canalway—these objectives kept park staff busy through the turn of the century. The
Lowell community reaffirmed its belief in planning with two citywide conferences:
"Lowell: 2000 and Beyond" addressed ways to take the city as a whole to the next
orbit, and "2001: A Cultural Odyssey" aimed to strengthen the arts and humanities.

To look at the Lowell: Beyond 2000 agenda is to see how disciplined Lowell has
been in its redevelopment efforts. Mayor Eileen Donoghue and City Manager Brian
Martin joined with UMass–Lowell, Middlesex Community College, the Lowell Plan,
Inc., and NPS to sponsor the all-day program for 350 people at the Doubletree Hotel (originally the Hilton) at the Lower Locks complex. By this time, the conference
sponsors had become the go-to partners for major initiatives of this kind. Speakers
such as Ray Suarez of National Public Radio's "Talk of the Nation," Kati Haycock of
the Education Trust, and award-winning architect William L. Rawn III offered insights
on reconciling suburban growth and small cities, the critical role of urban schools,

The Canalway along the Eastern Canal at Massachusetts Mills
Tory Germann

the benefits of inner-city waterways, the economic impact of higher education, neighborhood vitality as an essential asset, and the social and economic value of cultural activity. Suarez said the previous fifty years had been bad for cities, but that the rising cost of transportation, the aging cohort of baby boomers, and fundamental desire to live closer to other people would help turn the tide back to city living. The key, in his view, would be for cities like Lowell to provide a wide set of choices for living, "a broad continuum of housing"—and, he stressed, the more prosperous among us must "get beyond feeling contempt for low-income working people."[44]

The sessions extended the community dialogue begun in the mid-1960s when Lowell started to climb back up the hill. Martin closed out the day with a panel of local people talking about what they heard and what next steps Lowell should take. The event was classic Lowell civic engagement, a trait that has come to characterize the "New Lowell" as much as the vaunted formula for mass-production of textiles known as the Lowell System defined the prototypical mill city of the 1840s.

A few years before, in 1997, a sprawling, brightly illustrated blueprint for improving natural assets like rivers, parks, and the state forest was brought forth by some of the same activists who had fostered the urban cultural park idea twenty years before. Called Lowell: The Flowering City, the plan was shaped by more than 100 community volunteers in a three-day community charette enriched with landscape architects and urban affairs scholars. In all these activities, top park staff members rolled up their sleeves alongside neighborhood-group leaders, city planners, bank presidents, artists, teachers, and others. The intangible benefit of resident NPS experts in history, preservation, urban planning, public administration, and resource management has become so much a part of how Lowell functions that at times the non-park members of the community can overlook the special circumstance that is everyday Lowell.

Lowellians have largely overcome their early skepticism of park personnel as outsiders whose agenda might be to turn the local heritage into "zoo exhibits," but there remains in segments of the community a gap in familiarity with the park and its staff day to day. Some observers think it may be time to turn the fully built park "inside out" and increase the street-level visibility of the operation. The museum and educational facilities add much to the way residents and visitors encounter the city, however, the Lowell's national-park identity is not as evident as it might be.

Alexis de Tocqueville did not go to Lowell on his notable visits to America in 1831 and 1833, unlike other Europeans of the time like Charles Dickens, British social reformer Harriet Martineau, and political economist Michel Chevalier of France. In *Democracy in America*, published in 1835, Tocqueville commented on the inclination of people in the new United States to organize and act in groups. He wrote:

> Americans of all ages, all conditions, all minds constantly unite. Not only do they have commercial and industrial associations in which all take part, but they also have a thousand other kinds: religious, moral, grave, futile, very general and very particular, immense and very small; Americans use associations to give fêtes, to found seminaries, to build inns, to raise churches, to distribute books, to send missionaries to the antipodes; in this manner they create hospitals, prisons, schools. Finally, if it is a question of bringing to light a truth or developing a sentiment with the support of a great example, they associate. Everywhere that, at the head of a new undertaking, you see the government in France and a great lord in England, count on it that you will perceive an association in the United States.[45]

The Lowell community that brought a national park to its city and the Lowell of twenty-first-century America offer plentiful evidence that this civic impulse has not dimmed. Contemporary Lowell is powered by people meeting day and night; community organizations are the manufacturers of social glue and public action. Collective action is necessary in a place where most people are of modest means. There are few public initiatives driven by one man or one woman. Lowellians combine first when there is a dream or a problem, whether that means the Lowell Canalwaters Cleaners, who took it upon themselves to address chronic fouling of the canal system, or the Angkor Dance Troupe, who determined to preserve an art form and earned a White House award for young artists. A familiar face at the early canal clean-ups was Nancy L. Donahue, one of the city's leading philanthropists and strongest advocates for culture. Her involvement sent a powerful message about the importance of maintaining the historic canals. This activism is physical evidence of the soul of the city, the spirit that animates the cooperation between actors in the public sector, government and community affairs, and in the business or private sector.

At a White House ceremony in 1999, the Angkor Dance Troupe received the presidential "Coming Up Taller Award," the nation's highest recognition for arts groups serving young people who are at risk.

James Higgins

Nancy L. Donahue and George Duncan represent the longevity of the Lowell renaissance, both of them involved from the start. From canal clean-ups to commissioning artworks, they lead by doing. Donahue and her husband, Richard K. Donahue, are major philanthropists in the city. With Duncan, founder of Enterprise Bank of Lowell, they helped establish the Greater Lowell Community Foundation and have played essential roles in the cultural revival, notably the success of Merrimack Repertory Theatre. Duncan also championed the creation of the Lowell Development & Financial Corporation as a tool for investing in local rehabilitation.
Jennifer Myers

The "Partnership Park" got a literal partner in 2000 when community activists formed the Lowell Heritage Partnership (LHP), an alliance of more than twenty people affiliated with institutions, agencies, and organizations invested in the idea of Lowell as a special place. The catalyst for organizing was the perceived threat to one of the earliest factory complexes, the Appleton Mills, close to the park Visitor Center. The Appleton wound up being a showcase of adaptive reuse in the Hamilton Canal District redevelopment described ahead. In a twist on the typical preservation society, the LHP embraced a holistic approach to historic preservation, environmental protection, and cultural conservation. Its motto is "Caring for Architecture, Nature, and Culture." Members are associated with the Lowell Historical Society, Coalition for a Better Acre, Lowell Parks & Conservation Trust, Light of Cambodian Children, Greater Lowell Chamber of Commerce, and other entities. The organization is the financial host for the Lowell Historic Board's successful annual preservation outreach program "Doors Open Lowell" and has supported programs that cultivate young leaders and spread the preservation word into the neighborhoods.

In 2008, LNHP's thirtieth anniversary, the LHP was acknowledged in the anniversary report as an important community ally of the park. Once a month, park staff members and these community advocates meet to discuss needs and opportunities, filling in to a degree the gap left by the sunset of the Lowell Historic Preservation Commission as a federal agency. From 1978 to 1995, the business of the park was the subject of a monthly open meeting with representatives from several federal agencies and local stakeholders. One LHP achievement was marshaling community support to persuade the City Council to expand the Lowell Historic Board's oversight to include new construction and demolition of structures in the seven areas in the city's neighborhoods that are on the National Register for Historic Districts.

The LHP was formed shortly before Patrick McCrary became superintendent at Lowell. He had come to LNHP from the Oklahoma City National Memorial. He had led the NPS effort to work with state and local partners to build the memorial and a museum commemorating the lives of the 168 persons killed in an act of domestic terrorism. The bombing of the Alfred P. Murrah Federal Building on April 19, 1995, by antigovernment extremists was on McCrary's mind when he began talking about a "museum of social conscience" in Lowell. Touched by the stories of survivors of the Khmer Rouge genocide as he met members of the Cambodian American community in Lowell, McCrary wondered if the immigration theme embedded in the interpretive mission of LNHP could be the basis of a larger dialogue about mass violence, prejudice, and psychopathic hatred of others. The Irish immigrants in Lowell at one time were told that they "need not apply" for jobs, local Armenians carried the scars of ethnic-cleansing attacks, Jewish residents included survivors of concentration camps in Eastern Europe—one after another, ethnic, racial, religious, and political groups had suffered from discrimination and worse.

While the social-conscience museum concept remained an idea, McCrary moved to heighten community involvement in the park when he hired local historian Mehmed Ali to be the first director of the Patrick J. Mogan Cultural Center. Ali sparked a resurgence of heritage activism with his innovative and tireless promotion of the Lowell story. For several years, while funding was available, the Mogan Center boasted a series of exhibits developed by the community, a Scholar-in-Residence program, plus mini-grants for folklife events, history activities, publications, and research projects. With his doctorate in history completed, and after missing election to the City Council by 200 votes, Ali in 2010 responded to a State Department request for federal-agency administrators willing to serve in Iraq. He worked in Baghdad and in eastern Afghanistan on provincial reconstruction efforts and other projects, including rudimentary historic preservation initiatives in war-ravaged Baghdad.

Michael Creasey landed in Lowell on Valentine's Day, 2005, to start what would be a seven-year run. He left a large imprint on the park. Superintendent Creasey "worked big." He helped launch Public Matters, a leadership development program for emerging community leaders, in partnership with the Lowell Plan; the Public Matters cohort by 2013 had reached ninety-three members. He backed major museum initiatives such as the exhibition of Jack Kerouac's legendary *On the Road* scroll manuscript in 2007, which drew 25,000 people to the Boott Cotton Mills Museum, and the "Dickens in Lowell" project at the Boott Museum in 2012, commemorating Charles Dickens's 200th birthday and the author's notable visit to Lowell in 1842. Both the Kerouac and Dickens projects earned national awards.

Michael Creasey, LNHP superintendent, 2005–2012
Meghan Moore

Creasey's gumption also helped cement a daring collaboration in 2007 that brought to Lowell the world premiere of *Where Elephants Weep*, a genre-bending Cambodian rock opera built around a classic love story. Along with the park, the co-sponsors were UMass–Lowell, Middlesex Community College, COOL (the Cultural Organization of Lowell), the Cambodian American community, and the Theodore Edson Parker Foundation. More than 4,000 people attended the performances at Lowell High School's auditorium; the audiences were among the most diverse seen at large-scale performing arts events in the city in recent memory. He worked with park partners to expand the already successful Lowell Folk Festival and pushed to complete more segments of the Canalway paths, allowing people to follow the canal routes throughout the city.

In 2010, he invited the director of the National Park Service, Jonathan Jarvis, to give the keynote speech at an international conference on Innovative Cities held downtown at the UMass–Lowell Inn & Conference Center. After spending a year at Harvard University on a prestigious Loeb Fellowship at the Graduate School of Design, Creasey returned to Lowell for a short time before being appointed superintendent of Marsh-Billings-Rockefeller National Park and the NPS Conservation Institute in Woodstock, Vermont. The NPS director asked him to strengthen the think-tank operations at the Institute and create a leadership development program for managers.

As of this writing, Superintendent Celeste Bernardo occupies the corner office of the Agents' House at Paige and Kirk streets, across the street from Lowell High School, with its more than 3,000 students. Each school day she sees the Lowell story in progress in the youthful faces. A former ranger in Lowell who was in charge of the

YELLOWSTONE AND LOWELL

In January 1872, Senator Samuel Pomeroy of Kansas and Representative Henry L. Dawes of Massachusetts brought forward legislation in the U.S. Congress calling for an expanse of land "near the headwaters of the Yellowstone river" in the Wyoming territory to be "reserved and withdrawn from settlement, occupancy, or sale under the laws of the United States, and dedicated and set apart as a public park or pleasuring ground for the benefit and enjoyment of the people." Without extensive debate, the act of Congress was approved in both houses and signed by President Ulysses S. Grant on March 1, 1872. As Dayton Duncan and Ken Burns write in *The National Parks: America's Best Idea*, "this would be a *national* park—the first national park in the history of the world."[1] Yosemite Park, created by Congress, predated this decision, but the state of California managed Yosemite and had been doing so since 1864. Yellowstone is the beginning for *national* parks. In the years leading up to the establishment of Yellowstone, the country had learned about its stunning vistas and wilderness through the printed illustrations, photographs, and paintings of artists such as Thomas Moran and William Henry Jackson. As with Yosemite, the natural features of Yellowstone compelled those encountering them to want to convey to others what they had experienced, to somehow capture in line, form, and color the majestic character of the places.

By 1872, Lowell had been a visitor attraction for more than fifty years. From the start people behaved toward Lowell as if it was a place "apart," something new in form, scale, and purpose. In the first painted view by Benjamin Mather in 1825, ranged around the riverine edges of what had been Cheever's Farm and Fletcher's Farm are the multistoried redbrick Merrimack Manufacturing Company, Lowell Machine Shop, and related boarding houses set among valley trees. A parade of oil painters and illustrators followed Mather from the mid-1820s through the 1850s, in particular. Their renderings of the factories and urban scene were portrayed with all the care and reverence that one sees in depictions of mountainsides and cataracts out west.

In Thomas Moran's epic tableau *The Grand Canyon of the Yellowstone* (1872), based on his sketches from an excursion in 1871, the view is from a ledge that came to be known as Artist Point. Two figures dwarfed by massive trees and rock formations contemplate Nature in its glory. "All my tendencies are toward idealization," wrote Moran. The same is true for the praising-pictures of early Lowell, including David Claypool Johnston's engraving of the "mile of mills" from the north bank of the Merrimack River in 1850. Formally dressed figures on promenade in the foreground regard the industrial marvel and gesture toward the long red wall along the river under a tall sky and grand clouds. At the bottom left, bent over his work is a man in a cap making his own version of what we are looking at in the image. This high-ground vantage on the Dracut side of the river could be Lowell's Artist Point.

---

1. Ken Burns and Dayton Duncan, *The National Parks: America's Best Idea* (New York: Knopf, 2011).

The Grand Canyon of the Yellowstone by Thomas Moran, 1872
Department of the Interior Museum, Smithsonian American Art Museum, Washington, D.C.

Merrimack Prints, Lowell, Massachusetts, by David Claypool Johnston, c. 1850
Lowell Historical Society

new Boott Cotton Mills Museum soon after it opened, Bernardo had overseen New Bedford Whaling National Park and had a top post at Boston National Historical Park. Her deep knowledge of the history and cultural heritage of the region, as well as her experience in urban park settings, make her an excellent match for Lowell. Those high school students are not only part of the park's constituency, but also are seen as central to the park experience going forward. Bernardo sees major program themes in the open-ended process of industrialization and innovation, the immigration experience and exploration of ethnic identity, and the dynamic case study of Lowell's reclamation, both physical and cultural.

NOTES

1. Ken Salazar, commencement address at UMass–Lowell, author's notes.
2. Alexander Brash, Jamie Hand, and Kate Orff, eds., *Gateway: Visions for an Urban National Park* (New York: Princeton Architectural Press, 2011), 89.
3. Brash, Hand, and Orff, *Gateway*, 195.
4. Lawrence Gall, letter to the author.
5. *Working Together: The Story of the Lowell Model Cities Program* (Lowell Model Cities, 1971), n.p.
6. *Working Together*, n.p.
7. *Working Together*, n.p.
8. *Human Services Corporation*, n.p.
9. George O'Har and Gray Fitzsimons, "Lowell National Historical Park Administrative History," February 2004, 15.
10. Gall, letter to the author.
11. Brendan Fleming, interview with Maryrose Lane.
12. Patrick J. Mogan, "Renewal Process in Lowell, Massachusetts: Toward an Ecologically Sensitive Educational Model," University of Massachusetts–Amherst, 1975, 134.
13. *Lowell Urban Park* (Lowell: Human Services Corporation, 1973–1974), 48.
14. O'Har and Fitzsimons, 18.
15. Fred Faust, interview with Mehmed Ali.
16. Faust, interview with Ali.
17. Mary Ellen Fitzpatrick, interview with Ali.
18. Marty Meehan, interview with the author.
19. Faust, interview with Ali.
20. O'Har and Fitzsimons, 19.
21. O'Har and Fitzsimons, 20.
22. Richard Arenberg, interview with Ali.
23. *Paul Efthemios Tsongas, 1941–1997: Late a Senator from Massachusetts, Memorial Tributes in the Congress of the United States* (Washington, D.C.: U.S. Government Printing Office, 1997).
24. National Parks Conservation Association, http://www.npca.org/news/media-center/fact-sheets/anilca.html.
25. Fred Faust, letter to the author.
26. Niki Tsongas, interview with Ali.
27. Human Services Corporation and Page One Productions, *Roots of an Urban Cultural Park*.
28. Faust, letter to the author.
29. Gall, letter to the author.

30. O'Har and Fitzsimons, 2.5.
31. Gall, letter to the author.
32. O'Har and Fitzsimons, 4.6.
33. Steve Conant, interview with the author.
34. O'Har and Fitzsimons, 8.1.
35. O'Har and Fitzsimons, 8.1.
36. Gall, letter to the author.
37. O'Har and Fitzsimons, 9.4.
38. Mike Wurm, letter to the author.
39. O'Har and Fitzsimons, n.p.
40. Charles Parrott, *Lowell Then and Now: Restoring the Legacy of a Mill City* (Lowell: Lowell Historic Preservation Commission, 1995), vi.
41. O'Har and Fitzsimons, 11.3.
42. O'Har and Fitzsimons, 11.4.
43. Gall, letter to the author.
44. Ray Suarez at the Lowell: Beyond 2000 conference, author's notes.
45. Alexis de Tocqueville, *Democracy in America*, ed. Richard Heffner (New York: New American Library, 1956), 198.

CHAPTER 4

Bricks and Mortar, Then and Now

Charles Parrott

During the decades of the twentieth century, the fortunes of America's older cities spiraled downward as urban disinvestment and decline became a familiar pattern. Regardless of specifics, social and economic forces stripped our urban centers of the civic focus and presence they once held. Lowell has been no exception to this phenomenon. One of Lowell's approaches to revitalization has been the systematic architectural rehabilitation of its many historic downtown buildings. The rehabilitation approach contained a central idea: to return the building to economic viability while also preserving and enhancing its inherent historic character. Because these structures are also intended to serve an interpretive function as either background or landmark buildings within the park, the rehabilitation scheme arrived at for each building has been an attempt to enhance as fully as possible the general historic appearance of the building during Lowell's textile mill heyday. To achieve that look, traditional design has been advocated for replacement architectural elements, such as storefronts and windows. However, because downtown Lowell continues to be an active, working, economically striving city, no museum-like, exact-point-in-time exterior restoration is desirable or has been performed. Preexisting irreversible alterations usually have been accepted and accommodated in the rehabilitation design. Historic preservation and modern functional needs have been equally considered in arriving at each rehabilitation treatment. Building interiors have generally been done in a much freer, modern way except in a few cases where extraordinary interior elements encouraged some level of preservation. Following are examples of some of the more significant building rehabilitation projects. Although much new information about many of these buildings has been discovered in the course of time and the work on them, a great deal of the basic historical information has been obtained in the *Lowell National Historical Park and Preservation District Cultural Resources Inventory* by Shepley Bulfinch Richardson and Abbott. This massive effort of research and writing put together in a few short months in 1979 has proven to be almost error-free even when considerably more information about a particular building subsequently has come to light.

LOWELL MANUFACTURING COMPANY
(MARKET MILLS/CANAL PLACE)

Off Market Street

Many obsolete textile mills in New England have been rehabilitated for new uses since the 1970s. In the early years of the adaptive reuse movement, their preservation was often accomplished at the expense of their historic appearance. This usually was due to the developer's choice of new windows, configured quite differently from those traditionally used. However, on the typically plain, unrelieved facades of textile mills, the historic patterns of the windows are the principal character-defining element. Windows installed during the 1980s in buildings of the former Lowell Manufacturing Company offer contrasting examples of sensitivity to this characteristic.

1884: The Lowell Manufacturing Company was founded in 1828 as a producer of both cloth and hand-woven carpets. As a result of Erastus Bigelow's development of the power carpet loom here around 1840, the company evolved primarily into a producer of woolen carpets. In 1882, the No. 1 Brussels Weave Mill was built in the early part of a thirty-year campaign that almost completely replaced the original buildings with the larger ones now needed by a big carpet mill. The increased width of this mill over many earlier mills was reflected in the very large twelve-over-twelve windows. They were made about as big as practical for double-hung sash in an attempt to maximize light penetration into the interior. Later buildings in this complex that survive had their even-larger window openings divided into a pair of manageable four-over-four sash with transoms. This design was used in the adjacent Mill No. 2 of 1902, also a Brussels carpet mill, and the Worsted Mill of 1906.

Lowell Historical Society/UMass–Lowell Center for Lowell History

1979: The firm founded by Erastus Bigelow after he left Lowell turned full circle to take over the Lowell Manufacturing Company in 1899. However, in a surprise move in 1915, just after the building campaign ended, the Bigelow Company closed the Lowell plant. This action ushered in a long period of decline during which the buildings were divided into several ownerships and were used by a succession of smaller industrial concerns. Gradually, the property fell into disuse. In later years the buildings in the eastern half of the densely packed site were demolished, and others were at risk of being razed, especially the fire-damaged Mill No. 2.

James Higgins

2011: In one of the earlier large mill rehabilitation projects in this region, Mills No. 1 and 2 were cooperatively redeveloped in 1980–1981. With the new name of Market Mills, the complex provides private subsidized rental housing on the upper floors and public-sector mixed-use rental space at the street level. Institutional uses in the public area include the Lowell National Historical Park Visitor Center. Although this program was innovative and crucial to the buildings' preservation, the loss of architectural character generated by the replacement window choice is evident. In contrast, the Worsted Mill, located behind the two carpet mills, had windows identical to those of the No. 2 Brussels Mill. In 1986–1987, other owners rehabilitated the Worsted Mill for market rate housing, naming their development Canal Place. They maintained the historical appearance of the building by using replacement windows that represented newer technology.
James Higgins

1924: The building is a good example of a clapboarded-frame, five-bay, center-hall house of the late Federal style. After Kirk Boott's now-demolished mansion, it was one of the most substantial houses of Lowell's first generation, and yet it appears modest by today's standards. A double parlor and paired drawing and dining rooms flanked the stair hall, with the kitchen in a single-story rear ell. The few exterior changes over the years consist primarily of the addition of an entrance canopy, probably constructed in the 1850s, a second story on the ell, and a large dormer on the back slope of the roof.
Lowell Historical Society/UMass–Lowell Center for Lowell History

MOODY-WHISTLER-FRANCIS HOUSE
(WHISTLER HOUSE MUSEUM OF ART)

243 Worthen Street

The Moody-Whistler-Francis House, now the home of the Whistler House Museum of Art, is probably the most intact architectural example of Lowell's earliest period. In addition to being the birthplace of the celebrated American artist James McNeill Whistler, it is a major monument to the most important engineers associated with the seminal industrial endeavors undertaken in Lowell. In this house, built circa 1825 by the Locks and Canals Company for corporate engineering managers, lived Paul Moody, George Washington Whistler, and, later, James B. Francis, all major contributors to American civil and mechanical engineering practice in the nineteenth century. Whistler's famous son, the expatriate painter, was born in the house in 1834.

2011: The Lowell Art Association acquired the building in 1908 and has maintained it as an art museum ever since. The Association's stewardship undoubtedly accounts for this house being the sole survivor of the once-numerous single and double frame houses built by Lowell's earliest industrial corporations during the 1820s along Worthen and Dutton streets. The house's historic fabric was almost entirely intact in the late 1970s, but it was in need of restorative maintenance and repair. Successive small projects through the last decade began to bring back the building's earlier luster. The slate roof has been repaired. The original cornice, along with the siding and trim, has been restored, and original blinds (shutters) have been rebuilt.

James Higgins

FISKE BUILDING

217–227 Central Street

The Fiske Building represents the peak of the architectural exuberance during Lowell's Victorian era. In 1877, it was counted among the important buildings that were transforming the look of the city center from the provincial neoclassicism of the early years to the richer architectural expression of the industrially mature city. The building was probably designed by the architect Otis Merrill, who opened an office in the building. The eclectic treatment was likely encouraged by the owner, William Fiske, whose business included sash and door manufacturing, painting, and paperhanging services.

1890: Although the exterior treatment mixed stylistic devices and materials, the overall composition was graceful and coherent. Notable elements included the powerful storefront, which combined bold cast-iron columns with early examples of large plate-glass shop windows, and the interesting vertical gradation of the fenestration, which was perhaps encouraged by Fiske's knowledge of the latest window types. This display of window types moved upward from the still-novel shop windows to large vertical-pivot windows in the floor above, then to paired pivot windows with arched transoms, and culminated with arched-top hung sash. The most expressive element of all, however, was the building's cap. Here a heavy bracketed cornice supported a low mansard-roofed eave that ended in a Victorian parapet consisting of pinnacled pedestals and gables linked by a balustrade of iron cresting.

Lowell Historical Society/UMass–Lowell Center for Lowell History

2011: A fire destroyed the elaborate parapet and much of the interior in 1923. During the early twentieth century, the original storefronts, including all but one of the massive cast-iron columns, were removed to make way for modern storefronts. A major rehabilitation in 1987 virtually duplicated the lost design of the ground-floor facade and gave a proper base back to the building. Although the columns were replicated in painted glass-fiber-reinforced concrete, they match the original cast iron except for the foliated capitals, which were excluded. The remaining original upper facade was renewed as well, retaining its look except for the second-floor windows, which had to be replaced in a different configuration to satisfy building code requirements for housing on the upper floors. Although it was too costly to replace the missing parapet, the historic integrity of the building has been preserved and substantially enhanced.
James Higgins

DARIUS YOUNG HOUSE

72–76 Gorham Street

The Darius Young double house was one of the handful of pre–Civil War buildings in Lowell with a cut-granite facade, and was probably the only one of those
built solely for residential occupancy. That the house was built of stone may have
resulted from the probable involvement of two local stonemasons in its development. Erected in 1830 or 1831, the siting of the house directly on the street line
suggests the density and urban character that was already emerging within two or
three blocks of the mills. The surviving building fabric and an early deed referring
to one side of the building as a "stone house" indicate that it originally was configured as a pair of two-story townhouses. Sometime later, probably in the late 1800s,
the original windows were replaced and shop fronts were introduced when several
stone piers were replaced with iron columns and wooden beams.

1979: By the late 1970s, cheap hardboard paneling and an aluminum storefront had been
inserted into the ground-floor facade. A fire in 1980 seriously damaged the structure,
jeopardizing its preservation for some time. The fire had burned through the roof and
destroyed some of the granite veneer on the left side of the second story. The building was
boarded up in the hope that it could still be saved.
LNHP

2011: Preservation came to the building in 1984, when a new owner rescued and rehabilitated it. Because the building was to house a commercial enterprise, the shop aspect was retained in the new wooden storefront system, with the later framing members enclosed by wooden column facings and a false transom. The paired doorways of the original houses are recalled by the dual entrance to the new store. All of the fire-damaged granite was replaced with new matching stone and the rest, including the rough squared stone of the other three facades, was carefully restored. The windows were replaced with new wooden ones of the probably original six-over-six configuration. A new slate roof completed the resurrection of this small, but significant, historic building.

James Higgins

BOSTON AND MAINE RAILROAD DEPOT
(MIDDLESEX COMMUNITY COLLEGE)

238–254 Central Street

Through their early decades of operation, railroads, like airlines later, experienced increasing competition as multiple carriers began serving certain markets. In 1876, the forty-year monopoly of the Boston and Lowell between those two cities ended with the Boston and Maine's entry into Lowell at a new depot on Central Street at Towers Corner. The B & L years before had chosen to approach the city by

1880: Boston and Maine Railroad officials apparently felt that an architectural embellishment of the new depot would help establish the company's contending status. The terminal-type layout consisted of a lavishly detailed head-house fronting a 450-foot-long train shed that stretched back the long block to George Street. The High Victorian Gothic head-house was symmetrically arrayed except for the obvious emphasis on the corner tower nearest the open square. The extra stage of this tower contained clock faces on at least three of the four sides. Rich polychromed masonry, cast-iron colonnettes, and iron roof cresting were some of the features that also helped make this building a local landmark.
Lowell Historical Society/UMass–Lowell Center for Lowell History

1980: From 1921 to 1960, the building housed the Rialto Theatre, which was well known to generations of Lowell movie-goers for its second-run and Saturday children's features.
James Higgins

an overland route farther west that was better positioned for serving the railroad's envisioned market—mills needing to be supplied with bales of raw cotton. In contrast, the B & M trackage followed the Concord River into downtown Lowell. Four decades later, the B & M was intent as much on commuting and day-tripping passengers between Lowell and Boston as it was on freight.

APPLETON BLOCK

166–182 Central Street

As one of the Boston-based investors who initially developed Lowell, Nathan Appleton commanded enough local reverence for his name to be applied to a new bank founded in 1847. The original Appleton Block was built in 1848 to house the Appleton National Bank and tenants such as the equally new City Institution for Savings. It was typical of the plain, redbrick, gable-roofed, flat-granite-trimmed buildings constructed before the 1850s. Both financial institutions prospered at this site into the twentieth century. In 1870 Putnam and Son, a clothing retailer, was to begin its own long tenure here.

2011: Railroad competition ended in Lowell in 1887, when the B & L was absorbed into the B & M system. For operational reasons the older B & L station locations on Merrimack Street and on Middlesex and Thorndike Streets (the Northern Depot) were retained. The railroad ceased operations of Towers Corner in 1895 and disposed of the building. Except for the introduction of storefronts into the ground floor front, the building survived tolerably well into the 1950s, when the towers, front cornice, central gable, and the rear half of the train shed were demolished. From 1921 to 1960 the building housed the Rialto Theatre, which was well known to generations of Lowell moviegoers for its second-run and Saturday children's features. The remaining portion of the train shed, which had housed the theater auditorium and later a bowling alley, was taken down in 1985. The building was slated for demolition in 1989. The daily newspaper endorsed the teardown in an editorial. In an effort to save the structure, the owner approached the Lowell Historic Preservation Commission about accepting a donation. Unanimously, the commissioners took the building as a gift to the government. Step by step in the following years, federal money and much staff work made possible the reinstated towers and rehabilitated exterior. The park in 2007 transferred ownership of the depot to Middlesex Community College for development as a fine arts center. With $11 million in higher-education bond funding from the state and $3 million of its own, the college in 2013 announced a plan to create a theater and dance studio for academic classes and performances. The building is scheduled to open in 2017.

James Higgins

1880: The need to express a more modern image after the Civil War probably explains the replacement of the old three-and-one-half-story building with the new four-story Appleton Block in 1879. The building maintained the same footprint, with the main block fronting Central Street and a long wing on Warren Street. The banking establishments and the clothing store occupied the same locations as in the earlier building. The structure's change from vernacular Greek Revival to High Victorian Gothic, however, clearly indicated the need for these businesses to keep up with the times. Some of the more prominent features are the parapet's gables, finials, and iron cresting, along with the polychromed masonry and extensive use of pointed arches, including an arched corbel table at the fourth-floor line, and an arched and gabled entryway to the banking room.

Lowell Historical Society/UMass–Lowell Center for Lowell History

1979
LNHP

2011: The gables, finials, and cresting of the parapet as well as the original plate-glass and cast-iron storefronts were all stripped away in the early twentieth century, leaving the building without design unity at both top and bottom. A Moderne-style storefront remodeling of cast stone was given to the bank corner of the building. The new retail shop front at the other end was treated with even less sympathy. The greatest transformation, however, took place around 1960, when a black aluminum screen was installed over the most prominent portions of the second- and third-floor facades and top third of the storefront level. The top-floor masonry was painted rather than screened. In 1980, the banking corporation then owning the building agreed to remove the screen to reveal the historic facades underneath. The removal of the screen was widely lauded, and did improve the character of the streetscape. Unfortunately, the facade project did not include an appropriate restoration of the much-altered walls. The facade was cleaned using a somewhat damaging sandblasting treatment, and no rehabilitation was carried out to visually enhance either the truncated top or the disharmonious storefronts. A more complete recapturing of the building's historic character must await another day.
James Higgins

BON MARCHÉ BUILDING

143–153 Merrimack Street

Before there were suburban malls, America's city downtowns served that concentrated shopping function. Like a mall, the commercial district was organized around anchor department stores. In the early twentieth century Lowell had three such establishments: Bon Marché (meaning "a good bargain" in French), Pollard's, and Chalifoux's. Each of these four-to-six-story complexes offered almost every product a family needed. As a branch of the regional Jordan Marsh chain, the Bon Marché complex housed Lowell's last department store until it closed in 1990.

1900: The central section of the complex was built in 1892, linking it to the 1887 Mitchell Block around the corner on Kirk Street, also built by the proprietors of the Bon Marché, brothers Frederick and Charles Mitchell. Designed in the Commercial Renaissance Revival style, the Bon Marché was Lowell's second yellow-brick facade. The original main- and upper-floor stair doorways were located beneath the two oriel windows. The Railroad Bank Building of 1874, with its mid-1890s remodeled facade, was incorporated into the complex on the right.
Lowell Historical Society/UMass–Lowell Center for Lowell History

2011: The Bon Marché company continued to enlarge the complex and modify the facade in the twentieth century in an effort to stay competitive. The two-bay Lovejoy Annex was built on the left starting in 1923. At the same time, wooden storefronts and two of the cast-iron columns were replaced with a bronze-framed system with inset steel columns, and doorway locations were shifted. Later, the traditional use of awnings on the sunny side of the street gave way to a suspended steel sidewalk canopy. However, the most noticeable change was the complete painting of the entire Merrimack Street facade above the canopy with a coat of white paint, apparently in an attempt to unify the separate facades and block out unwanted windows. The work of recapturing some of the lost historic character of the street front began in 1983. The white paint was chemically stripped from the facade, revealing the original masonry materials, and then the wooden and metal elements were repainted. A temporary canvas awning replaced the canopy and covered the transom-level scar where it had been attached. Although the building was subsequently vacated, retail and office activity did resume and the Bon Marché was reestablished as an architectural titan downtown.

James Higgins

1992: In the 1840s, on both sides of the three short blocks that comprise Kirk Street, neat and stylish brick townhouses were erected to serve the middle class that had been attracted to the quickly growing factory town. A group of five such houses, three of two and one-half stories followed shortly by two of three and one-half stories, were built southerly from Lee Street in circa 1846–1847. Before 1876 the taller houses at the corner had lost their gable roof, probably to fire, and the shorter houses were Victorianized with a mansard roof and two-over-two windows. They remained like this until sometime in the mid-twentieth century, when the southerly four houses were gutted, reframed in steel, and extended vertically and at the rear to serve as a warehouse for an adjacent department store. This was as close to demolition as they could come while still retaining some sense of their original makeup.

LNHP

2013: With the department store gone, a Catholic religious organization (priests and brothers of the Missionary Oblates of Mary Immaculate—O.M.I.) associated with the adjacent St. Joseph the Worker Shrine obtained the buildings for the purpose of developing a retirement home for its members. With prompting from preservationists, the organization agreed to a historical reconstruction, and the four heavily altered houses emerged in 1993. Masonry cornices and gable walls, and most of the chimneys, were rebuilt on all five houses. Blocked windows and doors were reopened, and all the altered masonry was reconstructed. The more tenacious portions of the cement-based paint that coated the masonry were unfortunately sandblasted off when some of it did not immediately come off using gentler chemical methods. A slate roof was provided, along with enough period dormers to make the attic of the lower houses usable. New wooden windows, more or less based on historical forms, along with reproduction doors and window blinds, were installed. Although several elements were improperly proportioned, historically based plans were either not fully developed or not followed in all cases, and some technical preservation standards were violated, what was done to this building still led to a vast visual improvement.
James Higgins

WETHERBEE, KELLEY, ROSE, MAYNARD, AND DAY HOUSES (MISSIONARY OBLATES OF MARY IMMACULATE [O.M.I.] ANDRÉ GARIN RETIREMENT RESIDENCE)

21–27 Kirk Street

Like infinity, historically accurate reconstruction can be approached, but never reached. Assuming that one can get close, the question is, does it matter how close? Most serious preservationists think it does, but in recent years they have avoided the issue by rationalizing reconstruction out of their repertoire on the philosophical ground that it is nearly impossible to know how precisely a building looked, and on the pragmatic ground that even if one does, it is too expensive to achieve those results. To this might be added that, presuming one can come to a conclusion on what it looked like, it might be wise to avoid reconstruction when that is not on everyone's agenda.

BOOTT COTTON MILLS

Foot of John Street

Lowell's classic example of a fully developed nineteenth-century textile factory is the Boott Cotton Mills, named after Kirk Boott, the powerful manager of Lowell's first textile enterprise, the Merrimack Manufacturing Company. The first four of the Boott mills were built in the late 1830s to use the waterpower brought to the site by the new Eastern Canal. The buildings were placed end to end in a row between the canal and river. The parallel arrangement of these buildings and their water courses exemplify the ideal siting of a textile manufacturing complex for optimal use of direct-drive waterpower. Although periodic building additions and replacements through the rest of the century greatly increased the density of the site, the configuration of the original mill yard remains readily evident. The initial open rows of gable roofed, redbrick mills and their supporting structures along the canal evolved into the flat-roofed buildings that enclosed the upper and lower mill yards.

1870: When the company shut down during the Civil War, the four original buildings were joined in two pairs by linking structures that were framed by wooden Italianate stair/freight-elevator towers. With its three large clock faces and a bell cupola, the tower of Mill No. 2 exemplified corporate control of the worker's time. In a more purely aesthetic way, each tower was also crowned by a giant balustrade with ball finials on the corner pedestals. Although the stair tower was a typical feature of nineteenth-century New England textile mills, even more standard was the uniform grid of twelve-over-twelve-light sash windows.

1899: Around 1880 the gable roofs were removed from the four original buildings and a flat-roofed fifth story was added to both increase the usable space and reduce the risk of fire. The Italianate segmentally arched windows of this new top story contrast with the plain flat granite lintels of the original openings. Throughout most of the textile manufacturing period, the general historical configuration of the Boott mill yard was retained, although now minus its trees, as was the sloping bank which formed an areaway for the basement windows.

Lowell Historical Society/UMass–Lowell Center for Lowell History

1928: Although obsolete by the twentieth century, the buildings continued to be used for active textile production until the mill closed in 1954. Some details, such as the wooden tower balustrades and the mill yard bollards, had been removed, and many of the twelve-over-twelve windows replaced with ones of a six-over-six configuration, but otherwise the buildings survived intact with minimal maintenance through the early twentieth century. The owners made no major investment in the physical plant or production equipment, but stockholders received dividends without fail. Ironically, although the company's directors ran the mill into the ground, their practices preserved the nineteenth-century buildings.

Lowell Historical Society/UMass–Lowell Center for Lowell History

2011: A few years before the mill closed, the basement windows on the courtyard facades of the Mills No. 1–4 were blocked up, the areaways filled, and the courtyard completely paved in order that truck traffic be better accommodated. Numerous insensitive alterations and removals were made along these facades to provide loading docks as well. The Mill No. 3 stair tower was completely removed and a loading dock shed built in its place. Windows, doorways, and entrance canopies in the remaining towers were altered or removed. The top stories of the two octagonal brick towers of Mill No. 6 were demolished around 1950. After the mill closed it was used as industrial space for various tenants. This more marginal use, coupled with long-term vacancy in parts of the mill complex, resulted in more than thirty years of deterioration, along with the loss of more historic building fabric. In 1989–1990 new owners began a historically sensitive rehabilitation of the Boott Mills for use as office and technology business space. The facade work on the four principal mills that face the upper mill yard included the removal of shed appendages, chemical cleaning and repointing, the reconstruction of the missing stair tower, and restorations of the other three towers, whose original doorways and entrance canopies were also reconstructed. All of the windows on these facades were also replaced with either wooden or aluminum twelve-over-twelve windows, except in the few yet-unrestored masonry openings of Mills No. 1 and 2. The replacement window design that had been used earlier at the Wannalancit Office and Technology Center was taken a big step forward: the provision of the true-divided lights in the top three stories was achieved through an innovative new aluminum window that virtually duplicated the detail of the original wooden windows. The canal-side buildings were similarly treated, including the separately owned Mill No. 6, whose exterior was rehabilitated in 1980–1981 with new matching windows and masonry repointing. In 1992, after extensive interior work, this building opened as the Lowell National Historical Park's Boott Cotton Mills Museum.
James Higgins

2011: Boott Cotton Mills clock tower, restored.

James Higgins

BOOTT COTTON MILLS BOARDING HOUSE
(PATRICK J. MOGAN CULTURAL CENTER)

40 French Street

The long brick boarding house block made to house mill operatives is Lowell's singular contribution to architectural history. Although the early mills themselves were equally noted in their day, their form and function had been previously perfected in the second mill of the Boston Manufacturing Company. That mill was built in Waltham in 1817, five years before the erection of the first Waltham-type mill in Lowell. The first of Lowell's block-long boarding houses were those of the Hamilton Manufacturing Company, built in 1826 and 1827. Those of the Boott Cotton Mills were constructed ten years later. The eight Boott boarding house blocks were classically sited in rank, all perpendicular to the Eastern Canal and directly across it, opposite the mill yard. The early introduction of this tight row-house form indicates the prescience of Lowell's developers toward the emerging urban density of their successful industrial enterprise.

1927: Each block of Boott boarding houses contained eight units: four mill-girl boarding houses located in the middle two-thirds of the building, and four single-family "tenement" houses located in pairs fronting each end of the building. The blocks were of the form and style of most of Lowell's corporate housing: three and one-half stories, made of common brick with plain granite trim, a slate roof, and parapet-connected chimneys. The Yankee mill-girl era was winding down by the time of the Civil War, and the textile corporations sold many of the remaining boarding houses in the 1890s. Industrial encroachment had already resulted in the demolition or severe alteration of some of the buildings at the time of this photograph, but the original concept was still evident.

Lowell Historical Society/UMass–Lowell Center for Lowell History

1980: By the 1950s all of the Boott boarding houses had been demolished or irreversibly modified. Only this one, the seventh building from Bridge Street, remained, although its original front was exposed and it was so severely altered as to be almost unrecognizable. Of the approximately sixty boarding house blocks that once graced the city, only two others survived elsewhere with their original roof form into the late twentieth century.
James Higgins

2011: Because of Lowell's early-nineteenth-century contributions to the nation's Industrial Revolution and the historical importance of the corporate boarding house system, the building was reconstructed to its original exterior appearance in 1985. The work was undertaken by the Lowell Historic Preservation Commission as part of a federal program to develop the Lowell National Historical Park. A modern interior and a new rear addition completed in 1987 together house the cultural and interpretive functions of the Patrick J. Mogan Cultural Center. The Center is named in honor of the educator and planner who is recognized as the foremost advocate for the creation of an urban park based on the city's heritage. One of the units houses an exhibit of a partial reconstruction of a typical boarding house interior of the mill-girl era.
James Higgins

c. 1980: Boarding House Park, adjacent to the Mogan Cultural Center, before.
James Higgins

c. 2000: Boarding House Park, adjacent to the Mogan Cultural Center, after.
James Higgins

SUFFOLK MANUFACTURING COMPANY
(WANNALANCIT OFFICE AND TECHNOLOGY CENTER)

600–660 Suffolk Street

Following the Market Mills project, another development group rehabilitated the factory complex of the old Suffolk mills in 1982–1983. Operated from 1950 to 1980 as the Wannalancit Textile Company, this complex was Lowell's last weaving operation to use the old technology of the shuttle loom. Again the principal historic preservation issue involved the window treatment. Preservationists were dissatisfied with the visual results at Market Mills, which led them to a resolve to do better on the window design of the next mill project, which turned out to be the transformation of the old Suffolk mills into the Wannalancit Office and Technology Center.

c. 1880: The first Suffolk buildings had been erected in 1831–1832 with two mills of the original Waltham-Lowell type: relatively narrow and short with low floor-to-floor height. Linked in the mid-1840s, they proved adequate for the operational strategies and machinery sizes of the early period. However, within thirty years they were obsolete. After shutting the mills down due to a cotton shortage during the Civil War, the owners made the radical decision to completely replace the manufacturing building with a new one of the latest size and design. Additional mills were built through the remainder of the century, completely enclosing the mill yard and expanding onto adjacent land.
LNHP

2011: Early in the design process for the Wannalancit Office and Technology Center, planners determined that the appearance of the historic twelve-over-twelve double-hung sash windows would be reestablished in the new windows, while also achieving the operability, maintenance, and energy-efficiency goals set for them. Such a tall order had apparently not previously been met for any large-scale mill rehabilitation. It was necessary to develop such a window here for the first time. Essentially, the solution proved to be a simple incremental modification to the current aluminum window technology. A strong grid of aluminum bars was provided on the exterior of the single light of double glazing in each sash. As applied in the project's 1,200 windows, including the reexcavated areaway, the solution made a giant stride toward achieving a much more historically sensitive result.

James Higgins

CHAPTER 5

The Economics of Heritage

"In the contemporary city's struggle to survive and renew itself, . . . it is becoming more apparent that decisions must include cultural and aesthetic considerations, that is, those things which may not have immediate or apparent economic return."

—Urban Design Study: Historical Survey, 1970

"Lowell is the premier example of rehabilitated gritty cities worldwide."

—Historic Preservation, 1990

"The reason many people supported the park was plain and simple economics."
—Marie Sweeney, Lowell Museum Corporation & Lowell Historical Society, 1991

URBAN DESTRUCTION

In the *New Lowell Offering*, Charles Gargiulo wrote in 1979 about his Aunt Rose, who, with her husband, Claurence, lived on the second floor of a tenement in the Little Canada neighborhood that filled the crook of the river's elbow where the Merrimack bends before it rushes to the sea. Charles recalls his pious and introverted aunt. She was slightly crippled and spent most of her time indoors, reading religious tracts and watching people outside her window. In his poignant remembrance, Charles brings the reader up short: "Until she was forcibly evicted from her apartment by Urban Renewal in 1965 (she died a week later), I never saw her leave her home."[1] There are other stories like this.

Reports on the razing of Little Canada in the early 1960s cover policy decisions and statistics, such as the number of blocks cleared or the commercial value of ninety-six acres of open land. What is so often lost is the human cost. For the impact on ordinary people, we look to historians, sociologists, novelists, and the chroniclers of daily life. For example, one woman described her youth in the neighborhood in an interview in 1975:

[A]ll the families got along beautifully and we were all French people. . . . Everybody helped everybody, which is not done nowadays like it was then, but, people that had the money—if one needed help that means they would get together and they would come over and help. The whole thing was that there were too many people in a small area.[2]

While acknowledging the stressful conditions of an aged, overcrowded neighborhood, historian Frances Early credits the intangible value of coherent communities.

111

"People found emotional sustenance, psychological security, and a sense of meaning in the Little Canada of the late nineteenth and early twentieth centuries, a truth which will never 'show up' in government reports and vital statistics records."[3]

Writing about his home city of Liverpool, England, Paul Du Noyer observes that misguided redevelopment ("official vandalism"), as happened there in some cases after World War II, destabilizes a community: "When you demolish familiar places, or obliterate old pathways, you deracinate people, cutting them off from the psychic roots that nourish our sense of belonging."[4]

In his detailed chronicle of Lowell's self-help efforts from 1920 to 1978, "To Save a City," Mehmed Ali, a former program manager at Lowell National Historical Park, quotes shoeshine parlor owner Eugene Berube reacting to news that Little Canada will be demolished: "I feel like I'm losing part of my life."[5] Helen Ninteau was worried: "Did you ever try to find an apartment, with nine kids?"[6] These voices are just two among an estimated 2,500 residents, most of French Canadian descent, who occupied some 325 buildings marked for destruction, including 110 businesses, like Mr. Berube's shoeshine place on the main commercial way, Moody Street.

Between August 1964 and the summer of 1966, heavy-equipment operators in wrecking-ball cranes and bulldozers wiped out a dense swath of tenements and mill structures from the riverside to the doorstep of Lowell High School on the Merrimack Canal. Today, Little Canada is memorialized on Aiken Street in a modest bronze plaque mounted on a granite foundation stone rescued from one of the last buildings to go. On the plaque are the dates 1875–1964, a list of neighborhood streets, and the words of the motto of the province of Quebec, Canada: "Je Me Souviens! Lest We Forget!"

The fate of Little Canada was not the first traumatic tearing of the social fabric of the city, and it was not the last of the late twentieth century. Between June and December of 1939, more than 2,000 residents in the Acre neighborhood just northwest of downtown had been evicted to make way for a federally funded public-housing development, North Common Village. The blocks slated for removal were declared blighted and expendable. North Common Village was one of thousands of New Deal public infrastructure projects set in motion to try to prime the national economic pump in the depths of the Great Depression. The displaced persons included many from the Greek American enclave along Market Street.

One memorable photograph of Jefferson Street in the 1930s shows the names of Greek American businesses and families: Giavis Market, Karellas General Store, Palkos Barbershop, Panagiotareas, Kirkiles, Capilianis, Paleos, Lambus, Avramides, Eliopoulos, Tsandikos, Stephanopoulos, Karabatsos, Dabilis, and Sarris. In this project, nearly 150 buildings were wiped off the city grid. The local diaspora forever changed the Hellenic character of that part of the city—even though two beautiful churches remain in the area, Holy Trinity and the Transfiguration Greek Orthodox.

In 1966, a section of the Lower Highlands neighborhood came under the urban renewal sledgehammer. The district, southwest of downtown, was near the principal railroad line and close to a new multilane access road bringing traffic in from Routes 3 and 495: the Lowell Connector. Known as Hale-Howard for two of its busy streets, the sub-neighborhood had been home to many Jewish families, businesses, and synagogues since the 1880s. There was also a concentration of African Americans in the area. Again, urban renewal project managers identified the densely

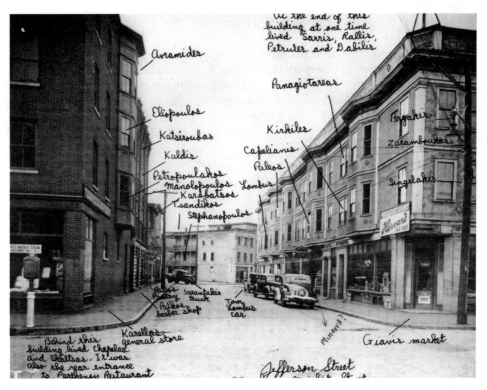

Jefferson Street in the Acre neighborhood was Greek American to the max in 1939. In 1980, collaborating with Charles Nikitopoulos on a book about the Greek experience in the city, artist Leo Panas wrote the names of families and businesses on this photograph—from memory.
UMass–Lowell Center for Lowell History and Charles Nikitopoulos

settled area as blight and began the demolition process across forty acres. About one-third of the 188 families forced to move were black or Hispanic.

Sociologist Shirley Kolack framed the movement of Jewish families away from the original "Little Village" (in Yiddish, *kleine shtetl*), as they called their cultural locus around Hale and Howard streets. Describing a sequence of changes in synagogues in the Highlands neighborhood, she writes:

> The dramatic residential shifts tied to synagogue renewals was poignantly symbolized in 1971 by a parade of members carrying the torahs from the old Montefiore Synagogue on Howard Street up Westford Street to the [upper] Highlands for the dedication of the new Montefiore Synagogue. This dispersion . . . left only the most pious elderly Jews on Howard Street.[7]

As in the Little Canada decision, city leaders argued that more open land was needed to attract manufacturing firms and other businesses to Lowell. People needed jobs, and land like this was primed for creating industrial parks and space for new companies. At least that was the thinking at the time, but policy decisions have social consequences. Lowellians began asking themselves, "What is the price of progress?" and "Where should we draw the line in obliterating what we recognize physically as Lowell?"

FEAR NOT PRESERVATION

Little Canada and Hale-Howard were two of the three large urban renewal projects put on the drawing board by city leaders in 1960. The third encompassed the massive industrial footprint of the Merrimack Manufacturing Company, the first cloth-production business in Lowell. Between 1822 and the 1840s, Merrimack Manufacturing grew, sprawling outward from the south bank of the river. The mill-scape stood at the terminus of the first canal, the Merrimack Canal, to branch off the main inner-city water artery, the Pawtucket Canal. In addition, the Merrimack Canal ran under Market, Merrimack, and French streets to the mill complex. Boarding houses on Dutton Street flanked one side of the Merrimack Canal, opposite today's Lucy Larcom Park. The company housing built here proved to be a flashpoint for preservation consciousness in Lowell.

With Little Canada chewed up by backhoes and wrecking cranes in 1965–1966, and several boarding houses already torn down, community leaders like Lydia S. Howard stepped forward to draw a line at the historic boarding houses. Married to lawyer Woodbury Howard, elected mayor in 1942, she formed the Lowell Committee for Fair Urban Renewal and Historical Restoration. Her group included Lowell Technological Institute faculty members Brendan Fleming, Richard Olney, John Goodwin, and Ernest James, as well as the library director, Joseph V. Kopycinski,

Demolition near the Northern and Merrimack canals, c. 1965
LNHP

and local history advocates Catherine Goodwin and Arthur L. Eno. A tireless organizer, she enlisted preservation and history scholars and rallied the residents to ward off destruction of the boarding houses. She wrote to the *Lowell Sun*:

"Every major city is attempting to save all historic buildings that it is feasible to rehabilitate. Have we no pride in our great past?" She added in another letter, "Lowell had achieved world fame not only for the boldness and brilliance of its technology and economic organization, but also for the enlightened nature of its social planning."[8]

The campaign to save the row houses (as people began to call them) drew support from out of state. George Stoffers of New York City decried the demolition plan in a letter to the editor of the *Sun* newspaper, warning that Lowell "will soon find itself indistinguishable from East Podunk or Kalamazoo."[9] On the other side, George K. Tsouprakos in a person-on-the-street interview told the *Sun*, "I think the old row houses should be torn down. They are a reminder of a past that might better be forgotten, at least the part represented by the houses. The mills are dead and gone, and Lowell cannot live in the past. The future lies in modern construction—and thought."[10]

Francesca Morse, the wife of then-Congressman F. Bradford Morse, spoke in favor of preservation. She wrote, "I fear that if Lowell continues on its present course one will be hard pressed to explain to his children why his ancestors came to the city. It is beginning to look as though the only reason anyone ever came to Lowell is to park his car."[11] U.S. Representative Morse not long afterward would introduce the first federal legislation calling for the protection of Lowell's historic assets.

An anonymous proponent of removal gave a very personal opinion: "Bravo! Finally the row houses are going to the devil—and the sooner they get there, the better. I'm 78, and I have known them for the past 53 years. I even roomed at Number 8 for a while, and I'd feel pretty bad if these lousy things were left there." The letter was signed, "Citizen."

Citizen saw his wish come true, for the row houses were no more by late summer 1966. The issue was a catalyst, however, for action on preservation. The local conversation turned to a discussion of balancing the forecast of jobs and the value of memory. At this time, the fact that the School Department eyed some of the Merrimack's boarding house land for a new high school building had made the policy question even more complicated. Columbia University scholar Loretta Ryan unpacked the row house issue in her PhD dissertation about Lowell. She wrote in one related book chapter:

> Had new federal subsidies for housing programs or preservation legislation been in place by August 1966, the short-term outcome vis-à-vis the row houses might have been different, but the long-term effects may have remained the same. The controversy laid the groundwork for future preservation efforts. It served to create a distinction in people's minds between urban renewal and historic preservation. It effectively separated the interests of preservation and those opposing federal intervention in local affairs and displacement of the poor. It suggested that preservation projects which worked with rather than against federal and state development programs had a chance to win powerful supporters.[12]

By 1970, the City Development Authority had completed an "Urban Design Study" as part of the Lowell Community Renewal Program. Paid for in part with U.S. Department of Housing and Urban Development funds managed by the state, the report notes that "Lowell has no historic preservation ordinance, although state enabling legislation was passed in 1955" to allow cities to establish historic commissions and designate preservation districts. A prerequisite to local action is the appointment of a study committee charged with "making an investigation and report on the historic significance of the buildings, structures, features, sites, or surroundings included in any proposed district."[13] The study must be followed by a public hearing. A two-thirds vote of the city council is necessary to establish a protected district.

The authors of the report used strong language in describing what was at stake if Lowell collectively did not confront the challenge of protecting its built environment. "It wasn't until after World War II," they wrote, "that the impetus and guidelines for historic preservation were provided by the National Trust for Historic Preservation and the National Park Service."[14] More specifically: "Fear sometimes is expressed that historical preservation can go to the extreme, shackling development and preserving useless structures," the authors warned.

> But in this country, and certainly in Lowell, there is a long way to go before we reach that point. In fact, it is becoming more apparent that if present trends continue the nation will have only a very few of its significant historical features left. These will be located in special places and will not be an integral part of the urban fabric of our cities. . . . Most cities, including Lowell, have suffered great losses of historic and architecturally significant buildings. They have been torn down indiscriminately with the mediocre and the bad. Few people realize that architecture is art that cannot be collected in a museum, but must live on in the building itself, preserved as part of the city. . . . It is said that we face the prospect of historical and "architectural sterility." It is not sterility alone, however, but the plague of an ugly and inarticulate environment. . . . Our environment is becoming a constant assault on our aesthetic sensibilities (not to mention our other senses).[15]

The report authors go on to assert that local architecture must be protected, otherwise "we may never be able to make significant progress in improving our visual environment." The suggested means for preservation include laws, zoning ordinances, building codes, and community education about the "long-term cultural and economic benefits"[16] of thoughtful preservation efforts.

Among the recommendations were: designate all category 1 (worthy of preservation) structures and sites for preservation; establish a "mill museum" in an actual mill to tell the story of the beginnings of the Industrial Revolution in Lowell; and create a historical district encompassing the area around City Hall. Three years later, in August 1973, the Lowell City Council voted in favor of two historic districts subject to design review by a historical commission. One district radiated from City Hall, and the second was a "Mill and Canal" district. New downtown street improvements took notice of the historic character of locations, and owners of historic buildings were eligible for design assistance from City of Lowell staff. The previous year, the City Council had made "the historical park concept" the central theme for economic development strategy. History, heritage, preservation, an urban park—these were the prevailing ideas among a core group of decision makers in Lowell less than ten years after federally funded urban clear-cutting had decimated parts of the city. It was a sea change, or a river change, of attitude caused by serious self-reflection, pragmatic policy reassessment, and tireless consciousness-raising by community activists.

ADAPTIVE-REUSE ECONOMICS

Peter Aucella was on his second stint as acting superintendent of LNHP in March 2012, keeping the park operations humming while the search was on to replace Superintendent Michael Creasey. When the Lowell Historic Preservation Commission's term of operations expired in 1995, after a seventeen-year run, Aucella moved across the street to the National Park Service. He had joined the commission as executive director in late 1986. Previously, he had been the City of Lowell director of planning and development and statewide economic development director for Paul Tsongas's U.S. Senate Office in Massachusetts. Aucella had grown up in Malden, Massachusetts, but, like Pat Mogan, Nancy L. Donahue, and others not born in the city, he became a key figure in Lowell's renaissance. As one of the best spokespersons about the Lowell revival story, he is regularly called on to speak about the comeback. Pat Mogan had his slideshow, and Peter is known for his PowerPoint presentation with dramatic "before-and-after" views of Lowell buildings.

Peter Aucella
Kevin Harkins

On this day, he welcomed to the park's administrative office students from Scotland's University of Aberdeen graduate program in planning. They were in Lowell to see the results of intensive urban planning and to ask questions of one of the masters. The group included planners from Scottish Natural Heritage and the Town and Country Planning Department of Ghana and a landscape architect from Tartu, Estonia.

Sitting near Aucella was Steve Stowell, longtime director of the Lowell Historic Board and a former park ranger. A graduate of Columbia University's School of Architecture, Planning, and Preservation, Stowell enforces the preservation standards in the Park and Preservation District, rules that the City of Lowell was expected to adopt as law in concert with the original federal authorization of $40 million for the development of the park. At the start, the LHPC staff, chiefly the planning director Sarah Peskin with planner Nancy Woods and architect Chuck Parrott, had devoted ten years to designing and implementing the historic-board regulatory structure as well as the standards that have served Lowell so well.

Since 1984, explained Stowell, approximately 2,500 construction projects, large and small, have received permits from the Historic Board. More than 70 percent can be characterized as preservation projects. "The Lowell Historic Board was established in 1983 to guarantee that private investment in properties in the historic district is not inconsistent with the federal investment," Aucella emphasized. "This is a critical element in the Lowell method."

Beyond large construction projects like hospital and university expansion, the regulatory process accounts for a large percentage of improvements in buildings in the downtown core and historic district, Aucella said.

> It's always a challenge, but the regulatory program in Lowell is effective. We are very knowledgeable now about the adaptive reuse of historic structures. We've shown that you can use historic preservation to jump-start a city whose pulse is very weak. When I came to Lowell in 1984, there was scaffolding on half the buildings downtown. Renovation was in full swing. Today, rehabilitation has overtaken decay.

When Kwasi Agyeman of Ghana asked about the local mechanisms that make preservation work in Lowell, Aucella talked about the Preservation Commission, pointing out that between 1978 and 1995, the commission awarded $5.4 million in preservation grants and loans, and leveraged $52 million in private capital for the renovation and reuse of sixty-three structures deemed to be of national importance

Downtown
deterioration,
Middlesex Street,
c. 1980
Lowell Historical
Society/Lowell Sun
Collection

based on early surveys of Lowell's architecture. In this case, federal investment yielded $9.60 for each public dollar. Taking Lowell's Preservation Loan Program as another measure of return-on-investment, Aucella calculates that the initial federal appropriation of $750,000 for loans has leveraged more than $130,000,000 in development dollars—or $173.77 for each federal dollar.

With its fifteen-member board representing local, state, and federal interests and a professional staff of architects, planners, project managers, and cultural affairs specialists, the commission was empowered to move in ways unheard of in most national parks up to that time. Part of the genius of the legislation that created the park is the provision for such a commission designed to function as a sister agency of the NPS during the intensive development phase of the new park.

Aucella also summarized the creation of the innovative Lowell Development & Financial Corporation (LDFC), a kind of public-interest bank set up at the insistence of newly minted Congressman Tsongas in 1975. Using his influence as a member of the Banking Committee of the U.S. House of Representatives, Tsongas railed against stingy local bankers and then called for a closed-door meeting of nine bank presidents to discuss ways to loosen up lending for projects in downtown Lowell, where property owners had been regularly denied loans in what amounted to what the industry refers to as "redlining" or marking certain areas as too risky for financing, usually unfairly. More than once he showed up at a public meeting to berate bankers and commercial property owners for not moving fast enough on development projects. Banker Jack Perry remembered the scene: "Paul brought us together, all the banks, and said, 'If you don't do this, I'll go to the newspaper and say you're all bums.' We did it."[17]

At the time more than twenty downtown buildings were boarded up. To reduce the exposure of banks worried about "throwing good money after bad," Tsongas suggested pooling funds. Five percent of their current deposits would be available for loans through a new entity, a nonprofit organization to be called the Lowell Development & Financial Corporation. Tsongas's allies included then-president of First Bank, George Duncan, and a young attorney he had strategized with, Michael Putziger. The money would be designated for downtown historic-building projects only. The stockholders were to be the investing banks and the Center City Committee. A broad forty-member board of directors would guide policy.

Combined, the banks bought $300,000 of shares to capitalize the LDFC. The initial interest rate was 3 percent, and the money was available as second mortgage financing. The banks wrote off their contributions as a loss. It took more than a year for the first loan to go out the door. The building was on the edge of the downtown and not historic, Barney's Deli on Middlesex Street near Jackson Mills, but it was a good enough start. When the owner's photograph appeared in the newspaper, other property owners asked, "How come he's getting money?" There was a bit of momentum. More loans were written. More publicity was had. A second stock sale added $300,000 more to the pool.

When the City of Lowell received a $5 million Urban Development Action Grant (UDAG) as an incentive for computer-maker Wang Laboratories to build its world headquarters in Lowell in 1978, City Manager William Taupier worked with the Lowell City Council to direct the grant to the LDFC rather than to the Wang corporation. The LDFC money was lent to Wang at 4 percent, which was a 60 percent discount on the prevailing prime rate. The repaid money was then put into the loan pool and made available at 0 to 3 percent. Today's LDFC has a $14 million revolving loan pool. The LDFC also manages a separate fund for historic preservation loans dating from the days of the Preservation Commission, which had its own arrangement with the LDFC. Among the LDFC's aid programs is one for down-payment assistance for homebuyers.

In *Renewing Cities*, urban policy scholar Ross J. Gittell wrote in 1992:

> The LDFC appeared to improve the city's positioning with regard to factor prices by reducing capital costs and financial risk of firms locating in Lowell and increasing the supply of funds available to local firms. Without the LDFC, Lowell's development leaders would have been considerably less effective deal makers. They would not have had a local institution to provide "creative" financing for Wang, Hilton [downtown hotel project], and other deals and would not have been able to react as expediently to developer requests and the priorities of federal program officials.
>
> The LDFC appears to have been particularly effective in the initial 'momentum-building' deals, which were undertaken when the city was still economically stagnant and conventional loans were not forthcoming. Two years after the LDFC was organized, a ten-year period began in which . . . Lowell experienced significant growth. Without the LDFC in place, local banks would not have had a vehicle to spread and share (with each other and the public sector) the risks and benefits associated with the Wang and other momentum-building deals and might have still been reluctant to invest in the city. [Between 1975 and 1984, seventy-five properties were built or renovated.][18]

Focusing on the mill properties, Aucella noted that of the 5.1 million square feet of mill buildings existing when the park was established in June 1978, most were either vacant or underutilized. The park would eventually rent 42,000 square feet on the first level of the Market Mills (Lowell Manufacturing Company) and purchase Boott Cotton Mill No. 6 and the counting house for its own uses, another 117,500 square feet. (The federal mill-property ownership is only 3.8 percent of the 5.1 million square feet.) That left millions of square feet for others. By the end of 2015, 95 percent of the mill real estate will be developed, according to Aucella's projections. If remaining parts of the Massachusetts Mills and Hamilton Mills are renovated by 2017, the completion figure will rise to 99 percent—an extraordinary accomplishment in forty years. The factories that produced cloth, shoes, and later plastics and light electronics have been transformed into places to live (from low-cost to high-end), businesses, health-care centers, nonprofit organization offices, and artist studios. By 2013, the total development value of mill space estimated by the Park Service was approaching $1 billion.

"THE LONG VIEW"

Charles "Chuck" Parrott has been on the park beat since before the beginning—which would be 1974–1975 when he was a member of the Historic American Building Survey/Historic American Engineering Record team that catalogued and assessed the condition of Lowell's industrial structures. He was one of the first persons hired for the staff of the Lowell Historic Preservation Commission in 1978. Like Aucella, he shifted to the National Park Service when the LHPC reached its sunset date. No historic architect has spent more time and contributed more expertise to the Lowell reclamation project than Parrott. There is hardly a building in the historic district that he has not had a hand, and his mind, in improving visually. He has been the conscience of historic preservation in Lowell.

LOWELL: BY THE NUMBERS

Population
1950	97,249
1960	92,107
1970	94,239
1980	92,418
2010	106, 519

Population by Race & Ethnicity (%)

Year	Total Population	White	Black	Asian	Other	Hispanic/Latino
1980	92,418	92.5	1.2	.7	1.1	5
2010	106,519	52.8	6.8	20.2	3.6	17.3

Population Over 65 Years
1980	13%
2010	10.1%

Persons Employed in Lowell (resident and nonresident)
1980	41,621
2010	50,859

Persons Employed in Manufacturing
1980	41.6%
2010	17.5%

Unemployment Rate
1980	4.8%
2010	6.4%

Median Family Income
1980	$17,942
2010	$51,471

High School Graduates among Residents
1980	57.7%
2010	78.3%

Sources: U.S. Census, Bureau of Labor Statistics, City of Lowell Division of Planning & Development)

HERITAGE RECLAMATION: PUBLIC-PRIVATE SECTORS, INVESTMENT/DEVELOPMENT

Lowell National Historical Park (federal appropriations, 1979–2012): $242,446,000
Lowell Preservation Loan Program (1983–2012):
   $709,400 in loans repaid
   $38,366,000 project investment
   $1,347,200 in active loans
   $88,275,314 in active project investment
   $2,481,620 in loans made
   $131,077,314 total project investment
   $377,527 in loans defaulted
Private Investment in Historic Preservation (through January 2014): $811,740,000+
Canalway/Riverwalk (federal appropriations, through January 2013): $35,565,000
Canalway/Riverwalk (state and local funds, through January 2013): $16,824,000
Canalway/Riverwalk Adjacent Development Spin-Off: $527,303,000 (through January 2013)

Source: Lowell National Historical Park

Resources are finite. You have to fight every preservation fight, knowing that you will lose some of the contests. What's important is the long view. The ultimate goal is to maintain the critical mass of structures so that the place in question, in our case Lowell, retains its distinctive character.[19]

One of the contests lost almost as soon as the park was established involved the Butler House in the city's Belvidere neighborhood. One of the most striking pre–Civil War homes, the mansion on a twelve-acre lot dated from 1843. The house was built for up-and-coming attorney Benjamin F. Butler (1818–1893), who would become one of the most accomplished persons and colorful personalities in the city's history, from Civil War general to governor of Massachusetts.

In 1979, the Butler estate was purchased by a developer for home building. For months, preservation activists unsuccessfully attempted to stave off the demolition and subdivision in a losing battle. There was no private or public entity ready to acquire and save the estate. The issue sounded an alarm among preservation advocates and illustrated what was at stake in operating a national historical park premised on an extensive preservation agenda.

Another high-profile loss was the cathedral-like St. Peter Church on Gorham Street, on the outskirts of the downtown historic district. Like many older inner-city parishes in the Boston Archdiocese, membership and Sunday Mass attendance at St. Peter declined in the closing decades of the twentieth century. The church leaders began to consolidate services and strategically close parishes. St. Peter was a particular challenge because the stone exterior needed repair. Church authorities chose not to invest in the structure and proceeded with a request for demolition. A lengthy conflict ensued, with parish stalwarts and local preservationists arguing to keep the church standing. The Preservation Commission revised the boundary of the Preservation

Charles "Chuck" Parrott
LNHP

Eastern Canal gatehouse
restoration near
Massachusetts Mills
James Higgins

District to encompass the church in the hope of saving it and making it eligible for
financial assistance. Nothing worked, and the building was torn down in 1996.

As groundbreaking as the Lowell park was and is, Parrott said, "It has not caused
a major change in the National Park Service's view of parks in general. The park
culture is still oriented to the West and wildlife."[20] While many historical parks were
created by the NPS after Lowell, few have a specifically urban focus and sweeping
mandates for federal involvement as seen in Lowell. Nor has the kind of power
wielded by the Lowell Historic Board (LHB) been adopted as standard procedure
in the new heritage areas that encompass broader regions, such as that in the
Blackstone River Valley National Heritage Corridor that runs from Massachusetts
to Rhode Island. In Lowell, federal officials were not charged to regulate design in
the Park and Preservation District; city officials were required to do so by enabling
legislation for the park—in collaboration with NPS and state officials as outlined in
the LHB ordinance.

Parrott works closely with the LHB and joins the regular design review sessions in
preparation for board meetings and hearings.

The enabling legislation for the Lowell Historic Board required that it be a police power control board—the board members enforce laws when they apply the Preservation Standards in their decisions. After Lowell, we did not see other park units requiring other localities to adopt the kind of strong controls that we have in Lowell. This is true in the new heritage areas, for example. On balance, our Historic Board has been successful.[21]

PRESERVATION TAX CREDIT TOOL

One of the most significant and customized tools of contemporary historic preservation takes the form of a system of tax credits. The National Park Service administers the Federal Historic Preservation Tax Incentives program, which provides a 20 percent income tax credit to property owners who rehab "historic, income-producing buildings" that the NPS categorizes as "certified historic structures." An individual cannot obtain these tax credits for his or her own home. Since the establishment of the program in 1976, the tax credits program has helped make possible $62 billion in private-sector spending on the adaptive reuse of historic buildings. The NPS and various state preservation offices manage the program, with additional help from the Internal Revenue Service, whose staff reviews expenditures to which the credit is being applied. There is also a 10 percent tax credit program for pre-1936 buildings that do not meet the federal standards for "historic" classification.

Taya Dixon Mullane and her husband moved to Lowell in 1992 because her husband had grown up nearby and housing prices were affordable, plus the city had a train line. They did not choose Lowell primarily for its history, but the city meshed well with Dixon Mullane's work as a historic preservation consultant for Epsilon Associates of Maynard, Massachusetts.

"I set out to be an architect, but I found out that I liked old buildings," Dixon Mullane said. She not only served on the Lowell Historic Board but also became a leader in her sub-neighborhood of the Lower Highlands. She helps property owners and developers statewide rescue and improve historic structures. "Without the federal and state tax credits, many buildings would not have been rehabilitated or, if they were renovated, the work would not have been up to the highest preservation standards."[22] She admires the quality of the preservation work throughout the Park and Preservation District and said much of the success is due to the talent and experience of park staff.

> Chuck Parrott can never go. His institutional knowledge, his consistency, is invaluable. When I was working with a developer on the final section of the Boott Cotton Mills to be redeveloped, Chuck's knowledge about the complex and how the mill yard evolved and was used was priceless.[23]

In Massachusetts, after Boston, Lowell ranks among the most active places where developers have used the preservation tax credits. The 2005 program introduced by the state as an economic development booster has seen accelerated use in Lowell. The Appleton Mills would not have been salvaged without state and federal credits, in Dixon Mullane's view. "I can't imagine how else it would have worked." The Appleton rehab, combined with extensive Boott Cotton Mills and Lawrence Mills renovations, "added two million square feet of renovated space representing $150

Checking the details
James Higgins

million in private investment, more than 1,500 new housing units, and countless new jobs,"[24] reported architect Robert Verrier on the *Preservation Nation* blog of the National Trust for Historic Preservation. Since 1996, Lowell projects have received a total of $324 million ($158,000 completed; $166,000 in process) in federal tax credits. Between 2004 and 2012, Lowell projects were awarded $39,880,000 in State Historic Tax Credits.

Given the starting condition of Lowell and what has been accomplished, when Parrott thinks about exemplary preservation work in Lowell-type cities in Europe and elsewhere he doesn't see anything comparable to what this city has done. Why has historic preservation worked in Lowell? Parrott pointed to both the smallish scale and compactness of Lowell's historic district. In a bigger city the effect would not be as visible, he said. There would be less of a chance to present it and experience the place as a comprehensive system, from energy production and manufacturing sites to residences, churches, and commercial buildings, as well as street patterns and green areas. Lowell grew so early and adapted to the existing landscape, the existing Pawtucket Canal, and the bend in the river. It's not a rational layout. The "tall fall" of the wide river tied to a canal system was something new. This was determined by the topography. It is what makes Lowell a special place.

In 1990, then-Congressman Chet Atkins said, "Lowell delivers two messages. First, is that historic preservation is for everybody, not just for the elite. There is an awful lot of blue-collar pride in historic preservation and an enormous interest in people preserving the heritage of working communities. And the second thing is that historic preservation is good for business."[25]

TWO CASES: MARKET MILLS AND
THE HAMILTON CANAL DISTRICT

Market Mills

From 1982 to 1992, the center of gravity for park activity was in the former Lowell Manufacturing Company complex at Dutton and Market streets downtown. A pair of factory buildings from 1882 and 1902 constituted more than 280,000 square feet of fire-scarred and largely derelict space when park and Lowell Historic Preservation Commission staff began to think about how to create a visitor center there, as recommended in "the Brown Book." Planning Director of the LHPC Sarah M. Peskin said Paul Tsongas "was instrumental in putting together this first large project of those called for in the park legislation."[26]

"The Brown Book" authors described this complex as forming "one end of the industrial mill wall which once encircled downtown Lowell." Its location off Dutton Street is significant because the road is considered to be the "historic gateway" as early as the 1820s, running alongside the city's first power canal and later the Boston and Lowell railroad line. Founded in 1828, the Lowell Manufacturing Company made cloth and hand-woven carpets. The current address on Market Street was once called Lowell Street. By 1882, the No. 1 Brussels Weave Mill on this site was producing woolen carpets on powered carpet looms invented by Erastus Bigelow. A second carpet production building was added twenty years later, followed by an associated Worsted Mill in 1906. All of these operations ended in 1915, when the Bigelow Carpet Company owners closed the business. In the 1920s, this was the site of the Lowell Silk Mills operated by the Newmarket Manufacturing Company. The Silk Mill was shut down in 1954. Smaller companies in various industries filled in the building through the later decades, but the physical plant continued to degrade from lack of maintenance and a large fire in 1979.

The first attempt at renovation was proposed by Edward Fish and Gerard Doherty, Braintree, Massachusetts–based developers, who intended to build housing for low-income families and elders. They had a commitment from the federal department of Housing and Urban Development for subsidies under the Section 8 program. Tsongas opposed the idea of a residential-only complex, realizing the street-level activity would be a key factor in recharging the downtown. Lowellians remembered the front mill as the location of Stuart's discount department store.

Lowell's vaunted public-private partnership ethic can be traced along one branch of its root system to the Market Mills project. Once the developers, organized as Market Mills Associates, and government struck a hard-fought deal to codevelop the complex, the work began. The multiuse project would feature street-level activity developed by the LHPC (42,000 square feet under a forty-year lease, 1982–2022) and apartments in all floors above, with a new public mill yard between the two buildings. Peskin described the process:

> This basic arrangement was to require countless hours of negotiation, complex agreements. Historic preservation concerns had to be weighed against cash-flow needs, public access against tenant privacy, and one designer's wishes against another's. When the process seemed to be getting mired, Tsongas frequently intervened, his energy and vision refocusing the parties on the common goal.[27]

Sarah M. Peskin was the first planner for the LHPC (1979–1989), where she oversaw its master plans, directed land acquisition and design for Boarding House Park and the Lowell Park Trolley system, and wrote the establishing ordinance for the Lowell Historic Board. She championed the development of the Canalway in Lowell, a network of waterside paths, and later served as chief of planning and legislation for the National Park Service's North Atlantic Region. Applying lessons learned in Lowell, she helped create Weir Farm National Historic Site and Boston Harbor Islands National Recreation Area. She is the author of *Guiding Growth and Change: A Handbook for the Massachusetts Citizen.*
Kevin Harkins

Opened with great fanfare in the spring of 1982, Market Mills became the southern anchor of the historic downtown, drawing in visitors off the highway who followed the familiar brown NPS signs into the core of the city and a free parking lot off Dutton Street that serviced the Visitor Center. The LHPC incubated a commercial venture in the space opposite the Park Visitor Center fronting on Market Street—a multiethnic food emporium called The Melting Pot. Intended to cater to both park tourists and residents looking for a new food experience downtown, The Melting Pot was Lowell's microscale answer to Boston's Quincy Market and other festival marketplace projects that were popular at the time. More or less successful for about twenty years, the quick-food restaurants were unable to compete long-term and the space today is the home of a state-of-the-art community cable TV operation, Lowell Telecommunications Corporation. Across the mill yard, LHPC staff worked with the local artists' community to create the Brush Art Gallery and Studios (originally called A Brush with History). For thirty years, "the Brush" has operated steadily, usually with a full complement of resident visual artists in small studios where they work in view of the public for certain hours each week. The facility includes a 3,000-square foot hardwood-floor gallery and wide corridor with studios on either side.

The Visitor Center, as envisioned in "the Brown Book," opened as a shared space with Lowell Heritage State Park but now is NPS-only. (The state contributed some $20 million to the development of park resources in Lowell, but funds for operation of state facilities became unpredictable after several years—this case demonstrates that all partnerships are not sustainable, especially when contingent on public money.) The facility includes orientation exhibits about the Lowell story, a newly renovated and expanded bookstore, and a 100-seat, two-level auditorium where visitors see a brief media production as an introduction to the park. People check in at the Center and then meet rangers for tours across the street at the Dutton

Market Mills
yard, before
and after,
1978 and
1982
James Higgins

Street trolley platform or fan out across the city on self-guided walks and further
explorations at places like the Boott Cotton Mills Museum. On the east end of the
complex is a small green space, Market Mills Park, which features the *Homage to
Women* sculpture by Mico Kaufman, dedicated in 1984. During the annual Lowell
Folk Festival, this area is packed with people who come to enjoy performers on the
Market Mills Stage.

In addition to the $1 million Visitor Center, the LHPC provided $1.5 million to
develop the first-floor spaces and the brick-and-landscaped mill yard. The complex
includes 230 housing units (82 for families and 148 for elders). Total cost of the
building project was $14 million. Market Mills Associates was able to avail itself of
Federal Tax Act incentives for "certified rehabilitation" of properties in a National
Historic Landmark District.

When the Boott Cotton Mills Museum on John Street, across the downtown from
Market Mills, opened in 1992, that building, combined with the adjacent Boarding

House Park and Mogan Cultural Center or Boott Mills Boarding House, shifted the park's center of gravity toward the river's edge. Ten years before, however, walking through the archway of one mill building and through the mill yard to the Visitor Center gave people a sense of the scale of factory production and that renovated mills could be a plus for the city's future.

Hamilton Canal District

The rehabilitation of the second-oldest mill district and the last large unimproved section of the downtown core began with a funky project title, the JAM Plan, in 1998. Named for Jackson, Appleton, and Middlesex streets, the area resembled what a lot of the downtown looked like in the 1970s: decay, dark alleys, overgrown empty lots, low-grade residences, and marginal small businesses. There were bright spots like favorite eateries (Elliot's Hot Dogs, Major's Café, and the Owl Diner), The Club fitness center, Riverside Glass Company, the Salvation Army headquarters, Washington Savings Bank, and Guy Lefebvre's Lowell Gallery. But the gaps in the streetscape, the rooming houses, a nighttime homeless shelter, and its out-of-the-way vibe suppressed redevelopment prospects.

The JAM Plan was one of two urban redevelopment plans that City Manager Brian Martin submitted to the state department of Housing and Economic Development for approval; the other was the Acre Plan, which covers a section of the historic neighborhood that lies in part within the federal Park and Preservation District. Martin and his successors, John Cox and Bernie Lynch, stuck with the redevelopment roadmap. They systematically purchased eighteen acres of land and properties, part of which would become the Hamilton Canal District (HCD), bundled them, and then bid the package as one consolidated redevelopment project to be overseen by a master developer. State funding for the project to date has been either project-specific competitive grant funding or legislative earmarks. The JAM area encompasses the HCD, fifteen acres on the edge of downtown envisioned as a residential and commercial sub-neighborhood whose western front is at one of

Hamilton Canal District, looking east, c. 2012
Tory Germann

Adam Baacke
Kevin Harkins

the most prominent gateways to the city. Here, four waterways converge, the Pawtucket, Western, Merrimack, and Hamilton canals, forming a kind of hydro-cloverleaf.

Adam Baacke was hired as Lowell's neighborhood planner in 2000 and seven years later was named by City Manager Bernie Lynch to be assistant city manager for planning and development. Baacke had also held the chief planner and deputy director positions. Before coming to Lowell, Baacke has been a designer and consultant for museums, theatres, and special events projects, mostly in the higher-education sector. His interest in building a more lasting relationship with a place led him to planning work. Reflecting on his time in Lowell, he said, "Lowell is just the right size—big enough to attract significant resources to get things done, but small enough that a person can have a meaningful role in many things."[28]

Baacke has seen the HCD project unfold from idea to reality. He helped write the JAM Plan that was approved by the state, giving the city expanded powers for eminent domain and real estate transactions to put together the fifteen acres. A pivotal moment in the process came when one of the major property holders in the designated area, Freudenberg Nonwovens, told city officials that the company would close its Lowell operation. To their credit, the owners asked what they could do to assist the community on their way out—and the city asked for the land on which four buildings sat. Freudenberg could not donate the property, but the owners agreed to sell to the city at a discount. Those parcels would constitute 40 percent of the HCD. The conversation with the Freudenberg owners was "the catalyst" for HCD, in Baacke's mind.

In 2003, the Fund for New Urbanism, a prominent group that included planner Jeff Speck, advertised in planning magazines in search of potential development sites. Baacke answered the ad. Soon, Speck and others came to Lowell to look at what they later described as "the best brownfields site in America." Speck and his partners thought the mills were spectacular; they loved the Market Mills archways and portal to downtown, and saw the proximity to Boston as a big plus. While the Fund for New Urbanism did not see the Lowell project through, the group's interest was national validation for what Baacke and others saw as a possible transformational project for Lowell. New City Manager John Cox and planning director Matt Coggins in 2004 presented to the City Council the HCD plan, which they anticipated would require $19 million in municipal funding (bonds, income from property sales, and other sources). To date, the City has spent $11 million, half of it in the form of state and federal grants.

One of the distinguishing elements of the HCD project is the use of form-based code for zoning, meaning that the use of land is not the only consideration when determining what is allowable. With form-based code, planners and developers factor in how the privately built and owned properties interact with the public realm—the common spaces where people gather, move through, do business, and relax. This approach emphasizes design of structures and spaces rather than dimensions and the end use, whether residential, commercial, or industrial. Lowell was the first city in Massachusetts to employ this New Urbanist planning process, which combines the charrette method (an intensive group planning and design workshop) with form-based code for zoning designation. More than 250 people attended multiple HCD workshops in 2007–2008. The goal with HCD was to provide to the master developer, which turned out to be Trinity Financial of Boston, land and buildings that were "fully entitled," eliminating the need for discretionary permits for individual projects in the district. Baacke called the original city councilors "courageous" for approving the proposal.

> It was a big risk, but by 2012 the project was already generating $100,000 more annually in property tax revenue than it was before the project began, from $181,000 in 2005 to $295,000. I think they were able to show that courage because the market for downtown property had proved itself by then and people before them had taken on big ideas that had worked out successfully—the park, the downtown hotel, the civic arena. People in Lowell believe it can work here because they have seen it. People in other places have seen disinvestment. That's a difference.[29]

The price tag for the HCD redevelopment is pegged at $800 million, and when completed the area could bring 1,800 jobs. The strategy is a public-private sector one again; one of the anchor buildings will be a $175 million "Judicial Center" with new courts for the county and district as well as facilities for supporting operations. Adjacent to the district is the new $42 million home of the Lowell Community Health Center at the former location of Adden Furniture in the Hamilton Mills complex.

In late summer 2012, public officials and developers cut a ribbon for the next phase of the Hamilton Canal District: converting a former textile plant, Freudenberg Nonwovens, into office space. The 1920s-era building harks back to the Saco-Lowell machine-shop compound that occupied the area from Swamp Locks to the Lowell Manufacturing Company mill that fronts on Market Street. From the late 1940s to 2003, Freudenberg made Pellon, a brand-name synthetic batting-type material used for stiffening or stabilizing with other fabrics or related uses. There was a time in Lowell in the 1960s when a remnant roll of Pellon in the cellar was almost as familiar and versatile as duct tape.

The $8.5 million renovation will yield 55,000 square feet of commercial space. On top of master developer Trinity's $2.5 million, TD Bank lent $4.5 million and the Lowell Development & Financial Corporation provided a $250,000 loan. Additionally, New Market Tax Credits were allocated by the Massachusetts Housing Investment Corp. for the 110 Canal Street project. At the ribbon cutting, Congresswoman Niki Tsongas not only praised the vaunted public-private cooperation in Lowell, but also underscored the results that can be achieved when local, state, and federal governments act as partners.

For its part, the City of Lowell spent $4 million in federal and state grant money to build a bridge over the Hamilton Canal and upgrade Jackson and Revere streets in the HCD. The LNHP staff had already conceptualized the Canalway in the area and produced designs for the Canalway from Canal Street (formerly Revere Street)

The Canalway in the Hamilton Canal District
James Higgins

to Marston Street. The trestle bridge and Canalway west of Canal Street were designed by consultants to the park under a separate funding source and constructed by the Massachusetts Department of Transportation with federal money obtained by the park. The state also provided $500,000 for the project in the form of a grant to the city that was assigned to the developers. On the drawing board is an extension of the National Park Service's historic trolley system. The visionary transit plan would connect the nearby Gallagher transportation hub with rail service to Boston and regional bus routes to the downtown core and beyond—to UMass–Lowell and Middlesex Community College and the sports and entertainment complex composed of UMass–Lowell's Tsongas Center hockey and events arena and LeLacheur baseball stadium, home of the Lowell Spinners, a minor-league Red Sox team.

The proposed seven-mile Lowell Trolley system would carry inbound rail commuters to and through the HCD before splitting into the three lines that serve the education and events nodes at terminus points. The core service area overlaps with the Park and Preservation District. Effectively, the start-up historic trolley system installed for park visitors would become a public transportation alternative in a city once thronging with streetcars. With twenty station stops and nine historic-replica trolleys running at ten-minute intervals, planners are aiming for a user-friendly option that should eliminate lots of cars in the central business district and offer immediate "green" benefits. Importantly, rides would be free for college and university students, faculty, and staff (the costs covered by the institutions). When fully operational, the trolleys would replace the city's current "Downtown Circulator" and campus shuttle buses—cutting CO_2 emissions significantly. Eventually, the electric trolleys could be plugged in to renewable energy sources.

The Appleton Mills, before redevelopment, c. 2009
James Higgins

The Appleton Mills, after redevelopment, c. 2012
James Higgins

Traffic engineers estimate a twenty-five-minute ride for anyone using the trolley from end to end, say, the train station to the baseball park, factoring in waiting time. As with the cable cars in San Francisco, speed is not the only consideration for users. Community advocates see the Lowell Trolley as integral to "the next generation of downtown revitalization with a core focus on livability and walkability."[30]

Trinity vice president Abby Goldenfarb expressed optimism about filling the space even as the Great Recession stubbornly refused to give way to a full-on upswing of the business cycle. The building is a few hundred paces from the refurbished Appleton Mills, which went from blight to a world-class example of adaptive reuse of a historic structure. The $64 million project, including a $13 million loan from the state's Growth District's Initiative, provided 130 units of affordable housing; bona fide artists were given the first shot at the apartments. Dozens of photographers, writers, sculptors, dancers, musicians, filmmakers, and painters grabbed the opportunity to settle downtown.

The Historic Board's Stowell put the historic preservation effort on the Appleton project in perspective:

> The rejuvenation of the Appleton mill yard was unprecedented in Lowell in terms of the level of work needed to rescue the remaining severely deteriorated buildings. While the finished product looks like a typical mill rehabilitation with a few contemporary twists, the condition of the buildings required design and engineering efforts of an order that we had not seen in Lowell. Historic masonry walls required extensive engineering to temporarily shore them up, allowing deteriorated structural elements and roofs to be removed while recycled and new, sound structural elements were installed.
>
> The architects also introduced contemporary industrial design elements such as metal panel systems that clad several exterior walls along the inner courtyard. This approach was a first in Lowell and only possible at Appleton due to extensive elevational voids left over from prior demolitions. Without documentation on how these walls should be treated, we endorsed an approach that distinguished the historic, rehabilitated elevations from the new, contemporary infill treatments. The end result is a unique blend of the old and new.[31]

Historic preservation consultant Taya Dixon Mullane said: "It's such an important piece of the streetscape, the combination of mill and canal. The area would have had a very different feel on the canal side without the mill. The Appleton is the front door of this old section of the city."[32]

The next phases of work for Trinity will bring on line two new residential buildings, each with at least fifty units, and a building with office and retail spaces at the west end of the HCD near the Judicial Center. The City of Lowell is expected to acquire the current NPS parking lot off Dutton Street to enhance business development in the HCD. Special congressional legislation was required to allow for the acquisition in exchange for equal value property that meets the needs of the park.

Both the past and the potential for areas like the Hamilton Canal District are imbued with their own kind of power. Michael Leary has been inspired by the industrial vistas of Lowell. He is a senior lecturer in the Department of Urban, Environmental, and Leisure Studies at London South Bank University in England. Leary has visited Lowell several times to do research for a book about preservation-based urban regeneration in Lowell; Manchester, England; and the Gastown district of Vancouver, British Columbia. During his Lowell stays, Leary begins and ends the day at the same place.

Coming from Manchester, England, the place that I found most moving was the site of the former Lowell Machine Shop. This is a rather overly modest, diffident name for a colossal engineering, technological innovation, and manufacturing complex covering many acres. As the sun passes over this semi-wild cityscape, half returned to nature, during the day and early evening the site changes its visual character. Under the dark gray of a stormy blue sky the site is full of industrial doom. Early evening can see it bathed in a warm golden hue of endless optimism. From present disused dereliction it transforms into a fascinating wildlife sanctuary and reminder of a once-world famous industrial past.

Nowhere is the past more evoked than looking east over the canal junction of Swamp Locks. Here, when the sun is right, light, water, and sky combine to produce fantastic reflections. Here, too, the complexity of the canal system and ingenuity of the nineteenth-century hydraulic engineers can be grasped instantly. The remnants of the rail tracks hint at the huge amounts of raw material brought in and the array of heavy machines and locomotives sent out. Spending time early in the morning with a red-tailed hawk that has a penchant for patrolling the sky overhead was a wonderful experience.[33]

STANDOFF AT THE DAM

One aspect of Lowell's special character has been under siege for the past decade—an international energy company that owns the hydropower plant in Lowell has been pushing to replace the current water-control technology at the Pawtucket Falls Dam with a motorized system of air-filled rubber bladders to manage the height of water held behind the dam—and pooling all the way north to holding lakes in the White Mountains of New Hampshire. The existing system involves steel pins that bend and segmented wooden "flashboards" made to break away under the gradually building force of water flowing downstream. The proposed bladder dam or crest-gate dam, a version of which is in place downriver at Lawrence, Massachusetts, would eliminate natural variables in controlling the water level and fundamentally change the character of the historic dam in place when Congress established the park.

On top of the preservation issues is a serious concern of property owners upstream, who have experienced severe flooding twice since 2000, in effect, two comings of the proverbial 100-year flood. Residents favor the self-regulating flashboard system that responds to increased water flow and gradually drains the upper portion of the watershed. Relying on company supervisors at the hydropower plant whose primary goal is increased energy production makes the residents worry about the prospects of longer periods of high water behind the dam that will back up into low-lying riverside land.

The National Park Service on May 24, 2012, hosted a meeting of the senior staff of the Federal Energy Regulatory Commission (FERC) with city planners; preservation program managers from Washington, D.C., and Boston; the town manager of Chelmsford, Massachusetts; Congresswoman Niki Tsongas's district director; and representatives of the Department of the Interior, Lowell Historic Board, and Enel Green Power, the owner of the hydroelectric plant. The FERC official in charge said it was a "technical meeting" to discuss the impact of the proposed changes to the dam on the historic structure. Enel had a proposal on the table that called for brown-painted rubber bladders with restraining straps mimicking the pin-and-board system, a large building for an air compressor to inflate and deflate the bladders, and an outdoor display panel on the grounds near the dam with historical information and images.

Pawtucket Falls
James Higgins

After much back and forth about perceived or not perceived negative effects of
the mechanized dam being proposed, the opponents and proponents seemed to
find a way out of the dilemma. Enel manager Victor Engel suggested that he and his
colleagues would be willing to look at replacement of the entire granite capstone
section of the dam, which would allow for redrilling of holes for the steel pins in
order to make a more stable and predictable system. The preservationists were open
to this approach and had, in fact, suggested it previously. Another option surfaced.
Perhaps one section of the dam could be replaced with a deeper gate on the north
end that would allow more water to be released. The preservationists had to think
about whether one end of the dam or the other was more valuable. Clearly, the
south portion took precedence. The gatehouse is a scientific time capsule of hydraulic experiments, an Interior Department official said: "The gatehouse is the oldest
surviving hydraulic research laboratory in the United States, the site of James B.
Francis's experiments."

LNHP Acting Superintendent Peter Aucella reminded everyone of what was at
stake. "This is a national issue. The Director of the National Park Service and a

Deputy Director have been out to see the dam."[34] Secretary of the Interior Ken Salazar, on a visit to Lowell a week later, would make his own pilgrimage to the falls and weigh in with his concerns about changing the character of the place. NPS managers from Washington said that without discussion of alternatives they would not accept Enel's proposal. The attorney from FERC said a decision on historic impact would wait until the park staff and Enel explored the replacement of the capstone atop the dam, which would mean keeping the flashboards. The National Park Service and Department of Interior staff continued to point to the authorizing law for the park, which states:

> No federal entity may issue any license or permit to any person to conduct an activity within the park or preservation district unless such entity determines that the proposed activity will be conducted in a manner consistent with the standards and criteria established pursuant to section 410 cc-32 (e) of this title and will not have an adverse effect on the resources of the park and preservation district (16 USC, sec. 410 cc-12).[35]

The meeting closed with comments from the thirty people in the audience. John Hamblett of the Pawtucket Congregational Church across the river from the dam objected to the proposed bladder dam for how it would degrade the "view-shed" enjoyed by church members and others, as well as to a noisy air compressor running twenty-four hours a day. "This is a cultural and natural resource for all of us, and it must be protected." Linda Harvey of the Pawtucketville Citizens Council extolled the value of Pawtucket Falls and the historic dam as a tourist attraction and noted the "significant contributions" made to Lowell by the NPS. Others reminded Enel

Viewing the Pawtucket Falls Dam: U.S. Representative Niki Tsongas of Lowell, Secretary of the Interior Ken Salazar, LNHP Superintendent Celeste Bernardo, and LNHP Assistant Superintendent Peter Aucella, 2012
LNHP

and company of the "catastrophic damage"[36] incurred by homeowners during the floods of 2006 and 2007.

Chuck Parrott reached higher in arguing for the value:

> The Merrimack still has a natural feeling because of the vernacular dam. There would be a loss of character with the loss of the seasonal water falling and pouring white foam through and over the flashboards. The current dam at Pawtucket Falls has the quality of a craft object, an artisanal operation so to speak, and there is value in experiencing its workings. People also are fascinated by the sight and sound of falling water. It's elemental. Picture Niagara Falls at the extreme scale. Why do people flock there? The encounter is inspiring.[37]

The hydropower company rejected both alternative options for the dam. On April 18, 2013, FERC issued a License Amendment Order allowing the company to proceed as it wished. But on November 18, 2013, the U.S. Department of Justice filed suit in the 1st District U.S. Court of Appeals, seeking to enforce the federal act authorizing the establishing of the park.

PUBLIC-PRIVATE PARTNERSHIP

Jim Cook hasn't worked anywhere else but Lowell since graduating from Northeastern University in Boston with a degree in political science with a minor concentration in urban planning. He was hired in 1990 as executive director of the Lowell Development & Financial Corporation and Lowell Plan, Inc. He had run the City of Lowell's planning office since 1986. From the front yard of his boyhood home he watched the demolition of the Hale-Howard area of the Lower Highlands. "It didn't seem like the best approach," Cook said, with a grin.[38]

Formed in 1980, the Lowell Plan provides a "big table" around which decision makers from business, government, education, health-care, and other fields gather every month for confidential discussions about the condition of the city. It is Exhibit #1 in the case for Lowell being the epitome of public-private partnership innovation. After City Hall, the Lowell Plan/LDFC office is usually the second stop for any visiting urban planner, business association leader, economic development director, or journalist seeking to understand the Lowell "mojo" that accounts for the storied revitalization. Combined, the Lowell Plan and LDFC function like the Swiss Army Knife of Lowell redevelopment efforts. At various times one or the other has purchased endangered properties, commissioned education reform studies, hired consultants to prepare downtown retails strategies, provided first-time home-buyer down payment assistance, incubated the city's original cultural affairs operation, and even presided over its own small navy when a host was needed for assembling the national park's beginning fleet of canal boats.

> Growing up in the 1950s and '60s, I sensed things weren't going well in Lowell. When I got to college I was drawn to planning because it seemed like a fun way to get something done and see the results in your own city. What better place to start than in a place that seemed to have nothing going for it?[39]

HIGH-TECH HIVE

On August 2, 2011, Lowell residents woke up to learn that *Forbes* magazine had named their hometown the sixth geekiest city in the country, not far behind San Jose, California, Boulder, Colorado, and Durham, North Carolina. The city of innovative mechanics in the nineteenth century had come full circle with this offbeat designation. Based on National Science Foundation figures for concentrations of college-educated science and technology workers, Lowell (and environs) reclaimed its place as a haven for inventors and engineers. A chunk of the 14.1 percent of the Lowell area's geek workforce can be found at Wannalancit Mills. One of the city's earliest adaptive reuse projects was this complex on Suffolk Street, on the perimeter of downtown. The owners of the Suffolk Textile Company, which was founded in 1830, built the factory complex and operated it until 1926. Another textile operation, Wannalancit Mills, took over the buildings in 1950 and produced cloth until 1981. In the modern era, the complex has housed the Lowell Museum Corporation, the startup Lowell campus for Middlesex Community College, and research centers of UMass–Lowell like those on atmospheric matters, medical devices, and sub-millimeter wave technology.

Owned by Farley White Interests of Boston today, the Wannalancit complex is a high-tech hive with a cluster of small companies whose combined innovation is reminiscent of the Lowell Machine Shop in its heyday. The names are Xenith (ultra-safe sports helmets), Metabolix (biodegradable plastics), Qvidian (cloud computing sales software), Blackmagic Design (video technology), Operon (bio-manufacturing workforce agent), Watermark (environmental engineering and construction management), and Kallidus (construction engineering). In late 2012, the technology space was 97 percent occupied. The City of Lowell's economic development director, Theresa Park, attributes the success to "location, price, unique building features, management, and amenities."

One Metabolix employee told Park that the rent at Wannalancit is less than what the company paid for parking when they were in Cambridge, Massachusetts. She said that Xenith, in particular, wanted the look that the renovated mill offers—exposed brick-and-beam finishes, huge windows, and large interior spaces. The location and amenities are a package. In the 1820s, the river made all the difference. In the car and truck era, being close to routes 495, 3, 128, and 93 is a plus in business; a bonus for employees is the commuter rail connection to Boston. Getting in and out is important, but the home base is even more so. The people who work at Wannalancit enjoy being close to the historic downtown with its world-cuisine eating places, national park and network of small museums, a baseball stadium with a Red Sox minor-league team, an attractive Riverwalk, big-time entertainment events at the Tsongas Center, and a university campus.

Jim Milinazzo and Jim Cook, c. 1978
Kevin Harkins

Cook started as a research assistant in the city's planning office in late 1977. The first thing he was given to read was "the Brown Book" of the Lowell Historic Canal District Commission.

> I had seen articles about some kind of urban park in the *Sun*, and I remember thinking that the idea had a touch of Disney to it. It didn't seem realistic that crowds of tourists were expected. With the bias of a Lowell resident, I wondered if local people would buy into this city being a national treasure. My grandparents worked in the mills—and how would they feel about a national park? Six months later President Carter signed the park bill.[40]

Three key changes in the 1970s altered the course of modern Lowell history in Cook's view; two of them he considered bigger than the park news.

> When Lowell State College and Lowell Technological Institute merged in 1975, the fact that we now had a university instantly elevated Lowell. I had high hopes for the impact.
> Second, the decision by Wang Laboratories to build a corporate tower on Industrial Avenue off the Lowell Connector was enormous. It was the first business tower to go up in Lowell, and it was many times taller than the mills. With the tower construction came the $5 million Urban Development Action Grant that the City Council voted to assign to the LDFC. Wang wound up with an extremely good deal. It was very inventive for City Manager Bill Taupier to recommend converting the UDAG grant to a loan that would be the basis of large pool of revolving funds. Lowell was the first community in the country to figure out that it could make the money work over and over and multiply the benefits. The U.S. Department of Housing and Development was so struck by the innovation that once the initial value of the grant was repaid to the LDFC, the government didn't consider it federal funding anymore.

So, Wang was building a tower, the University of Lowell [now UMass–Lowell] was accepting applications under its new name, and the park had moved from concept to reality, but was yet to be a proven asset.[41]

The excitement and resources generated by the passage of the park legislation proved to be a plus for developers and real estate business people who were looking at possible reuse of buildings now that there were some financial incentives. Properties that the city acquired for lack of tax payments were available for renovation. Low-interest loans and preservation tax credits (which are administered by the NPS) made the difference between a building standing vacant and construction sign going up in front.

The park's impact on the bricks-and-mortar assets of the city has exceeded my expectations. In thirty-five years, more than 400 buildings in and around the commercial core of the city have been improved and in some cases rescued from the junk heap. But the promise of high level tourism day-to-day that I took from reading the Brown Book has yet to be realized. We get hundreds of thousands of people at special events and festivals, which is wonderful, but we have not seen the kind of sustained daily tourism needed to drive a thriving retail district in a recharged downtown. That said, Lowell would be much worse off if we were not a national park community.[42]

The tourism point was not lost on Paul Tsongas. As early as 1981, in his book *The Road from Here*, Tsongas wrote, "As the primary deliverer of Lowell National Historical Park, I remain highly enthusiastic about its impact on the city. Since its delivery, however, I have come to understand its very real limitations."[43] He acknowledged the importance of federal funds in sparking a turnaround, but knew the public-dollar stimulus was just that, a way to provoke business investment.

Government money has but one purpose—to foster an environment that will attract private money, giving disadvantaged sectors of society a chance to reap the rewards provided by economic growth. . . . The trick is to encourage the private sector, feed it, and channel it, without getting bitten. The private sector is robust and cruel. I have been the victim of its cruelty (in the decline of both my family's business and that of the city I grew up in), so I will forever feel a distance from it. But I know that it's a necessary component. If this fact is ignored, efforts to revitalize . . . will not be sustained.[44]

Tsongas was always a multilateral actor. He courted industry for Lowell and pushed for public school improvements but also touted the economic and quality-of-life benefits of the arts at places like Merrimack Repertory Theatre. Around the time of his presidential bid in 1991–1992, he decided it was time to add muscle to Lowell as a destination city. He wasn't going to wait for history tourists to fill the canal boats and cobblestone streets. The Lowell Plan in 1993 hired Coopers and Lybrand consultants to plan a civic arena for sports and entertainment. Within five years, the 6,500-seat arena and a 5,000-seat baseball park would put Lowell on the map of minor-league sports.

The route was far from smooth, however, and the arena issue proved to be a critical test of the community's fortitude and self-confidence, culminating in a nonbinding public referendum on the city ballot in the November 1994. The vote to approve "expending public funds, in any amount, for the purposes of participating in the construction and/or development of the proposed multi-purpose arena"[45] prevailed by a 53 to 47 percent margin—"after months of debate, information gathering, procedural concerns, and a shoving match" (in the City Council chamber).[46]

Brian Martin, former mayor
of Lowell and a city councilor,
was named headmaster of
Lowell High School in 2013.
Lowell Sun

Cook notes that the arena vote is pivotal on the long trail of recovery because it stands out as a rare instance when Lowell voters as a body were asked their opinion on a specific development decision. It was close, 10,637 to 9,747, but the people who believed the Lowell pie could grow won the day. The community rancor did not subside, and a slate of anti-arena candidates tried a political route to reach their goal. New City Manager Brian Martin in early November 1995 risked his job by naming names in a passionate letter published in the *Lowell Sun* in which he put the question of city progress squarely at the head of an election that was only days away. It was shocking to see a City Manager endorse candidates and thrash others.

> I feel compelled to write this article because I think this Tuesday's election is one of the most crucial in the history of Lowell. First of all, let me say that I love this city and I love this job. Lowell has been home to the Martin family for over 100 years, and I hope it will be for the next 100 years. . . . Our agenda in the next two years should be to move Lowell into the twenty-first century as one of the premier American cities. . . . I see a city where families can enjoy a quality of life without leaving the city boundaries. First and foremost: safe streets and a second-to-none school system. I see a thriving downtown with a farmer's market and top specialty shops and restaurants to attract customers from all over; a cultural smorgasbord that boasts a national park, a world-class folk festival, fascinating museums, award-winning theatre and entertainment, top-notch sporting events from our very own high school right up through minor-league hockey and base-ball. . . . Lowell in 1995 is a far better city than it was when I was growing up. . . . I need your support, and I am counting on you to endorse my leadership.[47]

The voter turn-out was 44 percent of the electorate: 5,000 more people voted than in the preliminary election in which anti-arena candidates had stormed to the top and scared the incumbents. The arena proponents prevailed and would constitute a majority on the new council.

The River Hawks, UMass–Lowell's Division I ice hockey team, play at the arena, now called the Tsongas Center at UMass–Lowell
James Higgins

LeLacheur Park, home of the Lowell Spinners, a minor-league affiliate of the Boston Red Sox
James Higgins

There was a national park connection here as well, an Aucella connection. At the request of City Manager Martin, Aucella became an executive-on-loan to a new Arena Commission charged with overseeing the construction of the civic arena and the baseball park that was soon added to the job list. Aucella and the commission composed of city and university appointees brought both projects in on time and on budget, the Paul E. Tsongas Arena opening in January 1998 and Edward A. Le-Lacheur baseball stadium in June 1998.

Including $24 million from the state and UMass–Lowell, plus a $4.9 million City of Lowell bond, the arena area development investment exceeded $78 million. This included entry road construction, redevelopment of the adjacent post office, and improvements to segments of the Canalway and Riverwalk adjoining the arena. The funds were almost exclusively local, state, and federal government monies, ranging from state highway funds and a U.S. Environmental Protection Agency Brownfields grant to National Park Service construction money.

Paul Tsongas died in 1997 from health complications related to a return of the cancer that had first made him sick in 1983. Niki acknowledged the community's respect for her late husband at the standing-room-only inaugural hockey game at the arena. When Edward LeLacheur's namesake ballpark hosted its first Lowell Spinners game, the former baseball catcher and longtime state representative from Sacred Heart parish threw out the first ball with style.

The new cultural industry formula was taking shape: a national park with a robust school program and top-notch music festivals, plus minor-league sports teams, plus cultural pillars like Merrimack Repertory Theatre, New England Quilt Museum, Whistler House Museum of Art, and American Textile History Museum, and Lowell Memorial Auditorium—all the activity playing out in a waterfront setting that looks like a redbrick museum without walls. The economics of cultural tourism became more promising as the pieces were moved into place.

Cook said the Lowell comeback has been a team effort all along:

The city councilors through the years do not get enough credit. Every big project that came before the council was approved. They had to vote on all the components of Lowell's comeback, from pursuing the urban park concept through the zoning changes to allow artists to live in their studios downtown. Sometimes we had to go back with some changes, but the lesson is that things do get done if people vote on the merits.

Also sometimes overlooked is the role of the state, particularly as federal money has been less available. We would not have the arena (now Tsongas Center at UMass Lowell) or LeLacheur ballpark without the University as a state-funded entity. The widening of Route 3 was a huge transportation improvement for Lowell and made it less of a burden to commute from Lowell to metro Boston. Parking garages downtown? Thank the state representatives and senators for bringing home that bacon. A landmark judicial center being built at the central gateway into the city—another investment by the state—to say nothing of the generous school building fund that got us new schools in the 1980s and '90s and the additional money that came with the Education Reform legislation.[48]

Jim Milinazzo has been friends with Jim Cook since their high school days. Milinazzo studied urban planning in graduate school at Penn State and earned a master's degree in public administration from Suffolk University. Both of them signed up for the Lowell revitalization project early on and have stuck with it. Milinazzo was director of the city planning department ahead of Cook's tenure and saw Cook succeed him as head of the Lowell Plan and Lowell Development & Financial Corporation. He also served as executive director of the Lowell Housing Authority. Cook stayed in the administrative trenches, but Milinazzo later in his career ran for office, serving several terms on the City Council and once being elected mayor by his colleagues on the council. When he describes today's Lowell System—a nineteenth-century term used to describe Lowell's successful manufacturing formula—he emphasizes the public-private partnership ethic and the "can-do" attitude among the day-to-day public administrators who are charged with implementing plans.

> We, the planners and administrators, didn't have to get credit. The political "delivery system" got the credit, the state and federal office holders who brought home the essential public dollars. Not that there were no egos among the planners and managers. But we needed to let the elected officials get recognized.[49]

Milinazzo started in the city planning office in 1978, where he shared an office with Cook. Two years later, when he was twenty-six years old, City Manager Joe Tully named him to succeed the outgoing director of the division of planning and development, Bob Gilman. The park was in place by then, and in Milinazzo's view City Hall leaders "saw the park as cash coming in to the city, a federal funding source for big bricks-and-mortar projects."[50]

He cited the importance of Lowell's planning culture in the sustained redevelopment of Lowell. Almost everything that has transpired has been put down on paper and illustrated with conceptual drawings, maps, and photographs. In 1980, the American Cities Corporation came to Lowell at the behest of Tsongas. They were associated with the Rouse Company, which had developed Faneuil Hall in Boston and the Inner Harbor redevelopment in Baltimore. With the Lowell Plan and City of Lowell splitting the $250,000 fee, the American Cities staff produced a downtown redevelopment plan that called for a first-class hotel, better and more retail stores, a renovated public auditorium, an access road for a hotel, and an international training center for Wang Laboratories. The future training center would help close the deal on a Hilton hotel downtown, but Wang's business stumble in the late 1980s shuttered the training center and undermined the Hilton franchise. On the housing side, Milinazzo points to the comeback of downtown as a mixed-income residential neighborhood and the remaking of the troubled Shaughnessy Terrace housing complex as River's Edge, with single-family and duplex homes offered at affordable prices. The project was not without controversy and required the utmost of Lowell's vaunted public-private sector collaboration, but the results have been encouraging. Milinazzo stepped back and assessed the work:

> The major projects were accomplished, including the roadway to a downtown hotel. Developer Arthur Robbins had told City planners that he did not want one traffic light between the Lowell Connector and his hotel, which now houses 500 UMass Lowell students as the campus Inn & Conference Center. The infrastructure improvements are always a worthwhile investment. Lowell has been successful when everyone comes together around ambitious ideas and follows the plan through to completion. That faith in good planning has been one of the factors that has distinguished Lowell among the other cities in Massachusetts that we now group as Gateway Cities. We stand out in the state, and we have earned ourselves a reputation across the country and around the world.[51]

In the 1970s, the city's problems were fairly described as Lowell's own, but the people who live and work in the city overcame its own demoralizing past. Today, the city faces serious challenges, some similar and others different in Milinazzo's view. They are not unique to Lowell, but rather national and global in origin and largely due to economic megatrends. Lowell has positioned itself to compete, and that is an advantage over where it was in 1970. After being defeated in a race for reelection in 2011, Milinazzo rallied his supporters and sought to return as a city councilor in 2013. State Senator Eileen Donoghue of Lowell welcomed his return to the political arena at a fund-raising event at Long Meadow Golf Club, where more than 100 people had gathered. She said, "We need councilors with Jim Milinazzo's stature because there is so much more that Lowell can do. Among the older cities in Massachusetts, those portals for newcomers and new ideas, Lowell stands out—but the city cannot stand still if it expects to be competitive and successful."[52] He won.

CREATIVE PLACE-MAKING

In the spring of 2012 Lowell hosted leaders and activists from twenty-four communities identified by the state as Gateway Cities, most of them being the same as or similar to the small to mid-sized postindustrial cities that formed the network of Heritage State Parks in the 1970s. These are entry-level places with old bones of built environments and churning populations continually refreshed by newcomers. Among the new arrivers in Lowell are Iraqis, Burmese, Bhutanese, Nigerians, and Brazilians. Fundamental challenges remain—the need for better-paying jobs, consistently excellent schools, and a broadly healthy community, including less crime and less abuse of addictive substances. As an alternative to the conventional manufacturing plants that once charged these cities' economic batteries, many of these communities are looking to the creative industries as a supplemental economic energy source. Lowell has led the way in developing the creative strands in the local economy, going back to the establishment of state and national parks in the 1970s and publication in 1987 of the state's first comprehensive cultural development plan for a city, *The Lowell Cultural Plan*. Lowell continues to be intentional with this approach, completing in 2008 a development strategy explicitly for the creative economy: *On the Cultural Road: City of World Culture*. In Massachusetts, the governor's creative economy council defines the creative economy as "the many interlocking industry sectors that center on providing creative services such as advertising, architecture or creating and promoting intellectual property products such as arts, film, computer games, multimedia, or design."[53]

In 1987, the predominant thinking about the cultural sector in Lowell was that it was characterized by nonprofit organization activity and heavily dependent on philanthropy. By 2008, the conversation was a more balanced discussion about creative industries, earned income, sustainable operations, and entrepreneurship—and a much looser construction of what is cultural and creative, encompassing tech start-ups, artisanal bakeries, video producers, and the like. This more businesslike vocabulary is a better fit for community development policy, which explains in part why more than 200 people would convene at the UMass–Lowell Inn & Conference Center to share ideas about "creative place-making" and learn from the best-practice examples put forth on PowerPoint presentations.

In 2012, Lowell's City Manager Bernie Lynch hosted officials from the Chinese Ministry of Finance who visited City Hall to learn about successful municipal budget processes and financial management practices. A career public administrator, Lynch was city manager from 2006 to 2014.
Jennifer Myers

Lowell City Manager Bernie Lynch welcomed the audience. The sponsors were MassINC, a progressive think tank; the Massachusetts Cultural Council, the state agency promoting the arts, humanities, and interpretive sciences; and the Executive Office of Housing and Economic Development, whose cabinet secretary chairs the Governor's Creative Economy Council. The progressive-minded leaders of the Lowell-oriented Theodore Edson Parker Foundation also contributed money for the event. Lynch laid out the rationale and results when it comes to the creative economy in Lowell:

> We're convinced that employers are drawn to locations with a base of talented, creative individuals who are in the current workforce or available for an expanding workforce. These employers want to be in places that are vibrant, diverse, and authentic, and which possess the amenities and walking-friendly environments that complement creative lifestyles—hence, our city marketing slogan: "Alive. Unique. Inspiring." We work every day to make Lowell a distinctive destination with a genuine sense of place.
>
> Since 2000, when the City adopted a creative economy strategy for downtown revitalization, we have seen 1,454 new housing units built or renovated and occupied, 94

State Senator and former Lowell Mayor Eileen
Donoghue
Kevin Harkins

units are under construction, 749 more units have been granted permits. Another 157 residential units are being reviewed for permits at this time. Developers have renovated about 2.6 million square feet in dozens of vacant buildings. Under construction or under permit now are projects totaling 750,000 square feet of property. We also are seeing new construction—700,000 square feet of office, commercial, and research and development space either already under permit or in the process. That's the evidence of people and businesses on the ground. The quality-of-life activity that we believe accounts in large measure for this strong real estate interest has equally impressive statistics.[54]

What are the metrics? In 2012, there were 440 artist studios, 190 of which are live-work housing units. The city had ten theater and performing arts spaces; sixteen museums, galleries, and cultural centers; and five rehearsal and recording studios. The Lowell Folk Festival attendance each July exceeds 100,000, the Lowell Summer Music Series draws some 30,000 people each year, Lowell Memorial Auditorium puts tens of thousands of people in seats, and the Tsongas Center at UMass–Lowell attracted more than 70,000 people in 2011–2012. There are dozens of creative-economy businesses, like film industry prop-makers Ymittos Candle on Dutton Street downtown, whose products were featured in *The Pirates of the Caribbean* and *Lincoln* movies. The city's ethnic cuisine spans the world, from American diner food and Irish pub grub to Indian and Brazilian delights.

State Senator Donoghue in 2012 chaired the legislature's Joint Committee on Tourism, Arts, and Cultural Development. The former city councilor and mayor of Lowell champions the creative economy. Tourism is a $15 billion industry in Massachusetts, the third largest economic cluster in the state. Lowell National Historical Park itself in 2010 generated a $35 million impact on Lowell and the surrounding region by attracting more than 540,000 visitors to its sites and events. The economic activity accounts for 467 jobs, according to an analysis by Michigan State University economists under contract for the National Park Service countrywide.

On a morning panel at the summit, Donoghue talked about an old building on Middle Street downtown that became a "pigeon roost." She described how the city in the early 2000s took a derelict building in its possession due the owner's failure

Lowell's visual art history is anchored in the birthplace of James McNeill Whistler (1834–1903), remembered in a contemporary bronze sculpture by Mico Kaufman, a respected Lowell area artist.

James Higgins

to pay property taxes and issued a call for proposals for developers to convert the structure to loft-style residences. The sale price was one dollar. These would be homes and production studios for people who could prove they were creative-industries workers of some type. The city offered small incentive grants to assist with set-up costs in the spartan spaces. "The idea was to attract artists downtown," Donoghue said. "We didn't know if it would work but we were hearing from artists in and outside the city that they wanted places where they could live and work. They couldn't afford two rents." Providence, Rhode Island, had had some success developing an artists' quarter downtown. The mayor there joked about artists being "the Marines of the city," for their willingness to establish a beachhead in rundown urban districts.

Renamed Ayer Lofts, the artist live-work space venture opened with full occupancy. The success made believers of other housing developers who were curious about the potential of a downtown that by then had been at the center point of a national park for more than twenty years. Lowell was still figuring out what it meant to live in a place with rangers leading tours and replica trolleys tooting whistles at the intersections. The Ayer Lofts project made it look like something more was possible in making Lowell a cultural destination.

Going back to 1981, the Lowell Historic Preservation Commission had stimulated the development of an artist-studio project on the ground floor of the Market Mills complex, across from the Visitor Center, the previously mentioned Brush Art

Gallery and Studios. The project was modeled on the Torpedo Factory in Alexandria, Virginia, which Fred Faust had visited while working on Paul Tsongas's staff in Washington, D.C. The Torpedo Factory's operational twist is that resident artists are required to work in view of the public for a certain number of hours each week in exchange for a more affordable rent. When "The Brush" opened in 1982, it was a fraction of the Torpedo Factory size and provided space for about a dozen artists in windowed studios arranged on either side of a corridor. In exchange for modest rent paid to the LHPC, the original Brush artists agreed to keep their studio doors open for a certain number of hours per week. The arrangement was not a fit for every artist, but there were many in the area who were willing to try the formula. For the LHPC and park, the project provided a much-needed additional visitor draw in the early years, before museum displays opened at the Boott Mills Boarding House (Mogan Cultural Center) and Boott Cotton Mills Museum.

Part of the Brush Art Gallery root system stretches back to an earlier organization, Art Alive!, a cooperative of more than fifty artists who had been allowed to use a former clothing store that the NPS had bought with the intention of removing it because the modern building did not conform to the historic streetscape in the middle of Merrimack Street. From 1979 until the mid-1980s, Art Alive! was an important space for local artists to meet and display their work.

The Brush Art Gallery celebrated its thirtieth anniversary in June 2012, a remarkable achievement for any arts center. The pioneering efforts of the artists at Art Alive!, The Brush, and Ayer Lofts showed a way forward that has led to Lowell now being a magnet for painters, musicians, dancers, writers, and other creative artists. Some 500 working artists in the city have given a new meaning to the city motto, Art Is the Handmaid of Human Good. Western Avenue Studios on the Pawtucket Canal is the largest concentration of artists' studios in the northeast of the nation. Once a statement of belief in the social value of artisanship and a tribute to the industrial arts as exemplified in high-end manufacturing, the city seal has taken on a fine-arts shine.

At the Creative Place–making Summit, Senator Donoghue said community leaders looking for a way forward should assess carefully their own strengths and weaknesses. "In Lowell we realized that we have to be who we are," she said. In Lowell's case, there was and is a lot to work with because of the rich history, social mix, and certain advantages that come with being a locus of higher education and situated at transportation crossroads. The region matters also, which is what one of her fellow panelists emphasized.

Former mayor of Meridian, Mississippi, John Robert Smith is as eloquent a spokesman for the virtues of cities and the arts as one might meet. He told the summit attendees the story of Meridian remaking itself into the intellectual and cultural hub of its region. He contends that cities must offer excellent artistic experiences to both children, as a way to nurture their aspirations, and also to business CEOs who crave inspiring moments in their own lives. He believes that people want to live in places whose residents care about questions like "Where do we come from?" and "Who are we now?"—places that have a sense of their own identity and a coherent presentation of themselves in everyday life, not places where residents try to imitate a prefab formula from away or react defensively to the way they think others view them. He showed a slide of a marketing poster from Mississippi with a headline acknowledging the prevailing view of it as a lagging state. "Yes, we can read. A few of us can even write." was the headline under which were the faces of about twenty authors: William Faulkner, Eudora Welty, John Grisham, Natasha Trethewey, and others. The words "Mississippi" and "poor" don't have to mean poor self-image or poor prospects, he said. And, it does not hurt to show that you have a sense of humor.

Returning to his point about aspirations, Smith said, "You have to remain focused on a point in the future you will not occupy. I see that point in the eyes of my grandson." In his closing, Smith lifted up the audience when he cited the Persian poet Sa'di on the human need for "loaves and hyacinths" to feed body and soul and quoted the Illinois poet Vachel Lindsay's poem "On the Building of Springfield."

> We should build parks that students from afar
> Would choose to starve in, rather than go home,
> Fair little squares, with Phidian ornament,
> Food for the spirit, milk and honeycomb.
>
> We must have many Lincoln-hearted men.
> A city is not builded in a day.
> And they must do their work, and come and go
> While countless generations pass away.

GATHERING THE LOWELL HONEY

One of the city's estimable historical figures, Benjamin F. Butler, said many notable things, but one of them resounds loudly. In 1876, on the fiftieth anniversary of Lowell's founding as a town, he reminded his listeners that "Our city has been a hive of industry, and, as a rule, the honey has been gathered by others."[55] He was referring to the financial heyday of Lowell, when the vast profits from the textile industry flowed to investors outside of Lowell. As has been tracked by Robert Dalzell in his book *Enterprising Elite*, the "honey" from Lowell enriched the original industry founders, the so-called Boston Associates, and their descendants. The wealth created by cloth production workers found its way into banks and railroads via investors and enhanced institutions in Boston such as Massachusetts General Hospital, Harvard University, and the Boston Athenaeum. According to Dalzell, in the mid-1800s "[t]here was no way of calculating just how much money the combined endowments of Boston's major charitable and philanthropic institutions represented, but the total ran into the millions."[56] Little of the profits remained in Lowell. The only substantial foundation whose grant-making concentrates on Lowell is the Theodore Edson Parker Foundation; Lowell did not have its own community foundation until 1997.

The turn to heritage as an economic engine was an attempt by Lowellians to leverage the value of their own assets, those things that could not be picked up and taken away to a Southern town like a textile factory. Lowellians in the 1970s had a kind of collective "scales falling from the eyes" experience as they saw anew their rivers and forests, architecture, pluralistic population, and city story—natural resources that were there to stay. The question was, how best to transform these resources into wealth-generators that would help make their city vibrant and optimistic.

One of the beauties of a national park solution is that all Americans own the national parks. Lowell became one of a 402-part common that stretches from the pine-lined coast of Maine in Acadia to the glowing lava streams of Hawaii volcanoes. This is a forever solution. There is no plant-closing in the future, no anxiety about outsourcing of the service, no potential corporate takeover. The promise is based on the full faith of the United States of America, the people of America who own these special places and who have charged the National Park Service with being custodians of certain natural places and heritage sites—and their stories. Lowellians, with the support of fellow Americans, changed the course of their city's future and ensured that an important piece of the national narrative would be securely in place and protected for the benefit of present and future generations.

In *The Inner City: A Handbook for Renewal,* Paul M. Bray takes on the topic of urban cultural parks, citing Lowell and a network of towns in New York State as examples of this concept: "These communities have pursued the vision of the urban environment itself as a park, seeking to transform themselves into places where everything is interesting. They have expanded the notion of the park to include inhabited portions of the city."[57] Galen Cranz extends the definition, saying that in these cases "the city was in fact a work of art worthy of appreciation and objectification."[58]

These are huge ideas. Lowell, collectively, has made manifest the concept put forward by local activists and their urban design allies of the 1970s. Some forty years later, observers are trying to understand the implications. The choices that were made changed lives. The priorities that were set and pursued by decision makers and those without official power made some people winners and others losers in the contest for resources. In Cranz's view, "The potentiality of parks to shape and reflect social values is still by no means fully understood."[59] Some opponents of the Lowell park idea maintain that the city would have been better with a shopping mall downtown and more parking garages. On balance, at the beginning of the twenty-first century, Lowell is more stable, productive, and coherent in meaning than most cities in its category. Some holes in the fabric show, but that only makes the people who care get busy fixing the holes.

NOTES

1. Charles A. Gargiulo, "Aunt Rose," *New Lowell Offering* 3, no. 1 (Spring 1979): 28.

2. Frances H. Early, "The Settling-In Process: The Beginnings of Little Canada in Lowell, Massachusetts, in the Late Nineteenth Century," in *The Little Canadas of New England: Third Annual Conference of the French Institute/Assumption College (Worcester, Massachusetts, March 13, 1982),* ed. Claire Quintal (Worcester: Assumption College, 1982), 23.

3. Early, 36.

4. Paul Du Noyer, *Liverpool: Wondrous Place, Music from Cavern to Cream* (London: Virgin, 2002), 9.

5. Mehmed Ali, "To Save a City: From Urban Renewal to Historic Preservation in Lowell, Massachusetts, 1920–1978 (University of Connecticut, 2006), 205.

6. Ali, "To Save a City," 205.

7. Shirley Kolack, *A New Beginning: The Jews of Historic Lowell, Massachusetts* (New York: Peter Lang, 1997), 12–13.

8. "The Preservation Movement: Then and Now," exhibit text.

9. "The Preservation Movement."

10. "The Preservation Movement."

11. "The Preservation Movement."

12. Loretta A. Ryan, "The Remaking of Lowell and Its Histories," in *Lowell: The Continuing Revolution: A History of Lowell, Massachusetts*, ed. Robert Weible (Lowell: Lowell Historical Society, 1991), 380.

13. *Urban Design Study* (City Development Authority, Lowell, Massachusetts, March 1970), 30.

14. *Urban Design Study*, 5.

15. *Urban Design Study*, 5.

16. *Urban Design Study*, 5.

17. Jack Perry, Lowell Development & Financial Corporation, meeting notes, 2011.

18. Ross J. Gittell, *Renewing Cities* (Princeton: Princeton University Press, 1992), 83.

19. Charles Parrott, interview with the author.

20. Parrott, interview with the author.

21. Parrott, interview with the author.

22. Taya Dixon Mullane, interview with the author.

23. Dixon Mullane, interview with the author.

24. Robert Verrier, "Human Energy (and Historic Tax Credits) Help 'Re-Boott' Historic New England Mill," *Preservation Nation Blog*, March 1, 2013.

25. Allen Freeman, "Lessons from Lowell," *Historic Preservation*, November–December 1990, 35.

26. Sarah Peskin, "Lowell, Massachusetts: Preservation Key to Revitalization," Institute for Urban Design, Project Monograph no. 2, March 1985, 5.

27. Peskin, "Lowell, Massachusetts," 5.

28. Adam Baacke, interview with the author.

29. Baacke, interview with the author.

30. *Lowell Trolley Study*, n.p.

31. Stephen Stowell, letter to the author, 2013.

32. Dixon Mullane, interview with the author.

33. Michael Leary, letter to the author, 2012.

34. Peter Avcella, meeting notes, author.

35. Meeting notes, author.

36. Meeting notes, author.

37. Parrott, interview with the author.

38. Jim Cook, interview with the author.

39. Cook, interview with the author.

40. Cook, interview with the author.

41. Cook, interview with the author.

42. Cook, interview with the author.

43. Paul Tsongas, *The Road from Here: Liberalism and Realities in the 1980s* (New York: Knopf, 1981), 21.

44. Tsongas, *The Road from Here*, 20–21.

45. Michael J. Paglia, "The Paul E. Tsongas Arena: Building a Legacy," UMass–Lowell, Economic and Social Development of Regions Master's Degree Program, April 2012, 16.

46. Paglia, "Paul E. Tsongas Arena," 23.

47. Brian Martin, "It's Time to Take a Stand," *Lowell Sun*, November 5, 1995.

48. Jim Cook, interview with the author.

49. Jim Milinazzo, interview with the author.

50. Milinazzo, interview with the author.

51. Milinazzo, interview with the author.

52. Eileen Donoghue, meeting notes, author.

53. https://MaLegislature.gov/Laws/SessionLaws/Acts/2008/chapter54.

54. Bernie Lynch, meeting notes, author.

55. Arthur L. Eno Jr., ed., *Cotton Was King: A History of Lowell, Massachusetts* (Lowell: Lowell Historical Society and New Hampshire Publishing Company, 1976), 145.

56. Robert F. Dalzell Jr., *Enterprising Elite: The Boston Associates and the World They Made* (Cambridge and London: Harvard University Press, 1987), 159.

57. Paul M. Bray, "Urban Cultural Parks," in *The Inner City: A Handbook for Renewal*, ed. Roger L. Kemp (Jefferson, N.C.: McFarland, 2001), 225.

58. Bray, 223.

59. Bray, 223.

CHAPTER 6

Telling the Story

"From its advent as the foremost cotton manufacturing center in the nation, through its decline, and into its revitalization, [Lowell] foreshadowed the industrialized, urbanized lifestyle characteristic of today and helped an agrarian people adapt to a new way of life. Through interpretation, Lowell can offer a unique insight into the broader consequences of the industrial revolution."

—General Management Plan, *Lowell National Historical Park,* 1980

". . . Lowell's citizens experienced the extremes of the advance of American society and economic structures. Because Lowell's life as a city is so dramatic, changes in this archetypal community clarify trends that more moderated experiences in other communities might obscure."

—*Marc Miller,* The Irony of Victory: World War II and Lowell, Massachusetts

IF THE FALLS COULD SPEAK

The National Park Service had a robust partner in its early efforts to collect, preserve, and present the Lowell story. The Lowell Historic Preservation Commission by 1980 was actively fulfilling its charge in the park legislation to "provide for educational and cultural programs to encourage appreciation of the resources of the park and preservation district." That one clause, combined with the authority to "make grants to any person or any public or private entity to provide for (i) educational and cultural programs,"[1] made the agency a local powerhouse. It was like having miniature national endowments for the arts and the humanities oriented solely to Lowell. In seventeen years, hundreds of thousands of dollars in cultural grants flowed to Lowell cultural organizations and individuals who had passion, ability, and a good idea. Between 1989 and 1995, during its first and only reauthorization period, the LHPC invested nearly $3 million in cultural programs in the form of cooperative agreements with nonprofit groups, events at Boarding House Park, public art, and a start-up folklife center.

Although more identified by its bricks-and-mortar responsibility to assess the condition of historical structures and act to preserve them, the LHPC embodied the Mogan mindset that "the buildings are the props around which the story will be told"—so much so that the agency took as the theme for its roadmap, *The Preservation Plan* (1980), the following: "To tell the human story of the Industrial Revolution in a nineteenth-century setting by encouraging cultural expression in Lowell."[2] It would be expression in the form of preserved architecture, to be sure, but expression also in the form of theater, history, music, educational activities, literature, folklore, visual art, crafts, and dance.

Most of the LHPC's results came about through incentives for the community to tell its own story: direct grants, partnership agreements tied to funding (cooperative agreements, in federal government vocabulary), and pilot projects seeded with LHPC money. All this activity was meant to augment the operational program of the park, whose much larger staff was charged with developing an "interpretive program" for the new park, building museum sites, designing and delivering tour experiences, and figuring out how to present the Lowell story to the visitors who were expected in increasing numbers. With its ranger corps and in-house planners, historians, curators, and other staff with specialized expertise, the NPS was the mainstay of the core historical presentation in Lowell while the LHPC primed the cultural pump and tested what might or might not work in the form of cultural programs.

One of the LHPC's performing arts initiatives in the early 1980s was outdoor theater on a small empty lot on Shattuck Street across from the agency's administrative offices in the Lowell Gaslight Building. Construction company owner and former Lowell mayor Armand W. LeMay brought in a crew to build an impromptu stage for summer productions of *The Fantastiks* and *A Funny Thing Happened on the Way to the Forum*, again with Merrimack Repertory Theatre featured. Evening crowds jammed the seating area and overflowed onto the cobblestones of the closed street. These were not history shows, but the event brought people into contact with the historical resource, the distinctive nineteenth-century setting that is the context of the park. Today, the Lowell Summer Music Series at Boarding House Park, on the other side of downtown, draws more than 30,000 people to a beautifully restored

The Shattuck Street Stage in action, c. 1980
James Higgins

area of the park where they enjoy the music of Joan Baez, Lyle Lovett, Ziggy Marley, Buddy Guy, and the B-52s, among other stars old and new.

In the second floor stairwell at park headquarters on Kirk Street hangs a framed poster for "The Lowell Play," a pageant of history selected as the winning entry in a national competition sponsored by the LHPC. On February 12 and 13, 1982, students in the Lowell High School Performing Arts Program brought to the stage *If the Falls Could Speak* by David Riley, a Vermont-based journalist and playwright. His previous play, *Ethan*, about Revolutionary War hero Ethan Allen, had toured Vermont as part of the national observance of America's Bicentennial in 1976. The Lowell Play poster is a condensed view of the city's history designed as a mock front page of a newspaper plastered with headlines such as "Hub Men Plan Mill, 1821." In two acts, Riley paraded the founders, mill girls, and strikers across the stage, followed by representative immigrant workers with their travails and triumphs and then voices from the road to recovery as the feel-good ending.

The play had premiered in May 1981, in a downtown event center, produced by Merrimack Regional (now Repertory) Theatre and featuring professional actors. That first production was a high point of the citywide Lowell Festival '81. Riley had already written about Lowell in a lengthy cover story for the *Boston Globe Magazine* in July 1980: "The Rebirth of Lowell: A Beacon for Revitalization." His article was a no-holds-barred account of Lowell's struggle to get back on its feet in the 1960s and 1970s.

> The number of downtown residents shrank from 17,000 to 1,700 in the last twenty years. Of the huge textile mills that had put the city on the map, only two remained open, partially used by smaller companies. Hell's Angels paraded through the streets. . . . Lowell's Merrimack River was one of the country's most polluted rivers. And urban renewal had destroyed two cohesive communities in Lowell, one demolished to make way for an industrial park that no one would build on. . . . It was a town to be laughed at.[3]

Between 1970 and 1980, however, much had changed. Frank Keefe, chief planner for Massachusetts, a former head of city planning in Lowell, told Riley that Lowell is "the beacon to the whole new movement of urban revitalization," and Mayor Robert Maguire added, "Our major problem is keeping up with the progress."[4] If the actual Pawtucket Falls could have spoken in 1970, the story would have been wildly different, and the playwright might have had a hard time attracting an audience instead of Riley's play filling the seats at Lowell High for all three shows.

There is a view locally that 1975 is the modern era's turning point. It was the year of despair and the year of new hope. The convergence of bad and good factors seemed to shake the city out of its past and set it going in a new direction. Lowell historians are familiar with a stark photograph of a 1930s building displaying a huge sign that read: We Tried/We Failed/We Quit. In 1970s Lowell, however, the psychological climate had changed. A growing number of people were determined that the cyclical boom-bust outcome would be different this time. Robert Gilman, a planner and banker in Lowell who played a hands-on role in the change process, summed up the trouble:

> The 13 percent official unemployment rate was the worst in the state. A dozen major commercial properties downtown were in the hands of City Hall because the owners could not pay taxes due. The city's population had been dropping by about 1,000 a year since 1960.[5]

Abandoned mill space had once hummed with textile machines and shoemaking
James Higgins

Conversely, 1975 was the year when Governor Frank Sargent, a Massachusetts Republican, signed the legislation that established Lowell Heritage State Park as the first in a network of similar parks in small postindustrial cities. Another piece of state legislation that proved to be more important to Lowell in the long run also made its way to the governor's desk: the law effecting a merger of Lowell State College and Lowell Technological Institute to form a new University of Lowell with buildings ranged along the north and south banks of the Merrimack in the area of Pawtucket Falls. The third winning move involved the formation of a quasi-public bank called the Lowell Development & Financial Corporation (LDFC), which was paired soon after with the Lowell Plan, Inc., a nonprofit economic development group.

Reconnecting with the story of Lowell was a challenge for a long time. Notwithstanding Lowell's distinctive place in the American narrative, between 1920 and 1976 not one new general history of the city was published. Bracketed by Frederick Coburn's *History of Lowell* (1920), and the Lowell Historical Society's multiauthor *Cotton Was King: A History of Lowell* (1976), there were Margaret Terrell's *Lowell: A Study of Industrial Development* (1940) and John Coolidge's *Mill and Mansion* (1942), but these are specialized titles. Newspapers of the period provided the proverbial "first draft of history," and the city had a robust paper-reading public that bought the *Lowell Sun, Courier-Citizen, L'Éoile,* and more in English and other languages. John L. Kerouac's *The Town and the City* (1950) contributed a fictional account of city life from the 1920s through the World War II era. Kerouac went on to publish four more novels set largely in Lowell that double as a social history of his youth. These books would later help justify a $100,000 federal grant to create a sculptural tribute to the author in the heart of the national and state parks.

By the 1960s, with the economic fortunes of the city in long decline, it was not unusual to hear a Lowell resident reply "North of Boston" when asked "Where are you from?" Ten mill companies were sold, closed, or moved from 1899 to 1958; the basis of Lowell's claim to national and world historical significance faded.

The litany of losses on the wall in the Boott Cotton Mills Museum tracks the decline:

Lowell Mfg. Co., sold, 1899.
Middlesex Mfg. Co., closed, 1919.
Hamilton Mfg. Co., closed, 1926.
Lawrence Mfg. Co., sold, 1926.
Tremont Mfg. Co., sold, 1926.
Suffolk Mfg. Co., sold, 1926.
Appleton Mfg. Co., moved, 1927.
Massachusetts Cotton Mills, closed, 1928.
Boott Cotton Mills, closed, 1954.
Merrimack Mfg. Co., closed, 1958.

An anonymous quipster summed up Lowell's misfortune this way: "The Great Depression hit Lowell earlier than anywhere else in the country and lasted longer here than anywhere else." During the depths of the national economic trough, some 40 percent of Lowell residents received "relief" checks or support of some kind from the government. Census schedules show a loss of 20,000 city residents from 1920 to 1960, the high-water mark having been 112,000. It would take until 1990 for the city to again top 100,000.

As the community regained its collective confidence, more people embraced what was fundamentally theirs. Patrick Mogan often said, "A city that has no past cannot have a future." He meant that an unmoored, alienated local population is unlikely to act in a coherent, positive fashion. Community social psychologists would say that a community disassociated from its identity, at odds with its own story, cannot be expected to function as a competent entity. Until Lowell found its way back to its storied beginnings and reconciled the successes and the damages, the city was not able to move forward. Conventional wisdom defined Lowell downward through most of the twentieth century.

In 2010, the official population figure was 106,519, but knowledgeable observers say that figure is low because the neighborhoods include thousands of uncounted persons. Between 1980 and 2000, Greater Lowell surged from 226,000 to 270,000. A regional boom in computer technology businesses and the arrival of thousands of refugees from the war zones of Vietnam, Laos, and Cambodia recharged the city's figurative batteries. Essential factors in Lowell's newfound momentum were the reappraisal of its history, a renewed appreciation for the significant role it had played in the national experience, and a practical assessment of the value of that indigenous resource—a story, unlike a mill, that could not be torn down, sold, or otherwise taken away.

A COUNTER-NARRATIVE

There is a counter-narrative, however, one that today is subordinated to the distilled script of urban rise, fall, and resurrection. Even with jobs hard to find and stubborn social problems, the city functioned well enough for many families and individuals who remained rooted through the middle decades of the century.

John Leite was fifteen years old in 1948 when he started blowing his horn at the Cosmo on Market Street. He and two friends asked the musicians' union for special permission to play because every other performer in the union local had plenty of work. In those days there were 500 musicians in the union. Places like the Flamingo, Laconia, Silver Star, Mirror Lounge, and Laurier Supper Club with its hydraulic stage lit up the downtown on weekend nights. "People wanted to go out after working all day," Leite said. "And they could afford the prices."[6] Small-time players and big-name artists came to Lowell, like Louis "Satchmo" Armstrong at the Lowell Memorial Auditorium and jazz singer Billie Holiday, who gave her last nightclub performance at the Blue Moon in May 1959.

A graduate of Lowell High School, Leite joined the army and played bass trombone with the 7th Army Symphony in Europe, including for operas at festivals in Germany, and for a time performed with David Amram, a prominent composer and instrumentalist. In 1955, Leite enrolled in the Music Education program at Lowell State College.

John Leite on the way to Germany to join the 7th Army Symphony on bass trombone, c. 1950

John Leite

I'm a freshman in line waiting to sign up, and I hear, "John!" I turn around, there's Frank Page. I went to high school with him. He was a couple of years younger, and had gone into the 18th Army band at Fort Devens in Ayer, Massachusetts. Frank Hickey, who had graduated in '49, a year before me, went into the Navy and was on the ship *Wasp* all over the world. Bob Leclair, also from '49, was an Army entertainer in Korea, and sang with Richie Dee after college. So, I meet these guys on the first day; we had all come back, and wound up as freshman music students, alongside veterans from other towns. This was the first time that Lowell State had seen so many men in the music program.[7]

Leite had a hand in the urban cultural park planning years later, when he designed an illustrated Model Cities program report for Pat Mogan that was instrumental in advancing the park concept.

Twenty years after Leite's days at Lowell High, when Marty Meehan was growing up on London Street in Sacred Heart Parish, the community music scene was still lively, from choirs, like the Catholic singers at the Immaculate Conception Church, to garage bands of aspiring rock stars and traditional marching bands. Meehan played drums in the popular Sacred Heart School Band. "Imagine what an opportunity it was for a working-class kid to march in the St. Patrick's Day parade in New York City? We stayed in the Abbey Victoria Hotel—five times before I started high school. It was a big deal,"[8] Meehan said. The former congressman who became Chancellor of UMass–Lowell in 2007 had a paper route by the time he was nine years old. His father was a printer at the *Lowell Sun*. His parents were able to raise seven children on a printer's income, and after forty-three years there was a fair pension to be had. Meehan rode his bike downtown every Saturday to settle up accounts at the newspaper's business office. He got a closeup look at the boarded-up buildings and gaps in the streetscape.

Meehan echoes many Lowellians when he says that although the city's economy was depressed, community life was vigorous. The high school offered endless opportunities for motivated students. Winners of the prestigious Carney Medal each year went on to elite colleges. As president of the student council, Meehan learned early about leadership, and these skills would serve him well as he extended his reach.

Through the 1950s, 1960s, and early 1970s, across the city there were movies, talent shows, concerts. The Commodore Ballroom featured big bands such as Stan Kenton, Ray Anthony, and Buddy Rich, singers Connie Francis and Fabian, and later rocking pop groups like the Doors, Cream, and the Beach Boys, as well as local favorites Little John and the Sherwoods. The storied dance hall closed in 1972.

Beginning in the early 1900s, Lowell has had more than forty movie theaters. That statistic was a big find for journalist Nancye Tuttle, when she researched the city's cultural history for a special museum exhibit about city theaters for the Mogan Cultural Center in 1993. Some of the older names like La Scala and Alhambra gave way to places called the Rialto, Crown, and B. F. Keith's. The State or Gates Theater on Back Central Street began as the Opera House in 1887 before being converted to a movie house. A few venues doubled as vaudeville stages for stars like W. C. Fields. Keith's, which opened in 1911, at one time offered three performances a day with silent pictures and a live orchestra in a pit.

"I had a standing 'date' with my dad in the 1930s, when the newest musicals came to town starring Fred Astaire, Ginger Rogers, Alice Faye, and Eleanor Powell and played in Lowell's first-run houses," Dolores Dion told Tuttle. Charles Tsapatsaris liked the cowboys: "We saw Westerns at the Royal—Tim McCoy, Buck Jones, Tom Mix, and Ken Maynard. There were Frankenstein movies and gangster films and the animal trainer, Clyde Beatty. We got in for a dime."[9] The last downtown theater to show films was the Strand, which closed in 1968 and was later demolished to make way for a new Hilton Hotel in the mid-1980s.

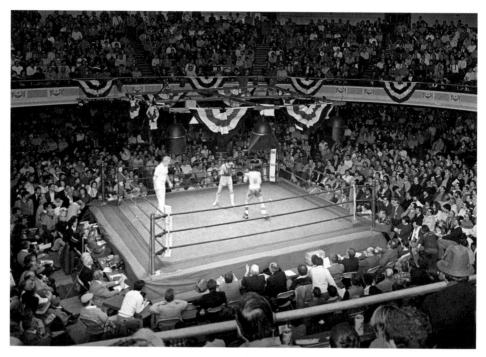

Golden Gloves boxing has had enduring appeal in Lowell.
James Higgins

Many Lowellians today have fond memories of life in the city from the 1950s through the 1980s. A vintage photograph of the Bon Marché building on Merrimack Street posted on the web in the spring of 2012 generated dozens of comments. Sandra Smith Houle was nostalgic for the Bon Marché department store at Christmastime: "It was so very special with all the decorations downtown." Rachel Bergeron Fisher worked in a coffee shop downtown during the holidays around 1980. "People would come in from shopping, and at night the lights were beautiful," she said. Alice M. Le-May loved the big holiday bell hung in the middle of Kearney Square. Marina Cacici would sit on the curb in front of Bon Marché to watch the holiday parade go by.[10]

Despite the ups and downs and daily struggles from the Acre to Belvidere, Lowell had a certain something that was fascinating. In 1962, Jack Kerouac sat for a rambling interview with Professor Charles Ziavras and Attorney Jim Curtis on their weekly book discussion program on local radio station WCAP. He was in town to promote a new novel and offered this judgment: "In my opinion, Lowell, Massachusetts, is now the most interesting city in the United States of America."

The average family income in Lowell in 1973 was $10,242, the lowest in its region. People in the suburbs, many of them former Lowellians, earned $12,000 to $14,000 annually. City Hall on Merrimack Street was flying a banner from the previous year that proclaimed Lowell an "All-American City," thanks to the National Municipal League. The designation recognized the quality of community participation in "solving urban problems." (In 1999, Lowell again earned the All-American City award; community leader Mary Bacigalupo choreographed an inspiring river-themed performance at the final presentations in Philadelphia.)

Raytheon Missile Systems employed 2,000 at its South Lowell plant. Computer maker Wang Laboratories was up and coming in nearby Tewksbury. Joan Fabrics and Pandel-Bradford manufactured synthetic materials for shoes and car seats. The ubiquitous trailer trucks emblazoned with the words "Wednesday is Prince Spaghetti Day" carried tons of Lowell-made Prince pasta to markets in those years. Honeywell Information Systems had a large facility near Appleton Mills. Employees of banks, printers, supermarkets, hospitals, utilities, retailers, and other small- to medium-sized businesses made up most of the workforce. The Chamber of Commerce touted "a broad-based economy," keenly aware of the danger of again loading the eggs in a single basket. There was another lesson of heavy industrial activity, an awareness of what kind of work was desirable. "Through foresight and strict planning, the area has attracted clean industries and demanded that they remain so by building in safeguards against pollution and contamination."[11]

Absent the park, however, it would have taken more time for Lowell to be considered a "national" city once more. By 1992, the Lowell story had reemerged in local and national consciousness so prominently that the lead editorial of the *New York Times* on Labor Day was titled "The Mills Weren't Made of Marble." The *Times* writer singled out the park as an exception to the rule of heritage sites that typically showcase lavish homes and civic monuments:

> America's working men and women have a starring role in the epic called "The Industrial Revolution." A thundering score sets the mood, provided by 88 belt-driven looms in an unusual factory museum. . . . This is an American past that many grandparents lived, and still remember. Youngsters who experience even for a moment the gloom of these old mills will better understand why trade unions sprang into being to check rapacious capital. The Lowell park and museum realize an imaginative scheme put forward in the 1970s. . . . Restoring the old canals and the long-shuttered mills has given new hope and dignity to a Lowell now entering the post-industrial revolution.[12]

How much easier it was to raise the Lowell flag and take ownership of the local address when the city's story was back in the national conversation in a positive tone.

"THE DANGER OF A SINGLE STORY"

"History is story. It means nothing else as a noun. Herodotus was the first to use the word . . . and he used it as a verb: to find out for oneself. Then you tell."

—*Charles Olson*, The Special View of History *(1970)*

Duey Kol came to Lowell for the first time in 1999 to see the Southeast Asian Water Festival on the north bank of the Merrimack River above Pawtucket Falls. This wide, relatively straight section of the river has been called one of the best stretches for rowing in the country. For years, the community has hosted competitions like the Textile Regatta. Every August, the Southeast Asian Water Festival draws tens of thousands of people to the riverside for music, dancing, food, people watching, and the Khmer long-boat races similar to those held on the Mekong River. Kol was born in a refugee camp in Thailand while her parents waited for an opportunity to move to a safe new home. Their next stop was another camp in the Philippines,

Duey Kol of the National Park Service
LNHP

and then in 1984 on to Chelsea, Massachusetts, which, like Lowell, had become a place where Cambodian families were resettling in increasing numbers. Her family was sponsored for resettlement in the United States by Boston Catholic Charities. She was three and a half years old when she arrived in America with her parents and younger brother and sister. For the first six months the family lived on welfare payments and shared a three-bedroom apartment with two other Cambodian families.

As a youth she learned traditional Khmer dance and performed with the Reaching Out for Chelsea Adolescents Dance Troupe. Her mother had been a dancer before the Khmer Rouge overran Cambodia. Along the way, Kol met members of the acclaimed Angkor Dance Troupe of Lowell. She remembers her high school teacher Sylvia Schernbaum urging her and fellow students to "Think big, dream big." She did just that, winning acceptance to Simmons College in Boston. After graduation she worked for a time as an insurance agent in Waltham, Massachusetts, concentrating on the immigrant and refugee communities in Lowell and Lynn, Massachusetts.

In 2004, she was recruited by George Chigas of the Angkor Dance Troupe to help manage the organization. With a Theodore Edson Parker Foundation grant, Chigas and Samkhann Khoeun of the Cambodian Expressions project of Middlesex Community College brought her on board as a shared program manager. The dance group was based on the top floor of the park's Mogan Cultural Center. Observing the cultural activities being organized by the park staff, she told Mogan Center director Mehmed Ali: "I want your job. Teach me how to do it."

When the park advertised a special events position, Kol applied and was selected. She worked on the Lowell Folk Festival, Lowell Summer Music Series, and other events. She earned a master's degree in community social psychology at UMass–Lowell, and was promoted to assistant director of cultural programs. A rising star, Kol was recruited in 2012 to work in the office of the assistant director of the National Park Service in Washington, D.C., which oversees interpretive and education policies. She already had been helping with the agency's nationwide Diversity and Inclusion Project. The topic could not be more personal:

> Those of us who are bicultural have to create a separate idea that is not one or the other—we have to manage a blended identity. It's important to develop year-round relationships with the people whose cultural traditions we promote on special days. We have to get beyond celebration. We of the park staff must be able to exist in a condition

like the state of "therapeutic irritation" that comes with holding a new and different pose in yoga. We should be able to hold ourselves in that place that is uncomfortable and to be okay with that. At the same time, visitors should be comfortable asking difficult, complicated questions on tours, in museums, and at public activities.[13]

Kol is a strong advocate of multitrack storytelling.

We have to ask ourselves, how do you decide what to present? Which stories do you choose to tell? We need the best storytellers, more people who have lived the stories. With a topic like immigration, we can be relevant in what we talk about. And what happens to people not interested in displaying their culture in a public demonstration?

It's our responsibility to explore and probe, to record more stories in Lowell because this is where we have been asked to preserve part of America's history and relate it to people. There's a TED talk (Technology, Entertainment, Design) online by Nigerian novelist Chimamanda Adichie in which she cautions listeners about "the danger of a single story" and how this can lead to a fundamental lack of understanding of another person or place. She says, "The single story creates stereotypes, and the problem with stereotypes is not that they are untrue, but that they are incomplete. They make one story become the only story."[14]

THE POWER OF WATER

For $250, a visitor to Las Vegas can take a Papillon Company helicopter tour above and below the West Rim of the Grand Canyon; for another $50 the helicopter will land on the canyon floor so passengers can take a half-hour look around the magnificent setting. If one were available, a helicopter would be the best way for a visitor to enter Lowell National Historical Park, choppering down the blue channel of the Merrimack River from the north, dipping low over the Pawtucket Falls to see the dam, gatehouse, and blacksmith shop, and then ascending over downtown for a bird's-eye view of the latticework of canals that make up the engineering marvel that is the Lowell waterpower system. After seeing the system of canals feeding water into the mill district downtown, a visitor would be more prepared to encounter the ground-level components of the intricate industrial mechanism. A map is a poor second if someone has the aerial view on video.

The Merrimack's watershed encompasses more than 5,000 square miles of New Hampshire and Massachusetts. It rises in the White Mountains of New Hampshire where the Winnipesaukee and Pemigewasset rivers meet in the town of Franklin. The river provides habitat for eagles and salmon, and drinking water for hundreds of thousands of people. It amounts to the fourth largest basin in New England, after the Kennebec and Penobscot in Maine and the Connecticut River that traverses New Hampshire, Vermont, Massachusetts, and Connecticut. The Merrimack runs 115 miles from source to sea, fifty miles of it in the lower valley of Massachusetts—from Tyngsborough to the mouth where fresh water meets salt, between Newburyport and Salisbury. The spring-fat Merrimack rushes to Lowell at 22,000 cubic feet per second.

The founders of Lowell harnessed it like a mythical-sized draught animal that pulled American textile manufacturing into a whole new era. They would speak of "a millpower" instead of horsepower. The best authority on Lowell's waterpower system is Patrick M. Malone of Brown University, who defines a millpower as "the amount of water power required to drive a textile mill, in this case the second mill at Waltham. . . . For the Merrimack [mills] directors, a millpower was 25 cfs of water on a 30-foot drop. That was equivalent to 85 gross, or theoretical, horsepower."[15] (Waltham, Massachusetts, was the site of the Boston Manufacturing Company on the Charles River, the first venture of Francis C. Lowell and partners.)

In early New England the river drew newcomers to its banks the way waterways always have. Family farms led to villages, which grew to towns. Transportation in particular put the Merrimack in play in the late seventeenth and early eighteenth centuries. From the dense northeastern woodlands, timber was carried down on boats to Newburyport, soon known for its small forest of masts. "By 1880, more than 1,600 trading vessels had been built on the Merrimack," according to Kathy McCabe, writing for the Merrimack River Watershed Council.[16]

The utility of the Merrimack literally took a turn in 1792, when digging began for the Pawtucket Canal a short distance upriver from the travel barrier of the Pawtucket Falls at then-Chelmsford. With its completion in 1796, boats and barges could side-step the falls and continue to the sea at Newburyport. The Pawtucket was followed by a second Lowell–Boston connection, the Middlesex Canal, which was opened full-length in 1803, providing upcountry traders a shortcut to Boston wharves through the interior that lopped off miles of river navigation. With the advent of locomotives, the railroad trumped the slow canal barges. The Pawtucket, which was underperforming as a shipping lane, later offered a ready-made watercourse for hydro-driven factories envisioned in 1821. The mill men needed only to excavate a few more canals to divert flow from the Pawtucket to flatland on the south bank of the Merrimack. There rose a great red wall of factories. Later, another megacanal, the Northern, would be dug to amplify the river's impact in the core industrial zone.

In late August every year, the Southeast Asian Water Festival on the north bank of the Merrimack River in the Pawtucketville neighborhood features community boat races in traditional long boats, similar to events on the Mekong River in Asia.
James Higgins

Writing in the *National Geographic Magazine* in 1951, Albert W. Atwood called the Merrimack River "a veritable slave in the service of industry."[17] The Lowell of the time gets short shrift in the article, whose sentences recall the pioneering exploits of the merchants and engineers of the mills' heyday. But by 1950, the river that had added so much value to the Lowell business ventures not only flowed past the city like so much opportunity lost, but the water was fouled by generations of misuse. Decades of toxic effluent from the mills and other riverside operations had contaminated the bed over which fresh current moved, often carrying pollutants that would not be prohibited until the passage of the Clean Water Act (Federal Water Pollution Control Act) of 1972. The black humor among boaters and rowers recommended a cleansing chemical shower for anyone unfortunate enough to spill overboard.

Adaptive reuse is a term employed to describe a combined preservation-renovation process that results in historic structures being recycled for contemporary activity, whether that end use is residential, commercial, educational, or something else. Adaptive reuse also applies to the Merrimack River, seen in its various reincarnations as fishing ground, liquid highway, and energy production source. In the 1970s, a new and different way of looking at the river gained popularity. Together with Lowell's canals, the river began to be talked about as a small-scale natural wonder and heritage jewel for its Genesis-like role in setting in motion the American Industrial Revolution.

RIDING THE *PAUL MOODY*

Getting on the water is a big draw at the park. The canals were Lowell's ticket to national park status. Although Lowell was called "The Venice of America" in the nineteenth century, nobody would have taken Lowell for the "floating city" of northeast Italy, dating from 421. There were no gondolas or even kayaks in Lowell's canals of the past, at least not legally.

Henry and John Thoreau did not ply the Lowell canals with their boat during their week on the Concord and Merrimack Rivers in 1839. They left the first river and meandered along the Middlesex Canal to get north of the rapids at Pawtucket Falls.

> We left [the Concord's] channel, just above Billerica Falls, and entered the canal, which runs, or rather is conducted, six miles through the woods to the Merrimack, at Middlesex [Village] . . . Pawtucket and Wamesit, where the Indians resorted in the fishing season, are now Lowell, the city of spindles and Manchester of America, which sends cloth round the globe. Even we youthful voyagers had spent part of our lives in the village of Chelmsford, when the present city, whose bells we heard, was its obscure north district only, and the giant weaver was not yet fairly born. So old are we; so young is it.[18]

His brother died a few years after the river voyage, and Thoreau took up the writing project as an elegy for John, which he synthesized with profound reflections on nature and spirituality. He wrote the book in the cabin at Walden Pond in 1845. Writer John McPhee and a friend retraced the Thoreau brothers' trip in August 2003. With the book as their map, the two men in a canoe paid homage to the early travelers all the way to Hooksett in New Hampshire. McPhee and his companion found the former junction of the Middlesex Canal and river at Lowell under a warehouse and railroad tracks opposite Hadley Field on Middlesex Street. "The Merrimack there is a thousand feet wide and subject to the winds if not of an ocean at least of a good-sized lake," McPhee observed.[19]

The Lowell canals were power canals, strictly for business, custom-made to direct the flow to turning water-wheels and turbines in the mill basements. To understand and enjoy the engineering marvel of the Lowell canal system in the context of a park experience, however, it was clear to everyone that people would have to ride boats in the canals. Some early commentators said this was the "Disney" element in the proposed Lowell park. This would be "the ride."

One late summer morning in 2011, Captain Tom Gallagher drove south from his home in New Hampshire to pilot a small boat in the canals. He knew what he would see when he got to Lowell. There had been ten inches of rain in the past week. Soil from the White Mountains and loam from farmland where rivers and streams had overtopped their banks had infused the canal water with dark earth. He could have used T. S. Eliot's words: "The river is a strong brown god." Ranger Krystal Vezina's group looked at the water as the captain gave safety instructions. She had twenty people for the morning tour, old and young, talkative and watchful. Several of the younger kids busied themselves filling in blanks in their scavenger-hunt books.

National Park Service canal boat at the Swamp Locks
James Higgins

Gallagher backed up the *Paul Moody*, named for the master mechanic who built the first American power loom. Two Evinrude 80 outboard motors propelled the boat forward. The point of the ride is not speed, but rather observation—and the ranger provides a running commentary, sometimes posing questions to the passengers. "Do you know how many hours a day the mill girls worked?"

"Fourteen," one man said. "And six days a week."

The *Paul Moody* set off on the Pawtucket Canal from its station at Swamp Locks—the locks being stone-lined chambers with wooden gates on both ends that allow vessels to rise or descend between sections of the canal system, which steps down three levels (and in reverse direction) between the upriver inflow and downriver outflow. The original Pawtucket was about ten feet deep. Mules tromped alongside on the towpath, pulling barges laden with cargo. Swamp Locks is one of the main terminals for boat and trolley passengers. The area was once a wetland of swamps, bogs, and a "mill pond" that fed water to branching canals.

Sun warmed the travelers. Seagulls squawked. The subterranean view of the city surprises most visitors, even longtime Lowell residents. Everything looks taller and more imposing, more muscular and formidable in function and form. On the water side of Western Avenue, steam pipes line one side of the canal, which sweeps in a long curve toward School Street. The stone walls rise almost ten feet above the water. The canal builders fit stone on stone so tightly that no mortar was required. Soon the boat passed under a large rusty railroad bridge tattooed with vintage names and symbols. A popular but unsanctioned swimming spot, in high summer the tourists sometimes get a wave and a wisecrack from the local Olympians.

"How much did the mill workers earn?" Vezina wondered out loud. "$3.50 each week, of which $1.50 went to the corporation for room and board. Their take-home was $2.00."

When asked, "Who replaced the mill girls when they began to leave after the working conditions got worse and they protested to shorten the work day?" A girl about twelve years old replied, "The strong men from Ireland took jobs in the mills."

The ranger nodded and said a little more: "Whole Irish families worked in the mills—women and kids as young as six years old."

After passing under the Korean War Veterans Bridge at School Street and another canal bridge at Broadway, the captain speeded up to enter the Guard Locks complex. Ordinarily, this tour would move through the locks and proceed to the inlet where the Pawtucket Canal meets the Merrimack, but the river was too high and choppy due to the heavy rain. Instead, the passengers disembarked to see the legendary gate that has blocked flood waters from engulfing the core of the city twice since 1852.

The "flood gate," Great Gate, or "Francis Gate" was constructed in 1850. Chief Engineer of the Locks & Canals Company James B. Francis knew his river culture. Francis has another informal title: Chief of Police of Water. The Merrimack was known to flood approximately every seventy years. The Lowell industrial plant had been functioning since 1823 without a flood. The clock was ticking. Francis ordered the gate to be built and installed, a massive portcullis of stacked Georgia Pine timbers weighing twenty-one tons and fastened in place by a fist-sized iron shackle. Ridiculed at first as "Francis's Folly," the gate was twenty-seven feet tall and twenty-five feet wide. In an emergency, a worker was expected to shinny up the beam in the gatehouse and break the shackle. Witnesses said it took five seconds for the miniature timber dam to plunge down into its channels and seal the canal shut.

Learning about the
Great Gate or
"Francis Gate"
James Higgins

The winter of 1851–1852 was a season *horribilus* with forty snowstorms followed by record spring rainfall. Lakes in upper New Hampshire swelled, and the
river bulged like a python ingesting a husky mammal. Rain poured on April 18,
19, 20, and 21. At 3:00 a.m. on April 22, 1852, Francis ordered the flood gate to
be unleashed. The barrier held. The water receded, and there was no more talk of
"Francis's Folly" at Guard Locks. To reload the gate, workers removed the roof of the
gatehouse and used oxen to raise it to its ready position. Although Lowell suffered
severe flooding again in March 1936, residents agree that the damage would have
been worse if the gate had not been dropped that year. The high water dates are
marked on the gatehouse. Seventy years after 1936 came the Mother's Day Flood of
2006. A new gate had been designed: stackable steel beams that are modular and
more easily moved. The steel device was required again in 2007. The original gate is
now treated as an artifact.

It was time to get back into the boat and reverse course on the Pawtucket. Downstream past Broadway, there is another type of energy produced by a cogeneration
plant that uses two jet engines to create electricity with steam. Ranger Vezina talked
about pollution and the river, describing how the Merrimack River forty years ago

was a Class D waterway. People were warned not to swim or fish in it. Thanks in large part to the federally mandated cleanup since 1972, the river today is ranked as a Class B resource, which means people can swim in it, fish freely, and eat what they catch. Lowell has a large water treatment plant on Pawtucket Boulevard on the north bank of the river, which yields some of the highest quality and best-tasting water in the region.

Back at Swamp Locks, the captain barked, "Hands off the gunnel" (the edge of the boat), as he took the boat into one of the recently renovated lock chambers going south. Three lock tenders swung into action. They turned wheels to open the wicket gates, which are like doggie doors at the bottom of the large gate. Water streamed into the chamber. The boat lowered quickly. As the boat dropped there was an illusion that the walls were closing in. When water on both sides of the southernmost gate leveled off, then the doors opened. The boat nudged forward, going under another structure, moving toward the far gate, dropping more. Towering above was one of the vacant buildings in the Hamilton Canal District redevelopment zone, featuring an enormous banner that read "54,000 SF Available," with the development company's phone number. Through the gate, the boat motored toward the Industrial Canyon, a stretch of the Pawtucket lined with four- and six-story buildings, former mills, shoe factories, and other commercial structures. Vezina used this opportunity to talk about the preservation movement in Lowell and how the city's economy recovered from a trough in the 1970s in large part because real estate value

Lock tenders on the Pawtucket Canal
James Higgins

began to be extracted from the many damaged or abandoned buildings in the core of the city.

The Industrial Canyon was an invention of park planners. To create a memorable vista up and down the Pawtucket at Central Street, two single-story modern-era buildings, a furniture store and clothing shop, were purchased by the federal government. They were removed to reveal a signature industrial scene up-canal and the Lower Locks complex downstream, arguably the most visually impressive location in the historic district downtown.

The junction of the Pawtucket and Eastern canals and the final leg of the Concord River before it merges with the Merrimack speak to the ambition of the city-making gesture at Lowell. The convergence of waterways and two late-twentieth-century edifices marks this as the change-over-time place. In the 1790s, the Lower Locks was built as the southernmost of four locks on the Pawtucket Canal. The first known business was Frye's Tavern and stagecoach stop, the meeting place for mill agent Kirk Boott and Hugh Cummiskey in 1822, when they discussed hiring Irish immigrants for construction projects in the new factory town. Frye's was the victim of creative destruction as business improved and the old tavern made way for the redbrick American House hotel on Central Street, which served guests until the 1940s. As East Chelmsford, this area saw early industrial activity: small textile and grist mills, a machine shop, and stores dating from 1813. The second major mill complex in Lowell rose along the locks, the Middlesex Manufacturing Company, a woolen producer. On the north side of the canal was Prescott Mills for cotton fabric.

The Lower Locks today is home to the Lowell campus of Middlesex Community College (MCC)—a second campus is in Bedford, Massachusetts. At this spot, MCC

The Industrial Canyon
James Higgins

Lower Locks complex, before redevelopment, c. 1980
James Higgins

Lower Locks complex, after redevelopment, c. 2010
James Higgins

acquired the former international training center for Wang Laboratories, now a multistory hexagonal brick academic building, as well as an early-twentieth-century post office (later a federal office building), across Merrimack Street. On the west embankment at Lower Locks is the UMass–Lowell Inn & Conference Center (ICC), constructed as a Hilton Hotel in 1986 and sold to the university in 2008. The ICC houses 500 students and offers guest rooms year-round. It has become a hub of social, educational, and cultural activity, hosting major conferences and public events. Here the tour ended, and Vezina summed up: "Not everyone thinks of urban places when they hear the words 'national park,' but Lowell has something in common with natural wonders like Cape Cod Seashore and the Great Smoky Mountains. Our history is the wonder."

MILL WORK

"I started in the Merrimack mills when I was 15. . . . I married when I was 20. . . . [My husband George and I] both worked and struggled and helped the children whenever we could. We started at six and we had two shifts. . . . My boys got the G.I. bill, and my daughter graduated from state teachers' college and was a school teacher. I have a boy who is a scientist and worked at the Department of the Interior in Washington. He has a Ph.D. from Georgetown.

—*Mabel Delehanty Mangan* (b. 1901), spinner, Lowell millworker for 50 years[20]

As a visitor enters the Boott Cotton Mills Museum through the nondescript wooden door of the stair tower in Boott Mill No. 6, the space feels like an airlock between the mill yard outside and whatever is on the other side of the door leading into the factory. A lot is going on in this space. The white-painted stairwell takes the visitor's eye up five floors, the worn metal-capped treads stamped with "Boott Cotton Mills" and spiraling up around an oval opening reminiscent of a cross-sectioned chambered nautilus. One doesn't expect this moment of beauty in a factory.

The swirly attraction was too appealing to resist for twelve-year-old Lizzie M. Ryan in 1869, when she tried to ride the banister down and landed senseless at the bottom, having crashed through a lower railing. A local newspaper chastised her and her nameless coworkers for playing on the property even as the report described her condition as possibly fatal. This was a whole different sort of industrial accident.

Affixed to the side of the staircase is a poem by George Chapman from 1938, a newspaper poem in the days when newspapers printed poems. Chapman was one of the *Alentour* poets associated with the contemporary poetry magazine published in the city from 1935 to 1943. He writes that the workers are "one with the mills"—"one with the travail of labor, the honors of the trade." He describes the dust, the steam, the stench, "the shuttles' thunder" behind the gates that swallow workers who are "buoyant as the dawn" and "heavy as the night."[21]

The poem is displayed under a sign that reads Regulations of the Middlesex Company, July 1840; turning around in the stair tower, one sees on the wall a Notice from the Boott Cotton Mills agent Linus Childs, from July 1852, which sternly warns that "no one, on any account, shall bring within the Yard or into any Building any Lucifer or Friction Matches, Pipes or Cigars."[22] Boott Mill No. 6 was built between 1871 and 1873, creating a third line of mills in the complex, whose earliest foundation stones were laid in 1835. There were 950 women and 120 men at the Boott when the first cloth was produced, a plain and coarse fabric with which the owners hoped to dominate a segment of the textile market—and which they accomplished for several decades.

The Boott's numbers are high: 155,000 yards of cloth each week in 1840; 2,400 looms operating in 1868; 450,000 yards weekly by 1905; 3,500 looms in 1910. There were more than 200 types of jobs in the mill in 1910—hoop man, doffer, yarn girl, trucker, wheel and dynamo oiler, harness mender, night fireman, burler, blacksmith, piper helper, creeler, spindle setter, draftsman, runner, and warper-tender. The mill has its own culture, the job names as peculiar as those on a ship. In fact, the mill can feel like a ship, a five-story, redbrick, hard-edged container with power generated down below and transferred upward, the whole operation a complex fitting together of equipment and workers concentrated on the output of a tangible object that can be used and sold. Cloth.

A word to the uninitiated: in the industry the word "textile" is pronounced "tek-stul," not "tek-style," which is often the way the word is said in Lowell. The late John Goodwin, Lowell native, Lowell Historical Society stalwart, and engineering professor at UMass–Lowell for decades,

Loom operator in the Weave Room
James Higgins

could always be counted on to kindly correct the parvenu on the industrial history scene.

The scale of the operation impresses the observer. This is a place of mass volume and multiples of component parts. Black-and-white photographs on the staircase leading to the second floor of the exhibit share a motif: posed workers and views of machines in ranks and thread spools in rows. The operation is about the efficiency of sameness. The mills are almost carbon copies, the windows repeating in their regularity, suggesting simplicity but also a comment on the interchangeability of parts. The goal is to be practical and productive. The fire buckets are red and spaced

WALK THIS WAY: A CANAL HIKE, 2010

The two hikers set out on a pure blue near-spring morning for a Sunday walk that would loosely trace the rough-cut of a stretch of walkway along the midsection of the Pawtucket Canal. Starting on Jackson Street near the commercial core of the city, they traversed the Hamilton Canal District, where large-scale construction would start in six or eight months. There's a mini-industrial canyon vista up the Hamilton Canal with two remaining suspended walkways over the water. The area was quiet at 8:00 a.m.—the Charter School on Jackson not in session and upper-story residents sleeping in. Photographer Jim Higgins calls this area the "last frontier" of Lowell's mill-scape. Once redevelopment begins, changes will be swift and dramatic. The plan calls for extensive preservation and adaptive reuse, and even the protection of some factory ruins as architectural evidence of the scale of production. These are the early mills: Hamilton Manufacturing Company (1825), Appleton Company (1828).

The companions walked west over the Louis Lord Overpass and crossed the invisible line between the Acre and the Lower Highlands neighborhoods. The sidewalk overlooks a subterranean section of Middlesex Street. Of note is the Nobis Engineering building, a historic rehab of the former Davis & Sargent Lumber Company, which is being certified by the U.S. Green Building Council as a Leadership in Energy and Environmental Design or LEED project. The side closest to the Boys and Girls Club is clad in corrugated metal that complements the cleaned-up brick and stone exterior of the original structure. The property backs up to what will be the Canalway path on the upper Pawtucket Canal. Birds sang loudly in the trees. Kenny's Cleaners, a leather and suede specialist, occupies the adjacent brick building whose weathered green window bays jut out, flanking a stone archway above the door. Behind the club is a back lot of jungle-thick twisted thickets and branches that could hide any kind of wildlife.

The walkers popped out on the side of the club, opposite Palin Plaza with its Asian building accents and commercial cluster (Angkor Wat Realty, New Palin Jewelry, White Rose Restaurant, H & R Block, etc.). Clemente Park across the street is one of the most active parks in the city: basketball, skateboarding, volleyball, swings. Tom Clark wrote a poem about the baseball legend Roberto Clemente of the Pittsburgh Pirates that recalls the ballplayer's death in a plane crash at sea (near the so-called Bermuda Triangle) while on his way to deliver disaster relief supplies to earthquake victims in Nicaragua in 1972. The Puerto Rican native was renowned for his charity. Clark's poem, called "The Great One" concludes:

> No matter how many times
> Manny Sanguillen dove for your body
> the sun kept going down
> on his inability to find it
>
> I just hope those Martians realize
> they are claiming the rights to
> far and away the greatest rightfielder
> of all time.[1]

---

1. Tom Clark, *Fan Poems* (Plainfield, VT: North Atlantic Books, 1976).

The Pawtucket Canal curves broadly around Western Avenue on the other side. In the early days of the park, tourists in the canal boats swinging up this way would often get waves from the workers in the Joan Fabrics plant when the windows were open. Hundreds of artists now work in studios in the vast industrial structure.

Past Clemente Park, the travelers slid down a side street, Saunders, which dead-ends at the canal—there is an old taxi barn for Yellow Cabs—and proceeded on Payne Street. Here, it looks like Lowell might be the auto-body-repair-shop capital of the northeast—Le's, Vo's, M & R, and James Trinity bunched up. At the corner is School Street Light Truck Parts with a neat, compact operation. Truck cabs and rear ends are stacked three high just like the shelves of boats at a marina. A green canopy shields a row of tires. On the next building are signs for car accident repair and a chiropractor—one-stop shopping. They turned north and cross the Korean War Veterans Bridge, passing through the National Grid complex behind the Stoklosa School. Gone from the complex are the reddish-brown behemoth gas storage tanks of the Lowell Gas Company that some people used to eye warily.

The walkers wound their way back up Willie and Franklin streets, noting two small stone houses on either side of a wooden house with a roof detail that reads "1902." They picked their way back to a recently completed section of the Canalway along the Western Canal at Suffolk Street, all shiny railings and smooth pavement, behind the American Textile History Museum, and then crossed Dutton Street to the Swamp Locks and their starting point. The mid-March ice had not given up its hold on the Merrimack Canal, where a beat-up blue rowboat was trapped against the canal wall.

evenly between the windows in the weave room exhibit with its eighty-eight looms (a fully operating weave room at the Boott had about 100 looms).

The profuse list of jobs cited above contrasts sharply with textile manufacturing operations today. Examining American competitiveness and factory culture in the twenty-first century, Adam Davidson wrote, "There's a joke in cotton country [in South Carolina] that a modern textile mill employs only a man and a dog. The man is there to feed the dog, and the dog is there to keep the man away from the machines." The textile companies that shed Lowell for more lucrative financial circumstances in the South had about an eighty-year run in places like South Carolina. "Hundreds of mills here once spun raw cotton into thread and then wove and knit the thread into clothes and textiles," Davidson wrote.[23]

But the North American Free Trade Agreement and relaxation of trade relations with China changed everything. Labor-intensive operations were cheaper to operate overseas and across the Rio Grande River in Mexico. Segments of the industry in the United States concentrate on specialized materials that come out of factories with computer brains and robotic arms. With all the macroeconomic changes, however, America still holds first or second place in global manufacturing. Increasingly, however, a manufacturing job that pays well requires technical skills that must be gained through classroom and hands-on education or an apprenticeship. There is less opportunity for walk-ons with minimal ability.

Wu Chunming was a "factory girl" in 1990s China, a seventeen-year old villager who went to the city, in her case Dongguan, like the Yankee farmers' daughters from New Hampshire and Vermont who found their way to the Spindle City in the mill rush after 1820. She worked in a toy-making plant, but others like her were textile mill girls. Her diary from 1994 reads like a document from the "Mill Girls" museum exhibit in a reconstructed boarding house across the canal from the Boot Cotton Mills Museum.

> We start work at seven in the morning and get off work at nine at night. Afterward we shower and wash our clothes. At around ten, those with money go out for midnight snacks and those without money go to sleep. We sleep until 6:30 in the morning. . . . Those who want breakfast use ten minutes to eat, but I have seen many people not eat. . . . I certainly would not ignore my health for the sake of thinness or saving money. After all, what is the point of doing migrant work? Can it be that it is just to earn this bit of money?[24]

The Lowell mill girls or factory operatives usually stayed for about three years before choosing other paths. They came to Lowell hopeful about the opportunity, and willing to work and live by the company rules—up to a point. More than twenty years into the Lowell venture, in 1846, 4,000 workers, many of them young women, joined the fight to reduce the work day from twelve and fourteen hours to

Entrance to the Mill Girls exhibit

James Higgins

ten hours. The corporations prevailed, however, and that fight was not won until 1874. These facts and others are presented in the "Mill Girls" exhibit, a re-created 1840s-era section of a boarding house on two levels. Downstairs is a dining room and kitchen, upstairs a bedroom with lighting and audio components that allow visitors to eavesdrop on imagined young women during quiet time.

Adjoining the "Mill Girls" area and following somewhat chronologically in the social history of the city is a section of the museum exhibit about the immigrant experience in Lowell. In an impressionistic fashion, the social history of people from dozens of ethnic groups is told through the use of photographs, videos, and artifacts. The exhibit makers sought to answer four questions about the individuals and families who settled in the city: Who came to Lowell? Why did they come here? How were they changed by Lowell, and how did they, in turn, change the city? On a two-level wall in large letters is the wording from the public law creating the Lowell park that cites the existence of a distinctive urban culture in the neighborhoods of Lowell, the social manifestation of multi-ethnicity. The opposite wall is filled with names taken from Lowell City Directories, mapping the process of population change. A banner from a Franco-American church, a Spanish-language pamphlet, political campaign materials for a Greek American, a video about Cambodian refugees starting over in Lowell, an Irish American store sign—pieces of material culture fit together to make a city story.

Outside in the Boott Mills yard, passersby hear the one-two, one-two, one-two of the banging shuttles; inside the noise is assaulting even with about ten looms in action. Cushioned by earplugs, visitors keep to the safety of the railed-off aisle and look over the Draper Model E. looms that were brought to Lowell for the exhibit from Tennessee to demonstrate the technology in action and to produce plain weave and herringbone cloth. The effect is like being underwater while somebody is shouting at you.

Throughout the museum the voices of past workers make a chorus of commentary. They appreciate the employment, complain about conditions, and are resigned to the limited local opportunities. In text and on tape they bring alive the day-to-day drama of mill work—both stultifying and rewarding—a path to a paycheck that allowed for a home, a family, and some measure of independence.

On the second floor of the Boott museum the visitor finds an in-depth presentation of the American industrial experience seen through the filter of the textile industry. The merchants took Alexander Hamilton's side in the debate about manufacturing vs. farming that challenged Thomas Jefferson's agrarian vision for democracy. The innovative bale-to-bolt integrated production process is illustrated wonderfully in a substantial see-through mill model. Videos loaded with point-and-counterpoint views allow for choosing sides in disputes between management and labor. Peak business success is evidenced in displays of colorful fabrics, machinery inventions, and marketing materials. There's a busy-ness to the second floor that conveys a sense of prosperity even as the industrial edges begin to fray when competition heats up and technology improves. The story winds down with a litany of mill companies that were shuttered or sold or moved away between 1899 and 1954. The narrative thins further and attempts to set the Lowell experience in a global context before it swings upward with the news that the city found a future in its past.

For ten years Mike Wurm helped plan the exhibits at the Boott Cotton Mills Museum and Mogan Cultural Center. Reflecting on the Boott Cotton Mills exhibition, he said,

The faces and voices of the workers eventually brought the exhibit alive, and proved to be the most moving and memorable elements, especially the "Decline" video in which workers talked about one mill after the other being shut down or moving south as they hung on barely in the twentieth-century hard times in Lowell. . . . It is rather amusing and satisfying both to think that Lowell has the only working factory in the National Park Service, the restored weave room, and that people have to visit our museum to learn about what it was like to work in a factory, when not that long ago, that was the predominant experience for people in Lowell and America.[25]

Bob Weible is state historian for New York. He was the historian at Lowell National Historical Park when the Boott exhibition was conceived but before it was installed. Noting that the museum exhibit received the Dibner Award for Excellence from the Society for the History of Technology, Weible pointed out that there were critics of the original closing section of the exhibit. Instead of a hard-hitting wrap-up that connected the textile industry experience with turmoil in the high-tech sector in the early 1990s, especially in Massachusetts, the final segment took an upbeat look at economic prospects in the city at the moment. The ending was rethought in the mid-2000s and replaced with a display referencing the city's revival and posing questions about the interconnected global economy and sustainable urban living.
All in all, the National Park Service saw the project as a success by 1994.

Visitation was good. The press remained supportive. The agency could take credit for interpreting industrial history. And even those insiders who still regarded Lowell's history as only marginally significant recognized that the park's management structure was viable and could be replicated elsewhere. New parks, such as Martin Luther King National Historic Site in Georgia and Women's Rights National Historical Park in New York, addressed socially relevant themes while promoting economic development—as did a number of politically popular heritage parks.[26]

THE CITY AS A CLASSROOM

"It is time that we had uncommon schools, that we did not leave off our education when we begin to be men and women. It is time that villages were universities. . . ."

—Henry David Thoreau, from "Reading" in *Walden* (1854)

Michael Southworth needed a place to test his nascent ideas about "an integrated urban education network comparable to a traditional national park."[27] He was a doctoral student at the Massachusetts Institute of Technology in the mid-1960s, studying urban design and planning with Kevin Lynch. Southworth was exploring the possibilities of what he called "the educative city," an innovative concept that flowed from his research on "the communications functions of the built and natural environment." He approached Boston Children's Museum director Mike Spock, who it turned out was not in a position to launch an initiative of this kind. Spock advised him to go to Lowell and speak to Pat Mogan, who was investigating alternative methods of teaching and learning. He did.

I vividly recall my first visit to Lowell, arriving by train from North Station in Boston on a bleak winter day just before Christmas 1967—a Dickensian experience with all of the

MOULIN ROUGE

Moulin rouge means "red mill." A visitor to the Montmartre district of Paris in 1889 would have seen a four-story red windmill incongruously standing between two commercial buildings in an area that was a magnet for the "creative class" of the day. The spirited "red mill" cabaret synonymous with "can-can" dancers and painter Toulouse-Lautrec is a cultural galaxy away from the iconic red mills of Lowell. But a mill is a mill is a mill, to borrow from Gertrude Stein—or is it?

What a simple word, almost too short to notice and soft when pronounced: *mill.* Yet this is the basic fact of the city named Lowell. Mill is an old word, Old English "mylen" and before that Latin "millesimum." From the same root come the words mild, melt, mold, meld, maul, milt, mull, malt, and mulch. It is a verb and a noun, the action word giving rise to the thing we call "mill," a combination of process and place having to do with grinding—and then making, manufacturing. The meaning circles back to the red mill in Paris, not an actual windmill but pretending to be for the village aura of Montmartre. The original windmills had wind-spun, tower-mounted crossed blades (or sails) whose rotation turned a grain-grinding wheel inside to make "meal" (sounds like "mill") or coarse baking flour. Any operation driven by a turning wheel, whether driven by wind or water, took on the mill name. Sawmills cut huge logs into boards. Later, mill was applied to a place of production in general, such as a steel mill. The Lowell mills carried the wheel-driven-production meaning at first and later stood for the broader meaning: place of manufacture or factory. The Lowell mills stretched along the edge of the Merrimack for about a mile and dispersed slightly inland on a spider web of canals. If a rider was approaching Monument Valley National Monument in Utah and saw the red sandstone buttes, some of which are blocky, resembling buildings, and others attenuated like spires and towers, the rider would not automatically think of the nineteenth-century redbrick mills of Lowell. But if later two panorama views of the scenes were compared, the similarity would be striking: the saturated magnesium-oxide color, boxy shapes punctuated by tapered uprights, and fortress-like objects lined up across the landscape.

nearly abandoned mills. Pat was immediately excited by the ideas I had sketched and wanted to try them in Lowell.

In the 1960s, many school systems were experimenting with ways of making learning more engaging for children, and some were taking learning into the city. A prime example was the Parkway program in Philadelphia, but there were others. John Dewey, in an earlier era, was doing similar things around the country; in fact, Kevin Lynch had gone to a Dewey elementary school in the 1920s. My focus was on how the city might be designed to promote learning and development, while these programs were focused more on the classroom experience. When I met Pat Mogan, he was looking for ways of taking learning out of the school and into the city, so it was a perfect fit with my urban design interests at the time.[28]

Southworth and his wife, Susan, also an urban designer, were two of the many daring thinkers whom Mogan and his local collaborators invited to the city to help shape a vision for a new community that would emerge from the postindustrial crust. Southworth is now a professor of urban design and planning in the departments of City and Regional Planning and Landscape Architecture and Environmental Planning at the University of California–Berkeley. He said:

> Lowell would never have become an urban national park if it had not been for Pat Mogan. He was the coordinator, supporter, and glue over so many years to bring the idea to fruition. My involvement was at the beginning, but Pat converted all the skeptics who were intent on demolishing the mills and burying the canals in the rubble to provide parking lots. He was a magician at getting funding for Lowell from every conceivable source![29]

The park idea found its staunchest early advocates among teachers. Local educators were motivated by a desire to provide more meaningful and effective ways to foster learning among the young people of Lowell. Pat Mogan was fond of saying, "You'll find a lot of instruction in classrooms, but not a lot of learning."[30] He and others were convinced that an alternative setting was needed for education. They were talking about these ideas in the middle and late 1960s. Another word that was in the air in those days was "environment." Mostly, the word was used in relation to thoughts about nature and ecology, but it was sometimes used interchangeably with the notion of "place." Environment typically meant a place in a natural state. Mogan, Sister Lillian, Peter Stamas, Angelike Georgalos, and others in the Model Cities Education Component imagined the advantages of teaching in an alternative classroom, even an outdoor classroom—a classroom in the environment. They made a conceptual leap to the 1,140-acre state forest on the north bank of the Merrimack, the Lowell-Dracut-Tyngsboro State Forest. Planning began for an environmental classroom in the woods. Grants were sought and received. Stamas made a further associational leap: "We were talking about learning and the environment, and we said, 'Well, why does the environment have to be in the forest? Why can't the environment be right here in the city? Why can't the 'park' be in the city?'"[31]

Once the thinking came around to using the city as a classroom, pieces of the planning puzzle began to fit together. The idea of a city-scale lifelong learning laboratory gained momentum. The pedagogical method was to be experiential education—what has come to be called "hands-on learning." A critical step in imagining the shape of this city-scale learning experience was the hiring of the Southworths by the Model Cities education group. The big ideas came together in a manifesto printed as a colorful illustrated poster:

> The Lowell Discovery Network provides a continuous regional open space centered on the historic canal system, with continuous bicycle and pedestrian paths [including] a network of discovery centers at historic and industrial sites designed to communicate through direct experience the organization of the city and its history, industrial processes, and operation of the canal system. These centers are an extension of the school, an alternative to the school. The city discovery transit experiment will connect tourists and residents with learning centers and other points of interest.
>
> The Center for Human Development will provide a neutral ground which allows self-renewal through planning, programming, research, implementation, and evaluation. The human resources for learning will be utilized in a non-school setting; the Greek native who did herding in Greece or the old retired mill worker will share their experiences with students.[32]

Quoting from a report by the Education Facilities Laboratories about the pioneering urban education initiative in Lowell, the Southworths grew more expansive:

Lowell intends to turn this old industrial city into a huge human development center, a great educational complex which will cover everything from the school of expectant mothers and infant education through postgraduate college studies. The plan will provide a series of paths crisscrossing and furnished with all manner of informational settings, primarily related to the history of Lowell.

Outdoor digs and neighborhood museums, furnished with relics of Lowell's origins and past, will dot the landscape; an old mill will be converted into instructional centers, relating to the old and new industries in Lowell, as well as into workshops for every phase of learning. It is a project which will use found (old) space rather than building from scratch. It will use all the resources of the city: churches, historical architecture, railyards and factories, even its old jail, for a kind of total education of its citizens.[33]

The poster features fifteen detailed and annotated drawings of proposed discovery centers. The Water Discovery Center at a canal gatehouse would have a "water sculpture displaying hydro-dynamic principles" and an operational model of a dam with controls to be manipulated by observers. The Treetop Walk would take people through the upper canopy of the forest via an elevated walkway; along the way would be enlarged models of leaves and tree trunk cross sections for examination. See-through underground displays would reveal root structures and soil layers. The walkway culminated in a platform with telescopes to view the city and surrounding land. Planners called for a Mill Discovery Center with a working textile manufacturing operation and machine museum in the mill yard. There would be two large outdoor dioramas: one of the city street grid and the other of the canal system (fully functional). On the streets, people would find Urban Information Devices that allowed them to see inside various buildings to better understand the everyday business of the city. Platforms in certain spots would let people view a printer or a candle-maker at work. Like reverse drainpipes, periscopes affixed to buildings of cooperating companies would enable a person on the sidewalk to see activity on upper floors. The Migration Map was a mural on a side of an ethnic social club tracing migration routes, with dates of major waves of immigration.

The Lowell Discovery Network design was circulated internationally by the Southworths and others after being presented in Lowell. In 1972, the concept won the City Design Award from the Associazione per Il Disegno Industriale in Milan, Italy; the next year the Southworths received the Progressive Architecture Urban Design Award. The *New York Times, Boston Globe, Washington Post*, and European newspapers reported on this next new thing proposed for Lowell: an urban cultural park.

The cornucopia of ideas was almost overwhelming. Charles Nikitopoulos came to Lowell as a boy from Greece. The longtime professor of Community Social Psychology at UMass–Lowell remembers meeting Mogan around 1971, when Nikitopoulos was between work and had been directed by a friend to the Model Cities Program based in the Acre neighborhood. He listened to Mogan for about forty minutes, hearing about the grand plan for making over Lowell into an urban laboratory for learning. Mogan's advice for his visitor was to contact the staff at the Solomon Mental Health Center in Lowell, which eventually would be pulled in to the Mogan orbit as one of the many service organizations arrayed to assist in the schema designed to promote the community's well-being. Nikitopoulos used Greek mythology to make a point about Mogan.

I am sure that he infected me and much of my work at the University. In the same way that Zeus, the god of the sky, sneezed the clouds into existence, Mogan back then not only sneezed the droplets of myriad ideas that are still animating life in the city, but he also sneezed out a hundred Moganites who are still infecting the way people think.

Later, in the 1980s, I was chair of the Lowell Cooperative Learning Center, a kind of "free school." Pat had agreed to teach a course on the Educative City, but only seven people signed up. I told him he didn't have to go forward with the class, but he protested: "These seven people each know several other people, and if I can convert seven at a time, then I will eventually get my message across to enough people to make a difference."[34]

"THE EVERYWHERE SCHOOL"

In tandem with the macro version of an urban cultural park that Mogan and company were promoting, there was a more specific proposal for a new type of school in Lowell that was working its way through the state and local approval processes. In 1967, the Massachusetts legislature enacted a law that called for the establishment of three experimental schools. The Lowell Mayor's Committee on Model Cities, formed early that year to respond to the new federal program, had education as one of its interest areas, with Mogan leading the effort. Using Model Cities planning money from the U.S. Department of Housing and Urban Development (HUD), Mogan's subcommittee focused on developing a proposal for an experimental school to be called the Center for Human Development (CHD).

What exactly was the CHD? John E. Roche in 1979 prepared a thesis on the CHD as a student at the Boston Architectural Center. In the opening pages he described the vision:

> The Center for Human Development will be physically expressed as a facility in which various purveyors of education, health, mental health, and rehabilitation are brought together to stimulate motivation and development by recognition of Lowell's past virtues and present opportunities. In the process, by restoring and recycling historic buildings, specifically mills, we will stimulate an appreciation for Lowell's past, present, and future heritage in the form of an educational process serving all ages. The people want this facility to symbolize the revitalization of an old city.[35]

In 1974, in his own doctoral dissertation, Mogan wrote:

> The school envisioned must be more than a physical facility in order to accommodate the non-traditional syllabus for an education. The program and the facilities should contribute substantially toward providing students and local citizens with the opportunity to pursue individual goals through their own initiative, to participate meaningfully in community affairs.[36]

In 1972, the state education leaders endorsed the CHD blueprint and recommended it receive funding as one of its three experimental schools, under the name of "The Everywhere School." Architectural plans were prepared for the CHD, and the acting commissioner of education Thomas Curtin recommended $469,000 for its development in Lowell, but the governor and a new education commissioner failed to support the appropriation.

In July 1973, the Lowell advocates were told to seek funding elsewhere for the CHD. Mogan and his colleagues never abandoned the core thinking that informed the CHD plan. Two years before, he and his supporters had established a nonprofit organization, Human Services Corporation, which ultimately implemented many of the programmatic goals of the CHD—in a sense standing in for the CHD without a big box building for delivery of integrated assistance to families and individuals. The holistic approach to learning, well-being, and productivity, be it for one person or the community as a living organism, gave the city a new way of thinking about itself. This was an essential part of finding a new purpose for Lowell, a purpose defined by Lowellians themselves and not imposed from the outside; this way of thinking transcended the mentality that Lowell was nothing but a factory town, an intricate manufacturing device that yielded the most benefits for external investors.

TSONGAS INDUSTRIAL HISTORY (AND SCIENCE) CENTER

Director Sheila Kirschbaum of UMass–Lowell said flatly that no other national park in the country has been able to develop an educational program like the Tsongas Industrial History Center. Since 1991, this collaboration among the park, UMass–Lowell, and Lowell School Department has seen more than one million students and teachers participate in its innovative hands-on, place-based learning and teacher development programs. Reaching students from grade three to graduate school, the center has been studied by educators throughout the United States and from abroad. While "history" is in the official name, the TIHC promotes interdisciplinary education, connecting science and engineering to literature and history. As much as any other organization in Lowell and the park, the Tsongas Industrial History Center embodies the concept of the city as a classroom. Kirschbaum elaborated:

> In other parks, you will not see such a dependable partner for the park as we have in UMass–Lowell. There aren't educational programs in which the students are guided all day. They don't have the personalized learning that we offer here—and you won't see dedicated facilities like the one we have at the Boott museum, not to mention our access to other park sites and the UMass–Lowell Bellegarde Boathouse on the Merrimack.
>
> We are a model for the National Park Service. Staff from parks across the country shadow Tsongas Center staff members to learn our methods. We're especially active among parks in the Northeast.[37]

UMass–Lowell faculty members are more involved than ever. Working with park interpretive staffers in 2011, the TIHC helped organize park visits for 1,300 first-year university students. A new course called "Lowell as Text" and the Honors Program's "Text in the City" provide entrees to the heritage resources. A $3 million National Science Foundation grant for a Science of Rivers project allowed the TIHC to add digital water-quality testing to its longtime River as a Classroom program. Professors Fred Martin of Computer Science and Michelle Scribner-MacLean of the Graduate School of Education teamed with center personnel on the project. Professors David Kazmer of the Engineering College and Michelle Scribner-MacLean of the Graduate School of Education have used the resources of the center with UMass–Lowell undergraduate students in the UTeach program. Developed at the

Sheila Kirschbaum
Kevin Harkins

University of Texas–Austin, and being replicated nationwide, UTeach prepares STEM (science, technology, engineering, and mathematics) majors to become middle school or high school teachers. UMass–Lowell's UTeach undergraduates used the center's workshop spaces to plan and then teach a project-based instructional unit to Greater Lowell Technical High School students, central to which was the fieldwork at the TIHC.

The university's involvement with the center dates from before the official beginning. Educator Don Pierson was recruited in 1984 to coordinate a community-based study of the city's public schools that was being led by Mario D. Fantini, Dean of the School of Education at the University of Massachusetts–Amherst; M. Virginia Biggy, Dean of the College of Education at the then-University of Lowell; and Robert I. Sperber, special assistant to the president and professor of education at Boston University. Paul Tsongas had asked these three to guide the project and tapped the business community through the Lowell Plan, Inc., and City Hall for $150,000 to pay for it. Pierson would later become Dean of UMass–Lowell's Graduate School of Education and the vice provost for graduate programs.

Pierson knew about the stirrings of school reform in Lowell. In the 1970s, Pat Mogan and George Tsapatsaris of the Lowell School Department had visited him in Brookline, Massachusetts, near Boston, where he was an elementary school principal. Pierson and Sperber had been researching the benefits of school-based early childhood education, and the Lowell administrators were looking for models.

The overall goal of the project was to establish a process through which resources across the city would be brought to bear on achieving educational excellence. The project was called the Lowell Model for Educational Excellence, and it was not welcomed by the majority of the school committee and many administrators in the central office of the school department, including Superintendent Henry Mroz. The major recommendations urged continuous curricular improvement, a more open public process for the selection of school principals, and a higher level of involvement by parents and others in the community. In response, for its part the university established a Center for Field Studies and Services attached to the master's program in education that provides research and resources to support educational improvement in Lowell schools as well as those in districts around Massachusetts.

Brian Martin was a young mayor when the Lowell Model for Educational Excellence was released. He has public education in his blood. His mother, Katherine Martin, was a teacher who had served on the school committee, been an assistant superintendent to Superintendent Mogan, and pushed for reform in the system. A baseball star at Lowell High and UMass–Amherst, Brian Martin taught in the regional technical high school before jumping into politics himself in 1981, running for City Council. In Lowell's Plan E form of municipal government, the mayor chairs the school committee as an additional responsibility. Martin in early 1985 put the recommendations of the Lowell Model on the school committee agenda meeting after meeting and consistently had the same outcome, 6-1, with his vote the only Yes. The dynamic changed when the recommendation to open up the hiring process for school administrators came before the committee. The public took notice and signaled support. Momentum shifted, and Martin credits much of today's success in the school system to the improved process for selecting principals.

In the 1986–1987 school year, administrators were registering 100 new children each week, most of them from Cambodian refugee families. "We were placing them wherever we could, whether in spare areas in the schools or rented community spaces," George Tsapatsaris said.[38] He was in the school department's central office at the time. The problem was that the Asian students, especially, were being grouped in locations that were isolating them from the broad school population. The result was legal action by parents of Asian and Latino students, which resulted in a desegregation plan that was driven by a citywide school assignment process that is still in effect today. The voluntary desegregation plan was shaped by Tsapatsaris, then-Mayor Richard P. Howe, city solicitor Thomas Sweeney, and bilingual education coordinator Anne O'Donnell in consultation with attorneys, parents, and the federal court officials. Today, 56 percent of the students in the public schools are from minority racial groups.

In the early 1990s, Lowell rebuilt its school infrastructure thanks to a 90 percent reimbursement program offered by the state. Lowell went to that well more often than any city in the state. New facilities, such as the $40 million renovation of the high school, plus the state's Education Reform initiative with funding linked to student performance, enhanced the entire learning experience. In the late 1980s, 50 percent of Lowell's school buildings were pre–World War II vintage, and a number of them were nineteenth-century structures, such as the Coburn School that was built in 1848, during the presidency of James Polk. Lowell built or renovated twenty schools, a $300 million investment in education that cost the citizens of Lowell $30 million. Former School Superintendent Tsapatsaris coordinated much of the renewal, working closely with then-City Manager James Campbell. "We modernized buildings, generated enthusiasm, and unified the school system," the former superintendent said.[39] Better relations with the business community, a city-wide parent organization, and ramped-up involvement by the university all flowed from the tough work on the Lowell Model.

When Sandy Walter was named park superintendent in 1984, she called Pierson to talk about her ideas for education programs at the Boott Mills Museum. "We have the building, but we don't have the expertise," Pierson remembers her saying. Walter wanted to collaborate with the university and the local schools. If the Lowell Model for Educational Excellence was going to work, the park would have to be a key component. "Sandy was a bundle of energy and enthusiasm and very entrepreneurial," he said.[40]

A critical step in the development of the Tsongas Industrial History Center was a 1986 study trip to San Francisco taken by a couple of dozen Lowell movers and shakers, organized by the park and Lowell Historic Preservation Commission. The itinerary featured a visit to the highly regarded Exploratorium, an innovative science and technology center that had been created at the old Palace of the Arts. Many of the exhibits are interactive, encouraging people of all ages to get their hands on scientific and engineering principles. At the time the various displays included a label headlined "What's Going on Here?"—followed by a brief explanation free of scientific jargon. Walter had worked at Golden Gate National Recreation Area (GGNRA), which was known for its aggressive approach to partnerships. The Lowell group also visited the Headlands Institute on the Sausalito side of the bay, a nonprofit environmental education organization that uses old military facilities managed by GGNRA. As well, Walter, Pierson, and state Representative Susan Rourke of Lowell went to Colonial Williamsburg in Virginia to see the role-playing approach used there for presenting and teaching history. Old Sturbridge Village in Massachusetts was known to them, another site with costumed staff in period settings. Sturbridge's director of educational programs, Peter O'Connell, helped shape some of the early thinking for the center and later served many years as the TIHC director. Representative Rourke and state Senator Paul Sheehy proved to be key allies early on when Lowell's legislative delegation was able to secure state funding for the center for many years through the university budget.

With the center's first director, Ed Pershey, the tone was set for hands-on learning. The concept rhymed with Mogan's views about education outside the classroom. Teachers were afforded an opportunity to break out of the fifty-minute lecture class format and would prepare students for the site visits. Pershey talked about "doing history" in the same way that teachers talk about "doing math." What sets Lowell apart, Pierson said, is that the students don't simply walk around and have

Learning how to weave
James Higgins

experiences. "In Lowell you spend an hour *doing* something. The young people get emotionally involved in programs like Workers on the Line when they find themselves confronting labor conditions."

Every student in the Lowell public schools visits the center in grades 3, 4, 5, 8, and 11. There are more than 13,500 students in the system. Also, the center's staff members visit students in grades 3 and 8 in some schools. This is an extraordinary extension of the learning experience for these young people. Consider how enmeshed in the story of the city the typical student is by the time she or he graduates from high school.

Yellow buses stop at the top of Boarding House Park just before 9:30 a.m. each school day from September through June. The passengers step out at this focal point of LNHP. The roster of hometowns is not dissimilar from the towns and cities from which industrial Lowell drew its early workforce: eighth graders from Goffstown, New Hampshire, registered for the Power to Production workshop; fifth and sixth graders from Townshend, Vermont, for Engineer It!; third graders from Lawrence, Massachusetts, for Change in the Making; a group of homeschoolers from Portsmouth, Rhode Island, who will do the Bale to Bolt workshop; classes from Dedham, Massachusetts, headed for Yankees and Immigrants; three groups of eighth graders from Merrimack, New Hampshire, the town where most of Lowell's red bricks were made in the nineteenth century; and six homeroom classes of eighth graders from the Kathryn B. Stoklosa School in Lowell, whose students will fan out into two different workshops—Bale to Bolt and Power to Production.

Paul Levasseur, tall, lean, and gray-haired, is on his toes watching for the first buses of the day. He is one of twelve museum educators—part-time teachers and one ranger who will guide more than 150 students through the Tsongas Industrial History Center programs on the last day of April. Each teacher carries a plastic clipboard emblazoned on the back with the center's logo. The sky is pure blue, playing off the dominant redbrick scene on French Street. In sight are a reconstructed 1840s mill workers' boarding house on Levasseur's right; the old trade high school, now Lowell High School Freshman Academy, in front of him, next to the park headquarters in a mill agents' house; and behind him the rosy sunlit façade of the Boott Cotton Mills. A green-uniformed staffer is mowing the grass at the outdoor performance park, base camp for the Lowell Summer Music Series. Flower-patterned banners on the light poles promote the entertainment: Blues-Folk-Rock-Celtic.

Levasseur was a history teacher and school administrator until he retired and joined the center's team in 2003. His avocation was Civil War reenactments, and these days he gives talks on World War I and II. He knows the morning drill. Four big utility carts are parked on the wide concrete frontage of Boarding House Park; these are for the students' bag lunches, which will be wheeled down to the mill. Everyone eats in a lunch room on the fourth floor of the mill called the Moody Street Feeder—the name is a pun referencing one of the hydropower connections in the city's canal system.

Today, Levasseur is meeting Phil Conners's homeroom students from the Stoklosa, one of Lowell's crop of new schools. The school stands at the corner of Broadway and School streets in the dense sub-neighborhood called the Lower Highlands. Of his 26 students, 24 are young people of color. Their names are Adam, Erica, Susie, Kelly, Alexis. They're dressed in jeans, light jackets, hooded sweatshirts, and sweaters. Only a few are sporting logotype: Aero, Abercrombie, New England Patriots, Lake Winnipesauke. For many of them, their parents or grandparents come from Asia, Africa, and Latin America. Most of the students were born in the United States. Conners teaches English, but he is here for an interdisciplinary day—science, history, language arts.

Along the sidewalk, students are disembarking for the day. One group follows a ranger toward the Boott Cotton Mills Museum. Other groups assemble with their respective instructors. Levasseur's group gathers in front of the large green steel silhouette of Francis Cabot Lowell at the northwest corner of Boarding House Park. The students talk and joke, calling each other's names to get a look. They quiet down when they hear,

> My name is Paul Levasseur, and I'll be your museum teacher today. Let's sit down on the steps near the stage while we wait for the trolley. You live in Lowell, and some people don't appreciate what happened here. Today, we're going to see how the people who built Lowell turned water into money.

It's busy in the Boott Mills yard with groups passing by the windows of the counting house, where Levasseur's group has assembled in front of a map on the wall. He shows them the Stoklosa School on the map to get them oriented to the downtown mill district. Guard Locks on the Pawtucket Canal near the school is the location of Francis Gate, which Levasseur says he wishes he could show them because it is "very cool."

"I want you to remember four letters today," said Levasseur. "I'll give you the letters one by one, and you tell me what they stand for. 'W' (and one kid said 'water'), 'P' (he got a shout out of 'power'), another 'P' (this one is harder, but he coaxed 'produce' from a girl after a verb-noun detour into grammar), and, finally, another 'P' (he asked for a fancy word for making money, and filled in with 'profit' to keep the discussion moving)." The words would later be seen by the group on a poster in the Water Room at the center where the students will apply in a lab situation the scientific principles they will soon engage on site in a nineteenth-century turbine pit.

Back outside, one of the park's replica trolleys, Number 4131, stopped in front of the museum to pick up the students, who had been watching a pair of mallard ducks frolicking in the Eastern Canal alongside the mill. Lowell's waterways provide appealing habitat for birds, including ospreys and eagles nesting on the banks of the Merrimack. Hawks and falcons perch on mill-tops as they scan for a pigeon lunch. Above the windows inside the trolley are photographs documenting the construction of the trolley in Ida Grove, Iowa, at the Gomaco Trolley company. Building these from scratch required the Lowell Historic Preservation Commission staff in the 1980s to find the local rail-matching undercarriages in Australia. The sixteen-ton yellow trolley rode the track alongside the Eastern Canal and past Lowell High School and the Ayotte Garage with its flowering trees, stopping at each road crossing—the flagmen hop off to signal Go or Don't Go.

Near the former site of the Tremont Mills powerhouse, the track ends at a wooden platform adjacent to a small brick gatehouse where the Northern and Western canals meet. The students stepped down from the trolley and gathered for a quick briefing about the next stop, straight ahead in the Wannalancit Mills complex, originally the Suffolk Mills. The complex was one of the earliest adaptive reuse projects in the city. Today, more than a dozen small tech companies fill most of the mill space while UMass–Lowell uses a portion of the complex for business incubator space such as the Massachusetts Medical Devices Development project (M2D2). Looming over the trolley terminus is one of the few contemporary office buildings added to the Lowell streetscape since the 1970s: the corporate headquarters of Jeanne d'Arc Credit Union (JDCU), one of the oldest banking firms in the city. JDCU moved into the new structure that was built by local business owner Will Soucy, who negotiated with state officials to acquire the right to build on the land. The agreement included a requirement that the basement of the one-time Tremont Mills powerhouse be kept intact so that people could see the enormous turbine pits that once helped drive the mill operations.

Levasseur asked the students what they see in the canal water. "Looks dirty," one boy said. "It's actually dark because of the recent rain," Levasseur explained. "We use the term 'silted up' when it gets dark like this. The rain washes debris, oil from roads, and soil into the river, which carries it downstream. After a week or so, the water clears up. It's not polluted, but it is dirty. You can see pollen on the surface, too, because of the spring blossoms."

Reviewing the geography of the river one more time, Levasseur said the water in the river drops thirty-two feet from the Pawtucket Falls upriver to the area close to where we are standing. He asked Kelly and Adam to work out a physics problem having to do with dropping a gallon of water (8.3 pounds) from the top of the mill. Closing the loop, the good teacher explained the difference between potential energy and kinetic energy and where gravity comes into the equation, and then brought things back around to the businessmen who calculated that they could power thousands of looms in textile factories feeding off the falling water at this bend in the river.

He led the group across Suffolk Street and down the Canalway path to a door in the middle of the mill. Inside the air is musty from decades of water in the basement. On the wall are maps of the city and canal-system diagrams. This is a park exhibition site, "The River Transformed," with machinery displays, a working power loom, and museum panels with historic photographs and explanatory text. The history-and-engineering lesson here lasted about an hour. The room includes a large opening in the floor exposing a working turbine and in the middle of the floor component parts of the same type of water turbine that reveal exactly how the machine functions. Water flows into the mill via huge tubes called penstocks and drops down onto the turbines to set them spinning. The turbines move large pulleys or flywheels that in turn transfer the energy to a series of small pulleys and leather belts connected to shafts that down the line are attached to the rows of looms in the weave room. Levasseur went into lesson mode:

> Picture a bicycle with all the parts connected, from pedal to gear to chain to the wheel. That's what is called "transmission of power." It's the same with this mill machinery, and all the math was figured out with a pencil and paper. No computer, no calculator in the 1820s.

Levasseur picked up a child's pinwheel toy and turned it on its side so that the plastic blades were horizontal.

> There was a problem with the hydropower technology in the early years. Vertical water wheels, called breast wheels or overshot wheels, were only about 70 percent efficient in extracting power from the water falling onto the wheels. The mill owners asked their top

engineer, James B. Francis, to tackle the problem. Francis knew of experiments in France involving a new design for water wheels. He came up with the mixed-flow turbine that drew almost all of the falling water into its spinning blades and could produce power at near 90 percent efficiency. Better use of the available water meant more output from the looms, and more profit.

The students descended the stairs close to the 28,000-pound flywheel, a megapulley that reaches speeds of forty miles per hour. This was a cue for Levasseur to remind students of their "simple machines" lesson in general science and go back to the "everything is connected" concept. The basement of the mill is a kind of ancient industrial tomb except that some of the workings are still active. Students moved through single-file, eyeing the aged walls and massive foundation stones. Someone joked about the antique leather-belt stretcher: "Have you ever heard of the rack?" Grimy metal barrels with spigots line the wall. The soundtrack is continuous running water. It is like walking inside a behemoth truck motor. The air is damp. Levasseur kept talking as students moved through the passageway and then up another set of wooden stairs to the ground floor where everyone had first entered. This mill used fifteen of the thirty-two feet of water coming down the falls; the remaining seventeen was channeled to the adjacent mill closer to the river. The Lowell mill plan was developed on two levels in order to squeeze the maximum energy out of the thrusting river. The introduction of steam power in the 1850s changed the operational plan, but the canals and buildings were in place by then.

Upstairs, Levasseur gathered his group in front of a single power loom fully loaded with thread. Holding a shuttle, he explained the "kiss of death" syndrome. Until the 1880s, loom operators had to suck a thread end from the spool inside the shuttle through an opening (the shuttle eye) to connect it to the working thread in the machine. At a time of highly infectious diseases like tuberculosis and different strains of flu, the fact that workers from different shifts put their lips on the same shuttle made for a public health nightmare. A mill mechanic in Massachusetts, J. H. Northrup, invented a shuttle-changing device in 1889 that greatly enhanced occupational safety. Another worry for loom operators was the static electricity created by the spinning leather belts. Imagine what that will do to a fourteen-year-old girl's long hair if it gets pulled up into the belt, Levasseur said. He inserted the shuttle and flipped a switch. The racketing noise filled the room: bump-it, bump-it, bump-it, bump-it—constant noise as the threads came together and added a half-inch of woven cloth, this type called "shirting," a plain weave that would have been printed with a design back in the day. The sound was as powerful a transporter as anything the students had experienced all morning. Closing their eyes, they could time-travel to 1831 when the Suffolk Mill was new. One of the original mill companies in Lowell, the Suffolk, later combined with the Tremont Mills, employed thousands of Lowellians through the decades and produced cloth until it shut down in 1926.

The Stoklosa students ended their morning with a trolley ride back to the Boott Mills Museum, where they were engulfed in the thunder of a small army of power looms banging away in the Weave Room on the first floor. After lunch in the Moody Street Feeder, Conners's class headed downstairs to the center's bustling base camp. Their destination was a room with a sign that reads "Power to Production," but that is commonly known as the Water Room or simply H_2O. This is a wet lab with six work stations: two canal system setups that resemble miniature, one-level water-park layouts about two and a half feet off the floor; and four upright machines

The Water Room
James Higgins

fitted with faucets and designed to accommodate different versions of plastic water-wheels.

The kids split into two groups, scientists and engineers, and got their instructions. The scientists were charged with creating a hydropower system that will take water from an imaginary lake (a square water container) and river (a plastic trough) and channel it through three different canals (more plastic toughs) so that it spins water-wheels linked to the mill component parts. The goal is to get all three power sources spinning at the same rate. Six students jump into the breach and start designing on a magnetized board with parts matching the water system components. Once designed and signed off on by the museum teacher, the students began bolting the canal sections together, jacking the mills up or down to meet the penstocks, and adjusting the flow from the "river" and between canals and mills with round plastic dams and gates perforated to adjust water flow. Instead of thirty-two feet from the Pawtucket Falls, these mini-models offer six inches of drop that must be engineered to drive three different "factories."

As one team hustled to adjust water flow and get their wheels spinning equally fast, Conners urged them to find answers by trial and error, moving gates and dams.

"Alexis, look at that wheel in the middle canal," he said.

"It's spinning too slowly, and I'm losing money!"

When the groups reported back on their success or lack thereof, Levasseur told them what a smart scientist will do:

"Test, examine results, test again, and compare results to identify the solution!"

Engineers paired up to test different water-wheel models on the upright machines. Each team analyzed the speed and strength of four different wheel designs (undershot, high breast, overshot, mid-breast) on red plastic bucket wheels and blue paddle wheels. This is all about efficiency, and the students are expected to defend their recommendations for the best of the eight combinations.

Around the room the students' eyes shone. Their clothes were wet, but not soaked. Everyone had been up and moving around for an hour. After seeing the industrial artifacts in the morning, they literally rolled up their sleeves and made simulated water-powered factories. The dictionary tells us that technology is "the practical application of knowledge." This "applied" behavior is central to the Lowell story, and every day of the school year students and teachers apply knowledge in authentic learning experiences in situ, whether on the venerable shop floors of Lowell mills or on the water in the River as a Classroom activities launched from the UMass–Lowell Bellegarde Boathouse above the Pawtucket Falls.

Education ranger Rebecca Lofgren came to Lowell in 2010 from the Mississippi National River and Recreation Area in Minneapolis-St. Paul, Minnesota. The Iowa native is a specialist in environmental education with a master's degree from the University of Minnesota. The Mill City Museum of the Minnesota Historical Society has a water room whose design is based on the Tsongas operation; the flour mills of the Twin Cities for a time were powered by a canal system. Boston investors who knew about the Lowell canals were behind the flour-making mills.

"Learning the history and science behind Lowell in a hands-on way, through the trial-and-error method that engineers experienced right here, is so entertaining that students cannot help but be pulled into it all," Lofgren said. After two years at the center, she can usually spot which student in a visiting class is the engineer in the bunch:

> The engineers tend to take the lead and have a very specific vision of how the canals are supposed to be built and why. It's especially endearing when one student, very often a younger student in the fourth or fifth grade, starts to explain the concept of why something was built in a certain way and clearly knows more about this than you![41]

The four wheel-testing machines are named for important engineers, three from Lowell's past and another of hall-of-fame ranking. They are Paul Moody, who "helped build the first American factory power loom" and was the chief engineer of the Locks & Canals Company from 1823 to 1831; George Washington Whistler, who served as chief engineer (1831 to 1837) and was a pioneering railroad designer; the previously mentioned James B. Francis, hydraulics genius and chief engineer in Lowell (1837 to 1885); and Uriah Boyden, born in 1804, who invented the outward-flow turbine. The Water Room is one of the lab areas in the third floor experiential learning center, among them Bale to Bolt with its sixteen one-person wooden hand looms, the Yankees and Immigrants role-play area, Workers on the Line with its cloth-printing operation that brings home the term "speed-up," and Engineer It! equipped with the building blocks of innovation used in the engineering design process.

Outside the Engineer It! workshop is a mini-exhibit illustrating a solar power system based on the actual photovoltaic panels atop the museum building, a display designed by UMass–Lowell engineering students as part of a community engagement project. The message is about sustainable energy, which is fitting for an industrial city first powered by water in a carbon-neutral process. Paul Tsongas would have enjoyed seeing this. He was an early proponent of solar energy even as he argued for the necessity of nuclear reactors being in the country's power mix. When the softball team of his congressional office ran onto one of the fields on the National Mall, their shirts read: Tsongas Tsolarstars.

Dean Anita Greenwood of the Graduate School of Education at UMass–Lowell guides the university side of the partnership that makes possible the Tsongas Industrial History Center. Since 2008, she has been on a mission to reorient the university's side of the collaboration toward more research projects that contribute to both progress at the center and faculty initiatives. A prime example is a 2011 grant for $1.3 million from the National Science Foundation awarded to computer science professor Fred Martin and Michelle Scribner-MacLean, a professor in Greenwood's School, for a "cyber-learning" project designed to train middle and high school students to be "data scientists" who are at ease sorting through and absorbing the blizzard of scientific information blowing across digital screens every day.

Using the Internet System for Networked Sensor Experimentation (iSENSE), students will learn "to create their own experiments, upload and tag data, and configure, save, and share dynamic visual representations of the data," Martin explained.[42] Classroom applications range from engineering surveys to environmental analyses. The center is a key partner in the work, as is a group called Machine Science Inc. in Cambridge, Massachusetts. Thirty teachers from the region will take part in the project over four years, training with iSENSE and bringing students to Lowell for hands-on projects like water-quality studies of the Merrimack River. Some 2,300 students stand to benefit from the project, which Martin and Scribner-MacLean hope to develop into a nationwide resource via the web. Greenwood added:

> We want to expand our collaboration with faculty in the School of Health and Environment and College of Engineering in the next few years. The National Science Foundation support should be a growth area because nearly all of the funded projects now have education components that address the public impact of research.[43]

Greenwood and others at the center work closely with the leadership of the Lowell Public Schools, particularly Superintendent Jean Franco, an alumnus of the university who graduated in the same class at UMass–Lowell Chancellor Marty Meehan. (These two and Bernie Lynch, the veteran city manager, all graduated in the same UMass–Lowell class—evidence that the local brain drain was over.) "The Lowell schools have really embraced the concept of place-based learning exemplified by Tsongas Industrial History Center programs," Greenwood said, an approach that Mogan had long advocated. The commitment means that students and teachers plug in to the program at the elementary, middle, and high school levels, each time with a different slant and for an experience shaped to meet curricular needs. Greenwood credits Kirschbaum with forging the strong relationship with Lowell school leaders: "Sheila is an example of the way success in Lowell often depends on special people who are deeply committed to the city. These partnerships depend on hard work over an extended period."[44]

LOWELL FOLK FESTIVAL

"Here we are dealing with living traditions. We know that the urge to preserve is based on the fact that we know the things that we are passing on have value, and we want to hold on to them. So we try to build continuity and to show continuity. We try to have people understand each other, and use the performing arts as an educational tool in preservation."

—Joe Wilson, Director, National Council for the Traditional Arts[45]

There is no better day in contemporary Lowell than the last Saturday in July during the annual Lowell Folk Festival. This is the fulfillment day—the day when the vision of the park-makers is fully realized. In the core of the mill district, from the four-way canal junction at the Swamp Locks to the iconic Boott Mills clock-and-bell tower, people fill the open spaces between the redbrick blocks and animate the scene. They are Shakespearean players for a day on that historic stage, bringing their tens

The festival in full swing at Boarding House Park, 2013
Tory Germann

of thousands of American stories to the industrial fountainhead. People, not cars, own the streets for the duration, sharing the pavement with essential support vehicles and electric carts.

For long stretches, the festivalgoer moves among the scores of restored buildings. The architectural fabric largely has been knit together—block after block painstakingly restored in synch with preservation standards applied by the city's Historic Board. At every corner, from entryway to roofline, the discerning visitor perceives the beauty and skill evident in the curve of crafted woodwork or clean line of windowsills. For all their practical forthrightness, the downtown facades express an artisanal building vocabulary, not prefabricated construction Muzak. The park has a cultural and visual theme without being pitched as a "theme park." The scene is real instead of "Main Street" at Disney and an authentic "Adventureland" with a hint of "Tomorrowland" for people who want the good things that small cities offer.

Consulting architects, urban planning graduate students, economists, and historians brought reserves of intellect and imagination to the local advance guard of park proponents. For all their expertise, however, these outside experts did not draw a blueprint for what is arguably the most important creation of reclaimed Lowell. Not the oracle-like "Brown Book" report of the Lowell Historic Canal District Commission, not the unconventional *General Management Plan* of the National Park Service, not the pioneering *Preservation Plan* of the Lowell Historic Preservation Commission—none of these documents called for a peak annual event in which all the social and physical capital of the park would be combined with the force of a moon rocket. One of the largest events of its kind in the country, the festival draws tens of thousands of people to the city for three days of roots music and dance, ethnic food, and craft demonstrations on stages, sidewalks, and city greens throughout the historic district downtown. (Nobody really knows the attendance because there is no gate or admission fee, but crowd estimates exceed 100,000.)

The festival comes from somewhere to be sure. Its outline was not sketched on a paper dinner napkin like another of Lowell's famed urban revival devices. From the 1970s on, the community's ambition had been growing in regard to presenting cultural experiences. Today's Lowell Festival Foundation is rooted in the Lowell Regatta Festival Committee organized in 1974 by restaurateur and Lowell booster Xenophon "Zenny" Speronis, business leader John Green, and journalist Richard "Dick" Taffe. Their original notion was to produce an event along and on the Merrimack River that would generate interest in Lowell businesses and raise the visibility of the then-Lowell Technological Institute rowing program (today's UMass–Lowell). Speronis described the impulse:

> The idea has its basis in the frustration of a businessman looking at the unused river all those years, the frustration of downtown businessmen realizing that the Dollar Day Specials weren't going to compete with the shopping malls, and the frustration of the people of Lowell about things not moving quickly enough in a positive direction.

Taffe knew the city had something special but undervalued in the river. "The Merrimack is the only river on the East Coast with a two-mile stretch upstream above a low-head dam without a major current."[46] He knew there was power boating at Lake Mead in the Southwest and water skiing in Fort Lauderdale, Florida. Could rowing be the next big thing for Lowell? One problem was the condition of the river, rated as one of the country's most polluted at the time.

Street games on cobblestoned Shattuck Street, 2013
Lou Neofotistos

At Speronis's Camelot-themed Speare House Restaurant on Pawtucket Boulevard on the river—on that long broad stretch described by Taffe—the trio brainstormed a plan for a few downtown events paired with Lowell Tech rowing events scheduled for May, August, and September 1974. "Within a matter of months we had three phenomenal festivals without a cloud in the sky and 80-degree weather." The culmination was "Octoberfest," attended by more than 100,000 revelers. They had planned a homecoming tribute for TV personality Ed McMahon, best known as Johnny Carson's sidekick on the long-running *Tonight Show*. McMahon was from Lowell. Comedian Jerry Lewis headlined a parade, and singer Della Reese performed. What followed were large-scale outdoor events that demonstrated Lowell's potential as a big arts and entertainment attraction. The committee's success in highlighting the river and Lowell as a destination later helped make the case to congressional leaders that Lowell had the potential for being a popular national park location. The Speare House was the preferred hospitality site when community leaders hosted state and national elected officials, urban specialists, and historians visiting Lowell to study the feasibility of a historical park in the city.

Between 1974 and 1990, according to its records, the Regatta Festival Committee produced or participated in more than 1,000 events. At its peak, the volunteer base numbered 400 people. From a community sailing program to charity efforts like Toys for Tots at Christmas, the group amounted to a blank check for community service. The call went out, and the helpers showed up like volunteer firefighters. Each January, Speronis hosted a party for them at the Speare House.

The committee was an early partner of the park, providing services through a "cooperative agreement" that included, for a time, operation of the canal boats. In 1986, the committee helped save the summer boat operation after the contractor withdrew from the program on short notice. Park Superintendent Chrysandra Walter reached out to Speronis and the leaders of the Lowell Plan, Inc., who solved the problem and kept the tour boats on the canals. Speronis in 1990 received the National Park Service's first North Atlantic Region Volunteer of the Year Award. Green later served on the Board of Directors of the National Council for Traditional Arts in Washington, D.C., by virtue of the committee's role in co-presenting the annual Lowell Folk Festival.

The high points of "Regatta" days were concerts on the river by the Boston Pops orchestra conducted by the charismatic Arthur Fiedler, known for his long white hair and penchant for fire engines. Tens of thousands of people would gather at the Charles G. Sampas Pavilion of Lowell Heritage State Park for rousing symphony performances that climaxed in Tchaikovsky's *1812 Overture* complete with cannon fire from the "Fiedler Battery" of the Army National Guard. The mid-section of Pawtucket Boulevard looked like Times Square on New Year's Eve, prefiguring the vast crowds at the Lowell Folk Festival in the years ahead.

After the park opened its Lowell door in 1978, the Regatta Festival Committee (now Lowell Festival Foundation) helped park staff organize summer weekend fairs in Lucy Larcom Park, which borders a section of the Merrimack Canal. These fairs showcased traditions of one or another of the city's fifty-something different ethnic groups. The canal-side events were genuine, but small. As the park gained momentum, occupied rehabilitated buildings, and extended its public activities, the missing ingredient in its cultural operations was scale—the park needed to "go big," as the Regatta group had done with some of its events.

There was another concern. Given how central the "human story" is to the historical narrative told by rangers, it was becoming increasingly clear by the mid-1980s that the park and community had to improve the presentation quality and substantive depth of the cultural heritage programs in the city. Lowell planners and administrators dealing with the park were not at first using the words "folklife" or "folklore." The terminology in Lowell was "ethnic" and "multicultural" when referring to the heritage of the people. In 1976, the U.S. Congress established the American Folklife Center (AFC) at the Library of Congress with a mission "to preserve and present" the traditional culture of the nation. The Archive of Folk Culture at the Library dates from 1928, and holds a vast amount of ethnographic data. Here is folklife defined by the AFC:

> The story of America is reflected in the cultural productions of ordinary people who live everyday lives, from cooking and eating meals, to the activities of work and play, to religious observances and seasonal celebration. Folklife includes the songs we sing, the stories we tell, the crafts we make.[47]

When the AFC was preparing a yearlong Lowell Folklife Study in 1986, Patrick Mogan read its one-page mission statement. He chuckled: "These people stole all our ideas."[48]

Soon, partnerships with the American Folklife Center and the National Council for the Traditional Arts (NCTA) offered Lowell, the park and the community, an opportunity to raise the bar for cultural heritage programs. Like preservation standards, the standards for community cultural presentations had to rise. Community arts activity has merit, but the level of action is more typically amateur or perhaps semiprofessional. A nation—and Lowell was now a major-league cultural site—must aim for excellence in national cultural experiences. This does not mean working exclusively with paid full-time professionals, but it does mean that the practitioners should exemplify the highest level of achievement in their respective fields, whether that of an experienced local cook from the Portuguese national parish of St. Anthony's in the Back Central neighborhood of Lowell or a visiting fiddle player from the Franco-American precincts of Maine.

There is also the quality of production to consider. Even at a free festival event, a visitor to a national park expects first-rate printed materials, an organized directional-sign system, high-quality audio and lighting equipment, informed program presenters, professional maintenance services, and well-trained production staff. The NCTA offered expertise and experience. The American Folklife Center, with its partner the Smithsonian Institution, had a record of success in producing the American Folklife Festival during the summer on the National Mall in Washington, D.C. With these collaborators, Lowell had an opportunity to step up its game. All along the way, however, Mogan cautioned program managers and funders. He warned them that the worst outcome of bringing the park to Lowell would be turning Lowell people into spectators of their own culture. He wanted to cultivate local knowledge, talent, and skills.

In September 1986, park Superintendent Walter led a four-person team from her staff and that of the Preservation Commission to Washington, D.C., to meet with Joe Wilson, director of the NCTA, and Vernon "Dave" Dame, chief of interpretation of the National Park Service. The purpose of the Lowell delegation's visit was to convince Wilson to bring the National Folk Festival to Lowell for a three-year run.

The "National" rolls out a welcome rug of traditional music, dance, crafts, and storytelling with talent scooped up from the Hawaiian Islands to East Harlem in New York City. The event originated in St. Louis, Missouri, in 1934, and moved around the country for the next few decades. In the 1970s and 1980s, the National Folk Festival was produced at the Wolf Trap National Park for the Performing Arts in Virginia and Cuyahoga Valley National Park in Ohio. In 1986, it had been staged in New York City to mark the restoration of the Statue of Liberty.

Wilson at the time knew just about every folk artist in the country. For decades, he traveled the blue highways and multilane freeways from coast to coast on NCTA business, talking to Cajun accordion players in the bayous, blues guitarists in the Carolinas, and dairy farmer-poets in Vermont. Wilson talked about the National like nobody else:

> The National Folk Festival is a concept first of all. It's a belief in our country—its ability to serve a plural society. It's a belief that the traditional arts and folk groups that make up our country are not going to die out, but that they will continue into the centuries ahead. . . . We take artists who have been playing in their living rooms and on their back

porches and for their families and neighbors and we put them up on a big stage and turn lights on them here where ethnography meets show business.[49]

Both Wilson and Dame embraced the idea of taking their cultural camp meeting to the still-new national park in Lowell. Notwithstanding the formidable industrial history in Lowell, some grassroots park supporters in the city claim it really exists as a tribute to the positive contributions made by the peoples of various ethnic and racial identities to the character of our United States—their labor being notable, but their humanity more so. Public Law 95-290 of the 95th Congress, the act establishing Lowell National Historical Park, acknowledges Lowell to be the "most significant planned industrial city in the United States" in the first item under Findings and Purpose; the second item reads: "the cultural heritage of many of the ethnic groups that immigrated to the United States during the late nineteenth century and early twentieth century is still preserved in Lowell's neighborhoods."[50] In those words is the justification for the Lowell Folk Festival.

Not quite a silent partner to the initial collaboration, but someone whose role is infrequently acknowledged, is the former congressman who represented Lowell in the late 1980s, Chester G. "Chet" Atkins of Concord, Massachusetts. His former aide, Steve Conant, remembered that Atkins encouraged this Washington-Lowell alliance and, as a member of the Appropriations Committee of the U.S. House of Representatives, he wielded important influence on behalf of Lowell's building and program developments.

With the NCTA's commitment secured, Walter assembled a steering group in Lowell, put together more than $100,000, and began shaping what would be Lowell's largest street party in memory. When the National kicked off in late July 1987, the park and Lowell had their "big bang" event, and every astute observer knew immediately that this venture was a keeper. Right off, the festival felt like a signature event, one that could define the city going forward. Like the interlacing canals that converted the force of flowing river water to power for machines that turned raw cotton into bolts of cloth, the festival channels the expressive tributaries of the American experience into an urban-set performance and exposition whose end product is inspiration.

The Lowell Folk Festival, under that name, grew organically from the three Nationals in Lowell. In that first year of the Lowell Folk Festival, local banks alone contributed some $200,000 to the cause. Lowell's festival is considered one of the most successful of the progeny of the National Folk Festival. The annual production has doubled as a laboratory for community partnerships, an area in which Lowell is now considered a distinguished model. Today, the festival is presented by Lowell National Historical Park, the City of Lowell, the Lowell Festival Foundation, Greater Merrimack Valley Convention & Visitor Bureau, Greater Lowell Chamber of Commerce, and the National Council for the Traditional Arts. As the centerpiece of the city's cultural calendar, the festival has created a perception of Lowell as a "festival city," bolstered by annual events such as the Southeast Asian Water Festival, Jack Kerouac Literary Festival, New England Quilt Festival, and Winterfest. The annual budget now exceeds $1 million ($450,000 cash from presenters and sponsors and the rest from donations in kind). The festival is a true joint venture and would not be possible without the tens of thousands of dollars contributed by the co-presenters and sponsors from the private and public sectors, as well as personal contributions by friends of the festival and donors at the event. City departments provide police

A Native American performer at Market Mills Park
James Higgins

and maintenance support. Volunteers organized by the Lowell Festival Foundation give of themselves, helping with everything from stage setup to guest services. The effort goes year-round to ensure an A-1 production each July.

The downtown business community embraced the festival, so much so that a "fringe festival" became a potent attraction starting in the mid-2000s. Every pub and eatery owner who can fit tables on the sidewalk outside the door and afford to hire a brace of folk singers says "game on" for the weekend. When the festival stages close down for the night, the party moves inside until closing time.

"We're a great stew of many different cultures, and we put it all together in this festival so people can sample a little bit of where everybody in this country comes from," Walter said.[51] Her work and life achieved splendid harmony after she married one of the stars of the early festivals, master musician Seamus Connolly. (Among other accolades, Connolly is the unmatched ten-time winner of the Irish National Fiddle Championships.) Sandy Walter died in 2011 after a long illness.

Each edition of the Lowell Folk Festival offers surprises. Veteran attendees reminisce about the instantly classic appearance by teen-aged Alison Krauss or the flying Celtic feet of Michael Flatley before he starred in "Riverdance." Reviewing the twenty-fifth anniversary festival in 2011, *Boston Globe* arts writer Stuart Munro reported that he was "bowled over" by the surprising performances of the Boston-based Debo Band with guest singers and dancers from Fendika of Ethiopia. At the Dance Pavilion in the park parking lot behind Market Mills, Debo and friends likely softened the asphalt under the wooden dance floor with their super-hot, funky jazz-inflected Afro-pop sounds. They had hundreds of people moving every which way and clapping on-and-off rhythm under what felt like a revival tent. Big blasts of golden horns, peppery runs

The Debo Band with Fendika, 2011
LNHP

on accordion keys, drumbeats that thumped in chest cavities, driving guitar licks, and jet-powered singing—all this from fifteen artists making one grand sound.

A person wants to see something new when walking around the festival, whether a closeup view of a man carving a wooden duck decoy or a different brand of banjo playing. When Fendika's lead singer, Melaku Belay, ecstatically shook in place at the climax of one of the group's towering numbers, most of those gathered around witnessed something new. It was "eskista," a traditional trance-dance of Ethiopia whose moves are the roots of breaking and popping—and the Harlem shake. He was like strawberries in a musical blender revving at top speed. When he peaked he just stopped and threw his arms wide. Everybody was spent.

Fendika had CDs for sale, but a plastic disc would not transmit anything close to what the crowd had experienced. The "live" aspect of the festival is the winning ingredient. The Quebe Sisters might make for pleasant listening on *Prairie Home Companion* radio waves, but a person has to lean on the black-iron fence at 1824 St. Anne's churchyard to soak up their harmonies for full effect. The same goes for the Rhythm of Rajasthan performers with their lush music from northern India and the gospel-singing Birmingham Sunlights of Alabama, both of whom enchanted audiences at Boarding House Park against the brick front range of the Boott Cotton Mills at the twenty-fifth festival.

The festival has become as much a delight for "foodies" as for music fans. At the Foodways Tent in 2011, Dorothy "Dottie" Naruszewicz Flanagan of Lowell and Carol Matyka of Boston taught onlookers how to make a favorite Polish-American food, pierogi or pierogies (because nobody can eat just one). Popular at Christmastime, they are on the menu in all seasons. These dumplings can be filled with cabbage and sauerkraut or a mixture of cheese, onions, and potatoes. "Every culture has its own version of this food, like Italian ravioli, Chinese pot stickers, and empanadas," Matyka noted. Other specialties included Pennsylvania Dutch chicken corn noodle soup, cold Cambodian noodle salad, and Jewish noodle kugel: the topic was "pasta and noodles around the world."[52]

Pauline Golec received a Lifetime Volunteer Award from the park in 2010. With a laugh, Golec explained, "When I was told about it, I wondered if someone knew something about my future that I didn't know—did it mean that my life of volunteering would soon be over or that I had to volunteer forever? Oh, well."[53] She was recognized not only for her work as a museum teacher at the Tsongas Industrial History Center, but also for service as "Ethnic Chair" of the Lowell Festival Foundation. As Ethnic Chair she coordinates the small army of community volunteers who staff the food booths. In 2009, the organizations that do the food presentations and sales were recognized with a Cultural Heritage Award from the National Park Service, presented to the Lowell Festival Foundation on their behalf.

Golec has been part of festival activities since the first Regatta Festival in May 1974. Asked what got her to the proverbial volunteer table, she said, "Ethnic pride, and I had friends who were involved, plus I love this city—and I'm a teacher."[54] For most of that time she held a dual role as cochair of the Lowell Polish Cultural

Pauline Golec with the Excellence in Cultural Heritage Award received by the Lowell Festival Foundation for outstanding achievement in presenting American ethnic culinary traditions at the Lowell Folk Festival
Kevin Harkins

Committee. She remembers walking Massachusetts Governor Michael Dukakis around the Polish Festival at Lucy Larcom Park one year in the mid-1980s. Golec also chairs the Festival Foundation Scholarship Committee, which makes awards to high school seniors or college students. In honor of the twenty-fifth anniversary of the Lowell Folk Festival, scholarships were presented to three young people who themselves have volunteered at the Polish, Filipino, and Burmese food booths.

Janet Leggat's involvement with the Regatta Festival Committee and later the Lowell Festival Foundation dates from 1988. She has been a volunteer, a part-time manager, a full-time executive director, and is now a member of the board of directors. Her sister, the late Susan Leggat, was involved in Regatta Festival Committee activities from the start, eventually joining the park staff as an administrative assistant and then events specialist. Susan left for a year in the early 1980s, joining former Lowell park superintendent Lew Albert at Cuyahoga National Recreation Area in Ohio. She was back a year later. Janet recalled her sister's vision:

> Susan and Joe Wilson had such a clear idea of what the festival should be. Lowell is the most successful spin-off of the National Folk Festival. Some things like the logistics are better handled by the local partners, but the National Council for the Traditional Arts is highly knowledgeable about the talent—they ensure the integrity of the artists. The local

Susan Leggat (1947–2003)
LNHP

ethnic food component, organized for years by Pauline Golec, has given the festival a distinctive character. A lot of people look forward to eating on that weekend.[55]

Peter Aucella, assistant superintendent of the park, called Susan "the conscience of the festival," saying, "She made sure it retained its integrity and didn't become a circus. You couldn't believe the cockamamie ideas she had to listen to. It is what it is because of her."[56]

Susan's friend Marie Sweeney remembered Sue's "happy warrior" qualities:

The pride she took in her job and in the many organizations she joined and supported was classic. Who could say "No" to her when she asked for help or to buy a ticket or asked you to join a board or committee or to be a festival volunteer? It wasn't for her, but for her cause, she'd say. But we did it for her, too. She was a pioneer and a role model for all of us, but especially for young women. . . . She had a strong will to do what was right—and to do it in the right way. She had a touch of kindness about her even when she had to say, "Not appropriate for this festival," or "No, they can't sell t-shirts." . . . She helped make Lowell not just a place, but a "community" of people working together for the good of all.[57]

Speaking to local video-documentary producers Ruth Page and Scott Glidden, Joe Wilson used a folksy metaphor in reflecting on culture and the preservation of traditional arts in America:

It's possible to think of the structure of culture in the United States today as an ice cream sandwich. Up at the top you have received culture that is transmitted through conservatories and great institutions. You have ballet here and symphony music and all the great works of the Western World. There was a time, a few centuries ago, when you only had this level of culture, elite culture, and all the rest of culture was folk culture, the thing that working folks did for their own enjoyment, the thing that they played for themselves and handed down through their families and communities. But a century or so ago, we started manufacturing culture. We started making records and books and other things that were sold en masse, and so we have popular culture now or mass culture, the middle part of our ice cream sandwich.

Folk culture is made by institutions, too, but small institutions. The family is the main institution of folk culture, and it's not created to make money. Sometimes people become professionals who do these things, but they do these things because they're good, and because they're beautiful, and because they should be passed on.[58]

TRADITIONS CONNECT US

One late winter evening in 2012, Jorge Arce overstuffed the stage in the Visitor Center auditorium at Market Mills with fourteen audience members equipped with sticks, a donkey's jaw, shakers and scrapers, bongos and conga drums, tambourines, musical gourds, and cowbells. Among the pickup ensemble were park Superintendent Michael Creasey, City of Lowell economic development specialist Theresa Park, the first executive director of the Preservation Commission Fred Faust, and *Preservation Plan* graphic designer Joan Ross, along with a rich mix of others. (Note the presence of Faust and Ross: Lowell has a way of holding people's attention for decades.) Two costumed carnival street dancers entered from the back door and joined the rhythmic section up front. Arce started a chant-along, teaching words to the forty people still in their seats—urging them to get up and throw their voices forward. At the end everybody joined in a carousing line dance that circled the room three times before the conductor wrapped up the show.

Earlier, Arce had taken the crowd on a geocultural voyage from western Africa to the West Indies to New York City.

> To become an actor, I had to become a historian. Africans have been in America for five centuries. The rhythms of Puerto Rican Plena dance, Desi Arnaz's Cuban conga drumming, and today's hip-hop music are all from the continent in which you could fit Europe five times. [He showed a map on-screen of Africa in actual-size proportion to the other continents.] This is the real flat map of the globe. We can bring people together and make the world one country—you have 2,000 years of history in your body.

A native of Puerto Rico, Arce has a degree in Musical Theater from the Boston Conservatory and a master's degree in education from Harvard University. He tours as an actor and musician, spreading the gospel of Afro-Caribbean music and dances such as the Bomba and Plena through performances and workshops at schools and festivals. He is one of the best known cultural ambassadors for the Puerto Rican community in America. He was at the park as a guest presenter in the year-round Lowell Folklife Series, organized by the park's cultural programs director Maggie Holtzberg, who is also the state folklorist for the Massachusetts Cultural Council. She has been at the park on a temporary assignment made possible by an intergovernmental personnel agreement. She talked about her work:

> Folklorists observe, document, present, and interpret forms of expressive culture in situ. We are interested in how people come to a tradition, how they learn it, and how their traditional art reflects the values of the community in which it exists.
>
> One way for the park to stay relevant is to better understand and interpret what's going on *now* in this post-industrial city. What is the immigrant urban experience like for people living in Lowell today? It is all around us—ready to be observed, questioned, told, and preserved. Think how many times we've wanted to know what life was *really* like for the Irish canal diggers of the 1820s? What was the texture of daily life? Nobody cared to record it. It is now lost. Our work revolves around what life is like for the many that make Lowell home, including those in underserved communities.[59]

In addition to Arce, the 2012 series featured four local cooks in an "Ode to Fat! Schmaltz, Salt Pork, Olive Oil, & Ghee"; songs of the Greek Asia Minor Refugees performed by the Sophia Bilides Trio; and a film about a neighborhood in Lawrence, Massachusetts, where residents are trying to hold together the community fabric.

Holtzberg's series is the latest attempt to make Lowell a hub of folklife activity throughout the year. People in folklife circles know about the festival in July, but it has not been easy to embed related activities into the park or community. In the early 1990s, the Lowell Historic Preservation Commission and Middlesex Community College incubated the New England Folklife Center, with offices and exhibit space on the top floor of the Boott Cotton Mills Museum. The LHPC was prolific in its cultural research-and-development initiatives, funding arts and humanities programs informed by the themes of the park. The center was not able to establish itself as the focal point for regional activities; funding for operations became increasingly difficult to obtain, and the center closed in 1996.

CULTURAL AFFAIRS

When the National Endowment for the Arts staff wanted to look back in 2012 and assess the impact of its grants since its establishment in 1967 (nearly 140,000 grants), they selected five recipients to highlight as examples of the difference NEA funding made "at critical points in their development, support that ultimately magnified the reach of their art." The awardees were profiled in a special issue of *NEA Arts*, the agency's magazine. Lowell as a community was chosen as one of the five national examples. The city was in good company in this special issue, alongside African American poet Nikki Giovanni, the Steppenwolf Theater Company in Chicago, the Mississippi Arts Commission, and the Mark Morris Dance Group.

Rebecca Gross's story "Building on the Past" in *NEA Arts* recounts the "creative rebirth" of Lowell, citing a 1974 grant of $30,000 to the City of Lowell for design of landscape improvements along the canal system. Another early grant awarded to the Human Services Corporation, headed by Mogan, provided $21,000 for a plan to transform the Boott Cotton Mills into a community cultural center. This design won a national prize. Other grant recipients through the years include Merrimack Repertory Theatre for play development and the Lowell Office of Cultural Affairs to commission sculptures for the Lowell Public Art Collection. Gross wrote:

> Although Lowell was beginning to gain recognition as a regional wunderkind, it was the National Folk Festival that transformed Lowell into a national destination overnight. . . . Today the annual three-day festival is the largest free celebration of its kind. . . . It has received continuous support from the Arts Endowment since its inception. [The Lowell Festival Foundation received $30,000 from the NEA for the 2012 Festival.][60]

The expressive road from Pat Mogan's early musings to this kind of national recognition forty years later is blessed by much hard work, some false starts and detours, and many feats of imagination—and it is layered with accomplishments. The Creative Economy is common parlance among urban planners thanks to Richard Florida's buzz-y analysis of the potential of a "creative class" to drive urban vitality and productivity (his success formula emphasizing the nexus of talent, technology, and tolerance). Lowell embraces the creative economy concept as part of the city's master plan, but the record shows that Mogan was onto the creative economy long before social scientists began massaging the idea.

In 1971, Mogan and fellow activists formed the nonprofit Human Services Corporation (HSC) to build "concrete economic and social programs" that would instill hope and determination in people. One document in the HSC Archives at the UMass–Lowell Center for Lowell History (in the Mogan Cultural Center) illustrates how broadly Mogan thought about the potential of culture as a way to spur economic growth and social vitality. By 1972, he had been appointed long-range planner for the city and set up shop with his brash crew. A favorite local anecdote recounts a story about a top city official who one day dropped by the planning office unannounced to find a man with his chin in his hand, staring at the wall. When asked what he was doing, the man replied: "I work for Pat Mogan. I get paid to think." The official shot back: "Well, I think you're fired."

Sometime that summer Mogan received a booklet from the National Endowment for the Arts. Leafing through, he saw possibilities for funding. He marked up the pages and then dashed off a memo to the Center City Committee, a nonprofit group that boosts downtown improvements. Here is an excerpt:

p. 14: Architecture and Environmental Arts Program—Development of basic environmental design criteria for the guidance of local officials. Could we design a special assessment area and allow people, according to these criteria, to enhance their property without increasing the taxes?

p. 12: Graduate Thesis Fellowships—"To assist thesis work in the fields of architecture, landscape architecture, industrial design, and planning, photography, purchase of materials, mock-ups." How about mock-ups for the canals, mills, the landscape along the V.F.W. Highway for pedestrians, bicycles trails, etc.?

p. 13: Pilot public school curriculum programs—Specialists to tie-in forest and city into the curriculum by utilizing the same classroom behavioral objectives and utilizing the environment as the context for learning.

p. 19: Could we get a dance company to have a home base in a mill, specialize in ethnic dance and swing out of this home base to serve a larger area?. . .

p. 31: "A limited number of grants may also be made to community-based cultural research organizations to provide information on regional and ethnic culture and cultural organizations." Possibility of a program to tie-in with experimental school by getting students to write their own family tree. . . .

p. 34: Poetry in the schools—"Placing professional poets and other writers in elementary and secondary classrooms."

p. 42: Conservation program—"Assistance to museums for conservation work on collections of works of art or objects of cultural significance."—What are the art pieces that portray the industrialism in Lowell? Are the portraits in City Hall and the artwork on the second floor of the library subjects for this Conservation Program? Could Lowell be a branch of some museum or start its own museum?

p. 65. Theatre Programs—"Community Service Projects, including programs designed to reach larger and more diversified audiences and educational programs involving joint planning and significant financial commitment from the educational community."

p. 69. Visual Arts Program, Photography Fellowships—Could John Gustafson of Carole Johnson Associates qualify for this? John has about 600 pictures of our canals, mills, and buildings—the project can contribute to the Urban National Cultural Park.

p. 71. Works of Art in Public Spaces—"Matching grants to cities and towns to commission American artists to create works of art in any medium (including photography) for specific urban sites." Could Lowell commission an artist to create the theme?[61]

Twenty years after Mogan marked up his copy of the NEA program book, Lowell boasted a robust cultural-affairs sector topped by a nonprofit organization, the Lowell Office of Cultural Affairs (LOCA), which was funded in part by City Hall and the Lowell Plan economic development group. LOCA supported those who "create, present, and preserve" the city's culture. Organizing and funding LOCA had been the primary recommendation of the *Lowell Cultural Plan* (1987), which was the first comprehensive cultural development plan produced by a community in Massachusetts. Looking at a selection of activities in a single issue of the *LOCAL* events calendar, one can understand why even today the Massachusetts Cultural Council refers to Lowell as its "poster child" for cultural affairs in the state.

LOCAL: **April–May 1992**

"Abstracts and Sculpture" by Vladimir P. Kozhemiakov of Russia (Brush Art Gallery and Studios).

"Moore on Lowell: Drawings and Prints by Janet Lambert-Moore" (Whistler House Museum of Art).

"Holland Travelogue" (Moses Greeley Parker Lectures).

Lowell Philharmonic Orchestra Concert (Durgin Hall, UMass–Lowell).

"Music and Dance of Ireland with Seamus Connolly" (Merrimack Repertory Theater).

"Florian Lambert: Chanson, Musique, et Poesie a Travers L'Histoire du Quebec" (Middlesex Community College).

Cambodian New Year Celebration (JFK Plaza, City Hall).

"Hands Across the City," ethnic dance and music by Lowell High School students.

April Kids Week programs (National Park Service and partners).

"Earth Day '92" (National Park Service and Lowell Heritage State Park).

"Shirley Valentine" (Merrimack Repertory Theater).

"Jazz Lab" of UMass–Lowell Music Dept. (Durgin Hall, UMass–Lowell).

"The Big Band Sounds of the '40s" (The Highland Players at Lowell Memorial Auditorium)

"History Factory Teacher Workshop" (Tsongas Industrial History Center).

Deadline for Fifth Annual City of Lowell Youth Film Festival.

Preservation Week in Lowell with tours, workshops, and kids' programs.

Billy Burr's Funorama carnival at Regatta Field.

"With Pen in Hand: Excerpts from Lowell Family Letters" (Lowell Historical Society program).

Tour de Lowell: *Lowell Sun* Bicycle Race.

Veterans Memorial Day Parade.

Community Sailing Summer Season Opening.

"A Light in the Attic: Treasures of City Hall" (Lowell Historic Board exhibit at the Mogan Cultural Center).[62]

LOWELL SUMMER MUSIC SERIES

"I took my nine-year-old daughter to see The Machine. She is a huge fan of Pink Floyd. It was her first concert, and we had an awesome time!"

—Maureen Newcomb, 2012[63]

Each summer since 1989, a beautiful park that was once a rundown parking lot turns the middle of Lowell into one of the most exciting performance venues in Massachusetts. The weekend evening concerts and daytime free shows for kids bring more than 30,000 people to the front of the pavilion that is the trademark of the Lowell Summer Music Series, a partnership of LNHP and the Lowell Festival Foundation. What is the National Park Service doing managing a pop music series, even one with a traditional arts twist? What began as a modest attempt to liven up the Park and Preservation District and stimulate tourist activity has become one of the city's cultural cornerstones, not as massive as the Folk Festival because of the limitations of the downtown green, which holds about 2,000 people comfortably.

What is really going on from the Park Service's perspective, however, is that music and dance are the media for relating to people and inviting them into the historic district, where they learn about what the NPS does in Lowell. When the stars appear over the iconic Boott Cotton Mills clock-and-bell tower, the audience gets a postcard view of a national park vista. When Ziggy Marley shouts out his father's words, "Get

Boarding House Park under the lights
James Higgins

up, Stand up, Stand up for your rights!" against the redbrick backdrop of the mill, and the entire audience shouts those words with him, it's not a big leap to imagine the mill girls "turning out" to protest a 20 percent cut in pay in 1834. They fought for their rights.

The list of past performers at the music series speaks for itself: Joan Baez, Lyle Lovett, The Brew, k.d. lang, America, Ziggy Marley, Beausoleil, Southern Rail, Wayne Toups, Kenny Loggins, Gaelic Storm, Marc Cohn, Eric Burdon and the Animals, John Mayall, Collie Buddz, Grace Potter and the Nocturnals, Mavis Staples, Indigo Girls, Béla Fleck and the Flecktones, Toad the Wet Sprocket, Rickie Lee Jones, Matisyahu, Herbie Hancock, Jimmy Cliff, Los Lobos, Ani DeFranco, Jakob Dylan and the Wallflowers, Lucinda Williams, the Neville Brothers, Richard Thompson, Levon Helm, Taj Mahal, Assembly of Dust, Arlo Guthrie, Marcia Ball, Buddy Guy, Roger McGuinn, Bob Weir and Ratdog, Davy Jones, Don McLean, the Clancy Brothers, Herb Reed and the Platters, the Dance Theatre of Harlem, Shakespeare's *Twelfth Night*, Preservation Hall Jazz Band, Seamus Connolly, Guy Clark, Eddie from Ohio, Sha Na Na, Joan Osborne, Sleepy LaBeef, Eileen Ivers, Inca Son, Angkor Dance Troupe, Buckwheat Zydeco, The Drifters, John Sebastian, J. Geils and Bluestime, ABBAmania, Dar Williams, Cake, Fab Faux, Joan Armatrading, The B-52s, Entrain, 10,000 Maniacs, the Robert Cray Band, Koko Taylor, Emmylou Harris and Rodney Crowell . . .

Joan Baez and her band
Ray Houde

SCULPTURE TRAIL[64]

Lowell was such a hotspot in the field of outdoor sculpture or public art in 1988 that Boston's Museum of Fine Arts and the Institute of Contemporary Art invited the local art community to be a satellite location for activities linked to an ambitious two-country art exhibition, "The BiNational: German Art of the '80s." The curators aimed to provide a platform "to examine important trends emerging in contemporary art in Germany and the United States." Lowell was asked to host artist Bruno K., of Berlin. He proposed an industrial-type assemblage made of heavy-duty construction materials like steel ventilation tubes to be mounted on exposed beams in the archway outside the Brush Gallery at Market Mills. In the gallery he would display a number of his recent works, including inventive vehicles and sculpture made of found objects. With the approval of the National Park Service, Bruno K. installed his sculpture in December, where it remained for more than a month. Related activities included a talk by the artist at the then-University of Lowell Art Department. A capacity crowd turned out for the exhibit opening at the Brush. Bruno K. described his approach:

> I've been working on the same theme for years . . . concerned with power, domination, heroism, and the products of our ancestors, such as trophies, medals, and victorious poses. . . . I've never sought out this theme, let along thought of it. It's far too much an integral part of me. In my parents' home, for example, war was always an important theme. . . . And certain patterns of thought and behavior from our grandfathers' generation have contributed to the present-day situation.[65]

Buddy Guy
Tim Carter

How did Lowell get to the front of the line in the public-art niche of contemporary sculpture? The city at the time had a modest collection of statuary and monuments, mostly war memorials and ethnic heritage markers, but few new works of art had been commissioned and installed between World War II and the 1980s. There had been a flurry of mural-making in the 1970s with Lowell artists Janet Lambert-Moore and Leo Panas leading teams of young people in summer jobs projects funded by the Neighborhood Youth Corps of Community Teamwork Inc. City history– and ethnic heritage–themed murals were painted on several building walls and a municipal parking garage. There were French-Canadian, Irish, Greek, and Portuguese tableaux. The parking garage that predated the current one on John Street featured a long upper-deck wrap-around narrative painting about the city's industrial past, from slave ships tied to cotton growing in the South to twentieth-century strike banners carried by mill workers.

Pat Mogan in 1972 had circled the topic "Works of Art in Public Spaces" in his National Endowment for the Arts program brochure, wondering if this was worth following up on. He often talked with local artists such as Richard Marion and Jeannine Tardiff about identifying motifs associated with Lowell, like the fishing shack in Rockport, Massachusetts, that has launched a million watercolor paintings. His first impulse always was to work with community artists, but he thought motifs like Pawtucket Falls or the Boott Mills clock-and-bell tower could draw artists from all over and result in Lowell images being as iconic as the Gloucester, Massachusetts, fisherman on the waterfront or Paul Revere on his bronze horse in the North End of Boston.

The idea for new large-scale outdoor sculpture in the historic district downtown, however, came from Paul Tsongas. Having lived and worked around Washington, D.C., for many years, he admired the profound national monuments and lively street sculpture in the capital city. He noticed how much his young daughters enjoyed seeing and engaging with artworks. Lowell could benefit from a little of this, he decided. Tsongas had good instincts on the cultural side, but he was the first to admit he had a lot to learn about contemporary art. He was as serious about culture as he was about energy and economics. In May 1984, Executive Director Faust of the Lowell Historic Preservation Commission introduced him to the commission's new cultural affairs director. Tsongas fixed his eyes on me: "Are you taking my job? Don't screw up."—and then he grinned.

Tsongas and Mogan did not agree about the public art initiative. Mogan was skeptical of Tsongas's approach, which he suspected as meaning that Lowell was lacking in culture. Culture was like water to fish for Mogan: it was all around, it was the "way of life," and artworks were expressions of culture, not the stuff of culture itself. He liked to quote a cultural policy statement from the Province of Quebec, Canada, in which culture was defined as "the harmonization of economic and human factors"[66]—in other words, the expressive elements of a people's way of life arose from nexus of making a life and making a living.

Mogan's understanding of culture is captured in this excerpt of Robert Cantwell's *Ethnomimesis: Folklife and the Representation of Culture*:

> Culture . . . passes secretly, even silently, telepathically, between a parent and a child who does not even realize that she has been looking on or listening until years later, when she somehow discovers what she has learned and can now do herself; it ripens, untended, often unconsciously, in dreams, suddenly and unexpectedly to reveal itself in an expression or a turn of phrase, in a way of relating to one's children or one's spouse, or, at another level, in our musical and pictorial preferences, in the narratives we construct about ourselves and others or to which we turn for understanding.[67]

This notion of culture was important to him because he vividly remembered what had happened in his youth in Norwood, Massachusetts, among the Irish Americans whom he believed had "killed their culture" in order to assimilate and get ahead in mainstream society. He was a fierce defender of Lowell's distinctive way of life that was shaped by the layered traditions, beliefs, and knowledge of people with roots in nations around the world. For generations they had made accommodation with the culture of their adopted homeland, a place they changed as much as it changed them.

The cultural affairs staff of the LHPC, in particular, helped provide a context for the public art initiative by establishing a framework for the contemporary sculpture. All the new sculptures would be expected to respond in some direct or oblique way to one or more of the themes of the park: Labor, Capital, Waterpower, Technology, and the Industrial City. From 1981 through the mid-1990s, the Preservation Commission helped drive the public art effort—in the later years allied with the Lowell Office of Cultural Affairs.

By 1995, the nine-piece Lowell Public Art Collection had been assembled, valued at about $1 million. The Department of the Interior, through the National Park Service and Lowell Historic Preservation Commission, had contributed approximately $500,000 in the effort to develop a series of linked sculptures in the vicinity of the inner loop of the Canalway network of walking paths. Each of the sculptures in its own fashion referenced an aspect of the city's story, whether Robert Cumming's manipulation of the iconic shapes of Lowell or Ellen Rothenberg's tribute to the women labor activists of the nineteenth century. After a hiatus of several years, public art reentered the scene in 2011 with plans for new work at Point Park, where the Hamilton Canal District redevelopment area terminates in a prominent wedge at Swamp Locks, in sight of the busy roadway bringing people into the historic zone.

One night in January 1983, the Citizens Advisory Board for Community Development Block Grant Funds met to consider the Lowell City Manager's request for money to commission a sculpture for downtown Lowell. In a nineteenth-century church converted to a community meeting hall, six men sat at a table in front of about twenty people. There was a small brown sculpture model on a stand in front of the room.

One board member asked, "Who brought that thing before us?"[68]

The City Manager himself had said the sculpture looked like two lobsters fighting, but advanced the proposal at Senator Tsongas's urging.

Homage to Women by Mico Kaufman was dedicated in 1984.
James Higgins

In support of the proposal, an advocate said that a sculpture like this could be "symbolic of Lowell's past and future," and described more abstract landmarks in Chicago and San Francisco.

Although the advisory board voted "No," the City Council, under pressure from the Manager, who in turn was being pressed by Tsongas, approved the funding: $25,000 (the total cost of the commission was $100,000). Sculptor Mico Kaufman scaled up the model into a monumental bronze work of five entwined life-sized bronze figures leaning forward and upward as if about to take flight. *Homage to Women* is a tribute to womankind, especially the women who composed the initial work force in Lowell's textile mills. The artwork is the dominant feature of a small park adjacent to the Market Mills complex on Market Street.

Tsongas had invited Kaufman to propose the first piece of what became the Lowell Public Art Collection. They met in the artist's studio in Tewksbury, a Lowell suburb. Tsongas listened, and then became a champion of the idea. A world-renowned medallion artist, Kaufman is a Romanian immigrant who survived three years in a World War II Nazi concentration camp. Among his notable achievements is being selected to design the official medal for President Ronald Reagan's second inauguration in 1985.

At the dedication ceremony in 1984, several distinguished women from the Lowell area helped unveil the sculpture. Tsongas said, "Great cultures aren't remembered for their business practices. They're remembered for their art." Tsongas didn't stop at one sculpture. He imagined an art collection that would be a point of community pride. He obtained commitments for funding from individuals, corporations, and public agencies in order to build the collection. So committed was he to the idea that he and his wife, Niki, commissioned a work in memory of their parents.

The Lowell Public Art Collection is distinguished by its thematic coherence. Encountered in the historic district, the pieces are visual commentaries on the issues arising from the themes of the urban park. The artworks have been integrated into small parks, plazas, public spaces, and structures, forming a linear collection loosely following the Canalway paths along the downtown or inner loop of the canal system.

The Lowell Sculptures by Massachusetts-born Robert Cumming were installed in the summer of 1990 around the perimeter of Boarding House Park downtown; they are simple forms based on Lowell symbols that have been combined in a modular design. The artist made the first of his many visits to Lowell in the fall of 1988 to begin the research that led to his proposal to create a sculpture for the city. Working at home in Connecticut or at his studio in western Massachusetts, he refined the concept. A model was presented to the project sponsors and approved in the summer of 1989. Describing the design process, the artist said:

> I was looking for a series of modular shapes that would represent Lowell and cities of the American Industrial Revolution. Using very recognizable elements seemed to make sense in a public project. One of the first shapes that came up was the thread spool, which is similar to a shape I've used in past work: a beehive. I rounded off the spool from the mills to make the shape more like a hive, and in so doing it became less a thread spool than a general shape that could be a beehive, an early American symbol for industry.
>
>   The second major piece is the silhouette of Francis Cabot Lowell, which I saw all over the city. I photographed a copy of it at the Pollard Memorial Library. Some of the other shapes came from the stonework around the locks and canals. If you see a set of

stairs going up an intricate form, there's an impulse to climb. The three sculptures are of human-scale, and I hope people will sit and stand on them. In order to play with the module idea and interchange the shapes in a great number of combinations, I made well over 100 pieces. It was like Santa's Workshop in my living room.[69]

Sculpture *One* is the centerpiece of the series. The most intricate of the sculptures, this piece includes the six-foot-high, six-ton granite silhouette of Francis Cabot Lowell faced on two sides with steel painted black. The elaborate red brick and gray granite base with steps is reminiscent of the rounded stair wall at the Guard Locks on the upper Pawtucket Canal. The third element is the notched granite thread spool or beehive form. The elements of this sculpture suggest basic building blocks of the city: the mind of Mr. Lowell, the built environment, and the product of industry. The structure offers a kind of observation deck made of "Lowell material" from which to view the heart of the industrial city.

The Lowell Sculptures by Robert Cumming at Boarding House Park were unveiled in 1990.
James Higgins

Sculpture *Two* is the tipped thread spool or hive shape mounted on a granite base near the corner of French and John Streets. Three tapered granite blocks are stacked to form the cone shape. The tip of the spindle is about nine feet high. Long steel pins anchor the top section. The sculpture includes a section of black granite polished to a mirror finish. Though the fanciful balancing act may draw a smile from the viewer, in the same moment there is an underlying suggestion of impending doom.

One of the challenges of working within a historic district such as Lowell's is that artworks are scrutinized as any other physical additions or alterations in the zone and subject to the same preservation standards. The Lowell Historic Board, a city agency, enforces strict preservation standards in order to protect the nationally significant architecture and help knit old structures and new construction into a harmonious setting. Working with arts administrators, artists, and planners from Lowell and beyond, the Historic Board reviews proposed designs, meets with artists, and issues permits for installation of new works in the historic district.

Preservationist views about the art are seen in a plan produced by the Lowell Historic Preservation Commission: "New public art should respect the historic setting of the industrial artifacts and have no tendency to overwhelm. Generally, the new art should . . . help define a sense of place at many locations along the canal system."[70]

Ellen Rothenberg was the first woman to complete a work for the collection. Other women had developed proposals of their own or with partners, but for various reasons the projects were derailed in the design process or otherwise not fabricated. Based in Chicago in the early 1990s, Rothenberg was invited to visit Lowell and propose a design for a specific location. She chose Lucy Larcom Park, between the Merrimack Canal and St. Anne's Church in the middle of downtown.

"Try Again," "Stick to Your Text," "Thy Sister's Keeper Thou Art!," "Truth Loses Nothing . . . Upon Investigation"—these and other statements of belief and advice are cut into stone and steel markers in her multipart sculpture *Industry, Not Servitude*. The visual and verbal information exists in a permanent "pause" ready to release its meaning to the next viewer moving through a slim landscape. Voices caught in granite and metal are activated by each passerby. This is an artwork with a voice, in a time, and of a place that can only be Lowell. The voices are pulled from the historic air, lifted from the dry papers. Voices stopped in full-throated command or cry or unsentimental statement. These are words that were not necessarily much heard, never mind heeded, in their time because they rose from marginal sources: women, poets and writers, workers, labor organizers. Decades later, the spoken and paperbound words are shiny and strong.

The artist's shapes and preserved language are part of the daily experience of the community, like doorways, sirens, street lamps, and bench talk. In Lowell's compact downtown, the historic district reveals a slice-of-nineteenth-century-life, from factory and church to boarding house and manager's residence. Only one other work in the Lowell Public Art Collection employs language, the *Jack Kerouac Commemorative*. Rothenberg's sculpture connects and extends two sections of the Lowell High School campus, a location that both benefits from the social and humane qualities of the sculpture and puts the artwork at risk of harsh use. The micro-community of the high school population, nearby workers, and property owners is challenged with allowing the artwork to exist in its midst. Of all the pieces in the collection, this one and the Kerouac sculpture bear the marks of some rough handling. Nicks, tags, and other wear-marks remind everyone why vigilant maintenance is required to assure the integrity of public art.

The voices embedded by Rothenberg in stairs and curved benches make her work familiar and embraceable. The artist gave some of Lowell's past good words back to the community. She named in public, for the first time, two important persons who should be remembered: author Lucy Larcom and labor activist and journalist Sarah Bagley. Although the park was dedicated to Larcom decades ago, there was no sign or marker on site until Rothenberg ringed a tree with her poetry, and Bagley had vanished to parts unknown, bereft of even a silhouette to pass on her likeness. Now Bagley is there with a quote: "Truth loses nothing upon investigation."

An alternative form of commemoration was tried at the Boott Cotton Mills. Volunteers worked with David Ireland, a San Francisco–based artist, to transform a nineteenth-century power house into a stabilized environment whose scale, volume, and light would evoke an industrial chapel. Ireland called his proposed artwork *The Generator Room*.

An early 1990s PBS television documentary about dinosaur hunters in China explained that "it can take a team of scientists 15,000 hours to dig out a dinosaur."[71] Another kind of excavation could be found for a while in the depths of the Boott. More than seventy persons on the *Generator Room* team logged about 3,000 hours in the first two years, cleaning, scraping, and varnishing the brick walls, concrete ceiling, skylights, steel trusses, and animal-like machinery in the three-story room. Led by Professor Jim Coates, the UMass–Lowell art department signed onto the project and offered a public-art seminar on site for three semesters running. More than any other, this urban archeology project signified how far the thinking about public art had advanced in a decade.

The Generator Room provoked a wider discussion about preserving interior spaces—most of the Lowell work to date had been about exteriors and building facades. Instead of sandblasting and dry-walling for interior renovations, with the "G-Room Project" Ireland pushed a new method for inside work. Unfortunately, the project became a casualty of the crushing regional recession of the early 1990s. The developers of the mill complex lost the building to their creditors, and the art team vacated the power house. Daily work schedules curled off the bulletin board, scaffolding gathered dust, and the water seeped in through cracked skylights. Surface improvements made by the volunteers deteriorated. To redeem the enormous effort, the project directors in 1999 produced a documentary book chronicling the *Generator Room* experience, paid for with grant money from the Andy Warhol Foundation for the Visual Arts.

In 1987, Paul Tsongas discussed with Dimitri Hadzi the growing art collection in Lowell. About a year later, the Tsongases asked the artist to begin thinking about a design for a tribute to their parents. Hadzi's sculpture was the first and remains the only entirely privately funded work in the Lowell Public Art Collection. Tsongas had tried to find a donor for a work by Hadzi, but could not close the deal with the business leader whom he had in mind. Exasperated, he asked Niki about doing it themselves. In quiet moments, Tsongas at the start of his public-art campaign sometimes wondered aloud if he and his coconspirators on the sculpture trail looked like "Texas oilmen" to skeptics of the effort—rounding up big pieces of art because they could. It was this worry that led Tsongas to reach out to David Ross, director of Boston's Institute of Contemporary Art, and art consultant Patricia Fuller for the latter phase of the project.

Hadzi was a distinguished artist. Following service in the air force in World War II and graduation from the Cooper Union, he was awarded a Fulbright Fellowship to study in Greece. In Athens he met Henry Moore and began a long friendship with the great sculptor. Hadzi then moved to Rome where his veteran's benefits helped support him and his new family as he studied casting and foundry work. He began to make his mark, shipping work to dealers and museums throughout Europe and across the Atlantic to America. In 1956, he was chosen to represent the United States in the prestigious Venice *Biennale;* a few years later Hadzi was again asked to represent the United States in Venice, this time along with Louise Nevelson. His reputation grew and his artistic powers developed. In 1975, Harvard University invited Hadzi to take up residence on campus, where he remained for many years. Asked about the responsibility of the public artist, Hadzi offered these thoughts:

> I can't always explain my work. I keep discovering things myself because a good part of what I'm doing is intuitive. I think the sculptor should carefully consider, without compromise, what he or she is creating for a public space. You have to try to be sympathetic to the public. They are trying to understand something. Of course, the other side of the coin is that people should make more of an effort to learn about contemporary art. After all, chamber music and poetry were very difficult for me. I have had to put a lot of time into it. Still, I do understand that contemporary art can be hard. Perhaps it is because there are so many baffling directions in sculpture right now.[72]

Speaking about the lengthy design process for the Tsongas's project, Hadzi said, "The two commissions that I have found most difficult were the doors of St. Paul's Church in Rome and this one. Unlike other commissions, I needed to get close to the people who commissioned me." In the end, Hadzi arrived at a solution that he described as "simple and embracing—the forms possibly suggest a family group or trees. There's a sense of something strong, yet warm."[73]

The bronze sculpture is a group of three elements, the tallest of which rises about ten feet. Hadzi used a translucent black patina to add crispness to the forms. The title, *agapétimé,* means "love and honor" in Greek. The work stands at the junction of the Pawtucket Canal and Eastern Canal at the Lower Locks complex off East Merrimack Street. A third water source, the Concord River, flows by within sight on its way to the Merrimack River. Nearby the sculpture is one terminus of the park's replica historic trolley line.

Anthropologist Claude Levi-Strauss put forward the concept that art ("savage thought") is like a national park of the "civilized mind." He was thinking of the wildness of a natural park, but it is an interesting link to have made. Conversely, can we say that a national park, a proscribed distinctive place set apart, is akin to an artwork? Cultural analyst and art historian Lucy Lippard agrees with that notion. She sees Lowell's national historical park as a large-scale public artwork. She makes a strong case for communities and individuals telling their own stories artfully. "Local knowledge and awareness contextualize historical information or images that might otherwise become detached as 'high art,'" she writes in *The Lure of the Local: Senses of Place in a Multicentered Society.* "In cities and large towns, the need to know others' histories as well as one's own is particularly urgent and particularly difficult because the geography encourages alienation."[74]

The National Park Service in Lowell keeps the story alive for people in every sphere—local, state, national, and global. Lippard highlights the park in her book, not without criticism, even though on balance she admires the impulse and pro-grammatic gestures:

> I like to think of installations from the New York Chinatown History Project (now the Museum of Chinese in the Americas) and the Lowell National Historical Park as "art-works" because they diverge from the conventional museum and historical society. They have more open-minded social analysis, accompanied by an experimental approach to didactic display.[75]

KEROUAC COMES HOME[76]

"Another Kerouac pilgrimage coming to an end, chasing the ghost of Jack in forlorn Lowell. Rejuvenation found in your hometown. In your beginnings we can find your truth, our own truth."

—Katie and Sam Costello of Hubbard, Ohio,
at the *On the Road* scroll manuscript exhibition, 2007

In early 1942, nineteen-year-old Jack Kerouac was hired as a sportswriter at the *Lowell Sun*. The Lowell High School athlete had used a scholarship as his ticket to ride to New York City, but was back home after dropping out of Columbia University. He had one goal—to be a recognized author: "I began to write a novel right in the City Room about Lowell and the three attendant ills of most middle-sized cities: provincialism, bigotry, and materialism."[77] Although he was soon gone again, Lowell stayed with him and fueled his soul and art until the end. He came back as a local-boy-made-good in 1950, signing copies of his first novel, *The Town and the City*, in a department store on Merrimack Street. He called Lowell "Galloway" in that book, a Romantic family saga set in the decades before and after World War II.

With his novel *On the Road* in 1957, Kerouac added a new voice to the country's literary mix. His gutsy, lyrical language was American speech, delivered in a rush and rhythm that sent readers into a spin. He chronicled his adventures coast-to-coast. Kerouac's America is made of stories from multiethnic, working-class Lowell along with tales of young writers, railroaders, spiritual voyagers, jazz revelers, and wanderers on the social fringe. Kerouac's books speak to people consumed with the big questions, like "How shall we live?"

Readers come to Lowell to touch a part of what Kerouac was. Much of Kerouac's Lowell remains: the Lowell High School of *Maggie Cassidy*; the river of *Doctor Sax*; the St. Louis de France church of *Visions of Gerard*. Much is gone as well, but visitors fill in the gaps. Many pilgrims stop at his grave in Edson Cemetery—some leave a rose or a wine bottle.

Like the Lowell Folk Festival and Lowell Public Art Collection, Jack Kerouac was not mentioned in the park's *General Management Plan*—but he was not excluded in any way either. A visitor to the park can fill a day, starting with the Visitor Center wall display about Kerouac that orients people to the key Kerouac places in the city; an allied brochure for a self-guided walking or riding tour provides more information about the author's life and literature. At the Mogan Cultural Center, a display case in the Immigrants Exhibit holds one of Kerouac's typewriters and the last green canvas backpack that he owned. A block away is the *Kerouac Commemorative*, with his words sandblasted into granite. After traveling the author's local road, from

Jack Kerouac (1922–1969) at his Florida home in 1958
Fred DeWitt; Orange County, Florida, Regional History Center

birthplace to gravesite, a visitor can return to the starting point where an evocative short film, *Lowell Blues* by Henry Ferrini, is screened every afternoon. Ferrini's "film poem" is a moody take on Kerouac's fantastical evocation of his early adolescence in Lowell, including the epic flood of 1936, spun out in the novel *Doctor Sax*.

The park staff has made a place for Kerouac, responding to strong public interest in this author. They collaborate with local organizers on Kerouac literary festivals in March and October. In 2007, they worked with scholars from UMass–Lowell to create a special exhibition about Kerouac for the Boott Mills Gallery on the first floor of the Boott Cotton Mills Museum. The centerpiece was the legendary *On the Road* scroll manuscript that was on a national tour for the book's fiftieth anniversary. For three caffeine-fevered weeks in 1951, Kerouac composed a revved-up version of the story he had been writing and rewriting for several years. The typescript stretches 120 feet—lengths of semi-transparent paper cut to size for feeding into the typewriter and scotch-taped together. Kerouac invented a form to match his creative surge, eliminating the need to interrupt the compositional flow by linking the sheets of paper. Prophetically, he anticipated the scrolling character of today's digital word processing. The scroll and accompanying display of images, artifacts, and illuminating text won a national award from the American Association for State and Local History, a prize shared by the park, UMass–Lowell, and city's cultural affairs office. The exhibit and thirty related events drew more than 25,000 people.

A week does not go by without a mention of Jack Kerouac in the major newspapers and magazines of the nation. The Lowell-born author's reputation has soared since his death in 1969. The Kerouac revival, which approaches a phenomenon in scope, has strong roots in Lowell. The scroll manuscript for *On the Road* sold in 2001 at a Christie's auction for $2.43 million, at the time the highest price ever paid for a manuscript of a literary work. In response, the *New York Times* wrote in an editorial, "What you sense in his prose is the freshness, the newness of the country" in the years after World War II. "Kerouac mapped a new geography, and he did it in an unparalleled three-week effusion that resulted in this typescript." The *Times* wrote about Kerouac's "breathless flux" as an "antidote to Hemingway," concluding, "when Kerouac shoots off sparks he still lights up the sky."[78] For critic Ann Douglas, "Kerouac's work represents the most extensive experiment in language and literary form undertaken by an American writer of his generation."[79]

Add such praise to the fact that Kerouac was named one of the most important figures of the past century by both *Life* magazine and *The Times* of London. The New York Public Library acquired most of Kerouac's manuscripts, typescripts, letters, and notebooks. The author's books are available in dozens of languages. The catalogue of activity and happenings is astonishing when one considers the low ebb of Kerouac's reputation when he died at the age of forty-seven in St. Petersburg, Florida. The Lowell-born author had left his imprint on the culture at the time of his death, largely through the impact of *On the Road*, but in death his legend has increased by leaps. The resurgence connects back to Lowell.

Some observers mark the beginning of the revival of interest in Kerouac to the posthumous release of his *Visions of Cody* (1972) while others credit Ann Charters's biography in 1973. Still others point to the gathering of Beat Generation authors and friends in Boulder, Colo., in 1982 in celebration of the 25th anniversary of Kerouac's culture-shaking novel *On the Road*. Not to be overlooked is Bob Dylan's performance at UMass–Lowell in November 1975, during a barnstorming northeast tour called the Rolling Thunder Revue. The star-studded concert in Costello Gymnasium was part of Dylan's pilgrimage to Kerouac's hometown. The visit to Lowell was reported in depth by *Rolling Stone* magazine, casting a new light on both Kerouac and Lowell.

The Kerouac connection at the university dates from 1967, when Kerouac had come back to live in Lowell with his wife, Stella, and ailing mother, Gabrielle. Professor Charles Ziavras was assigning *On the Road* in his English classes at Lowell Tech, one of the two root schools of today's university. He invited the author to lecture in his class: "What could be more ideal than to have the author interpret this classic for them?"[80] (Ziavras, who died in 2000, grew up in Lowell and was on the campus faculty for thirty-five years.)

Kerouac accepted the offer and even told Ziavras to pursue the idea of a writer-in-residence appointment. In a note he said, "I've had similar offers from other colleges round the country but to these seminars I could walk, over the Moody Street Bridge yet, and after the lecture I can always brood under the bridge or even jump in the river. . . . You can't learn how to write, but you certainly can learn why literature tells the truth at a given time."[81]

The plan fell apart when Kerouac told Ziavras that he could not go through with it. By the late 1960s, years of hard living and excessive drinking had taken its toll on the writer. Ziavras relates this episode and more in his *Visions of Kerouac* (1974), an early Kerouac biography.

Another key player in reviving local interest in Kerouac was Lewis Karabatsos, when he was director of the Lowell Museum in the Wannalancit Mills on Suffolk Street.

> In 1978, the Museum had a plan to highlight famous people who came from Lowell. Ben Butler, Lucy Larcom, and others came to mind, but we were also interested in doing something contemporary. Kerouac was an obvious choice: he was world renowned and visitors to the Museum always asked about him.
>
> Bob McLeod, who worked with me, and I started to pull together all the things on Kerouac we knew existed in the city. We also knew there was some sensitivity to the possibility of exploiting Kerouac's memory and what his work stood for. We decided to get an endorsement for the exhibit from Kerouac's widow, Stella, and contacted her through her brother John.

Karabatsos and McLeod set up fifty chairs—and more than 250 people showed up.

> We had so many people that we had to turn people away due to the fire code. People who couldn't get in were banging on the doors and windows and yelling. They said we were going against everything Kerouac stood for by keeping them out.[82]

One of the speakers was Paul Brouillette, a young writer and theater technician recently graduated from UMass–Boston. He had been a student of Kerouac's work since he was fifteen years old, when he had read of the Lowell author's death on the front page of the *Lowell Sun*. After UMass, he spent a summer at Naropa Institute in Colorado where he studied Beat Literature and was a research assistant for poet Allen Ginsberg. He wrote about the event:

> There were ghosts with us that night. The spirits of adolescents searching beyond horizon lines. The phantoms of men with loss in their eyes. . . . Our readings paled in comparison to *his* sound. Jack Kerouac narrating, no, spontaneously composing, the narrative to *Pull My Daisy* [the experimental film]. His voice surprised some people— playful and reassuring, like Brando's and Sinatra's when they, too, were young and not thickened by excess.[83]

Marie Sweeney served on the board of directors of the museum at the time. "It was clear to us that doing a Kerouac program would raise some controversy. It was the beginning of the well-attended, highly regarded celebrations of today."[84]

In 1985, Brian Foye put together an organization devoted to raising Kerouac's profile in his hometown: the Corporation for the Celebration of Jack Kerouac in Lowell (known today as Lowell Celebrates Kerouac! Inc.). Born and raised in Lowell, Foye had a keen interest in the Beat writers. During his college years he had met poet Allen Ginsberg, who urged Foye to do something ambitious for Kerouac back home. The intent was to produce literary events and establish a permanent tribute to Kerouac in some form. Foye's group would help plan the first Kerouac festival in 1988 and take the lead in following years—never missing a year to the present. He also published a book about Kerouac's literary places in Lowell.

An irreplaceable member of the organization is Roger Brunelle, a retired foreign languages teacher and Franco-American activist in the city. Responding to a request by Kerouac aficionados in Quebec who wanted to tour the sites in the author's books, Brunelle invented the guided tour of Kerouac places. Thirty years later, he has several specialized tours in his portfolio, including "Ghosts of the Pawtucket-ville Night" and "Mystic Jack," which he regularly offers for enthusiasts. Brunelle told author Jay Atkinson, "The *idea* of Kerouac is that anyone can become a writer, because everyone has a story to tell. The ones who are remembered are the ones who did it best."[85]

Around the same time that Foye put together the community organization, the staff and commissioners of the Lowell Historic Preservation Commission had begun talking about a permanent tribute to Kerouac in sculptural form, folding the project into the city's expanding public-art initiative. One of the LHPC's first cultural grants in 1981 had gone to the public library, Pollard Memorial Library, to publish a guide to Kerouac places in the city. Another grant had supported film director John Antonelli's documentary about Kerouac that premiered at Merrimack Repertory Theatre with three sold-out screenings. There was a track record leading to a more ambitious gesture, which came in the form of a national design competition for a sculptural tribute to Kerouac.

The decision to move forward with a Kerouac sculpture was daring. This was the era when Secretary of the Interior James Watt had banned the Beach Boys from performing on the National Mall because he did not feel that their "vibration" was a good one for mainstream America. When the LHPC voted to spend $100,000 on the project and make a grant of the same to the City of Lowell, the members knew the size of the grant had reached the threshold that required the secretary's approval in writing. In late 1986, one city councilor voted "No" on a motion to accept federal funding for a sculpture that would be installed in a new green space being developed by the city and state. The objection was based on disapproval of Kerouac's sometimes self-destructive behavior. That lone voice of dissent led to a media tempest. The real news was that Lowell, collectively, had said, "Yes" to Kerouac. The Secretary of the Interior signed off on the grant. In his own way, Kerouac had been all about "the department of the interior."

Kerouac always seems to be a topic waiting for a controversy. As a *Wall Street Journal* reporter told one LHPC staff member: "My editor is not looking for a story about consensus in Lowell; he wants me to get the controversy." It did not matter to the reporter that in the three Kerouac project motions involving officials of public entities in Lowell, the result had been two unanimous votes at the LHPC and one 7 to 1 outcome at the City Council. Opinion-writer George Will filled a page in *Newsweek* magazine with a satirical essay: "Daddy, Who Was Kerouac?"

On June 25, 1988, a crowd gathered in a new green space at Bridge and French streets to hear speeches and readings that marked the dedication of the *Jack Kerouac Commemorative*. The guest of honor was Mrs. Jack Kerouac, the former Stella Sampas of Lowell, whose support had been essential in moving the project forward from the start. Also in attendance were Kerouac's daughter from a previous marriage, Janet, and some of his closest literary friends, including poets Allen Ginsberg and Lawrence Ferlinghetti. Representatives from the Province of Quebec, Canada, and France brought greetings from their governments. Reporters from CBS television news and *New Yorker* magazine joined dozens of regional and international media representatives in covering the story.

Created by Texas artist Ben Woitena, the *Kerouac Commemorative* broke new ground in the way American writers are recognized. Typically, a birthplace is pre-served or a street is renamed for an author. The Kerouac sculpture blends into the landscape of a canal-side park designed by Brown and Rowe landscape architects

The Jack Kerouac Commemorative by Ben Woitena, 1988
James Higgins

of Boston. (Originally called Eastern Canal Park, the downtown green space soon after was renamed Kerouac Park by city officials.) Poet Michael McClure and former keyboardist of the Doors Ray Manzarek attended the ceremony, having performed downtown before 1,000 people the night before. A smiling McClure said it was "subversive" to have carved thousands of Kerouac's words into stone for the ages.

Eight triangular pillars of polished granite are inscribed with excerpts from ten of Kerouac's books. Resembling inverted books, the granite forms on the perimeter of the plaza feature the opening paragraphs from the author's five "Lowell novels" and *On the Road*. Chunks of text more metaphysical in nature appear on the inner ring of stone panels. The pavement and granite benches form circle and cross patterns, referencing the author's Catholic and Buddhist spirituality. The literature is presented in the open air, sandblasted into the reddish-brown granite. The sculpture is a portrait in language. For an artist who so loved the American landscape, it is appropriate that the *Kerouac Commemorative* is of the American earth. The granite was quarried in South Dakota; the stones were cut in Minnesota; West Virginian graphic designers worked on the text; and the sculptor is a Texan who studied art in Southern California.

Lowell was a wellspring of experience for Kerouac. He came back to the place, the people, time and again for his writing and personal sustenance. The Lowell books are a large part of the sculpture. Pawtucketville, Centralville, the South Common—the words are there. But the world is also there on the granite panels: baseball, Hemingway, freedom, Homer's *Iliad*, Los Angeles, Buddha, God, New York, the road.

Kerouac's characters seek truth, joy, and the ultimate ground of being—at times through contemplation on mountaintops, at other times through reckless physical indulgence. And sometimes his characters are sweetly even. His fiction foreshadowed major cultural shifts that altered our society in the 1960s and 1970s. He never denied his roots and branched farther than he might have guessed. The painter James McNeill Whistler, who did not claim Lowell as his native town, but whom the community wisely claims for his genius, had his birthplace preserved as an art museum in 1908. Eighty years later, Jack Kerouac had his big Lowell day.

Since 1990, John Sampas, the Kerouac Estate's representative and a brother-in-law of Kerouac's, has guided the publication of numerous Kerouac books: letters, novels, spiritual texts, poems, and more. A major donor to UMass–Lowell, his gifts have helped make possible a Kerouac Writer-in-Residence program, annual student scholarships, and the Jack and Stella Kerouac Center for Public Humanities. In the early 1990s, UMass–Lowell reinstated the English Department elective on Beat Studies that Ziavras had taught and also sponsored a recurring academic conference on Beat Literature. The first Kerouac Writer-in-Residence was Andre Dubus III, the best-selling author of *House of Sand and Fog* and *Townies* and now the anchor of a robust creative writing concentration in the English Department. In 2007, Sampas accepted on Kerouac's behalf an honorary doctor of humane letters degree from UMass–Lowell.

Photographer and writer John Suiter has documented Kerouac places from Lowell to the North Cascades National Park in the Pacific Northwest. His book *Poets on the Peaks: Gary Snyder, Philip Whalen, & Jack Kerouac in the Cascades* chronicles the experiences of the three writers as fire lookouts in the 1950s. Suiter is writing a biography of Snyder with the cooperation of the much-decorated poet and environmental thought-leader. Now based in Chicago, Suiter has witnessed a change in the hometown view of Kerouac. In the 1980s, local people that he encountered were often clueless about the author or they would scoff when Suiter told them that he was making photographs of places from Kerouac's life and writings. Many of them had heard about Kerouac's alcoholism; most were unaware that he had expressed his affection for Lowell in book after book. When Suiter returned to the city a few years later, he was encouraged by what he heard:

> I was back shooting for my "Rumors of Kerouac" exhibit at the Boott Mills Museum. I don't think there was anyone who hadn't heard of Kerouac, and the quality of what they heard was completely different, due largely I'm sure to the presence of the *Kerouac Commemorative* and the annual festivals. The clearest expression of the change came to me while I was making pictures of the Lowell High football team in 1992. I was trying to get something evocative of those great football scenes of Jack's in *The Town and the City* and *Vanity of Duluoz*. In the locker room at halftime, I asked one player what he knew about Jack Kerouac. "Kerouac? Oh sure—the poet," he said. "He used to play for this team." Jack would have loved that.[86]

NOTES

1. *Details of the Preservation Plan*, 173.
2. *The Preservation Plan, Lowell Historic Preservation Commission*, 2.
3. David Riley, "The Rebirth of Lowell: A Beacon for Revitalization," *Boston Globe Magazine*, July 20, 1980, 8.
4. Riley, "The Rebirth of Lowell," 9.
5. Robert Gilman, author's notes, 2012 meeting.

6. John Leite, interview with the author.

7. Leite, interview with the author.

8. Martin T. Meehan, interview with the author.

9. Nancye Tuttle, *Picture It: Lowell Goes to the Movies* (Lowell: Lowell Historic Preservation Commission, 1993), n.p.

10. "You Know You're From Lowell When . . ." https://www.facebook.com/#!/groups/242361685323.

11. *Greater Lowell Massachusetts, 1973*, n.p.

12. "The Mills Weren't Made of Marble," *New York Times*, September 7, 1992.

13. Duey Kol, interview with the author.

14. Kol, interview with the author.

15. Patrick M. Malone, *Waterpower in Lowell: Engineering and Industry in Nineteenth-Century America* (Baltimore: Johns Hopkins University Press, 2009), 39.

16. Andy Dabilis, Kathy McCabe, and Amy Sessler, *Rebirth of the Merrimack* (Merrimack River Watershed Council), n.p.

17. Albert W. Atwood, "The Merrimack: River of Industry and Romance," *National Geographic Magazine*, January 1951, 106.

18. Henry David Thoreau, *A Week on the Concord and Merrimack Rivers* (New York: Signet Classic/New American Library of World Literature, 1961), 61–62.

19. John McPhee, "1839–2003: Five Days on the Concord and Merrimack Rivers," *New Yorker*, December 15, 2003, 74.

20. Mary H. Blewett, *The Last Generation: Work and Life in the Textile Mills of Lowell, Massachusetts, 1910–1960.* (Amherst: University of Massachusetts Press, 1990), 93–96.

21. George Chapman, exhibit text, Boott Cotton Mills Museum.

22. Linus Childs, exhibit text, Boott Cotton Mills Museum.

23. Adam Davidson, "Making It in America," *Atlantic*, January/February 2012, 60.

24. Leslie T. Chang, *Factory Girls: From Village to City in a Changing China* (New York: Spiegel and Grau, 2009), 48.

25. Mike Wurm, letter to the author.

26. Robert Weible, "Visions and Reality: Reconsidering the Creation and Development of Lowell's National Park, 1966–1992." *Public Historian* 33, no. 2 (May 2011).

27. Michael Southworth, letter to the author.

28. Southworth, letter to the author.

29. Southworth, letter to the author.

30. Page One Productions, *Patrick J. Mogan: Visionary and Realist.*

31. Page One Productions, *Roots of an Urban Cultural Park.*

32. *Lowell Discovery Network.*

33. *Lowell Discovery Network.*

34. Charles Nikitopoulos, letter to the author.

35. John E. Roche, *The Center for Human Development*, 10.

36. Patrick J. Mogan, "Renewal Process in Lowell, Massachusetts: Toward an Ecologically Sensitive Educational Model," University of Massachusetts–Amherst, 1975, 78.

37. Sheila Kirschbaum, interview with the author.

38. George Tsapatsaris, interview with the author.

39. Tsapatsaris, interview with the author.

40. Donald Pierson, interview with the author.

41. Rebecca Lofgren, letter to the author.

42. Edwin L. Aguirre, "NSF Awards $1.3M to Transform Science Learning: Students to Become 'Data Scientists,'" http://www.uml.edu/News/stories/2011-12/Martin-NSF-Grant.aspx, September 16, 2011.

43. Anita Greenwood, interview with the author.

44. Greenwood, interview with the author.

45. Page One Productions, *Folk Culture in America.*

46. Rosemary Noon, "The Lowell Regatta Festival Committee," *LOCAL: Lowell Office of Cultural Affairs*, August–September 1990, 1.

47. *American Folklife Center*.

48. Mogan, conversation with the author.

49. Page One Productions, *Folk Culture in America*.

50. *Preservation Plan Amendment*, 70.

51. Page One Productions, *Folk Culture in America*.

52. Maggie Holtzberg, "The Pierogi Queen," *Keepers of Tradition: Traditional Arts and Folk Heritage*, July 19, 2011, blog.massfolksarts.org/blog/index.php/2011/07/the-pierogi-queen.

53. Pauline Golec, interview with the author.

54. Golec, interview with the author.

55. Janet Leggat, interview with the author.

56. David Perry, "Appreciation: Sue Leggat Recalled as Folk Fest's Conscience," *The Sun*, November 25, 2003.

57. Marie Sweeney, "I Remember Sue Leggat," remarks at Brush Gallery, June 2004.

58. Page One Productions, *Folk Culture*.

59. Holtzberg, letter to the author.

60. Rebecca Gross, "Rebuilding on the Past: The Creative Rebirth of Lowell, Massachusetts," *NEA Arts* no. 1 (2012).

61. Mogan, Memorandum to Center City Committee, August 1972.

62. *LOCAL: Lowell Office of Cultural Affairs*, April-May, 1992.

63. Maureen Newcomb, e-mail to Peter Aucella, 2012.

64. Some passages from this section first appeared in an article by the author in *Public Art Review*.

65. Bruno K, n.p.

66. *Culture: A Celebration of Lowell*, 8.

67. *The Lowell Cultural Plan Review Project*, iii.

68. Paul Marion, "Public Art in an Urban Laboratory: Lowell, Mass.," *Public Art Review* (Spring/Summer 1991): 14.

69. Marion, "Public Art in an Urban Laboratory," 14.

70. Marion, "Public Art in an Urban Laboratory," 15.

71. James Coates and Paul Marion, *Generator Room* (Lowell: Loom Press, 1998), 34.

72. Marion, *Dimitri Hadzi*, The Brush Gallery and Artists' Studios and the Hellenic Culture Society, October 12–November 11, 1990, n.p.

73. Marion, *Dimitri Hadzi*, n.p.

74. Lucy R. Lippard, *The Lure of the Local: Senses of Place in a Multicentered Society* (New York: New Press, 1997), 51.

75. Lippard, *The Lure of the Local*, 97.

76. Some passages from this section first appeared in an article by the author in the *UMass Lowell Magazine* and *Lowell Sun* newspaper.

77. Jack Kerouac, *Atop an Underwood: Early Stories and Other Writings*, ed. Paul Marion (New York: Viking, 1999), 179.

78. "Kerouac on the Block," *New York Times*, May 24, 2001.

79. Ann Douglas, "On the Road Again," *New York Times Book Review*, April 9, 1995.

80. Marion, "Kerouac on Campus: Roots of a Phenomenon," *UMass Lowell Alumni Magazine*, Winter 2002, 16.

81. Marion, "Kerouac on Campus," 16.

82. Marion, "Kerouac on Campus," 17.

83. Paul Brouillette, "Honoring Kerouac," 1.

84. Marion, "Kerouac on Campus," 17.

85. Jay Atkinson, *Paradise Road: Jack Kerouac's* Lost Highway *and My Search for America* (Hoboken: Wiley, 2010), 7.

86. Marion, "Kerouac on Campus," 18.

CHAPTER 7

Stewardship and Leadership

Writing about city renewal processes, Galen Cranz wonders about the possibilities inherent in urban cultural parks like Lowell's. Will they cause and sustain economic growth? Does the outcome reflect social values? Will the community enjoy a civic revitalization? This is work for the long haul, not like restoring a building or preparing a tour of labor history sites. This is about systemic change in the culture of a place. The work is on a generational scale—really, multigenerational. While the core idea can be a constant, the animating element, shaped by a place's internal conditions as well as the external factors, will change. Policies and approaches must be kept nimble and readily adaptable to new situations. Incumbents must be willing to make room for fresh takes while hewing to first principles that have borne success. None of this is automatic. Modern Lowell benefited greatly from continuity within its leadership network. Familiar names are links in the chain forged decades ago. And then something happened in the mid-2000s that demonstrated a deep level of self-reflection. Leaders began to address the challenge of succession.

Lowell movers and shakers now are intentional about transmitting the community story and helping other leaders in various stages of their professional development to learn how to convey their own stories and aspirations for the city. Something else also happened: younger activists began to organize themselves around projects. The synergy between structured programs and grassroots community-building signaled a new phase of community development. It was organic and of its time. The generational churn, the in-migration of younger doers, the maturing of Lowellians who had grown up enjoying a spunkier city—these factors changed the community condition. The organized efforts include Public Matters, a leadership development program of the Lowell Plan, Inc., and National Park Service; the Next Generation Giving Circle of the Greater Lowell Community Foundation; the Emergent Generation network and Foundation meet-ups, sparked by community organizers; the Paul H. Sullivan Leadership Institute of Middlesex Community College; the Young Professionals of Greater Lowell; and the Deshpande Foundation's Merrimack Valley Sandbox Leadership Institute for entrepreneurs in Lowell and Lawrence, Massachusetts. At the same time, the National Park Service cultivates young activists through various programs.

YOUTH STEWARDSHIP

Park ranger Amy Glowacki, LNHP's Youth Programs Coordinator, is more than pleased that Lowell is considered a leader among parks for the innovation and high quality of its youth programs. The Spindle City Corps, past recipient of a

231

congressional award, is a partnership program with Community Teamwork, Inc., that offers not only summer jobs but also year-round work that emphasizes job training, life skills, and leadership development. This is a program for young people aged fifteen to twenty-one. The Corps reflects the racial, ethnic, and economic mix of the city. Members address the most relevant environmental and social issues of today through theater programs in which they play nineteenth-century characters who pop up on the streets of Lowell and gritty maintenance work on visitor sites, a program funded by the Public Land Corps and Youth Conservation Corps. They learn their own history and how to appreciate the power of special places. Glowacki outlined the effort:

> We've been doing youth programs in Lowell for more than twenty years. Many of these young people have never been to a national park. Lowell is the gateway for them, not only as Americans who share in the ownership of the parks but also perhaps as a career. We reach out to schools and community organizations to connect with their internship and jobs programs.

Young people like Wesley McCants help to "spruce up" the park
LNHP

We see the youth experience of the park in a pyramid shape, starting with the broad constituency of students who experience the hands-on education programs at the Tsongas Industrial History Center. Our camps and after-school programs are the next stage for some of them, and finally there might be a summer job. The most promising among these young people can be identified for higher-level internships and even summer employment. At the top of the pyramid is the possibility of a permanent park job.[1]

Rhaissa Pereira Menezes was a Lowell High School student when she joined the Spindle City Corps. She worked the historic district downtown as a costumed interpreter for two summers, and sees the experience on a grand scale: "I hope one day to look back at my younger years and say, 'I worked for the National Park Service, and I helped change the world.'"[2]

PUBLIC MATTERS

In the park's thirtieth anniversary report in 2008, Superintendent Michael Creasey and his team called for the creation of a "National Park Community Development Academy," which was described as a six-month program for emerging leaders that would deepen their understanding of the values inherent in the park idea in Lowell and prepare them to be stewards of what has been built and formed. Creasey was frank in his assessment of the situation: "After three decades, the ranks of those who were involved with the establishment of the park are thinning, and many new residents have a limited perspective on the process by which the park helped to transform the city."[3] That insight led to the formation of Public Matters: Empowering Lowell's Leaders. Launched in 2009 by the park and the Lowell Plan, Inc., Public Matters has an ambitious goal—"to cultivate inspired stewards of our history, natural resources, social and cultural capital, and economic and government institutions."[4] By 2012, more than ninety-three men and women had completed the course that is grounded in the city's life and times, especially the recent past and present.

Creasey had come to Lowell in 2005 from Blackstone National Heritage Area, which takes in sites along the Connecticut River in south central Massachusetts and northern Connecticut. Blackstone had a successful leadership development program that Creasey believed could be a model for a similar initiative in Lowell. He organized focus groups to tease out what the best approach would be in Lowell and met with nonprofit organization managers, school administrators, and public officials. In 2008, Rosemary Noon joined the staff of the Lowell Plan as a project manager. A former park ranger and cultural programs administrator for the Lowell Historic Preservation Commission, the Lowell native with deep roots had been the city's first cultural affairs director in 1987 and later managed the Fine Arts Center of Regis College in Weston, Massachusetts. Her addition to the Lowell Plan team was a key to getting the leadership program started. Creasey and Lowell Plan executive director Jim Cook wanted to work together on a leadership initiative, and now Cook had someone who could drive the program. On the park side, partnership coordinator Sue Andrews and cultural-programs director David Blackburn were asked to work with Noon.

In January 2009, with the program still being shaped, the first class was selected through an open nomination process. The initial participants were like test pilots who gave the organizers vital feedback on the program, which uses Lowell history as a framework to discuss different leadership styles and models of community development. Each class numbers about twenty members. They come from the banks, Lowell Community Health Center, the National Park Service, the Visiting Nurses Association, technology companies, the city planning office, businesses, museums, the university and community college, social service agencies, and other organizations. There is a general but not in-depth understanding of the park among most Public Matters members. They are aware of the tours and museums, but it is often new for them to hear about the park's role in economic development, historic preservation, community partnerships, and sustainable environmental practices.

"The park's interest was tied to the huge investment in Lowell and assuring that in going forward there is a population here that is informed and understands what makes Lowell unique," Andrews said. "The local knowledge varies among the participants, and we definitely hear many people say they learned something new about the city, whether they were born here or are newcomers."[5]

Blackburn added, "To a person, the longtime residents will say, 'I didn't know that and I was always curious about it.' They are exposed to neighborhoods unfamiliar to them and to other people's stories. It's gratifying to see the longtimers, especially, getting new perspectives on the city."[6]

The half-year experience (January through June) is an immersion in civic culture and urban space, offering members intimate audiences with men and women who have played pivotal roles in the city's revival—people like former City Manager

Rosemary Noon of the Lowell Plan and David Blackburn and Sue Andrews of the park collaborate on the Public Matters leadership program.
Kevin Harkins

Brian Martin, playwright Jack Neary, and one-time president of the Lowell Museum Corporation Marie Sweeney. To the program's credit, each class looks like the city as a whole, an outcome that many community programs strive for but rarely attain. Participants engage the city as if they are tourists in their own town, visiting park sites and redevelopment projects with expert commentary from park administrator Peter Aucella and city planner Adam Baacke. One day is reserved for guided walking tours of neighborhoods that are not their own. In April, when the rapids are thrashing in the Concord River, everyone suits up in wet-gear for white-water rafting. For team-building, not much compares to pulling one of your seat-mates out of the foaming river. The sessions wrap up with a question: "What do we do now?" Working together, the class comes together around a "Promise of Commitment" that each of the members carries forward.

Members spend considerable time exploring the idea of "the story of self." One of the program's guiding documents is Marshall Ganz's "What Is Public Narrative?" Ganz calls public narrative a "leadership art," and says it is composed of three parts: "A story of why I have been called, a story of self; a story of why we have been called, a story of us; and a story of the urgent challenge for which we are called to act, a story of now."[7] By the midpoint of the program, each participant must prepare and present a three-minute narrative about himself or herself. These stand-up presentations are invariably dramatic. Noon described what happens:

> Members consistently tell us that creating and sharing their own "Story of Self" is the most inspirational element of the program. After hearing the powerful and transformative narratives of the guest panelists that we bring in, the members put themselves on the line when they candidly describe the routes they have traveled to get to this point in their lives. This is the point when people really find out who they have been sitting next to for weeks. Nobody leaves the room without having been emotionally and intellectually moved by what they have experienced.[8]

The next-to-last section of the Boott Cotton Mills Museum exhibition about Lowell's industrial history has a display titled "Dilemmas-Choices-Consequences," as these concepts apply to the changing position of Lowell in the national and global textile industry. These concepts are what Ganz is framing in his discussion about the "anxiety of agency, as well as its exhilaration" that a person feels when faced with an "urgent challenge."

For Noon, one of the compelling outcomes of the first four years of the program is the way alumni have formed a community of their own. They stay in touch on Facebook, organize meet-ups, and collaborate on special projects. And they pick each other out at community events.

Suzanne Frechette, deputy director of the Coalition for a Better Acre, wrote Noon a heartfelt message after a neighborhood cultural festival on the North Common in the Acre:

> As I looked around today, I couldn't help but notice all the Public Matters grads making our city a better place—and you were there! I think the prophecy of Public Matters and making those collaborations work has come true. Public Matters is a "we" project with an emphasis on collaborating and networking.[9]

In addition to the spin-off collegial benefit of the program, the Lowell Plan launched a mentoring program in 2011. They paired Public Matters graduates

Linda Sopheap Sou
Kevin Harkins

and selected other applicants with thirty mentors from the Lowell Plan board of directors and other veteran leaders in the city. Once-a-month meetings gave mentees a closer, inside look at what decision makers do every day. The program is evolving, and has as much to offer as a networking experience, Noon said.

Linda Sopheap Sou is a Public Matters graduate. She was born in Lowell to parents Tim and Kolab Thou, who had fled the Khmer Rouge genocide and resettled in Lowell in 1981. Her father is the founder of Angkor Dance Troupe, which he started in the refugee camps of Thailand and the Philippines. She started dancing with the troupe when she was three and is now president of the board of directors.

Inspired by her father's example of being true to his culture, Sou has become an important "connector" person through her work with teenagers at the Lowell Community Health Center. She said she learned from him that there are countless people who are missing opportunities and enriching experiences. Her passion is "bringing people together." If someone wants to know what is going on with youth in the city, she is a person to call. "I left the city to study sociology at the Massachusetts College of Liberal Arts knowing that I wanted to return to my wonderful city and contribute to its future—I cannot imagine working and living anywhere else."[10]

With roots in Lowell, but an upbringing in nearby Tyngsborough and college in upstate New York, Corey Sciuto had quasi-native credentials when he moved into a renovated mill building downtown. A software engineer with a passion for cities, he started taking pictures of life in Lowell and posting them online with historical notes. Before he knew it he was a blogger who had been featured in the daily newspaper.

"I got the attention of the Lowell Historical Society, and in 2010 was asked to present my documentary work at their annual meeting," he explained, "and was invited to join the board of directors." He emphasized how important it was that he was asked to get involved:

> It isn't just that I've traded thoughts and ideas with the movers and shakers in the fourth largest city in the Commonwealth, but I made the realization that individuals, when simply asked, can become empowered to use their passions and skills—perhaps undeveloped skills they didn't even know they had—to make a difference in their professional and civic community.[11]

Sciuto's willingness to help got him noticed by a Public Matters nominator. After his boss gave him permission to leave work early twice a month for the meetings, he told his coworkers, none of whom was from Lowell and many of whom are

Corey Sciuto
Kevin Harkins

apprehensive about the city, that Public Matters was the Lowell equivalent of the Skull and Bones Society of Yale.

Through anecdotes about Lowell's past and current leaders and discussions about our own strengths and weaknesses, I began to see how we each fit into the puzzle—what kind of leaders myself and my classmates could be. I found ways to contribute to our success as a group—for example, my Historical Society knowledge was needed from time to time. Other times, the detail focus that makes me a good engineer was of use. Others made their marks by being insightful, imaginative, charismatic, or organized—skills that I am less apt with.

I learned quite a bit about the importance of empowerment and synergies and am now better situated to ask others to participate. I was also able to bring the leadership skills I developed to my "day job" in software—I'm more confident and more interested in nurturing those key business relationships.

Programs like Public Matters and citizens like my classmates really help make Lowell a world-class, model small city. The city will move forward, always innovating, provided it has skilled and passionate leadership. We became not just twenty individuals with a nice certificate and some new skills. We're more than an alumni group that meets to reminisce. We emerged as civic leaders with the skills, passion, and network to do what needs to be done.[12]

Sovanna Devin Pouv is in his early thirties, but he has already covered a lot of territory in Lowell. He was born in Khao-I-Dang refugee camp in Thailand; his Cambodian mother was saved by his father, a Thai soldier, who found her in a ditch on the trail out of Cambodia. She had been shot and wounded. "They fell in love and, thus, had me."[13] From Southeast Asia, the family resettled in Chicago, and when Sovanna was eight years old moved to Lowell where his aunt was doing well. She was his mother's only surviving relative of the genocide. He went to Lowell High School and earned an associate's degree from Middlesex Community College at twenty-nine years old. He became a citizen in 2007 at a naturalization ceremony in Fenway Park. President George W. Bush welcomed the large group of new Americans on the jumbo-tron.

After several years working at the United Teen Equality Center (UTEC), Pouv took a job in marketing with Meerkat Technologies of Lowell, an online ticketing and marketing company. Pouv cites charismatic UTEC executive director Greg Croteau as a leadership role-model. "He taught me everything about being a community leader—how to get involved, how and when to be assertive, and how to create awareness of an issue."[14] At UTEC one of his responsibilities was to encourage people to register to vote and to promote the Vote 17 initiative, an effort to open municipal elections to seventeen-year-olds.

Pouv is a member of the Next Generation Giving Circle of the Greater Lowell Community Foundation, a philanthropic vehicle for young leaders. He helped organize

Sovanna Devin Pouv
Kevin Harkins

a different entity called the Foundation, which was intended to help bridge the gap between various downtown-interested groups and neighborhood-based groups. He wants to be a problem-solver, and, like Sou, he believes the first step is getting people together, particularly people from different spheres of city life. He is a social-glue manufacturer.

The Foundation Mixers provide an opportunity for 25- to 35-year-old like-minded folks to hang out, connect, and meet others who would not normally show up at networking events. My friends say these mixers are some of the best events they've been to and that they are pleased to meet so many great folks who are involved with the local politics and downtown excitement. I hope that people will develop the same passion that I have for this community. A lot of people aren't passionate because they don't know what to be passionate about—well, it's time for them to learn that Lowell is more than just a developing mill city. We're a family of immigrants from different generations.[15]

During the winter of 2012, Jim Cook of the Lowell Plan spoke to members of a Public Matters class who were sitting around the formidable conference table in the Lowell Plan office. Most of them were under forty years old. The topic of the workshop was the role that leadership has played in the city's revitalization. He said, "Unless people like yourselves want to live and work in Lowell and will buy houses, raise families, and send your kids to the Lowell schools, then all that has been done to bring the city back to life will have been for nothing."

Another guest that night was Bill Lipchitz, who managed Paul Tsongas's first campaign for Lowell City Council in 1969. He is the longtime clerk of the Lowell Development & Financial Corporation and since the 1970s has been a member of the Center City Committee.

The future of Lowell depends on the people who come into our city as well as those who are already here. The newcomers will have something to say about how things are done—just look at the furor about nightlife downtown and the new residents who weighed in on the topic at a City Council meeting. All those folks have an idea of what they want in Lowell, and it may well be quite different from what the "old guard" wants.

There will always be newcomers and immigrants who will assimilate in some ways and change things in other ways. The debate going on nationally today shows what the "old guard" thinks about changes and how they have dug in their heels. The old guard will eventually be the minority in this country, and they are not happy about it. We will always need new Pat Mogans and Paul Tsongases to articulate what can be done and to energize the rest of us to do it.

Remember Albert Biro, the formidable loom fixer on the cover of the *Report of the Lowell Historic Canal District Commission*? When Sovanna Pouv said Lowell is a family and not simply a cleaned-up pile of bricks, he sounded like Edward Glaeser in *Triumph of the City*: "The strength that comes from human collaboration is the central truth behind civilization's success. . . . Above all, we must free ourselves from our tendency to see cities as their buildings, and remember that the real city is made of flesh, not concrete."[16]

NOTES

1. Amy Glowacki, interview with the author.

2. *Pathways for Youth, Lowell National Historical Park*, n.p.

3. *Lowell National Historical Park, 1978–2008: 30 Years of Preservation and Innovation for Future Generations*, n.p.

4. Public Matters, http://lowellplan.org/content/public-matters.

5. Sue Andrews, interview with the author.

6. David Blackburn, interview with the author.

7. Marshall Ganz, "What Is Public Narrative?" n.p.

8. Rosemary Noon, interview with the author.

9. Suzanne Frechette, letter to Rosemary Noon, 2012.

10. Linda Sopheap Sou, letter to the author.

11. Corey Sciuto, letter to the author.

12. Sciuto, letter to the author.

13. Sovanna Pouv, letter to the author.

14. Pouv, letter to the author.

15. Pouv, letter to the author.

16. Edward Glaeser, *Triumph of the City: How Our Greatest Human Invention Makes Us Richer, Smarter, Greener, Healthier, and Happier* (New York: Penguin, 2012), 25.

Bibliography

BOOKS

Albert, Felix, *Immigrant Odyssey: A French Canadian Habitant in New England, A Bilingual Edition of Histoire D'Un Enfant Pauvre*. Translated by Arthur L. Eno Jr., with an introduction by Frances H. Early. Orono: University of Maine Press, 1991.

Atkinson, Jay. *Paradise Road: Jack Kerouac's* Lost Highway *and My Search for America*. Hoboken: Wiley, 2010.

Bedford, Henry F., and Trevor Colbourn. *The Americans: A Brief History*. New York: Harcourt Brace Jovanovich, 1972.

Blewett, Mary H. *The Last Generation: Work and Life in the Textile Mills of Lowell, Massachusetts, 1910–1960*. Amherst: University of Massachusetts Press, 1990.

——, ed. *Surviving Hard Times: The Working People of Lowell*. Lowell: Lowell Museum, 1982.

Blewett, Mary H., with Christine McKenna and Martha Mayo. *To Enrich and to Serve: The Centennial History of the University of Massachusetts, Lowell*. Virginia Beach: Donning Company, 1995.

Brash, Alexander, Jamie Hand, and Kate Orff, eds. *Gateway: Visions for an Urban National Park*. New York: Princeton Architectural Press, 2011.

Burns, Ken, and Dayton Duncan. *The National Parks: America's Best Idea*. New York: Knopf, 2011.

Chang, Leslie T. *Factory Girls: From Village to City in a Changing China*. New York: Spiegel and Grau, 2009.

Chigas, George. *Chanthy's Garden: Poems*. Lowell: Loom Press, 1986.

Clark, Tom. *Fan Poems*. Plainfield, VT: North Atlantic Books, 1976.

Coates, James, and Paul Marion, with text by David Ireland. *Generator Room*. Lowell: Loom Press, 1998.

Coburn, Frederick W. *History of Lowell and Its People, Illustrated*, vols. I, II, III. New York: Lewis Historical Publishing Company, 1920.

Cook, Patrick. *Middlesex Community College: Celebrating a Forty-Year Legacy of Learning*. Bedford and Lowell: Middlesex Community College, 2011.

Cowley, Charles. *A Handbook of Business in Lowell, with a History of the City*. Lowell: E. D. Green, 1856.

———. *Illustrated History of Lowell*. Boston: Lee and Shepard, 1868.

Dalzell, Robert F. Jr. *Enterprising Elite: The Boston Associates and the World They Made*. Cambridge and London: Harvard University Press, 1987.

Dickens, Charles. *American Notes for General Circulation* (1842). London: Penguin, 1985.

Drukman, Mason. *Community and Purpose in America: An Analysis of American Political Theory*. New York: McGraw-Hill, 1971.

Dublin, Thomas, ed. *Farm to Factory: Women's Letters, 1830–1860*. New York: Columbia University Press, 1981.

Dublin, Thomas. *Lowell: The Story of an Industrial City, Official National Park Handbook*. Washington, D.C.: National Park Service, U.S. Department of the Interior, 1992.

Du Noyer, Paul. *Liverpool: Wondrous Place, Music from Cavern to Cream*. London: Virgin, 2002.

Eno, Arthur L. Jr., ed. *Cotton Was King: A History of Lowell, Massachusetts*. Lowell: Lowell Historical Society and New Hampshire Publishing Company, 1976.

Federal Writers' Project of the Works Progress Administration for the State of Massachusetts, with a new introduction by Jane Holtz Kay. The WPA Guide to Massachusetts. New York: Pantheon Books, 1983, a reprint of *Massachusetts: A Guide to Its People and Places* (1937).

Flather, Roger. *The Boss' Son: Remembering the Boott Mills in Lowell, Massachusetts, 1937–1954, an Autobiography*. Bloomington: AuthorHouse, 2007.

Forrant, Robert, and Christoph Strobel. *The Big Move: Immigrant Voices from a Mill City*. Lowell: Loom Press, 2011.

Gittell, Ross J. *Renewing Cities*. Princeton: Princeton University Press, 1992.

Glaeser, Edward. *Triumph of the City: How Our Greatest Invention Makes Us Richer, Smarter, Greener, Healthier, and Happier*. New York: Penguin, 2012.

Goodwin, Doris Kearns. *Team of Rivals: The Political Genius of Abraham Lincoln*. New York: Simon and Schuster, 2005.

Grogan, Paul S. and Tony Proscio. *Comeback Cities: A Blueprint for Urban Neighborhood Revival*. Boulder: Westview, 2000.

Handlin, Oscar. *The Uprooted: The Epic Story of the Great Migrations that Made the American People*. Boston and Toronto: Atlantic Monthly Press Book/Little, Brown, 1951, 1973.

Higgins, James, and Joan Ross, with foreword by Sovann-Thida Loeung and introduction by Pho Tuyet-Lan. *Fractured Identities: Cambodia's Children of War*. Lowell: Loom Press, 1997.

Gross, Laurence F. *The Course of Industrial Decline: The Boott Cotton Mills of Lowell, Massachusetts, 1835–1955*. Baltimore and London: Johns Hopkins University Press, 1993.

Holden, Raymond P. *The Merrimack*. New York and Toronto: Rinehart and Co., 1958.

Hudon, Paul. *The Valley and Its Peoples: An Illustrated History of the Lower Merrimack*. Woodland Hills: Windsor Publications, 1982.

Johnson, Steven F. *Ninuock (the People): The Algonkian People of New England*. Marlborough: Bliss, 1995.

Kemp, Roger L., ed. *The Inner City: A Handbook for Renewal*. Jefferson: McFarland and Company, 2001.

Kerouac, Jack. *Atop an Underwood: Early Stories and Other Writings*. Edited by Paul Marion. New York: Viking, 1999.

Kolack, Shirley. *A New Beginning: The Jews of Historic Lowell, Massachusetts*. New York: Peter Lang, 1997.

Lane, Brigitte. *Franco-American Folk Traditions and Popular Culture in a Former Milltown: Aspects of Urban Folklore and the Dynamics of Folklore Change in Lowell, Massachusetts*. New York and London: Garland, 1990.

Larcom, Lucy, with an introduction by Charles T. Davis. *A New England Girlhood: Outlined from Memory*. Gloucester: Peter Smith, 1973, reprinted from Corinth, 1961.

Levine, Murray, and David V. Perkins. *Principles of Community Psychology: Perspectives and Applications*. 2nd ed. New York and Oxford: Oxford University Press, 1997.

Lippard, Lucy R. *The Lure of the Local: Senses of Place in a Multicentered Society*. New York: New Press, 1997.

Lowell Historical Society. *Lowell: The Mill City, Postcard History Series*. Charleston: Arcadia Publishing, 2005.

Macauley, David. *Mill*. New York: Houghton Mifflin, 1983.

Malone, Patrick M. *Waterpower in Lowell: Engineering and Industry in Nineteenth-Century America*. Baltimore: Johns Hopkins University Press, 2009.

Marchalonis, Shirley. *The Worlds of Lucy Larcom, 1824–1893*. Athens and London: University of Georgia Press, 1989.

Marx, Karl. *Capital: A Critique of Political Economy*, vol. II, *The Process of Circulation of Capital*. Edited by Friedrich Engels; translated by Ernest Untermann (1885). Chicago: Charles H. Kerr and Co., 1909. www.econlib.org.library/YPDBooks/Marx/mrxCpB21.html.

Marx, Leo. *The Machine in the Garden: Technology and the Pastoral Ideal in America*. London, Oxford, New York: Oxford University Press, 1964.

McNulty, Robert H., Dorothy R. Jacobson, and R. Leo Penne. *The Economics of Amenity: Community Futures and Quality of Life, A Policy Guide to Urban Economic Development*. Washington, D.C.: Partners for Livable Places, 1985.

Memorable Events: 100 Years of the Sun, 1978–1978. Lowell: Lowell Sun Publishing Company, 1978.

Menand, Louis. *The Metaphysical Club: A Story of Ideas in America*. New York: Farrar, Straus and Giroux, 2001.

Miller, Marc Scott. *The Irony of Victory: World War II and Lowell, Massachusetts*. Urbana and Chicago: University of Illinois Press, 1988.

Mitchell, Brian C. *The Paddy Camps: The Irish of Lowell, 1821–61*. Urbana and Chicago: University of Illinois Press, 1988.

Moran, William. *The Belles of New England: The Women of the Textile Mills and the Families Whose Wealth They Wove*. New York: Thomas Dunne, 2002.

Mrozowski, Stephen A., Grace H. Ziesing, and Mary C. Beaudry. *Living on the Boott: Historical Archaeology at the Boott Mills Boardinghouses, Lowell, Massachusetts*. Amherst: University of Massachusetts Press, 1996.

Norkunas, Martha. *Monuments and Memory: History and Representation in Lowell, Massachusetts*. Washington and London: Smithsonian Institution Press, 2002.

O'Connell, Shaun. *Imagining Boston: A Literary Landscape*. Boston: Beacon, 1990.

O'Dwyer, George F. *The Irish Catholic Genesis of Lowell*. Lowell: Sullivan Brothers, 1920, reprint by Lowell Museum Corporation, 1981.

Olson, Charles. *The Special View of History*. Edited by Ann Charters. Berkeley: Oyez, 1970.

Parrott, Charles, with Gretchen Sanders Joy. *Lowell, Then and Now: Restoring the Legacy of a Mill City*. Lowell: Lowell Historic Preservation Commission, 1995.

Paul Efthemios Tsongas, 1941–1997: Late a Senator from Massachusetts, Memorial Tributes in the Congress of the United States. Washington, D.C.: U.S. Government Printing Office, 1997.

Pendergast, John. *Images of America: Lowell*. Vols. I and II. Dover: Arcadia, 1996, 1997.

Pho, Tuyet-Lan, Jeffrey N. Gerson, and Sylvia R. Cowan. *Southeast Asian Refugees and Immigrants in the Mill City: Changing Families, Communities, Institutions—Thirty Years Afterward*. Burlington: Hanover and London: University Press of New England, 2007.

Purcell, Carroll, ed. *American Technology*. Malden and Oxford: Blackwell, 2001.

Quintal, Claire, ed. *The Little Canadas of New England*. Worcester: French Institute/Assumption College, 1983.

Robinson, Harriet H. *Loom & Spindle or Life among the Early Mill Girls*. Introduction by Jane Wilkins Pultz. Kailua: Press Pacifica, 1976.

Rosenberg, Chaim M. *The Life and Times of Francis Cabot Lowell, 1775–1818*. Lanham, MD: Lexington/Rowman & Littlefield, 2011.

Sampas, Charles. *That Was the Way It Was*. Edited by Marina Sampas Schell. Lowell: Marina Sampas Schell, 1986.

Saxenian, Annalee. *Regional Advantage: Culture and Competition in Silicon Valley and Route 128*. Cambridge and London: Harvard University Press, 1994, 1996.

Scoggins, Chaz. *Bricks and Bats: Professional Baseball in Lowell, Massachusetts*. Lowell: Lowell Historical Society, 2002.

Steinberg, Theodore. *Nature Incorporated: Industrialization and the Waters of New England*. Amherst: University of Massachusetts Press, 1991.

Temin, Peter, ed. *Engines of Enterprise: An Economic History of New England*. Cambridge and London: Harvard University Press, 2000.

Thoreau, Henry David, with a foreword by Denham Sutcliffe. *A Week on the Concord and Merrimack Rivers*. New York: Signet Classic/New American Library of World Literature, 1961.

Thoreau, Henry David. *Walden* and *Civil Disobedience*. Edited by Owen Thomas. New York: Norton, 1966.

Tocqueville, Alexis de. *Democracy in America*. Edited by Richard Heffner. New York: New American Library, 1956.

Trades and Labor Council of Lowell, Mass. *Lowell: A City of Spindles*. Lowell: Lawlor and Company Printers, 1900.

Tsongas, Paul. *Heading Home*. New York: Knopf, 1984.

———. *Journey of Purpose: Reflections on the Presidency, Multiculturalism, and Third Parties*. New Haven and London: Yale University Press, 1995.

———. *The Road from Here: Liberalism and Realities in the 1980s*. New York: Knopf, 1981.

Walter, E. V. *Placeways: A Theory of the Human Environment*. Chapel Hill and London: University of North Carolina Press, 1988.

Wang, An, with Eugene Linden. *Lessons: An Autobiography*. Reading: Addison-Wesley, 1986.

Weible, Robert, ed. *The Continuing Revolution: A History of Lowell, Massachusetts*. Lowell: Lowell Historical Society, 1991.

———. *Essays from the Lowell Conference on Industrial History, 1982–1983*. North Andover: Museum of American Textile History, 1985.

Weible, Robert, Oliver Ford, and Paul Marion, eds. *Essays from the Lowell Conference on Industrial History, 1980–1981*. Lowell: Lowell Conference on Industrial History, 1981.

Weisman, JoAnne B., ed. *The Lowell Mill Girls: Life in the Factory*. Lowell: Discovery Enterprises, Ltd., 1991.

Whittier, John Greenleaf. *Prose Works*, vol. II. Boston: Ticknor and Fields, 1866.

Year Book of the Lowell Board of Trade, 1911–1912. Lowell: Lowell Board of Trade, 1912.

ARTICLES

Aguirre, Edwin L. "NSF Awards $1.3M to Transform Science Learning: Students to Become 'Data Scientists.'" September 16, 2011. http://www.uml.edu/News/stories/2011-12/Martin-NSF-Grant.aspx.

Andreas, Peter. "Piracy and Fraud Propelled the U.S. Industrial Revolution." http://www.bloomberg.com/news/2013-02-01/piracy-and-fraud-propelled-the-u-s-industrial-revolution.html.

Atwood, Albert W. "The Merrimack: River of Industry and Romance." *National Geographic Magazine*, January 1951, 106–40.

Blackman, Ann. "Lowell's Little Acre: For Centuries, One Neighborhood Has Served as a Gateway for Immigrants." *Time*, June 23, 1993, 34.

Bray, Paul. "Urban Cultural Parks." In *The Inner City: A Handbook for Renewal*, edited by Roger L. Kemp. Jefferson, N.C.: McFarland, 2001.

Brewster, Mike. "An Wang: The Core of the Computer Era." *Business Week*, July 13, 2004. www.businessweek.com/stories/2004-7-13/an-wang-the-core-of-the-computer-era.

Brooks, David. "Digging Very, Very Slowly in a Lowell Churchyard Tells Something About Ireland." *The Telegraph* (Nashua, N.H.), July 23, 2012.

Cassidy, John. "The Greed Cycle: How the Financial System Encouraged Corporations to Go Crazy." *New Yorker*, September 23, 2002, 64–77.

Davidson, Adam. "Making It in America." *Atlantic*, January/February 2012.

Dornbusch, Jane. "A Market Where Beans Reign Supreme." *Boston Globe*, June 20, 2012, 12G.

Douglas, Ann. "On the Road Again." *New York Times Book Review*, April 9, 1995.

Douglas, Geoffrey. "'Desh' Despande: Philanthropist, Visionary, Venture Capitalist to the World." *UMass Lowell Magazine* 13, no. 1 (Winter 2010): 28–29.

———. "The Hogan Years: Four Decades of Reinvention." *UMass Lowell Magazine* 10, no. 1 (Winter 2007): 16–21.

Doyle, Katie. "Gateway Cities Partnership Seen Boosting Lowell." *The Sun*, October 18, 2012.

Early, Frances H. "The Settling-In Process: The Beginnings of Little Canada in Lowell, Massachusetts, in the Late Nineteenth Century." In *The Little Canadas of New England: Third Annual Conference of the French Institute/Assumption College (Worcester, Massachusetts, March 13, 1982)*, edited by Claire Quintal. Worcester: Assumption College, 1982.

Fedarko, Kevin. "Can I Copy Your Homework—And Represent You in Court?" *Time*, September 21, 1992, 52–53.

Fisher, Ian. "City Visit Billed as Inspiring Quest for Sculptors." *The Sun*, June 1, 1988.

Forman, Ian. "Lowell: Politics before Education." *Boston Globe*, April 2, 1963, 16.

Freeman, Allen. "Lessons from Lowell." *Historic Preservation*, November–December 1990, 32–38, 68.

Friedman, Thomas L. "Average Is Over." *New York Times*, January 24, 2012.

"Gang Distortions." *The Sun*, October 23, 2002, 7.

Gall, Lawrence. "National Park Sparks Lowell Renaissance." *Courier*, March 1988.

Gambon, Jill. "Digging for Lowell's Irish Roots." *University Relations*, UMass–Lowell, October 3, 2011.

Ganz, Marshall. "What Is Public Narrative?" 2008. http://grassrootsfund.org/docs/WhatIsPublicNarrative08.pdf.

Gargiulo, Charles A. "Aunt Rose." *New Lowell Offering* 3, no. 1 (Spring 1979): 28.

Gilkerson, Yancy S. "Textile Industry Meets Demand of Booming U.S. Population, 1887–1900." May 2, 2012. www.textileworld.com/textile_resources/history/1887-1900/Textile_Industry_Meets.

Goldberger, Paul. "Design Prize Reflects Resource Crisis." *New York Times*, January 24, 1974.

Goodheart, Adam. "How Slavery Really Ended in America." *New York Times*, April 1, 2011. http://www.nytimes.com/2011/04/03/magazine/mag-03CivilWar-t.html?pagewanted=all&_r=0.

Grady, John. "The Lessons of Lowell." *New Hampshire Seacoast Sunday*, June 26, 1988, 26–27.

Gross, Rebecca. "Rebuilding on the Past: The Creative Rebirth of Lowell, Massachusetts." *NEA Arts* no. 1 (2012).

Hall, Ann. "Lowell's a Desirable Address Again." *Boston Globe*, May 5, 1984.

Hanson, Karmen. "The All-America City and Youth." *National Civic Review* 88, no. 1 (Spring 1999).

Hebert, Ernest. "This New England: Lowell, Massachusetts." *Yankee*, November 1987.

Holtz Kay, Jane. "Lowell, Mass.—New Birth for Us All." *Nation*, September 17, 1977.

Holtzberg, Maggie. "The Pierogi Queen." *Keepers of Tradition: Traditional Arts and Folk Heritage*, July 19, 2011. blog.massfolkarts.org/blog/index.php/2011/07/the-pierogi-queen.

Howe, Richard Jr. "What was Lowell Before It was Lowell?" www.howlmag.com.

Hughes, Bill, and John Gohlke. "Weaving an Economic Rebirth, City's Survivors Cop an Attitude on Crime, and As the Golden Age Tarnished." *Herald News*, March 11 and 13, 2000. www.patersongreatfalls.org/news.

Howard, Marjorie. "Battle of the Parks Brewing." *The Sun*, November 5, 1978, B7.

Hyatt, Josh. "Wang: Who's to Blame?" *Boston Globe*, August 19, 1992.

Iven, Chris. "Lowell Center Puts Emphasis on Teens." *The Sun*, February 14, 1999, 13–14.

Karabatsos, Lewis. T. "Lowell Reborn." *National Parks & Conservation Magazine*, 1979.

"Kerouac Monument." *The Sun*, June 24, 1988.

"Kerouac on the Block." *New York Times*, May 24, 2001. http://www.nytimes.com/2001/05/24/opinion/kerouac-on-the-block.html.

Khan, Eve M. "An Experiment in Public Art." *Wall Street Journal*, October 21, 1991, A16.

Kirsner, Scott. "Tough Going for Start-Up Clusters Outside of Boston." *Boston Globe*, October 1, 2011. http://www.boston.com/business/technology/articles/2011/10/02/tough_going_for_start_up_clusters_outside_of_boston.

Klinkenborg, Verlyn. "Vermilion Cliffs National Monument: Rock of Ages." January 23, 2012. www.ngm.nationalgeographic.com/2012/02/vermilion-cliffs/klinkenborg-text.

Laidler, John. "Canal Project, Upgrades Advance." *Globe North, Boston Sunday Globe*, September 16, 2012.

Lavoie, Denise. "Nearly Two Decades After Death, a City Gives Jack Kerouac What Life Didn't—Recognition." *The Sun*, June 22, 1988.

Lee, Judith Yaross. "Lowell: Revisiting the Birth of Industry in America." *Invention & Technology*, Spring 1992.

Lehrer, Jonah. "Groupthink: The Brainstorming Myth." *New Yorker*, January 30, 2012.

"Lowell's New Era." *The Sun*, June 6, 1978.

MacDonald, Christine. "Escalating Gang Strife Raises Fears in Lowell." *Boston Globe*, February 15, 1999, B1, B6.

Marcus, Jon. "Meehan's House." *Boston Globe Magazine*, August 19, 2012, 20–23.

Marion, Paul. "Alentour: One of the Lost 'Little Magazines' (1935–1943)." *Massachusetts Review* (Summer 2004).

———. "Cut from American Cloth." In *The River Muse: Tales of Lowell & the Merrimack Valley, an Anthology*. Nashua: Sons of Liberty, 2012.

———. "Kerouac on Campus: Roots of a Phenomenon." *UMass Lowell Alumni Magazine* (Winter 2002).

———. "Public Art in an Urban Laboratory: Lowell, Mass." *Public Art Review* (Spring/Summer 1991).

———. "Stones that Speak of Kerouac and Lowell." *The Sun*, June 23, 1988.

Martin, Brian. "It's Time to Take a Stand." *Lowell Sun*, November 5, 1995.

McAdams, Sarah. "Killing Fields Survivors Tell Their Stories." *UMass Lowell Magazine* (Winter 2011–2012): 38–39.

McDonough, Jack. "Oyster Shells, Rusty Nails, and Rosary Beads: Irish Dig Reveals Clues to Lives of Nineteenth-Century Canal Builders." *UMass Lowell Magazine for Alumni and Friends* (Winter 2011).

McKean, David. "To Everything There Is a Season." *Lowell Irish*, July 20, 2012. irishlowell .blogspot.com.

McPhee, John. "1839–2003: Five Days on the Concord and Merrimack Rivers." *New Yorker*, December 15, 2003, 71–85.

Meyers, Jennifer. "Secretary of Interior Ken Salazar: 'Nobody Can Take Your Education Away From You.'" *The Sun*, May 27, 2012, 1, 5.

———. "Talks Under Way Over Lowell Dam." *The Sun*, May 25, 2012.

"The Mills Weren't Made of Marble." *New York Times*, September 7, 1992, 18.

Miskelly, Clodagh, Kirsten Cater, Constance Fleuriot, Morris Williams, and Lucy Wood. "Locating Story: Collaborative Community-Based Located Media Production." May 16, 2012. web.mit.edu/comm-forum/mit4/papers/miskelly.pdf.

Mooney, Brian C. "Life after Paul." *Boston Globe Magazine*, April 22, 2001, 12, 26–37.

Moore, Mary. "Greetings from Martyville: UMass Lowell Chancellor Has Significantly Grown the School's Size." *Boston Business Journal* 33, no. 17 (May 17–23, 2013): 1, 41.

Moran, Lyle. "Lawrence Mills Work Approved." *The Sun*, May 22, 2012, 3–5.

"National Trust Honors City for Excellence in Preservation." *The Shuttle: A Publication of UMass Lowell*, October 9, 2002, 3.

"New Low (Lowell, Massachusetts)." *Economist*, August 3, 1991.

"1990 in Review: Public Art (Robert Cumming, The Lowell Sculptures)." *Art in America, Art Guide*, 1991.

Noon, Rosemary. "The Lowell Regatta Festival Committee." *LOCAL: Lowell Office of Cultural Affairs* (August–September 1990).

Payne, Gary. "Venice of America." *Statesman* 1, no. 4 (Fall 1976): 10–12.

Pentland, William. "Geekville, USA: America's 20 Geekiest Cities." http://www.forbes.com/ sites/williampentland/2011/08/02/geekville-usa-americas-20-geekiest-cities.

Perry, David. "Appreciation: Sue Leggat Recalled as Folk Fest's Conscience." *The Sun*, November 25, 2003.

———. "From Mills to Microchips: Lowell is Geek Haven, UMass Lowell Feeding the Need for High-Tech Workforce." *UMass Lowell Public Affairs*, September 9, 2011.

Peskin, Sarah M. "Lowell, Massachusetts: Preservation Key to Revitalization." Purchase, NY: Institute for Urban Design, Project Monograph no. 2, March 1985.

Pizzi, Doug. "Few in Area Are Untouched by Wang's Descent." *The Sun*, August 19, 1992.

———. "Jack Kerouac Finds Peace and Honor at Last in Lowell." *The Sun*, June 26, 1988.

Powers, John. "Of Mills and Momentum: Why Is Lowell on the Upswing and Lawrence in the Doldrums?" *Boston Globe Magazine*, May 11, 1997.

Riley, David. "The Rebirth of Lowell: A Beacon for Revitalization." *Boston Globe Magazine*, July 20, 1980.

Rodriguez, Cindy. "Lowell Seeks Federal Help in Fight Against Gangs." *Boston Globe*, October 12, 2002, B1. www.register.bostonglobe.com/archives/cgi-bin/archives.dgi.

Rosenberg, Ronald, and Maggie Farley. "Can Wang Labs Make It? Life in Bankruptcy." *Boston Globe*, August 20, 1992.

Ryan, Loretta A. "The Remaking of Lowell and Its Histories." In *Lowell: A Continuing Revolution: A History of Lowell, Massachusetts*, edited by Robert Weible. Lowell: Lowell Historical Society, 1991.

Sato, Hiroko. "Freudenberg Redevelopment Kicks Off." *The Sun*, September 8, 2012.

———. "Key Piece of Renewal in Place." *The Sun*, August 31, 2012.

"Saving Lowell's Heritage." *Washington Post*, April 10, 1978.

Sayen, Harry. "A New England City Hits the Road Back." *Trenton Times*, May 11, 1978, A11.

Schecter, Dorothy A. "Lowell: Mill Town Renaissance: A Pioneering Spirit Prevails in Lowell." *Horizon*, June 1985.

Sciuto, Corey. "The Merrimack River—Renewable Energy." March 23, 2013. coreysciuto .blogspot.com.

Serafino, Phil. "Officials Fear Wang Cuts Will Ripple Through Area: Business Leaders See Jobless Ranks Growing." *The Sun*, August 19, 1992.

Sherburne, Rick. "Boarding House Park: What Does the Future Hold?" *LOCAL: Lowell Office of Cultural Affairs* (August–September 1992).

Sleeper, Peter. "Urban Park Now Reality as President Signs Bill." *The Sun*, June 5, 1978, 1.

Stanton, Cathy. "Serving Up Culture: Heritage and Its Discontents at an Industrial History Site." *International Journal of Heritage Studies* 2, no. 5 (December 2005): 415–21.

Stevens, Jay. "Classic Jack." *Yankee*, September 1994.

Stowell, Stephen. "Lowell's Look on Things." *The Alliance Review: News from the National Alliance of Preservation Commissions* (January/February 2000).

Sylvester, David. "Does Lowell Park Lack Leadership?" *The Sun*, December 4, 1978, 9.

Tsai, Joyce. "Salazar Praises Partnerships in Lowell's Revival." *The Sun*, May 26, 2012, 1, 10.

Tuttle, Nancye. "Lowell: Then and Now." *The Sun*, August 20, 1995.

Unger, Miles. "Lowell's Proud Past Brought Back to Light: Work Reveals Heroic Industrial Forms." *Boston Sunday Globe*, November 11, 1990, 14.

Valencia, Milton J. "Change at the Polls: Cambodian Voters are Making Themselves Heard in Lowell." *Diversity Boston, Boston Globe* (Summer 2011).

Verrier, Robert. "Human Energy (and Historic Tax Credits) Help 'Re-Boott' Historic New England Mill." *Preservation Nation Blog*, National Trust for Historic Preservation, March 1, 2013.

Wallace, Kendall. "Saturday Chat: Follow the Future Leader of Lowell." *The Sun*, March 10, 2012, 3.

Weible, Robert. "Lowell: Building a New Appreciation for Historical Place." *Public Historian* 6, no. 3 (Summer 1984).

———. "Visions and Reality: Reconsidering the Creation and Development of Lowell's National Park, 1966–1992." *Public Historian* 33, no. 2 (May 2011).

Wickenheiser, Matt. "Brick by Brick: Remaking Lowell's Mills." *The Sun*, May 11, 1999.

———. "To Raze or Restore: Leaders Make Passionate Arguments in the Name of Progress, Preservation." *The Sun*, September 13, 1998.

———. "Urban Planning Award to City, Historic Park." *The Sun*, May 5, 1998.

"A Working Woman. My Experience as a Factory Operative." *Daily Evening News*, February 23, 1867.

Yudis, Anthony J. "Living in the Park that Is Lowell." *Boston Globe*, May 23, 1982.

Zeiger, Dinah. "Telling Tales and Connecting Communities–Roadside Theater: ASU Community Story Telling." *Inside Arts* (November/December 1999). http://roadside.org/asset/ telling-tales-and-connecting-communities.

Ziegler, Bart. "Once Booming Wang Laboratories Failed to Heed the Changing Marketplace." *Seattle Times*, August 23, 1992. community.seattletimes.nwsource.com/archive?date =19920823&slug=1508984.

Zimmerman, Karl. "Cruising the Canals of Revitalized Lowell." *New York Times*, August 4, 1991, 20.

PAMPHLETS, NEWSLETTERS, AND BROCHURES

Acropolis of America: The Greek Community of Lowell, 1930–40, a Community Exhibit. Lowell: Lowell Hellenic Heritage Association, 1997.

Angkor Dance Troupe: Cambodian Classical and Folk Dance, 1999 Commemorative Book. Lowell: Angkor Dance Troupe, 1999.

Bever, Thomas D. *Economic Benefits of Historic Preservation.* Heritage Conservation and Recreation Service, U.S. Department of the Interior. May 1978.

Bruno K., BiNational: German American Art Now. Temporary Sculpture/Lowell, A Brush With History Gallery, University of Lowell Art Department, Lowell Historic Preservation Commission, Lowell Office of Cultural Affairs, Museum of Fine Arts, Boston, and Institute of Contemporary Art. December 17–January 29, 1988.

The Canal Packet. The Lowell Historic Canal District Commission. February 1976.

Canalway News. Lowell Historic Preservation Commission (Summer 1988).

City of Lowell and Lowell National Historical Park. Historic Massachusetts' 1998 Preservation Awards Dinner.

The Commission Bulletin 1, no. 1 (Spring 1979); 2, no. 2 (Spring 1980); 3, no. 3 (Winter 1981).

Conant, Stephen. *Bedrock, Bricks, and Rock Doves: The Natural History of Lowell, Massachusetts, An Exhibit by the Lowell Parks and Conservation Trust, Inc.* February 9–April 15, 1992. Patrick J. Mogan Cultural Center.

Dabilis, Andy, Kathy McCabe, and Amy Sessler. *Rebirth of the Merrimack.* Merrimack River Watershed Council, n.d.

The Early Automobile in Lowell: Marketing the Machine, 1896–1936. Introduction by Mehmed Ali. Lowell: Lowell Historical Society, 1998.

Emerging Technologies and Innovation Center: Where Ingenuity Meets Industry. UMass–Lowell, October 2012.

Ethnic Covenant Newsletter (Summer 1993).

Factory Tracts Numbers 1 and 2: Factory Life As It Is by an Operative. Lowell: Female Labor Reform Association, 1845; Lowell: Lowell Publishing Company, Inc., 1982 (facsimile reprint).

Greater Lowell Massachusetts. Chamber of Commerce of Greater Lowell, 1973.

Greater Lowell Massachusetts. Greater Lowell Chamber of Commerce, 1977.

Guide to the Merrimack River Valley. West Newbury: Merrimack River Watershed Council, Inc., 1984.

Hand-book for the Visitor to Lowell, 1848. Introduction by Mary H. Blewett and Arthur L. Eno Jr. Lowell: D. Bixby and Company, 1848; Lowell Publishing Company, Inc., 1982 (facsimile reprint).

Historic Lowell: Birthplace of the American Industrial Revolution, 1826–1976. The Official Tour Map of Lowell Sesquicentennial/Bicentennial Commission, Greater Lowell Regatta Festival Committee, Greater Lowell Chamber of Commerce, and Middlesex County Tourism and Development Council.

Human Services Corporation, Lowell, Massachusetts. 1980.

If the Falls Could Speak: A New Play by David Riley. Merrimack Regional Theatre, Lowell Historic Preservation Commission, and Lowell Plan. Smith Baker Center, May 28–31, 1981.

Johnson, Steven F. *New England Indians,* Series No. 1. Groton: New England Indian Literature, 1980.

Karabatsos, Lewis T., ed. *I Am a Factory Girl: Documents of Lowell's Nineteenth Century Working Women.* Lowell Museum Corporation, 1977.

LOCAL: Lowell Office of Cultural Affairs (April–May, 1992).

The Lowell Civic Collaborative: A Guidebook for Projects between Community Colleges and National Parks. Lowell National Historical Park and Middlesex Community College, 2006.

The Lowell Discovery Network: An Urban National Park. Planned by Michael and Susan Southworth for the Model Cities Education Component. Lowell: MCEC, 1972.

Lowell Historic Preservation Commission 1987 Newsletter.

Lowell: Lowell National Historical Park, Massachusetts. National Park Service, U.S. Dept. of the Interior, 1999.

Lowell Offering: Official Visitor Guide for 2011–2012. Lowell National Historical Park.

The Lowell Plan: A Fifteen-Year Partnership for Economic Development. October 6, 1994.

Lowell Urban National Cultural Park: UNCP Newsletter 1, no. 1. Lowell: Human Services Corporation, 1972.

Lowell: We Mean Business. The Lowell Plan and PageCrafters. 1993.

Malone, Patrick M. *Canals and Industry, Engineering in Lowell, 1821–1880.* Lowell: Lowell Museum, 1983.

———. *The Lowell Canal System.* Lowell: Lowell Museum in cooperation with the Slater Mill Historic Site, the Historic American Engineering Record, 1976.

Marion, Paul. *Dimitri Hadzi.* The Brush Gallery and Artists' Studios and the Hellenic Culture Society. October 12–November 11, 1990.

———. *Making the Lowell Sculptures: The Work of Robert Cumming.* Lowell: Lowell Historic Preservation Commission, June 30, 1992.

Market Mills in Lowell. Lowell Historic Preservation Commission, n.d.

Marty Meehan at 50. Lowell: Lowell Publishing Company, December 27–29, 2006.

Merrimack: A River Restored. Merrimack River Watershed Council, 1988.

Mill City Makeover: The Historic Preservation of Lowell. The Sun, May 13, 2011.

Nature along the Merrimack River: The Natural History of an Urban Park. Tsongas Industrial History Center, n.d.

Nesmith, Joseph A. *The Old Nesmith House and Some of Its Guests.* Lowell: John Nesmith House Alumni Foundation, 1989 (reprint of 1931 ms.).

Palermo, Barbara. *Lowell's Special Places: Exploring the Neighborhoods.* Lowell: Lowell Heritage Partnership, 2004.

Pathways for Youth, Lowell National Historical Park. Lowell: Lowell National Historical Park, 2010.

A Portfolio of Historical Maps of Lowell, 1821–1914. Lowell: Lowell Historical Society, n.d.

Preservation and the Tax Reform Act of 1976, a Preservation News Supplement. National Trust for Historic Preservation. November 1977.

River Environment Awareness Center (prepared by Harvard Graduate School of Design Community Assistance Program). Lowell: Lowell 2000 Corporation, n.d.

River's Reach: Merrimack River Watershed Council. Spring 1992.

Sarre, Louis Augustus, and David W. Malone. *How Sweet the Sound: The Story of a New England Congregation.* Lowell: Eliot Presbyterian Church, 2004.

Spindle City, 1820–1940, An Exhibit. The Lowell Museum Corporation. 1976.

Stachiw, Myron. *Negro Cloth: Northern Industry & Southern Slavery, an Exhibition by the Merrimack Valley Textile Museum.* Boston National Historical Park, September 1–November 1, 1981.

This Is Your City: Lowell. Lowell: League of Women Voters of Lowell, Massachusetts, 1958.

The Transformation of UMass Lowell. The Sun, September 18, 2012.

Tsongas Industrial History and Science Center, Field Trips and In-School Standards-Based Education Programs, 2012–2013. National Park Service and UMass–Lowell, 2012.

Tsongas, Paul E. *A Call to Economic Arms: Forging a New American Mandate.* Boston: The Tsongas Committee, 1991.

Tuttle, Nancye. *Picture It: Lowell Goes to the Movies.* Lowell: Lowell Historic Preservation Commission, 1993.

Walking Tours of Lowell (Downtown and Canals, West). Lowell Bicentennial/Sesquicentennial Commission, n.d.

REPORTS

Baker, Howard H. Jr., and J. Bennett Johnston. *Advancing the National Park Idea.* Washington: National Parks Conservation Association, 2009.

A Call to Action: Preparing for a Second Century of Stewardship and Engagement. Washington: National Park Service, August 25, 2011.

The Canalway: A Proposal, Draft Report of the Canalway Task Force. Lowell National Historical Park, June 1985.

Culture: A Celebration of Lowell, a Report on the Conference of November 22, 1986. Human Services Corporation, 1986.

Details of the Preservation Plan. Lowell: Lowell Historic Preservation Commission, U.S. Dept. of the Interior, 1980.

Duff, John B. *Preservation Plan: Lowell Historic Preservation Commission.* Lowell: Lowell Historic Preservation Commission, U.S. Dept. of the Interior, September 4, 1980.

Ethnicity in Lowell: Lowell National Historical Park Ethnographic Overview and Assessment. Prepared by University of Massachusetts Lowell History Department (Robert Forrant and Christoph Strobel). Boston: Northeast Region Ethnography Program, National Park Service, March 2011.

Fantini, Mario D., Virginia M. Biggy, and Robert I. Sperber. *The Lowell Model for Educational Excellence.* Executive Summary Report. Lowell: Lowell Model for Educational Excellence, January 1984.

Forman, Ben, and Tyler Creighton. *Building Vibrancy: Creative Placemaking Strategies for Gateway City Growth and Renewal.* Boston: MassINC and ArtPlace, July 2012.

The Future of America's National Parks: A Report to the President of the United States by the Secretary of the Interior Dirk Kempthorne, May 2007.

Hamilton Canal. Prepared by City of Lowell Division of Planning and Development, March 2004.

Hamilton Canal District Master Plan: A Vision Renewed. Prepared by Trinity Financial and Icon Architecture, September 2008.

Lane, Jonathan, and Dennis Frenchman. *Heritage Preservation and Development: A White Paper. 30 Years: Lowell National Historical Park,* 2008.

The Lowell Building Book. Prepared by City of Lowell Division of Planning and Development and Anderson Notter Associates, Architects and Preservation Planners, February 1977.

The Lowell Cultural Plan: 1987–1997, a Summary. Lowell: The Lowell Plan, Inc., 1987.

The Lowell Cultural Plan Review Project, Final Report. Lowell: The Lowell Office of Cultural Affairs and Human Services Corporation, 1994.

Lowell Downtown Evolution Plan: Actionable Executive Summary. Prepared by Speck and Assoc. LLC with AECOM and Rock Maple Studios, 2010.

Lowell: The Flowering City, a Report from the Project Anthopolis Charrette. Prepared by the Human Services Corporation. Lowell: Human Services Corporation, 1997.

Lowell Historic Preservation Commission, Annual Report 1982.

Lowell, Massachusetts: An Advisory Board Panel Report. Urban Land Institute, 2003.

Lowell National Historical Park, 10: 1978–1988.

Lowell National Historical Park, 2006 Annual Report: Lowell, New Rhythm of the River.

Lowell National Historical Park, 2007 Annual Report: Lowell, A City with Soul!

Lowell National Historical Park, 1978–2008: 30 Years of Preservation and Innovation for Future Generations. Lowell National Historical Park, June 2008.

Lowell National Historical Park, 2009: Lowell, Preservation and Innovation for Future Generations.

Lowell National Historical Park. Draft General Management Plan. U.S. Dept. of the Interior, National Park Service, May 1980.

Lowell: Stewards of Heritage, Lowell National Historical Park, 2011 Annual Report.

Lowell Trolley Study. Executive Summary. Prepared jointly by Lowell National Historical Park, City of Lowell, Lowell Plan, Northern Middlesex Council of Governments, Lowell Regional Transit Authority, UMass–Lowell, Trinity Financial, and the Seashore Trolley Museum, 2011.

Lowell Urban Park. Lowell: Human Services Corporation, 1973–1974.

Master Plan Developer Solicitation, Hamilton Canal. Prepared by City of Lowell Division of Planning and Development, June 2006.

Mofford, Juliet. *The Lowell Public Art Collection: Walking Tour.* Lowell National Historical Park, 1990.

O'Connell, Peter, and Gray Fitzsimons. *Public Presentation of Lowell's Stories: A White Paper. 30 Years: Lowell National Historical Park,* 2008.

O'Neill, Thomas P. III. *Lowell, Massachusetts: Report of the Lowell Historic Canal District Commission to the Ninety-Fifth Congress of the United States of America.* Washington: U.S. Government Printing Office, January 3, 1977.

On the Cultural Road . . . City of World Culture: Strategies for the Creative Economy in Lowell, Massachusetts. Prepared for the Lowell Plan, Inc., by Mt. Auburn Assoc. Lowell: Lowell Plan, 2007.

Preservation Plan Amendment. Lowell: Lowell Historic Preservation Commission, U.S. Dept. of the Interior, Lowell, Massachusetts, 1989.

Smith, Maura. *Revitalization Through Partnership: Public and Private Sector Investment in Lowell, Massachusetts.* Lowell: Lowell Historic Preservation Commission and Lowell Development and Financial Corporation, August 1984.

Thirty Pieces of Silver: A Report on Slum Housing in Lowell. Lowell Ethnic Covenant, June 1983.

Tsongas Industrial History Center Planning Report: Prepared for Lowell National Historical Park and University of Lowell. Center for History Now, March 1987.

The 22nd Annual Lowell Folk Festival: Annual Report 2008. City of Lowell, Lowell Festival Foundation, Lowell National Historical Park, National Council for the Traditional Arts, Greater Merrimack Valley Convention and Visitor Bureau, 2008.

Urban Design Study, Historical Survey: Lowell Community Renewal Program. City Development Authority, Lowell, Massachusetts, March 1970.

Working Together: The Story of the Lowell Model Cities Program. Lowell Model Cities. 1971.

UNPUBLISHED PAPERS, SPEECHES, JOURNALS, MEMORANDA, AND OTHER

Ali, Mehmed. "To Save a City: From Urban Renewal to Historic Preservation in Lowell, Massachusetts, 1920–1978." University of Connecticut, 2006.

Booras, Dimitrios. "Archaeology Reflections." September 2012.

Brouillette, Paul. "Honoring Kerouac." 1978.

Creasey, Michael. "Lowell Plan Breakfast: 30th Anniversary of LNHP." June 6, 2008.

DiStefano, Lisa J. "Tour Packet: Giving the City a Facelift, Art and Architecture in Lowell." 1986.

Forrant, Jean L., Robert Pyle, William Lazonick, and Charles Levenstein. "Sustainable Development for a Regional Economy: CITA Conference 2000 Background Paper." UMass–Lowell Committee on Industrial Theory and Assessment, University of Massachusetts Lowell, 1999.

LaPorte, Raymond. "My Story: Lowell–D.C. and Back Again, A Journal: January 24–May 15, 1978." Transcribed and annotated, October 17, 2011.

Leary, Michael. "Thoughts on Lowell, the Preservation Work in General." May 7, 2012.

Nikitopoulos, Charles. "On Patrick J. Mogan." September 30, 2011, letter to the author.

Meehan, Martin T. "College Town Speech at the Innovative Cities Conference," UMass–Lowell Inn and Conference Center. June 17, 2010.

Mogan, Patrick J. "Memorandum to Center City Committee, August 1972." Human Services Corporation Archives.

———. "Possible Funding Programs" [notes on National Endowment for the Arts funding programs]. August 15, 1972.

———. "Renewal Process in Lowell, Massachusetts: Toward an Ecologically Sensitive Educational Model." University of Massachusetts–Amherst, 1975.

O'Har, George, and Gray Fitzsimons. "Lowell National Historical Park Administrative History." February 2004.

Ostis, James. "Industrial and Cultural Heritage in Lowell, Massachusetts, and Its Role in Revitalization: Perspectives from Lowell's Leaders of Today." 2011.

——. "Peter S. Stamas: A Brief Biography for Consideration of the Lowell High School Distinguished Alumni Award." 2011.

Paglia, Michael J. "The Paul E. Tsongas Arena: Building a Legacy." UMass–Lowell, Economic and Social Development of Regions Master's Degree Program. April 2012.

Shams, Safi. "Bourdieu's Fields and Labor Agency: The Case of Lowell, Massachusetts, 1826–1845." Thesis Proposal, Dept. of Regional Economic and Social Development, UMass–Lowell. April 17, 2010.

Shatzer, Tess. "The Boott Cotton Mills Museum: An Exploration of Meanings, Connections, and Sense of Place Outcomes." Master's thesis, Stephen F. Austin State University. May 2007.

Sweeney, Marie. "I Remember Sue Leggat." Remarks at Brush Gallery, June 2004.

——. "Susan and Janet Leggat." Remarks at Salvation Army Breakfast, November 6, 2003.

Walsh, Bill. "Merrimack Street Businesses Listing, 1970–2012." November 28, 2011.

Yaro, Robert D. "History and Significance of the Lower Locks Area, Lowell, Massachusetts, and Lower Lock Restoration, Lowell Locks and Canals, Lowell, Massachusetts." Commonwealth of Massachusetts, Executive Office of Environmental Affairs, Department of Environmental Management, n.d.

VIDEOS, FILMS, AND OTHER MEDIA

Human Services Corporation and Page One Productions. *Roots of an Urban Cultural Park: A Community Change Process in Lowell.* Lowell: Human Services Corp. and Page One Productions, 1991.

Page One Productions. *Folk Culture in America.* Lowell: Page One Productions, 1989.

——. *Patrick J. Mogan: Visionary and Realist.* Lowell: Page One Productions, 1995.

——. *Roots of an Urban Cultural Park: A Community Change Process in Lowell, Massachusetts.* Lowell: Human Services Corporation and Page One Productions, 1991.

——. *Sightlines: Building the Lowell Public Art Collection.* Lowell: Page One Productions, 1991.

"The Preservation Movement: Then and Now." Exhibition in Boott Mills Gallery, Boott Cotton Mills Museum, May-September 2010.

WEBSITES

Coalition for a Better Acre, "History," http://www.coalitionforabetteracre.org/about-us/history.

National Parks Conservation Association, http://www.npca.org/news/media-center/fact-sheets/anilca.html.

Public Matters, http://lowellplan.org/content/public-matters.

INTERVIEWS

Andrews, Sue, with the author, September 24, 2012.

Arenberg, Richard, with Mehmed Ali, May 16 and June 23, 2003.

Aucella, Peter, with the author, 2011.

Baacke, Adam, with the author, September 26, 2012.

Blackburn, David, with the author, September 24, 2012.

Conant, Stephen, with the author, May 5, 2012.

Cook, James, with the author, 2011.
Correia, Richard, with Mehmed Ali, August 26, 2004.
Creasey, Michael, with the author, August 12, 2011.
Dixon Mullane, Taya, with the author, September 28, 2012.
Faust, Fred, with Mehmed Ali, February. 13, 2003.
Fitzpatrick, Mary Ellen, with Mehmed Ali, May 13, 2003.
Fleming, Brendan, with Maryrose Lane, March 29, 1994.
Glowacki, Amy, with the author, October 24, 2011.
Golec, Pauline, with the author, May 31, 2012.
Greenwood, Anita, with the author, July 24, 2012.
Kirshbaum, Sheila, with the author, May 18, 2012.
Kol, Duey, with the author, November 23, 2011.
Leggat, Janet, with the author, January 9, 2012.
Leite, John, with Gray Fitzsimons, August 10, 1999.
Leite, John, with the author, May 25, 2012.
Martin, Brian, with the author, May 30, 2012.
Mayo, Martha, with the author, September 6, 2013.
Meehan, Martin T., with the author, May 21, 2012.
Milinazzo, James, with the author, May 29, 2012.
Nikitopoulos, Charles, with the author, August 16, 2013.
Parrott, Charles, with the author, December 28, 2011.
Pierson, Donald, with the author, June 11, 2012.
Samaras, Bill, with the author, August 16, 2013.
Stowell, Stephen, with the author, 2012.
Tsapatsaris, George, with the author, August 16, 2013.
Tsongas, Nicola, with Mehmed Ali, February 11, 2003.

Index

Page numbers in *italics* indicate illustrations.

Abbott, Henry Livermore, 11
Academy Awards, 37
Acre, *10*, 128; AMNO, 42; CBA, 27–28, 30; immigration and, 13–14, 16, 29, *113*
Acre Family Day Care, 30
Acre Model Neighborhood Organization (AMNO), 42
Acre Plan, 129
adaptive reuse, 167
Adichie, Chimamanda, 165
AFC. *See* American Folklife Center
agapétimé (love and honor), 220
Agyeman, Kwasi, 118
Alaska National Interest Lands Conservation Act (ANILCA), 50
Albert, Lewis, 51, *55*, 59, 62
Alentour, 15
Alfred P. Murrah Federal Building, 74
Ali, Mehmed, 74, 112, 164
American Cities Corporation, 59, 145
American Cities Plan, 59
American Folklife Center (AFC), 199–200
American Notes for General Circulation (Dickens), 7
American Revolution Bicentennial Commission, *28*
"American Times," 37
America's Technology Highway, 33–34
AMNO. *See* Acre Model Neighborhood Organization
Amram, David, 160
Andrews, Sue, 233, 234, *234*
Andrus, Cecil, 52
Angkor Dance Troupe, 65, 72, *72*, 164, 236
ANILCA. *See* Alaska National Interest Lands Conservation Act
Antonelli, John, 225
Appleton, Nathan, 2, 4, 5, 92
Appleton Block, 92, *93–95*
Appleton Company, 176
Appleton Mills, 32, 73, 124–25, 129, *133*, 134

Appleton National Bank, 92
Arce, Jorge, 206–7
architecture, 15, 81; for creative economy, 146, 147; row houses, 114, *114*, 115; Urban Renewal Project, 16, 111–16. *See also specific properties*
Archive of Folk Culture, 199
Arena Commission, 144
Arenberg, Richard, 49, 53
Armstrong, Louis (Satchmo), 160
Arrangement in Grey and Black, 8
Art Alive!, 150
Artist Point, 76
Atkins, Chester G. (Chet), 61, 65, *66*, 125, 201
Atkinson, Jay, 225
Atwood, Albert W., 167
Aucella, Peter: Arena Commission work of, 142; on LHPC, 69; on Lowell Folk Festival, 206; Pawtucket Falls Dam and, *136*, 137; on preservation, 117–18, 120; Public Matters: Empowering Lowell's Leaders role of, 235
Ayer, J. C., 12
Ayer Lofts, 149

Baacke, Adam, *130*, 130–31, 235
Babb, Roger Sumner, 57
Baez, Joan, *212*
Bagley, Sarah, 219
Baker, Howard H., Jr., xi
Bale, Christian, 37
Bay State Street Railway, 63
Beast of New Orleans. *See* Butler, Benjamin F.
Belay, Melaku, 203
Bellegarde Boathouse, 62
Belley, Bernard A., 43
Bernardo, Celeste, *xi*, 75, 78, *137*
Berube, Eugene, 112
B. F. Keith's Theatre, 161
Bigelow, Erastus, *82–83*, 126

Bigelow Carpet Company, *83*, 126
Biggy, M. Virginia, 186
Bikila, Adebe, 25
"The BiNational: German Art of the '80s,"
   212
Biro, Albert, xii, *xii*, 239
Black, Chris, 47
Blackburn, David, 233, 234, *234*
bladder dam, 135–36, 137
Blake, William, 7
Blewett, Mary H., 14–15, *60*
Boarding House Park, 24, 60–61, 66, *107*
Bon Marché, 96, *96–97*, 162
Booras, Dimitrios, 30
Boott, Kirk, 8, *85*, 100, 172
Boott Cotton Mills Boarding House, 56,
   59, 64, 105, *105–7*
Boott Cotton Mills Museum, 100, *101–103*,
   104, 128; exhibits at, 74, 174, 175, *175*,
   177, *178*, 179–80, 222, 235; LHPC and,
   66–67; Mill No. 6, 58, 60, 61, 65, *65*,
   67, *103*, 120, 174–75; Walter's role in,
   65–66, *66*, 187; Weave Room, 16, *175*,
   192
Boston Associates, 151
Boston Globe, 17, 21, 157
Boston & Maine Railroad Depot, 36, 91,
   91, 92, *92*, 93
Boston Manufacturing Company, 4, 105
Boston Pops orchestra, 199
Boyden, Uriah, 194
de Brausch, Ted Santorelli, 63
Bray, Paul M., 152
Bread and Roses Strike, 14
British Legation, 13
Brooke, Ed, 53
Brouillette, Paul, 222
"the Brown Book," xii, 48, 126, 140
Brunelle, Roger, 224–25
Brush Art Gallery and Studios, 59,
   127–28, 149–50
A Brush With History, 59, 127–28,
   149–50
Building Conservation Branch, Northeast
   Cultural Resources Center, 65
"Building on the Past" (Gross), 208
Bundy, William, 23
Burchill, John, 59, 62, 69
Burns, Ken, 76
Burton, Phil, 49
Bush, George H. W., 24
Bush, George W., 25

Butler, Benjamin F., 11–12, 121, 151
Butler House, 122

Cables, Herbert, 62
Cacici, Marina, 162
A Call to Economic Arms (Tsongas, P.), 26
Cambodian Expressions project, 164
Cambodia Town, 32
Campbell, James, 187
Canal Place, *84*
Canalway, *70*, *132*; funding for, 121, 131,
   142; LHPC work on, 68, *127*, 215; pro-
   ponents of, 75, *127*
Cantwell, Robert, 214
Captain John Ford's Tavern, 5
Caret, Robert, 35
Carney Medal, 161
Carpenter, Karen, 52
Carr, Ethan, 40
Carter, James E., 22, 49, 50
Cartwright looms, 4
Cassidy, John, 4–5
Catholicism, 16
CBA. *See* Coalition for a Better Acre
Center City Committee, 43, 119, 208–9
Center for Human Development (CHD),
   42–43, 182–83, 184–85
Center for Lowell History (CLH), 64–65
166-182 Central Street, 92, *93–95*
217-227 Central Street, 86, *87–88*
238-254 Central Street, 36, 91, *91*, 92, *92*
Centralville, 14
Chalifoux's, 96
Chapman, George, 174
Charles G. Sampas Pavilion, 199
Charles River, 4
charrette method, 131
Chase Manhattan Bank, 67
CHD. *See* Center for Human Development
Chelmsford, Massachusetts, 1–2
Chen, Milton, xi
Chevalier, Michel, 71
Chigas, George, 164
Childs, Linus, 174
China, 177
Chunming, Wu, 177–78
Citizens Advisory Board for Community
   Development Block Grant Funds,
   215–16
City Development Authority, 115–16
City Hall District, 45, 116
City Institution for Savings, 92

City Poor Farm, 12
Civil War, 11–12, *101, 105*
Clancy, Jack, 35
Clark, Tom, 176
Clean Water Act, 167
Clemente, Roberto, 176
CLH. *See* Center for Lowell History
Clinton, Bill (William J.), 25
Coalition for a Better Acre (CBA), 27–28, 30
Coates, Jim, 219
Coburn, Frederick W., 158
Coggins, Matt, 130
"Coming Up Taller Award," 72
Commodore Ballroom, 161
Conant, Stephen, 61, 62, 201
Congress Group Properties, 66–67
Conner, Phil, 189, 193–94
Connolly, Michael, *22*
Connolly, Seamus, 202
Conservation Commission, 62
Conti, Silvio, 53
contraband, slaves as, 12
Cook, James, *140,* 144; career of, 138, 140;
    Public Matters: Empowering Lowell's
    Leaders role of, 233, 238
COOL. *See* Cultural Organization of Lowell
Coolidge, John, 158
Coopers and Lybrand, 141
Corporation for the Celebration of Jack
    Kerouac, 224
Costello, Clement, 47
cotton, 11
Cotton Was King: A History of Lowell, 158
Cowan, Carole, 36
Cowley, Charles, 11, 14
Cox, John, 129, 130
Cranz, Galen, 152, 231
Creasey, Michael, 58, *75;* career of, 74, 75,
    117; Public Matters: Empowering Low-
    ell's Leaders role of, 74, 233
creative economy, 146, 147, 208
Crockett, Davy, 8
Cronin, Paul, 45, 46
Crosson, County Tyrone, Northern Ireland,
    30
Croteau, Greg, 237
Cultural Organization of Lowell (COOL),
    75
Cultural Resources Inventory, 56, 58
Cumming, Robert, 215, 216–17, *217,* 218
Cummiskey, Hugh, 28, 30, 172
Curtin, Thomas, 184

Curtis, Jim, 162

Dalzell, Robert F., Jr., 151
Dame, Vernon (Dave), 200, 201
Darius Young House, 89, *89–90*
Davidson, Adam, 177
Davis, Jefferson, 11
Dawes, Henry L., 76
Debo, John, *55*
Debo Band, 202–3, *203*
Democracy in America (Tocqueville), 71
demolition by neglect, xix
Demonstration Cities and Metropolitan
    Development Act, 41
Denver Service Center (DSC), 43–44
Department of Environmental Manage-
    ment, Massachusetts, 59
Department of Housing and Urban Devel-
    opment, U.S. (HUD), 184
Department of Justice, U.S., 138
Dewey, John, 181
Dickens, Charles, 7, 71, 74
Dillon, Joseph T., 43
Dion, Dolores, 161
Diversity and Inclusion Project, 164–65
Dixon Mullane, Taya, 124, 134
Doctor Sax (Kerouac), 222
Doherty, Gerard, 126
Donahue, Matt, 62
Donahue, Nancy L., 72, *73*
Donahue, Richard K., 73
Donoghue, Eileen, 33, 70, 146, 148, *148,*
    149, 150
"Doors Open Lowell," 73–74
Douglass, Frederick, 11
Droney, Helen, 17
DSC. *See* Denver Service Center
Dubus, Andre, III, 227
Duff, John B., 51, 55, *56*
Dukakis, Michael S., 24, 36, 47
Duncan, Dayton, 76
Duncan, George, 15, *73,* 119
Du Noyer, Paul, 112
Dutton Street, 45, 126
Dylan, Bob, 223

Early, Edward J., Jr., 41
Early, Frances H., 111–12
East Chelmsford, Massachusetts, 5, 172
Eastern Canal, *70,* 100, *123*
Edinburgh, Scotland, 2
Edson, Theodore, 8

Eliot, John, 1
Eliot, T. S., 168
Emancipation Proclamation, 12
Emerson, Ralph Waldo, 8
Enel Green Power, 135, 136, 137
Engel, Victor, 136
Eno, Arthur L., 114–15
Enterprising Elite (Dalzell), 151
eskista, 203
Ethan (Riley), 157
Ethiopia, 25–26, 203
Ethnomimesis: Folklife and the Representation of Culture (Cantwell), 214
"The Everywhere School," 184
Excellence in Cultural Heritage Award, *204*
Exploratorium, 187–88

factory girls. *See* mill girls
Fantini, Mario D., 186
Farley White Interests, 139
Faust, Fred, 24; LaPorte and, 52, 53; at LHPC, 22, 23, 55, *56*, 206; Torpedo Factory and, 148; Tsongas, P., and, 22, 47, 48, 50
F. Bradford Morse Federal Building, 36
Federal Energy Regulatory Commission (FERC), 135–36, 137
Federal Historic Preservation Tax Incentives program, 124
Federal Writers' Project, 15
Fendika, 202–3, *203*
FERC. *See* Federal Energy Regulatory Commission
Ferrini, Henry, 222
Festival Foundation Scholarship Committee, 205
Fiedler, Arthur, 199
The Fighter, 37
First Nations, people of, 1
Fish, Edward, 126
Fiske, William, 88–89
Fiske Building, 86, *87–88*
Fitzpatrick, Mary Ellen, 47
Fitzsimons, Gray, 48
Flanagan, Dorothy (Dottie) Naruszewicz, 203
Flanagan, George, 41
Flatley, Michael, 202
Fleming, Brendan, 44–45, 114
flooding, 134–35, 169–70
Florida, Richard, 208
Flynn, Elizabeth Gurley, 14

Forbes, 139
Ford, Gerald R., 46
Forman, Ian, 17, 19
form-based code, 130
Forrant, Robert, 34
Fort Monroe, Virginia, 12
Fort Sumter, South Carolina, 11
the Foundation, 237–38
Foye, Brian, 224
Francis, James B., 85, 136, 169, 191–92, 194
Francis Floodgate, 16, 169–70, *170*
Franco, Jean, 195
Frechette, Suzanne, 235
Freedom Train, *28*
40 French Street, 105, *105–7*
Freudenberg Nonwovens, 130, 131
Frye's Tavern, 172
Fugitive Slave Act, 12
Fuller, Patricia, 219
Fund for New Urbanism, 129–30

Gall, Lawrence D., *41*, 57, 58; on LNHP attendance, 69; on NPS, 40–41, 43–44, 64
Gallagher, Tom, 168, 169
gangs, 31
Ganz, Marshall, 235
Gargiulo, Charles A., 111
Garrison, William Lloyd, 11
Gaslight Building, 55, 156
Gates, Bill, 24
Gateway Cities, 145
Gateway National Recreation Center, 40
Gatti, Arturo, 37
General Management Plan (GMP), 55–56, 59
General Order Number 28, 11
The Generator Room, 219
Georgalos, Angelike (Kay), 43, *56*
Gervais, Ricky, 36–37
Giavis, Vassilios (Bill), 58
Giavis Market, 58
G.I. Bill, 16
Gilman, Bob, 145, 157
Ginsberg, Allen, 224, 225
Gittell, Ross J., 32, 120
Glaeser, Edward, 239
Glidden, Scott, 206
Glowacki, Amy, 231, 232–33
GMP. *See* General Management Plan
Goldenfarb, Abby, 134

Golden Gate National Recreation Area, 40
Golden Gloves boxing, *162*
Golec, Pauline, 204, *204*, 205
Gomaco firm, 63, 64, 190
Goodwin, Catherine, 114–15
Goodwin, Doris Kearns, 12
Goodwin, John, *44*, 114, 175
72-76 Gorham Street, 89, *89–90*
The Grand Canyon of the Yellowstone, 76, 77
Grant, Ulysses S., 76
Graulich, Robert, 43
Greater Lowell, 16, 33, 159
Greater Lowell Community Foundation, 21, 73
"The Great One" (Clark), 176
Great Recession, 32, 33, 34, 134
Great Society program, 21, 41
Greek Americans, 112, *113*
Green, John, 197, 198, 199
Greenwood, Anita, 195
Grey Nuns. *See* Sisters of Charity of Montreal
Gross, Rebecca, 208
Growth District Initiative, 134
Guard Locks, 62
Guide to 1930s Massachusetts, 15–16
Guiding Growth and Change: A Handbook for the Massachusetts Citizen (Peskin), 127
Guy, Buddy, *213*

Hadzi, Dimitri, 219–20
Hale-Howard, 112–14, 138
Hall, Peter, 34
Hamblett, John, 137
Hamilton, Alexander, 2
Hamilton Canal District (HCD): Appleton Mills in, 32, 73, 124–25, 129, *133*, 134; Canalway in, 68, *70*, 75, 121, *127*, 131, *132*, 144, 215; renovation of, *129*, 129–32, *132*, 134
Hamilton Manufacturing Company, 105, 176
Hamilton Mills, 120
Hand-Book for the Visitor to Lowell, 7
Harper's Magazine, 14
Hartzog, George, 40
Harvey, Linda, 137
Hay, John, 12
Haycock, Kati, 70
Haywood, Bill, 14
HCD. *See* Hamilton Canal District
Heckler, Margaret, 53

Heritage State Parks, 59, 61, 63, 145, 158
H & H Paper Company, 56, 64
Hickel, Walter J., 40, 43, 46, 49
Higgins, James, 176
the Highlands, 113
Hilton Hotel, 62, 145, 161, 174
Hinojosa, Maria, xi
Historic American Buildings Survey, 46, 120
Historic Canal District Commission, *xi*, xii, 46, 47, 49
Historic Preservation, 32
History of Lowell (Coburn), 158
Hoar, Yvonne, 14
Hogan, William T., 33
Holiday, Billie, 160
Holtzberg, Maggie, 207
Holy Trinity church, 112
Homage to Women, 128, *215*, 215–16
Honeywell Information Systems, 163
Horrocks looms, 4
Houle, Sandra Smith, 162
Howard, Lydia S., 114
Howard, Woodbury, 114
Howe, Richard, Jr., 1–2
Howe, Richard P., 187
HSC. *See* Human Services Corporation
HUD. *See* Department of Housing and Urban Development, U.S.
Human Services Corporation (HSC), 24, 43, *44*, 45, 185, 208–9

ICC. *See* UMass–Lowell Inn & Conference Center
If the Falls Could Speak (Riley), 157
Immaculate Conception Church, 15–16
Independence National Historical Park, 40
Industrial Canyon, 171–72, *172*
Industrial Revolution, U.S., xi–xii, 7, 43, *106*
Industry, Not Servitude, 218–19
influenza, 1
The Inner City: A Handbook for Renewal (Bray), 152
Innovative Cities Conference, 35, 39, 75
Internal Revenue Service, 124
Internet System for Networked Sensor Experiments (iSENSE), 195
interpretive prospectus, 56, 58
The Invention of Lying, 36–37
Ireland, David, 219
iSENSE. *See* Internet System for Networked Sensor Experiments

Jack Kerouac Commemorative, 218–19, 221, 226, 227; dedication of, 64, 225, 226; funding for, 159; site of, 62, 225–26
Jackman, Elizabeth A., 7
Jackson, Andrew, 8
Jackson, Patrick Tracy, 5
James, Ernest, 114
JAM plan, 129–30
Jarvis, Charles, 162, 223
Jarvis, Jon, 39, 75
Jeanne d'Arc Credit Union (JDCU), 191
Jefferson National Expansion Memorial, 40
Joan Fabrics, 163, 177
John Nesmith House, 36
Johnson, Lyndon B., 41
Johnston, David Claypool, 76, 77
Johnston, J. Bennett, xi
Judicial Center, 131, 134

K., Bruno, 212
Das Kapital (Marx), 12, 13
Karabatsos, Lewis, 52, 224
Karam, Robert, 35
Kaufman, Mico, 128, *149*, *215*, 215–16
Kealy, William, 41
Keefe, Frank, 157
Kennedy, Ed, 52
Kennedy, Edward M. (Ted), 47, *51*, 61, 62
Kerouac, Jack (John), 15, 158, 162, *222*; exhibits on, 74, 221–22, 224; revival of, 223–24; sculpture tribute, 62, 64, 159, 221, 225–26, *226*, 227
Kerry, John F., 25, 45, 61
Khoeun, Samkhann, 164
King Philip's War, 1–2
Kirk Street, *98*
21–27 Kirk Street, 100
Kirshbaum, Sheila, 185, *186*, 195
Kirwin, John F., 43
"kiss of death" syndrome, 192
Kol, Duey, 163–64, *164*, 165
Kolack, Shirley, 113
Kopycinski, Joseph V., 114
Krauss, Alison, 202

Ladd, Luther, 11
Lambert-Moore, Janet, 213
Lamoureux, Lillian L., 43, 46, 50–51
language, 23
LaPorte, Raymond, 52–53
Larcom, Lucy, 219
Larter, Ted, 52

LDFC. *See* Lowell Development & Financial Corporation
Leary, Michael, 134
Lee Street, *98*
Leggat, Janet, 205
Leggat, Susan, 205, *205*, 206
Leite, John, 160, *160*
LeLacheur, Edward, 142
LeLacheur Park, 69, *143*, 144
LeMay, Alice M., 162
LeMay, Armand W., 47, 156
Leo, Melissa, 37
Levasseur, Paul, 189, 190, 191, 194
Levi-Strauss, Claude, 220
Lewis, Jerry, 198
Lezberg, Mel, 48
LHB. *See* Lowell Historic Board
LHP. *See* Lowell Heritage Partnership
LHPC. *See* Lowell Historic Preservation Commission
Lincoln, Abraham, 8, 12
Lindsay, Vachel, 150
Linus Childs House, 56
Lipchitz, Bill, 238
Lippard, Lucy R., 220–21
Little Canada, 14, 16, 17, 26, 111–12, 114
Little Greece, 16
Liverpool, England, 112
LNHP. *See* Lowell National Historical Park
LOCA. *See* Lowell Office of Cultural Affairs
Locks & Canals Company, 44, 46, 61, 85, 169
Locks & Canals Historic District, 45
locomotive, 61, *62*
Lofgren, Rebecca, 194
love and honor (*agapétimé*), 220
Lovejoy Annex, 97
Lowell, 2, *3*, *6*, *13*, *17*, 162; canal system, *9*, 16, 45, 48–49, 61, *67*, 68, *70*, 72, 75, 100, 121, *123*, *132*, 166, *166*, 167–68, *168*, 169–70, *170*, 171, *171*, 172, *172–73*, 174, 176–77; City Council of, 44–45, 116; during Civil War, 11–12, *101*, *105*; education in, 17, 19, 20, 21–22, 33–36, 42–43, 75, 181, 184, 185–95; employment in, 17, 24, 33, 41, 125, 130, 147–48, 157, 174–75; immigration to, 1, 13–14, 16, 29, *31*, 31–32, 65, 74, *113*, 145–46, 159, 163–64, 177–78, 179, 187, 189–90, 236, 237; labor force of, 6–7, 8, 10, 12, 14; in media, 36–37, 47, 53, 138, 157, 163, 167,

183, 202, 208, 223, 225; as model city, xix, 8, 19–22, 41–43; neighborhoods in, 13–14, 15–17, 27–29, 30, 32, 42, 45, 74, 111–12, *113*, 113–14, 121, 125–27, *127*, 128–29, *129*, 130–32, *132*, 133–34, 139, 176, 177, 189; origins of, xi–xii, 5–8, 10; population of, 31, 33, 157, 159; shopping in, 96, 151–52

Lowell, Francis Cabot, 2, 4, *4*, 6, *217*

"Lowell: 2000 and Beyond," 70–71

Lowell Art Association, *86*

Lowell: A Study of Industrial Development (Terrell), 158

Lowell Blues, 222

Lowell Canalwaters Cleaners, 72

Lowell Community Health Center, 131, 236

Lowell Community Renewal Project, 115–16

Lowell Connector, 112, 139

Lowell Cooperative Learning Center, 184

Lowell Cultural Plan, 146, 209

Lowell Development & Financial Corporation (LDFC), 27, 31, 73, 119–20, 158

Lowell Discovery Network, 182–83

Lowell Female Labor Reform Association, 7

Lowell Festival, 157

Lowell Festival Foundation, 197–99, 202, 204, 205

Lowell Folk Festival, 75, 196, *196*; attendance at, 69, 148; Aucella on, 206; budget for, 201; fringe festival of, 202; performers at, 198, 202–3, *203*; start of, 60–61, 201; volunteers at, 199, 202, 204, *204*, 205, *205*, 206; Walter and, 200, 201, 202. *See also* National Folk Festival

Lowell Folklife Series, 206–7

Lowell General Hospital, 33

Lowell Heritage Partnership (LHP), 73–74

Lowell High School, 75

Lowell Historical Society, 46, 64–65

Lowell Historic Board (LHB), 73–74, 117–18, 123, 218

Lowell Historic Preservation Commission (LHPC), 47, 51, 53, 207; Aucella on, 69; authority of, 57–58, 155; Boott Cotton Mills Museum and, 66–67; Boston & Maine Railroad Depot ownership by, 93; Canalway work by, 68, *127*, 215; Faust at, 22, 23, 55, *56*, 206; funding by, 68–69, 118–20, 129, 155, 156, 215; lifespan of, 50, 67–68, 74; Market Mills and, 126–28, 149; Meehan and, 68; New England Folklife Center and, 207; origins of, 48–49; Parrott at, 117, 120; Patrick J. Mogan Cultural Center and, *106*; public art and, 214–15, 218; reconstruction by, 64; St. Peter Church and, 122

Lowell Industrial Learning Experience, 59

Lowell Loom, 4–5, *5*

Lowell Machine Shop, 5, 7, 76, 134

Lowell Manufacturing Company, 58, *82*, *83*, 126

Lowell Model for Educational Excellence, 186, 187

Lowell Museum, 46, 58, 224

Lowell Museum Corporation, 139

Lowell National Historical Park (LNHP), 22; Artist-in-the-Park of, 58; attendance at, 69–70, 147; events at, 59–60; funding for, 61, 62, 67, 68–69, 117, 121; GMP for, 55–56, 59; legislation for, 49–51, *51*, 52–54, 201; Mogan's work on, 19–21, 41, *44*; origins of, 39–44, *44*, 45–51, *51*, 52–78; rangers, *57*; superintendents of, *55*, 59, 60, 65, 66, *66*, 69, 74, 75, *75*, 78, 117, 187, 200, 201, 202, 233; trolleys in, *63*, 63–64, 127, 132, 190; Tsongas, P., and, 48, 49, 50, *51*, 62, 67, 69; Visitor Center, 59, 128. *See also specific park properties*

Lowell National Historical Park and Preservation District Cultural Resources Inventory (Richardson and Abbott), 81

Lowell Offering, 7, 8

Lowell Office of Cultural Affairs (LOCA), 209–10

Lowell Parks & Conservation Trust, 62

Lowell Plan, Inc., 145, 186; leadership of, 138, 199; origins of, 27; *Public Matters: Empowering Lowell's Leaders*, 74, 233–34, *234*, 235–38

"The Lowell Play," 157

"Lowell: Politics Before Education" (Forman), 17

Lowell Preservation Loan Program, 119, 121

Lowell Public Art Collection, *215*, 215–17, *217*, 218–20

Lowell Publishing Company, 7

Lowell Redevelopment Authority, 45

Lowell School Committee, 17
The Lowell Sculptures, 216–17, *217*, 218
Lowell Spinners, *143*, 144
Lowell State Teachers College, 16
Lowell Summer Music Series, *211*; atten-
  dance at, 69, 148, 156–57; performers
  at, 157, 210, 211, *212*, *213*
Lowell Sun, 15, 25, 45, 47, 115, 142
Lowell Technological Institute, 44
Lowell Textile Institute, 16
Lowell: The Flowering City, 71
Lowell: Then and Now, 68
Lower Locks, 172, *173*, 174
Lucy Larcom Park, 16, *67*, 199
*The Lure of the Local: Senses of Place in a
  Multicentered Society* (Lippard), 220–21
Lynch, Bernie, 128, 147, *147*
Lynch, Kevin, 180, 181

M2D2. *See* Massachusetts Medical Devices
  Development Center
Machine Science, Inc., 195
Mack Building, 61
Mackintosh, Barry, 43–44
Maguire, Robert, 157
Mahoney, John, 41
Malavich, Bob, 48, 52
Malone, Patrick M., 165–66
Manchester, England, 4
Mangan, Mabel Delehanty, 174
Manzarek, Ray, 226
Marion, David, 26
Marion, Richard, 214
Mark and Elisia Saab Emerging Technolo-
  gies and Innovation Center, 34
Marker, Gordon, 43
Market Mills, 58, 120; history of, 126–27;
  LHPC and, 126–28, 149; Mill No. 1,
  83–84; Mill No. 2, *82–84*, *101*; No. 1
  Brussels Weave Mill, *82*, 126; No. 2
  Brussels Mill, *84*; renovation of, 126–
  28, *128*, 128; Tsongas, P., and, 126;
  Worsted Mill, *82*, *84*, 125. *See also* Boott
  Cotton Mills Museum
Market Mills Associates, 126, 128
Market Mills Park, 128, *202*
Martin, Brian, 70, 71, 129, *142*, 142,
  186–87
Martin, Fred, 185, 195
Martin, Katherine, 17, 186
Martineau, Harriet, 71
Marx, Karl, 12, 13

Massachusetts Bay Colony, 1
Massachusetts Medical Devices Develop-
  ment Center (M2D2), 34, 191
Massachusetts Mills, 66, 120
Mather, Benjamin, 76
Matyka, Carol, 203
Mayor's Committee on Model Cities, 184
MCC. *See* Middlesex Community College
McCabe, Kathy, 166
McCants, Wesley, *232*
McClure, Michael, 226
McCrary, Patrick, 74
McKean, David, 28, 29
McLeod, Bob, 224
McMahon, Ed, 198
McPhee, John, 167–68
Meehan, Martin T., 20, 39; LHPC and, 68;
  on Mogan, 47–48; as musician, 161; at
  UMass–Lowell, 33, 34, 35, *35*
The Melting Pot, 59, 127
Menand, Louis, 10–11
Menezes, Rhaissa Pereira, 233
Meridian, Massachusetts, 150
Merrill, Otis, 86, 89
Merrimack Canal, 16, 61, 68, 169–70, *170*
Merrimack Gatehouse, 56
Merrimack Manufacturing Company, 6, 17,
  76, 100, 114
Merrimack Repertory Theatre, 69–70, 73,
  156, 157, 208
Merrimack River, 1, *2*, 76, *77*; pollution
  in, 167, 170–71; size of, 165; Southeast
  Asian Water Festival on, 69, 163, *166*
143-153 Merrimack Street, *96–97*
Merrimack Valley Housing Partnership
  (MVHP), 31
Merroh Awke (strong place), 5
*The Metaphysical Club: A Story of Ideas in
  America* (Menand), 10–11
Middlesex Canal, 166
Middlesex Community College (MCC), 35;
  Boston & Maine Railroad Depot build-
  ing, 93; Cambodian Expressions project
  by, 164; enrollment at, 36; site of, 172,
  174
Middlesex Manufacturing Company, 172
Middlesex Street, 118
Migration Map, 183
Milinazzo, James, 20, *140*, 144, 145
Mill and Canal district, 116
Mill and Mansion (Coolidge), 158
Mill Discovery Center, 183

mill girls, 6–7, *8*, 10, 64, 178, *178*, 179
Mill Girls & Immigrants tour, 29, 179
millpower, 165–66
mills, xix, 2, 4, 181. *See also* specific mills
"The Mills Weren't Made of Marble," 163
minimum wage law, 15
Minute Man National Historical Park, 43
Mitchell, Charles, 96
Mitchell, Frederick, 96
Model Cities Program, xix, 21–23, 41–43, 182, 184
Moe, Richard, 32–33
Mogan, Patrick J., *22*, 32, 159; on AFC, 200; broadcasts by, 44; CHD and, 184, 185; on education, 20, 22, 23, 184; environmental education program of, 41; in HSC, 43, *44*, 45, 208–9; LaPorte and, 52; LNHP work by, 19–21, 41, *44*; Meehan on, 47–48; Nikitopoulos and, 183–84; Pierson and, 186; public art and, 213–14; Southworth, M., and, 180–81, 182; Tsongas, P., and, 214–15
"Mondays at Market Mills," 60
Montmartre, France, 181
Moody, Paul, 4, 85, 194
Moody-Whistler-Francis House, 85, *86*
Moran, Thomas, 76, *77*
Morse, F. Bradford, 41, 43, *44*, 50, 115
Morse, Francesca, 115
Mott, William Penn, Jr., 62–63
moulin rouge (red mill), 181
movie theatres, 161
Mroz, Henry, 186
Munro, Stuart, 202
MVHP. *See* Merrimack Valley Housing Partnership

National Council for the Traditional Arts (NCTA), 200
National Endowment for the Arts (NEA), 208–9
National Folk Festival, 200–1
National Geographic Magazine, 167
The National Parks: America's Best Idea (Duncan, D., and Burns), 76
National Parks Conservation Association, xi
National Park Service (NPS), xi; on Boott Cotton Mills Museum, 180; Boston & Maine Railroad Depot project, 36; Department of Environmental Management and, 59; Diversity and Inclusion

Project, 164–65; Gall on, 40–41, 43–44, 64; Historic Architectural Engineering Record, 46; Northeast Cultural Resources Center, 65; urban parks in, 40, 122; Walter on, 63
National Parks Second Century Commission, xi
National Register for Historic Districts, 74
National Trust for Historic Preservation, 32–33, 116, 125
NCTA. *See* National Council for the Traditional Arts
NEA. *See* National Endowment for the Arts
NEA Arts, 208
Neighborhood Youth Corps of Community Teamwork, 213, 232
Nesmith, Joseph A., 11
New Deal, 14, 15, 112
New England, *3*
New England Folklife Center, 65, 207
New England Regional Commission, 43
New Federalism, 68
New Lanark, Scotland, 2, 4
New Lowell Offering, 111
New Market Tax Credits, 131
New York Times, 163, 223
Nicolay, John, 12
Nikitopoulos, Charles, *113*, 183–84
Ninteau, Helen, 112
Nixon, Richard M., 46, 49
Nobis Engineering Company, 176
Noon, Rosemary, 59, 233, *234*, 235, 236
North American Free Trade Agreement, 177
North Atlantic Region Volunteer of the Year Award, 199
North Common Village, 16, 112
Northeast Housing Court, 30
Northrup, J. H., 192
Norwood, Massachusetts, 23
NPS. *See* National Park Service

O'Connell, Peter, 188
O'Connor, Sandra Day, xi
Octoberfest, 198
O'Donnell, Anne, 187
Old City Hall, 56, 59
Old Sturbridge Village, 188
Olney, Richard, 114
Olson, Charles, 163
O'Meara, George F., 41
O'Neill, Thomas P. (Tip), 46, 50
O'Neill, Thomas P., III, 46, 47

"On the Building of Springfield" (Lindsay), 151

On the Cultural Road: City of World Culture, 146

On the Road (Kerouac), 64, 74, 221, 222, 223

Outdoor Recreation Resources Review Committee, 40

Owen, Robert, 2, 4

Page, Ruth, 206
Panagiotakos, Steven C., 33, 34
Panas, Leo, *113*, 213
Pandel-Bradford, 163
Park, Theresa, 139, 206
Park and Preservation District, 117
Parrott, Charles, *122*, 124, 125; career of, 120; on LHB, 122; at LHPC, 117, 120; on Patrick J. Mogan Cultural Center, 64; on Pawtucket Falls Dam, 137
Partnership Park, 73
patent medicine, 12
Patrick, Deval, 32
Patrick J. Mogan Cultural Center, 21, 60, 64, 74, *106*
Paul E. Tsongas Arena, 141–42, *143*
Paul Tsongas Center, 39
Pawtucket, Rhode Island, 1
Pawtucket Canal, 166, 176, 177
Pawtucket Falls, 1, 5, 46, 62, *136*
Pawtucket Falls Dam, 68, 135–36, *137*, 137
Pawtucketville, 14
Pawtucketville Memorial School, 20
Pellon, 131
Perry, Jack, 119
Pershey, Ed, 188
Peskin, Sarah M., 63, 117, 126, *127*
Phillips, Frank, 47
pierogies, 203–4
Pierson, Donald, 186, 187, 188–89
Poe, Edgar Allan, 8
Poets on the Peaks: Gary Snyder, Philip Whalen, & Jack Kerouac in the Cascades (Suiter), 227
Point Park, 215
Polese, Mario, 34
Pollard, Mary, 19, *22*
Pollard, Samuel, 47, 52
Pollard's, 96
Pomeroy, Samuel, 76
Pouv, Sovanna Devin, 237–38, *238*, 239
power loom, 2, 4
Preservation Nation, 125

The Preservation Plan, 58, 155
Preservation Plan Amendment, 68
Prince Charles (Charles, Prince of Wales), 32
Providence, Rhode Island, 148
Public Law 95-290, 201
Public Matters: Empowering Lowell's Leaders, 74, 233–34, *234*, 235–38
Public Works Department, 27
Putnam and Son, 92
Putziger, Michael, 119

Railroad Bank Building, *96*
Rambur, Richard, 69
Rawn, William L., III, 70
Raytheon Missile Systems, 162
Reagan, Ronald, 68
"The Rebirth of Lowell: A Beacon for Revitalization" (Riley), 157
reconstruction, 64
red mill (*moulin rouge*), 181
Reese, Della, 198
Rees-Larkin Development, 67
Regatta Festival Committee. *See* Lowell Festival Foundation
Reilly School, 19
Renewing Cities (Gittell), 32, 120
Report of the Lowell Historic Canal District Commission, 239
"Report on Manufactures" (Hamilton), 2
restoration. *See* architecture
Rialto, *92*, 93. *See also* Boston & Maine Railroad Depot
Richard P. Howe Bridge, 33
Richardson, Shepley Bulfinch, 81
Riley, David, 157
River's Edge, 145
The Road from Here (Tsongas, P.), 141–42
Robbins, Arthur, 145
Roche, John E., 184
Rogers, Edith Nourse, 14–15
Rogers, John, 14
Roosevelt, Franklin D., 15, 40
Ross, David, 219
Ross, Joan, 206
Rothenberg, Ellen, 215, 218–19
Rourke, Susan, 188
Rouse Company, 145
Route 3, 33–34, 144
row houses, 17, 114, *114*, 115. *See also specific row houses*
Ryan, Lizzie A., 174
Ryan, Loretta A., 115

Salazar, Kenneth, xiii, 39, *137*, 137
Salem Maritime National Historic Site, 43
Samaras, William (Bill), 21, 22
Sampas, Charles G., 15, *28*, 36
Sampas, John, 227
Sampas, Stella (Kerouac), 223, 224, 225
Sampascoopies, 15
Sargent, Frank, 46, 158
sawmills, 181
Schernbaum, Sylvia, 164
Sciuto, Corey, 236–37, *237*
Scribner-MacLean, Michelle, 185, 195
sculpture, 212–15, *215. See also specific
    sculptures*
Sebelius, Keith, 53
Senate, U.S., 46
Shannon, James, 61
Shattuck Street Stage, 156, *156*
Shatzer, Tess, xix
Sheehy, Molly, 36
Sheehy, Paul, 36, 188
Sisters of Charity of Montreal (Grey Nuns),
    46
Skinner, Deborah, 6
slavery, 12
smallpox, 1
Smith, John Robert, 150
Smith Baker Center, 64
Social Security Act, 15
Solomon Mental Health Center, 183
Sou, Linda Sopheap, 236
Soucy, Will, 191
Southeast Asian Water Festival, 69, 163,
    166
Southworth, Michael, 180–83
Southworth, Susan, 181, 182–83
Spalding House, 62
Speare House, 198, 199
Speck, Jeff, 130
Sperber, Robert I., 186
Speronis, Xenophon (Zenny), 197, 198,
    199
Spindle City Corps, 231–33
Spock, Mike, 180
Spoons. *See* Butler, Benjamin F.
Sports Illustrated, 25–26
Stamas, Peter, 21, 43, 182
State Historic Tax Credits, 125
stock, sale of, 4–5
Stoffers, George, 115
Stowell, Stephen, 117, 134
St. Patrick Church, 10, 28–29
St. Peter Church, 122–23

streetcar No. 4131, 63, 190
strong place (*Merroh Awke*), 5
Suarez, Ray, 70, 71
Suffolk Manufacturing Company, 108,
    108–9
Suffolk Mill, 191–92
600-660 Suffolk Street, 108, *108–9*
Suffolk Textile Company, 139
Suiter, John, 227
Sumner, Charles, 10
sustainable energy, 195
Swamp Locks, 68, 135, *168*, 169, 171
Sweeney, Marie, 206, 224, 235
Sweeney, Thomas, 187

Taffe, Richard (Dick), 197, 198
Tardiff, Jeannine, 214
Taupier, William, 119, 140
Tavares, Jack, 41
tax credits, 124–25, 131, 141
TD Bank, 131
Terrell, Margaret, 158
Theodore Edson Parker Foundation, 75,
    147, 151, 164
Thirty Pieces of Silver, 30
Thoreau, Henry David, 8, 167
Thoreau, John, 167
Thou, Tim, 65, 236
TIHC. *See* Tsongas Industrial History
    Center
Tocqueville, Alexis de, 71
Torpedo Factory, 150
The Town and the City (Kerouac), 158, 221,
    227
Transfiguration Greek Orthodox Church,
    112
Treetop Walk, 183
Tremont Mills, 191
Tremont Yard, 59
Trinity Financial of Boston, 131
Triumph of the City, 239
Tsapatsaris, Charles, 161
Tsapatsaris, George, 21–22, 186, 187
Tsongas, Nicola, 33, 34, 39, 50, 131, *137*
Tsongas, Paul E., *26*, 32, 46, 141; ANILCA
    work by, 50; Costello and, 47; death of,
    144; Faust and, 22, 47, 48, 50; LaPorte
    and, 52; LDFC and, 27, 119; LNHP
    and, 48, 49, 50, *51*, 62, 67, 69; Lowell
    Public Art Collection and, *215*, 215–17,
    219–20; Market Mills and, 126; Mogan
    and, 214–15; presidential campaign of,
    24–25, *25*, 26

Tsongas Industrial History Center (TIHC), 189; inspiration for, 187–88; UTeach, 185–86; Water Room, 192, *193*, 193–95
Tsongas Tsolarstars, 195
Tsouprakos, George K., 115
Tully, B. Joseph, 27, 144
Tuttle, Nancye, 161
"2001: A Cultural Odyssey," 70

UDAG. *See* Urban Development Action Grant
Udall, Stewart, 40
UMass–Lowell. *See* University of Massachusetts–Lowell
UMass–Lowell Inn & Conference Center (ICC), 145, 146, 174
United Teen Equality Center (UTEC), 237
University of Massachusetts–Lowell (UMass–Lowell), 28, 62, 75; CLH, 64–65; hockey team of, 39, 69, *143*; Meehan at, 33, 34, 35, *35*; start of, 139, 140, 158; UTeach, 185–86
Uong, Rithy, 31, 32
Urban Design Study, 115–16
Urban Development Action Grant (UDAG), 119, 140
Urban Information Devices, 183
Urban Renewal Project, 16, 111–16
Usages and Abuses (Ayer), 12
U.S. News & World Report, 35
UTeach, 185–86
UTEC. *See* United Teen Equality Center

Vagos, Marc, 51, *57*
Vandenberg Esplanade, 46, 61, 62
Verrier, Robert, 125
Vezina, Krystal, 168, 169, 170–71, 174
Visions of Cody (Kerouac), 223
Visions of Kerouac (Ziavras), 223

Wagner Act, 15
Wahlberg, Mark, 37
Wallace, Kendall
Walter, Chrysandra (Sandy), 199; Boott Cotton Mills Museum role of, 65–66, *66*, 187; career of, 60; death of, 202; Lowell Folk Festival and, 200, 201, 202; on NPS, 63
Waltham, Massachusetts, 4, 6, 105
Wamesit, 1–2

Wang, An, 24
Wang Laboratories, 24, 36, 67, 119, 139
Wannalancit Mills, 16, 33, 34, 35–36, 138
Wannalancit Office and Technology Center, 103, 108, *108–9*
Wannalancit Textile Company, 56, 58, 108
Ward, Micky, 37
Washington, D.C., 40
Washington Post, 53
Water Discovery Center, 183
Watt, James, 225
WCAP radio station, 44, 162
The Wealth and Poverty of Regions: Why Cities Matter (Polese), 34
Weible, Robert, 40, 180
Western Avenue Studios, 32, 150
Wetherbee, Kelley, Rose, Maynard, and Day Houses, 100
Whalen, William (Bill), 48, 51
"What is Public Narrative?" (Ganz), 235
Where Elephants Weep, 75
Whistler, George Washington, 8, 85, 194
Whistler, James McNeill, 8, 85, *149*, 227
Whistler House Museum of Art, 85
Whitney, Addison, 11
Whittier, John Greenleaf, 6, 11
Will, George, 225
Wilson, E. O., xi
Wilson, Joe, 200–1, 206
windmills, 181
windows, 103
WinnDevelopment, 67
Wisconsin Glacier, 6
Woburn, Massachusetts, 1
Woitena, Ben, 225–26, *226*
Woods, Nancy, 117
Works Progress Administration, 15
World War I, 14
World War II, 16
Worthen Street, 8
243 Worthen Street, *85–86*
Wurm, Michael, 65, 66, 179–80

Xenith, 138

Ymittos Candle, 147
Yosemite Park, 76

Ziavras, Charles, 162, 223

About the Author

Paul Marion was born in Lowell, Massachusetts, in 1954. A graduate of the University of Massachusetts–Lowell, with degrees in political science and community social psychology, he also studied in the master's program in creative writing at the University of California–Irvine. In the 1980s, he was an administrator with the Lowell Historic Preservation Commission, U.S. Department of the Interior, helping to develop the programs and properties of Lowell National Historical Park. A cofounder of the Lowell Folk Festival and Lowell Heritage Partnership, he was also instrumental in the development of

Paul Marion
Kevin Harkins

the Lowell Cultural Plan, Mogan Cultural Center, Lowell Public Art Collection, and *Jack Kerouac Commemorative*. He is the author of several collections of poetry, including *What Is the City?* (2006), and editor of *Atop an Underwood: Early Stories and Other Writings* by Jack Kerouac (1999) and *French Class: French Canadian-American Writings on Identity, Culture, and Place* (1999). His work has appeared in *The Massachusetts Review, Slate, The Christian Science Monitor, Alaska Quarterly Review, Yankee,* and many anthologies. At UMass–Lowell, he is executive director of community relations and codirector of the Center for Arts and Ideas. He lives with his wife and son in an 1860s mill agent's house in Lowell.